W9-CTH-617

DATE DUE

			PRINTED IN U.S.A.

Authors
& Artists
for Young
Adults

ISSN 1040-5682

Authors & Artists for Young Adults

VOLUME 23

Thomas McMahon
Editor

GALE

DETROIT · NEW YORK · TORONTO · LONDON

Thomas McMahon, *Editor*

Joyce Nakamura, *Managing Editor*

Hal May, *Publisher*

Stephen Allison, Diane Andreassi, Ken Cuthbertson, Motoko Huthwaite, Arlene Johnson, J. Sydney Jones, Irene McKnight-Durham, Nancy Rampson, C. M. Ratner, Aaron Saari, Peggy Saari, Susan Reicha, Kenneth R. Shepherd, Tracy J. Sukraw, and Crystal Towns,
Sketchwriters/Contributing Editors

Victoria B. Cariappa, *Research Manager*
Cheryl L. Warnock, *Project Coordinator*
Gary J. Oudersluys and Maureen Richards, *Research Specialists*
Laura C. Bissey and Sean R. Smith, *Research Associates*

Susan M. Trosky, *Permissions Manager*
Maria L. Franklin, *Permissions Specialist*
Michele Lonoconus, *Permissions Associate*
Andrea Rigby, *Permissions Assitant*

Mary Beth Trimper, *Production Director*
Deborah Milliken, *Production Assistant*

Randy Bassett, *Image Database Supervisor*
Mikal Ansari, *Macintosh Artist*
Robert Duncan, *Imaging Specialist*
Pamela A. Reed, *Photography Coordinator*

The paper used in this publication meets the minimum requirements of American National Standard for Information Sciences—Permanence Paper for Printed Library Materials, ANSI Z39.48-1984.

Library of Congress Catalog Card Number 89-641100
ISBN 0-7876-1789-X
ISSN 1040-5682

10 9 8 7 6 5 4 3 2 1

Printed in the United States of America

Authors and Artists for Young Adults

TEEN BOARD

The staff of *Authors and Artists for Young Adults* wishes to thank the following young adult readers for their teen board participation:

Michael Arawy
Rebecca Athan
Andrew Bagley
Catharine Banasiak
Melissa Barnaby
Allison Barrett
Devin Barry
Amy Becker
Melanie Beene
Dara Bonetti
Jesse Bonware
Jessica Buchser
Emily Burleson
Dylan Burns
Annie Burton
Rachel Campominos
Abby Conover
Christy Cook
Teresa Copeland
Jordan Copes
Heather Lee Cordeira
Lin Costello
Kate Cottrell
John Crower
Jennifer Dennis
Joanne M. Dimenno
Alison Dougherty
Josh Dukelow
Joe Eckert
Ellis Farmer
Kylin Follenweider
Alda Fox
Michelle Gagnon
Sarah Gangstad
Mary Genest
Eric Gilbert
Kate Gunther

Grant Hamilton
Alice Harnisch
Mark Haseltine
Allen Heinecke
Erin Hooley
Laura Huber
Maeghan Hurley
Kristin Hursh
Kristina Ivanisin
Tom Ivers
Adam James
Amanda Joy
Austin Joy
Ian Kelly
Alysia Kulas
Sarah Kulik
Dana-Jean LaHaie
Rolland LaHaie
Sarah Lairy
Aaron Landini
Sarah Lawhead
Erin Lewis
Nisha Low-Nam
Jamie Luna
Chenda Ly
Lauren Makowski
Jaimie Mantie
Kimberly Marie Rutkauski
Jen Mathiason
Megan McDonald
Niamh McGuigan
Allison C. Mikkalo
Jocelyn Miller
Glynn Miller II
Neal Mody
Shannon Murphy
Jason Nealy

Pablo Nevares
Brittany Pagella
Carlene Palmer
Krista Paradiso
Daniel Pereira
Eric Peters
Brian Petersen
Leah M. Pickren
Anne Pizzi
Mike Quilligan
Jessi Quizar
Christina Rampelli
Matthew R. Reese
Eric Rice
Benjamin Rockey
Meghan E. Rozarie
Tony Ruggiero
Peter Ryan
Erica Sebeok
Amee Shelley
Elizabeth Shouse
Kersten Stevens
Erin Stick
Mark Strauss
Avery Thatcher
Adam Tierney
Dan Uznanski
Melissa Vosburg
Rebecca Weide
Jonathan Weinberg
Lynn Weisee
Joe Wenzel
Kenyon Whitehead
Alisson Wood
Brandon C. Wood
Ally Wright
Josh Yorke

Contents

Introduction

Authors and Artists for Young Adults is a reference series designed to serve the needs of middle school, junior high, and high school students interested in creative artists. Originally inspired by the need to bridge the gap between Gale's *Something about the Author,* created for children, and *Contemporary Authors,* intended for older students and adults, *Authors and Artists for Young Adults* has been expanded to cover not only an international scope of authors, but also a wide variety of other artists.

Although the emphasis of the series remains on the writer for young adults, we recognize that these readers have diverse interests covering a wide range of reading levels. The series therefore contains not only those creative artists who are of high interest to young adults, including cartoonists, photographers, music composers, bestselling authors of adult novels, media directors, producers, and performers, but also literary and artistic figures studied in academic curricula, such as influential novelists, playwrights, poets, and painters. The goal of *Authors and Artists for Young Adults* is to present this great diversity of creative artists in a format that is entertaining, informative, and understandable to the young adult reader.

Entry Format

Each volume of *Authors and Artists for Young Adults* will furnish in-depth coverage of twenty to twenty-five authors and artists. The typical entry consists of:

—A detailed biographical section that includes date of birth, marriage, children, education, and addresses.

—A comprehensive bibliography or filmography including publishers, producers, and years.

—Adaptations into other media forms.

—Works in progress.

—A distinctive essay featuring comments on an artist's life, career, artistic intentions, world views, and controversies.

—References for further reading.

—Extensive illustrations, photographs, movie stills, cartoons, book covers, and other relevant visual material.

A cumulative index to featured authors and artists appears in each volume.

Compilation Methods

The editors of *Authors and Artists for Young Adults* make every effort to secure information directly from the authors and artists through personal correspondence and interviews. Sketches on living authors and artists are sent to the biographee for review prior to publication. Any sketches not personally reviewed by biographees or their representatives are marked with an asterisk (*).

Highlights of Forthcoming Volumes

Among the authors and artists planned for future volumes are:

Tim Allen	Philip K. Dick	Donna Jo Napoli
Julia Alvarez	F. Scott Fitzgerald	Richard Peck
Alan Baillie	E. M. Forster	Tamora Pierce
Greg Bear	Russell Freedman	Frederick Pohl
Anthony Burgess	Joseph Heller	Carl Sandburg
Willa Cather	Ken Kesey	Robert Silverberg
Aidan Chambers	E. L. Konigsburg	Steven Spielberg
C. J. Cherryh	Jon Krakauer	Robert Louis Stevenson
Helen Cresswell	Mary E. Lyons	Marc Talbert
L. Sprague De Camp	Barbara Michaels	Edith Wharton
Samuel R. Delaney	Claude Monet	Oprah Winfrey
Farrukh Dhondy	Michael Moorcock	Paul R. Yee

Contact the Editor

We encourage our readers to examine the entire *AAYA* series. Please write and tell us if we can make AAYA even more helpful to you. Give your comments and suggestions to the editor:

BY MAIL: The Editor, *Authors and Artists for Young Adults*, Gale Research, 835 Penobscot Building, 645 Griswold St., Detroit, MI 48226-4094.

BY TELEPHONE: (800) 347-GALE

BY FAX: (313) 961-6599

BY E-MAIL: CYA@Gale.com@GALESMTP

Authors
& Artists
for Young
Adults

Margaret Buffie

■ Personal

Born March 29, 1945, in Winnipeg, Manitoba, Canada; daughter of Ernest William John (a lithographer) and Evelyn Elizabeth (Leach) Buffie; married James Macfarlane (a teacher), August 9, 1968; children: Christine Anne. *Education:* University of Manitoba, received degree, 1967, certificate in education, 1976.

■ Addresses

Home and office—165 Grandview St., Winnipeg, Manitoba, Canada R2G 0L4.

■ Career

Hudson's Bay Co., Winnipeg, Manitoba, Canada, illustrator, 1968-70; Winnipeg Art Gallery, Winnipeg, painting instructor, 1974-75; River East School Division, Winnipeg, high school art teacher, 1976-77; freelance illustrator and painter, 1977-84; writer, 1984—. *Member:* Writers' Union of Canada, Canadian Authors Association, Canadian Society of Children's Authors, Illustrators, and Performers.

■ Awards, Honors

Young Adult Canadian Book Award, 1987-88; Ontario Arts Council grants, 1987 and 1989. Works placed on Notable Canadian Young Adult Fiction list, Canadian Children's Book Centre Our Choice list, Canadian Library Association Notable Canadian Fiction list, and American Library Association Best Books for Young Adults list.

■ Writings

Who Is Frances Rain?, Kids Can Press (Toronto), 1987, published in United States as *The Haunting of Frances Rain*, Scholastic Inc., 1989.

The Guardian Circle, Kids Can Press, 1989, published in United States as *The Warnings*, Scholastic Inc., 1991.

My Mother's Ghost, Kids Can Press, 1992, published in United States as *Someone Else's Ghost*, Scholastic, Inc., 1994.

The Dark Garden, Kids Can Press, 1995.

■ Sidelights

Margaret Buffie is a popular Canadian author of fiction for young adults. She writes lively and entertaining ghost stories that combine elements of fantasy and reality; her books often fit into the traditional time-travel genre. The main characters in Buffie's novels are contemporary adolescent girls coping with family problems. These young women stumble onto a supernatural world that offers them solace from their troubles. Critics have praised the author for her ability to combine separate storylines and various images into coherent tales. Buffie won the Young Adult Canadian Book Award in 1987-88, and her works have been cited by prestigious Canadian and American literary associations.

Buffie's own life has had a noticeable impact on the plots of her novels. She was born on March 29, 1945, in Winnipeg, Manitoba, Canada, one of four daughters of Ernest and Evelyn Buffie. The family spent many summers at Long Pine Lake in Ontario living in a log cabin built by Buffie's grandfather in 1919. Buffie still cherishes memories of the Canadian wilderness that she fell in love with as a child. Unfortunately, when she was twelve, her father died of cancer, and her peaceful childhood came to an end. As a result, Buffie's mother had to work extra hard to keep the family together. Looking back, the author is not bitter about the experience of losing her father. In fact, as she told Dave Jenkinson in an interview for *Emergency Librarian*, "It's a time that's full of really rich memories for me that I've used or tried to use in the writing that I do."

Another influence on the subject matter of Buffie's novels was her childhood fear of the dark. For her, Buffie told Jenkinson, bedtime "meant being cut away from that warm light downstairs that my parents basked in while I dealt with the dark and dreadful things that flickered and slid through the blackness of my room at night." Buffie was afraid of going to bed alone until her parents gave her a copy of *Heidi* that she was allowed to read before going to sleep. This book became her defense against the unknown. She recalled, "I wasn't afraid anymore because I wasn't going to sleep all alone. I had Heidi with me. I *was* Heidi." The author also read the Bobbsey Twins and Nancy Drew books to occupy her time before going to sleep. Eventually, she said, "when I went to bed at night, I'd sort of rearrange the stories in my mind and make up my own."

Buffie was not always a writer; at first she was a painter. She did not begin to write until long after her marriage in 1967 to James Macfarlane, a high school art teacher. In 1971 she gave birth to a daughter, Christine Anne. When Christine became a teenager, the author began to remember her own childhood. Buffie stated, "I began to

---

If you enjoy the works of Margaret Buffie, you may also want to check out the following books and films:

Michael Bedard, *Redwork*, 1990.
Grace Chetwin, *Collidescope*, 1990, and *Friends in Time*, 1992.
Welwyn Wilton Katz, *False Face*, 1987, and *Time Ghost*, 1990.
The Navigator, a film about time travel, produced in New Zealand, 1988.

---

think about myself at 12 and how similar and different my daughter and I were. And I began to think about my father." It was at this point that Buffie began to write. At first she kept a journal in which she recorded her memories of the log cabin at Long Pine Lake, and of her father's death. Then Buffie began to read some of her daughter's books. "I became a secret YA reader . . . ," as she put it, "and I was well and truly hooked." After she realized that she enjoyed writing more than painting, Buffie finally began working on her first novel.

Haunted Tales

In 1987 Buffie published *Who Is Frances Rain?* (published in the United States as *The Haunting of Frances Rain*), the first in a successful series of ghost stories for young adults. *Who Is Frances Rain?* is about Lizzie, a fifteen-year-old girl who is confronting family problems. Her mother has just remarried, and Lizzie does not like her new stepfather. Nor does she get along with her brother and sister. To top it all off, she has to spend the summer with her family at their grandmother's cabin on Rain Lake in northern Manitoba, Canada. In order to get away from her family, Lizzie escapes to Rain Island, even though her grandmother has declared the place off-limits. Once there, Lizzie gets more than she bargained for after she finds a pair of wire-rimmed glasses. Through the glasses, Lizzie sees a hidden spirit world that is inhabited by ghosts that lived on the island sixty years ago. The ghosts have a message for Lizzie, and it is up to her to find out what that message is. As Lizzie uncovers clues about the spiritual world, she also discovers new ways of coping with her troubled family.

In *Who Is Frances Rain?*, Buffie combines several genres—mystery, ghost story, and time-travel fantasy—with a sensitive depiction of a fractured modern family. The result, according to Peter Carver in *Books For Young People,* is "a ghost story with much to reveal to the thoughtful reader about the turbulent emotions at work within families." Sarah Ellis, reviewing *Who Is Frances Rain?* in *Horn Book,* stated that the "time travel conventions are handled very delicately," and a *Kirkus Reviews* contributor praised the novel's "good sense of place and atmosphere" as well as the "all-too-realistic family friction and its heartening, less-than-perfect resolution. . . ."

The protagonists in Buffie's novels have much in common. Gwyneth Evans, writing in *Twentieth-Century Children's Writers,* observed that all of the main characters in Buffie's novels "are girls in their mid-teens who are seriously angry with their parents—and with good reason." Fifteen-year-old Rachel McCaw, the protagonist in *The Guardian Circle* (published in the United States as *The Warnings*), Buffie's second ghost story, is no exception. At the beginning of *The Guardian Circle,* Rachel's mother has run off and her father has sold their Manitoba farm to become a truck driver. Before leaving on a trip, Rachel's father drops her off at her Aunt Irene's house in Winnipeg. She is now stuck living with an odd assortment of old people whom she affectionately calls the "Fossils." These oldsters turn out to be part of a Guardian Circle, and they need Rachel's help to protect a magical stone, The Gregor Stone, from an ancient evil spirit. The story is, in the words of Peter Carver in *Quill and Quire,* "a classic struggle between good and evil, a struggle in which Rachel herself becomes the pivotal figure." According to *Voice of Youth Advocates* reviewer Catherine M. Dwyer, "Buffie has written a wonderful supernatural fantasy."

Although Buffie's novels examine the difficulties young women face while growing up, this does not mean that the other characters in her books are any less important. Buffie's third novel, *My Mother's Ghost* (published in the United States as *Someone Else's Ghost*), exemplifies this. Linda Soutar, a reviewer for *Canadian Children's Literature,* commented that this ghost story "breaks away from the alienated teen motif and allows for the incorporation of multiple perspectives while still focusing the story on the experiences of its young protagonist."

Rachel must help a group of her elders protect a magical stone from an ancient spirit in this 1991 supernatural fantasy.

In *My Mother's Ghost,* sixteen-year-old Jess is confronting difficult problems. Her little brother Scotty has just died, and her mother has lapsed into depression. To cope with their loss, the family moves out of Winnipeg to a ranch in Alberta. This time it is Jess's mother who begins seeing ghosts. She thinks it is the ghost of Scotty, but Jess finds out that it is actually the ghost of Ian, a young boy who used to live at the ranch. As Valerie White stated in her review for *Emergency Librarian,* "Buffie really tells two stories here: one is Jess's story in the present, the other is Ian's story from the past." Anna Santarossa, writing in *CM: A Re-*

viewing Journal of Canadian Materials for Young People, complimented the "interplay between past and present," adding that the two stories "are so interesting they could have easily stood alone. Together the stories create suspense and add another dimension to the novel."

Buffie's fourth ghost story for young adults is titled *The Dark Garden.* It concerns sixteen-year-old Thea who is recovering from amnesia that resulted from a bike accident. Not only must she recover from amnesia after returning home from the hospital, but she has to deal with a dysfunctional family, including neglectful parents. Thea is another one of Buffie's frustrated teenaged girls, and Joanne Stanbridge of *Canadian Children's Literature* stated that "Adolescents will sympathize with her moody defiance right up to the last page." Readers will also follow Thea's encounters with the supernatural world, especially the ghost of Susannah who contacts Thea and helps her uncover the secret behind a century-old tragedy. Stanbridge claimed that *The Dark Garden* is a challenging story that "requires an agile reader to keep up with the twists and turns of the plot." Nevertheless, she declared: "Buffie has once again written a book teenagers will love."

The discontent that Buffie expresses through the characters in her ghost stories is profound. It coincides with contemporary problems in the real world, and it relates to the author's life. The pain that Buffie's protagonists experience reflects the author's own tragic loss. A connection exists there, as Buffie herself once said, "I don't believe great lives die. There is a link between generations-characteristics passed on, stories told-and I explore those links." Buffie stories are not pure melodrama either. The author's tragedies are masked by a wry humor that will attract young readers. Furthermore, the combination of past and present in her novels will alert readers to the importance of history in their lives. As Peter Carver stated in *Quill and Quire,* "Margaret Buffie is a kind of literary archeologist exploring the people who occupy her stories. It's a search that's not likely to disappoint her readers."

■ Works Cited

Carver, Peter, review of *Who is Frances Rain?*, *Books For Young People,* October, 1987, p. 10.

Carver, Peter, "Margaret Buffie's Spirit Circle," *Quill and Quire,* November, 1989, p. 13.

Dwyer, Catherine M., review of *The Warnings, Voice of Youth Advocates,* June, 1991, p. 93.

Ellis, Sarah, "News from the North," review of *Who Is Frances Rain?, Horn Book,* May-June, 1988, pp. 390-94.

Evans, Gwyneth, *Twentieth-Century Children's Writers,* 4th edition, Gale, 1995, p. 165.

Review of *The Haunting of Frances Rain, Kirkus Reviews,* October 1, 1989, p. 1471.

Jenkinson, Dave, "Margaret Buffie," *Emergency Librarian,* January-February, 1989, pp. 58-62.

Santarossa, Anna, review of *My Mother's Ghost, CM: A Reviewing Journal of Canadian Materials for Young People,* November, 1992, p. 311.

Soutar, Linda, review of *My Mother's Ghost, Canadian Children's Literature,* Number 75, 1994, pp. 73-74.

Stanbridge, Joanne, review of *The Dark Garden, Canadian Children's Literature,* Number 82, 1996, pp. 84-85.

White, Valerie, review of *My Mother's Ghost, Emergency Librarian,* March-April, 1993, p. 61.

■ For More Information See

BOOKS

Children's Literature Review, Volume 39, Gale, 1996, pp. 10-28.

Something About the Author, Volume 71, Gale, 1993, pp. 38-39.

PERIODICALS

Booklist, March 15, 1991, p. 1464.

Books for Young People, October, 1987, p. 10.

Books In Canada, December, 1987, p. 11.

Bulletin of the Center for Children's Books, March, 1991, pp. 160-61; October, 1997, p. 45.

Canadian Children's Literature, Number 53, 1989, pp. 59-60; Number 68, 1992, pp. 43-49.

Children's Book News (Toronto), September, 1987, p. 13.

Children's Literature Association Quarterly, Winter, 1990, pp. 206-11.

CM: A Reviewing Journal of Canadian Materials for Young People, March, 1990, p. 71; January, 1991, pp. 63-65.

Horn Book, May/June, 1988, pp. 390-94; September/October, 1997, p. 568.

Kirkus Reviews, October 1, 1989, p. 1471; January 15, 1991, p. 105.

School Librarian, August, 1989, p. 112.

School Library Journal, September, 1989, p. 272;
  April, 1991, p. 141.
Voice of Youth Advocates, April, 1995, p. 19.*

—Sketch by Stephen Allison

Michael Cadnum

■ Personal

Born May 3, 1949, in Orange, CA; married; wife's name, Sherina.

■ Addresses

Home—Albany, CA. *Agent*—Katharine Kidde, Kidde, Hoyt & Picard, 335 East 51st St., New York, NY 10022; and Michael Thomas, A. M. Heath & Co., 79 St. Martin's Ln., London WC2N 4AA, England.

■ Career

Poet and novelist.

■ Awards, Honors

Creative Writing Fellowship; National Endowment for the Arts; *Poetry Northwest*'s Helen Bullis Prize; Owl Creek Book Award; Edgar Allan Poe Award

nominations, Mystery Writers of America, for *Calling Home* and *Breaking the Fall*.

■ Writings

NOVELS

Nightlight, St. Martin's, 1990.
Sleepwalker, St. Martin's, 1991.
Saint Peter's Wolf, Carroll & Graf, 1991.
Calling Home, Viking, 1991.
Ghostwright, Carroll & Graf, 1992.
Breaking the Fall, Viking, 1992.
The Horses of the Night, Carroll & Graf, 1993.
Skyscape, Carroll & Graf, 1994.
Taking It, Viking, 1995.
Zero at the Bone, Viking, 1996.
The Judas Glass, Carroll & Graf, 1996.
Edge, Viking, 1997.
In a Dark Wood, Orchard Books, 1998.

CHILDREN'S BOOKS

The Lost and Found House, Viking, 1997.

POETRY

The Morning of the Massacre (chapbook), **Bieler Press**, 1982.
Wrecking the Cactus (chapbook), **Salt Lick Press**, 1985.
Invisible Mirror (chapbook), **Ommation Press**, 1986.
Foreign Springs (chapbook), **Amelia Press**, 1987.

By Evening, Owl Creek Press, 1992.
The Cities We Will Never See, Singular Speech Press, 1993.

OTHER

Also contributor to story anthologies, including "Can't Catch Me," in *Black Thorn, White Rose,* edited by Ellen Datlow, Morrow, 1994; "The Man Who Did Cats Harm," in *Twists of the Tale: Cat Horror Stories,* edited by Ellen Datlow, Dell, 1996; "The Flounder's Kiss," in *Black Swan, White Raven,* edited by Ellen Datlow, Avon, 1997; "Touch Me Everyplace," in *Lethal Kisses,* edited by Ellen Datlow, Orion. Author of short essays, including "The Ghost and the Panda," in *Mystery Writer's Annual,* "Dreams with Teeth," in *Mystery Scene,* and a commentary to his poem "Sunbathing in Winter," in *Poet & Critic.* Contributor of poems to anthologies, including "Cat Spy," in *The Bedford Introduction to Literature,* and "Desert," in *Poets for Life,* Crown. Has also contributed to numerous periodicals, including *America, Antioch Review, Beloit Fiction Journal, Beloit Poetry Journal, Commonweal, Carolina Quarterly, Georgia Review, Kansas Quarterly, Literary Review, Midwest Quarterly, Mississippi Review, Poetry Northwest, Prairie Schooner,* and *Virginia Quarterly Review,* and occasional reviews for the "Read This" column in *New York Review of Science Fiction.*

■ **Work in Progress**

Heat, for Viking.

■ **Sidelights**

During the 1980s Michael Cadnum was a nationally recognized poet, publishing his work in prestigious literary journals. By 1990 he was also gaining wide acclaim for his suspense novels. On first consideration, Cadnum's transition from serious poetry to popular fiction would seem to be have been an unlikely leap. To the contrary, however, his experience as a poet was an asset to his work as a novelist, and within a few years he rose to his current position as one of the foremost writers of horror novels and psychological thrillers. Although Cadnum began writing for an adult audience and only later specialized in novels for young adults, his books have consistently appealed to teenagers who enjoy a scary story. Many of his horror novels are variations on standard tales about ghosts, werewolves, and vampires, but with a difference: he portrays complex characters and he uses a literary writing style. Critics particularly admire Cadnum's psychological thrillers, which address serious problems experienced by young adults. According to Patrick Jones, a reviewer for *Horn Book,* "Cadnum isn't offering simple tales of good and evil but complex stories written in simple yet tense prose about 'good kids' doing evil things."

The author of some of the most terrifying novels being published today also has a whimsical side, which was revealed during an interview with Peggy Saari for *Authors and Artists for Young Adults* (*AAYA*). Asked if he had any pets, Cadnum replied, "My current pet is a green and yellow parrot named Luke, who sometimes sits on my shoulder as I write and is one of my closest advisors." Cadnum grew up in Southern California. In the interview he recalled exploring the California shore: "My family spent a lot of time at the beach, the flat, sandy shore of Huntington Beach and Newport Beach. . . . Sometimes jellyfish washed up on shore, gigantic fried eggs with purple yolks. Sometimes there were sharks, cruising hammerheads the police tried to shoot from the pier. Late one afternoon everyone retreated from the water to watch a majestic dorsal fin slip majestically just beyond the breaking waves."

Cadnum had an early fascination with words. "The first word I learned to read was *We,*" he told *AAYA.* "I was sitting in the garage of my family home on Monrovia Street in Costa Mesa, California. A book was open in my lap, and my father pointed out the word. I liked the capital W, but I probably thought, as I think now, that a word with such a handsome beginning should be a little longer. *We* is such a short word, but it shows that in a small space a word can stand for so much." Like most teenagers, Cadnum watched television. Nevertheless he derived greater pleasure from reading, as he observed in the *AAYA* interview: "I have always felt our lives are too small, too thin and insubstantial. When we watch television—and I have always watched a lot of television—we are powerfully distracted from our routines, but only through reading are we really nourished."

The future poet and novelist was a voracious reader—"I always used to read everything I could get my hands on, from the steamiest trash to very difficult philosophy books I sometimes struggled to understand"—and through books he discovered the world. "By reading I was decoding the secrets the world around me did not want me to have," he told *AAYA*, "parting the curtain and seeing the other, full-color existence that did not try to sell me beer or a new car." For Cadnum the key to these secrets is the library. "To this day I love libraries, much more than bookstores," he continued, "because libraries are welcoming, the same way novels are welcoming. Books, like so much in the real world, give, and ask nothing in return."

"Not since the debut of Robert Cormier . . . has such a major talent emerged in adolescent literature. . . . There is the same oblique economy of language, the same startling richness of metaphor, the same depth of understanding of emotional pain."

—Patty Campbell on Michael Cadnum

Cadnum has also unlocked the secrets of the world through personal experience. "At one time in my career I ran a Suicide Prevention Center in Southern Alameda County," he said in the interview. "I listened to many unhappy people on the telephone, and I learned that everyone has a story to tell, confessions and insights no one wanted to listen to. Young and old, there are people out there who struggle to articulate their hopes." He added, "I feel that these people on the margins of life, young people, people just out of jail, extremely talented people estranged from their families, are not on the margins at all. They are where life really is." In fact, Cadnum concluded, "It is the so-called mainstream men and women, so-called normal people, who are in danger of living empty lives."

Ghostly Beginnings

In nearly all of his novels Cadnum portrays people who exist on the margins of life, such as successful professionals harboring unfulfilled desires or hidden demons and troubled teenagers coping with dysfunctional families. *Nightlight*, Cadnum's fiction debut, features Paul Wright, a restaurant reviewer who is bored with his job and has been haunted by a recurring nightmare. Paul is asked by his Aunt Mary to locate her missing son Len, an eccentric photographer who takes pictures of ghosts in cemeteries near his isolated cabin in northern California. When Paul invites his girlfriend Lise to go along on the trip he does not realize both Lise and Mary are having the same nightmare that torments him. Arriving at the cabin, Paul and Lise discover Len has disappeared, leaving behind all of his belongings as well as his tape-recorded conversations with a mysterious presence. Soon Paul and Lise are caught up in a series of unsettling events before they finally encounter Len's "companion." The plot builds to a frightening conclusion that leaves the reader wondering whether Len was insane or had actually been haunted by ghosts.

Nightlight was greeted with unanimous praise from critics. *Locus* reviewer Scott Winnett termed the novel "a remarkable debut," citing the ambiguous ending as evidence that the "worst ghosts of all are the ones inside yourself." Another *Locus* contributor, Edward Bryant, judged *Nightlight* to be "literary horror at a high level" because of "the author's use of a poet's precision to pick just the right words and images." Bryant urged other horror fiction writers to "[p]ay attention to Michael Cadnum." In a review for *Voice of Youth Advocates* (*VOYA*) Mary Lee Tiernan gave the first-time novelist a similar accolade, comparing him with Stephen King.

Cadnum delved into the supernatural again with his second novel, *Sleepwalker*, which features Davis Lowry, a famous archaeologist on a dig at an eighth-century bog in Yorkshire, England. Dreams of his dead wife compel Lowry to sleepwalk, and his work is interrupted by several accidents at the excavation site. Eventually he and his team unearth a 1,200-year-old Norse king, and when they see the corpse roaming the bog at night they suspect the mishaps and disasters were caused by supernatural forces. The story unfolds as Lowry and his colleagues try to solve the mystery. Eric W. Johnson recommended the book in *Library Journal* as "a richly textured and suitable mood study of revenge and terror" that is a "delicious blend" of "reality and the paranormal." Taking an opposite perspective in the *New York Times Book Review*, Ed Weiner found *Sleepwalker* to be only a

GHOSTWRIGHT

MICHAEL CADNUM

author of *Saint Peter's Wolf*

"A haunting thriller about the dark side of artistic impulse. Plenty of suspense and surprises."
—*The San Francisco Chronicle*

Haunted by the man from whom he stole ideas in the past, a successful playwright is confronted with a terrifying dilemma in this psychological thriller.

"slightly creepy, slightly musty" novel with an "unbelievable" ending.

Although Cadnum wrote *Saint Peter's Wolf* for adults, the book was placed on young adult reading lists. A retelling of the werewolf myth, it is the story of Benjamin Byrd, a proper San Francisco psychologist and art collector who is having marital problems. During a search for art treasures he finds a set of silver fangs. He then becomes obsessed with werewolves and is ultimately transformed into a beast that commits extremely violent acts. As Byrd changes back and forth from man to werewolf, he begins to appreciate the freedom and power he has as a creature of nature. He falls in love with Johanna, a woman who has also been transformed into a werewolf, and together they try to liberate themselves from their stifling human shapes.

During the interview with Saari, Cadnum discussed his purpose in writing the novel: "When I create a character like the psychologist in *Saint Peter's Wolf*, who finds himself able to change from an intelligent but constrained human to a werewolf, I am trying to celebrate our enormous potential for life. I think we are all deliciously complex, full of potential, part Sheriff of Nottingham and part Robin Hood." Don G. Campbell, a *Los Angeles Times Book Review* contributor, called *Saint Peter's Wolf* an "engrossing approach to a durable myth." Writing in *VOYA*, Delia A. Culberson was even more laudatory. She found the novel to be "a spellbinding *tour de force* in a rare blend of fantasy, horror, adventure, suspense, and passionate love. . . . A superb, fascinating book that subtly evokes that ancient, primal yearning in all living, breathing things for total, exhilarating freedom."

The YA Audience

Calling Home was Cadnum's first book published specifically for young adults. In the *AAYA* interview with Saari he revealed, "I wrote *Calling Home* thinking of it as a literary novel to be read by someone like myself. When it was accepted for publication as a young adult novel I was very surprised, because I had never heard of a young adult market." *Calling Home* is the story of Peter, a teenage alcoholic who accidentally kills his best friend, Mead. The boys are sharing a bottle of cognac in the basement of an abandoned house next to Peter's home, and in a moment of drunken anger Peter punches Mead. When he realizes his friend is dead he begins impersonating Mead in calls to Mead's parents, telling himself throughout the novel, "Impersonating the dead is easy." In the meantime he tries to lead a normal life through an alcoholic haze, keeping up the ruse that Mead has run away. Finally the pressure becomes unbearable and he confesses to another friend, Lani, whose lawyer father gets Peter the help he needs. Running through the main action are subplots about Peter's estranged parents and his girlfriend Angela, who contributes to his alcohol problem.

Calling Home was widely reviewed, gaining Cadnum recognition as one of the foremost authors for young adults. In *Wilson Library Journal*, Cathi Dunn MacRae noted that Cadnum "skillfully shapes suspense through masterful control of language," taking readers "so completely inside this disconnected boy, . . . they will never forget the experience." *Horn Book* reviewer Patty Campbell stated that *Calling Home* was an "exquisitely crafted work, a prose poem of devastating impact." Campbell added, "Not since the debut of Robert Cormier with *The Chocolate War* . . . has such a major talent emerged in adolescent literature. . . ." Roger Sutton observed in *Bulletin of the Children's Center for Books* that *Calling Home* offers "probably the truest portrait of a teenaged alcoholic we've had in YA fiction." *VOYA* reviewer Jane Chandra, however, considered it a "disappointing book" with "too many unanswered questions about Mead's death, the resulting investigation, and the (lack of) relationship between Mead's friends and his parents."

Cadnum's next novel, *Ghostwright*, is a psychological thriller about Hamilton Speke, a successful playwright. Speke's life begins to unravel after the appearance of serial killer Timothy Asquith, who had been his writing partner long ago. Claiming Speke stole his manuscripts, Asquith demands a share of the playwright's property. During a struggle Speke kills Asquith, then he buries the body, only to see the "corpse" lurking around the estate a few days later. When Speke digs up the grave and finds a rotting deer carcass, he learns Asquith had staged the murder. Determined to kill Speke, Asquith sets fire to the estate in a bloody climactic scene. As Marylaine Block stated in *Library Journal, Ghostwright* is a "fine novel of psychological horror" that "keeps readers as uncertain as Speke about what is real, what is only imagined. . . ." In *Publishers Weekly* Sybil Steinberg wrote, "From start to astonishing finish, this good old-fashioned thriller delivers." Larry W. Prater pointed out in *Kliatt,* however, that "the novel is perhaps too slow moving and too psychologically complex for many YAs."

Like *Calling Home*, Cadnum's next novel for young adults, *Breaking the Fall,* depicts a troubled teenager as the main character. Stanley North, a sophomore in high school, has difficulty coping with his parents' crumbling marriage and is doing poorly at school. He is torn between the worlds of his emotionally balanced girlfriend Sky, who urges him to return to sports, and his self-destructive friend Jared, who tantalizes him with the dangerous game of breaking into houses. Stanley becomes increasingly caught up in the thrill of stealing small items from homes while the occupants are sleeping. At the same time he attempts to free himself from crime by perfecting his burgling skills, but in the process he loses the respect of his parents and Sky.

"I want to give a voice to characters who ordinarily never have one. . . . I want to tell the secrets that are not told, and to see the world through new eyes."

—Michael Cadnum

Once again critics praised Cadnum's engrossing, suspenseful plot and his ability to evoke believable characters. In reviews for *Horn Book* Maeve Visser Knoth and Patty Campbell judged *Breaking the Fall* to be superior YA literature. According to Knoth, "The author writes truthfully about the seductive nature of power and friendships, recognizing the lengths to which young people will go in order to prove themselves," and Campbell wrote that Cadnum upheld the promising talent he exhibited in *Calling Home.* Susan L. Rogers noted in *School Library Journal* that "Some readers may be disturbed by this story, although mature teens may find it a more realistic reflection of a troubled world. . . ."

Breaking the Fall was followed by two psychological thrillers for adults, *The Horses of the Night* and *Skyscape.* In *The Horses of the Night* Cadnum gives a twist to the Faust legend in which a man sells his soul to the devil in return for power. Stratton Fields, a socially prominent San Francisco architect who "has it all," enters a contest to redesign Golden Gate Park. Plot complications multiply when he is accused of murdering the contest head. A *Kirkus Reviews* contributor noted that "Stratton wrestles with the questions of his sanity, while all along he grows in worldly and personal power— power that he can turn to good . . . or evil." *Locus* reviewer Winnett stated that Cadnum communicates a compelling message in *The Horses of the Night:* "dreams are never worth the price we pay for them. And you won't see the price tag until it's far too late."

Skyscape examines celebrity and media hype in the story of Curtis Newns, a world-renowned painter whose masterpiece, *Skyscape,* is mysteriously burned. Seeking help for a creative block from television psychiatrist Red Patterson, Newns becomes enmeshed in a spiraling descent into violence and death. In *Publishers Weekly,* Sybil Steinberg identified Patterson's "slowly revealed character" as "the novel's center," adding that "although the revelations threaten to oversimplify Cadnum's argument about fame and genius, they make for an arresting climax." *Library Journal* reviewer Robert C. Moore observed that Cadnum addresses "some weighty questions: Does the media create our stars or simply magnify their qualities? Does art belong to its creator or to society?"

Disconnected Youth

Cadnum again turned to young adult fiction with *Taking It, Zero to the Bone,* and *Edge.* In *Taking It* the author sensitively traces the psychological deterioration of Anna Charles, a seventeen-year-old kleptomaniac who is the daughter of wealthy, divorced parents. The story opens as Anna plays a game of wits with department store detectives while trying to resist the temptation to shoplift items she does not need. This compulsion reflects her low self-esteem and growing alienation from family and friends, which are caused by her mother's remarriage and her father's remoteness. Eventually losing control, Anna steals her best friend's dog then drives 500 miles to see her brother Ted, who was her childhood idol. When she realizes she can no longer communicate with Ted, she steals his savings and sets out for Las Vegas. The spree culminates in the desert with a car wreck and Anna's emotional collapse. The novel ends on a hopeful note, however, as Anna's father finally gives her a chance to express her feelings.

Becky Kornman stated in a *VOYA* review, "Cadnum realistically portrays an emotionally troubled teenager," noting that the reader "is drawn into Anna's mind and is able to experience her struggle. . . ." Praising Cadnum's "tight, beautiful prose" and his "finesse" in handling Anna's problems, *Booklist* reviewer Merri Monks concluded that *Taking It* "should not be missed." Diane

Roback and Elizabeth Devereaux were similarly impressed, observing in *Publishers Weekly* that Cadnum writes with "subtlety and tremendous insight" and "keeps readers on the edge of their seats with this taut psychological portrait."

Zero at the Bone is narrated by Cray Buchanan, a high-school senior whose sister, Anita, has disappeared. The novel examines the impact of this devastating event on Cray and his parents, who had all been productive, stable people. As they help the police search for Anita, their lives begin to unravel: they change as individuals, and they gradually question whether they really know one another. Upon discovering Anita's journal they realize they may not even have known her. A particularly compelling scene takes place in the morgue, as Cray and his parents wait to identify a body that turns out not to be Anita. Eventually the family pulls together again, although the mystery of Anita's disappearance is never solved.

The emotional anchor of *Zero at the Bone* is Cray, who has insight into the behavior of the people around him—in fact, he thinks he understands why Anita may have run away. As Carla A. Tripp notes in *VOYA,* "Cray possesses an uncanny sense about people. . . . So, even though he feels pain and emptiness (i.e., zero at the bone) left by his sister's disappearance, he *will* survive." Critics judged *Zero at the Bone* to be a riveting study of human relationships. Tripp termed it a "taut, psychological thriller," and *Publishers Weekly* reviewers Roback and Devereaux warned that "Fans of intense psychological dramas can expect to be emotionally drained by the time they reach the last chapter."

Family tragedy is also the subject of *Edge,* which Deborah Stevenson described in *Bulletin of the Center for Children's Books* as "a psychologically intense tale of inner struggle." Zachary Madison has dropped out of high school and works at a delivery job, yet he lacks direction. His life instantly becomes focused when his father, a successful science writer, is shot in a car-jacking and left paralyzed. At first helpless and disbelieving, Zach decides to seek justice after the man accused of attacking his father is set free. *Horn Book* reviewer Amy E. Chamberlain claimed that "it's worth the read to find out if he's capable of avenging his father's death." Although the novel "treads in the shadows," she wrote, "[it] breaks through the murk with a satisfying conclusion."

If you enjoy the works of Michael Cadnum, you may also want to check out the following books and films:

The works of Robert Cormier, including *I Am the Cheese*, 1977, *Fade*, 1988, and *In the Middle of the Night*, 1995.

Kathryn Lasky, *Prank*, 1984.

The works of Robert McCammon, including *They Thirst*, 1981, *Blue World*, 1989, and *Boy's Life*, 1991.

Over the Edge, Orion Pictures, 1979.

Stevenson also noted Cadnum's "dark narrative," but stressed that "measured, overdetermined prose suits the shadowy and searching mood."

Prior to *Edge*, Cadnum had published *The Judas Glass*, an adult novel based on the vampire legend. The complex plot revolves around Richard Stirling, an unhappily married attorney who falls in love with blind pianist Rebecca Pennant. He is shattered when Rebecca is found brutally murdered. After pricking his finger on an antique mirror and unwittingly taking the first step toward becoming a vampire, Richard himself dies when he crashes through a restaurant window. Clawing his way out of his coffin nine months later, he has the embalming fluid in his body replaced with human blood. Now a vampire, he resurrects Rebecca with his own blood and they revel in their superhuman existence. They soon realize their lives are unnatural, however, and Richard tries to become a human again. Critics remarked on Cadnum's continued virtuosity in giving a fresh perspective to old myths. Rachelle M. Blitz observed in *VOYA* that "This unique, sometimes puzzling novel offers horror fans a fresh approach to the vampire tale." Sybil Steinberg wrote in *Publishers Weekly* that "Cadnum brings an intensity of vision to this novel found in few other vampire stories," and she predicted that *The Judas Glass* was "bound to be one of the more provocative novels of 1996."

Expanding His Repertoire

In 1997 Cadnum published *The Lost and Found House*, a picture book for children about the ex-citing, and unsettling, adventure of moving to a new home. His poetic, evocative text is complemented with paintings by Steven Johnson and Lou Fancher that portray the experience through the eyes of an unnamed small boy. In the *AAYA* interview Cadnum discussed the autobiographical connection in the book: "My family moved several times during my childhood, much like the family in *The Lost and Found House*. I found the back gardens and new secret hideaways of the new houses fascinating. There were odd, lost treasures to be discovered—a discarded plastic soldier, a cat's eye marble—among the geraniums." Cadnum added that he wants to continue writing for children: "I enjoyed writing *The Lost and Found House*—and when I was a teacher I especially enjoyed working with very young children. I would very much like creating more such books."

Throughout his career as a novelist, Cadnum has continued publishing poetry and fiction in literary magazines, and several of his stories based on fairy tales have been published in anthologies. His thirteenth novel, *In A Dark Wood*, was set for publication in 1998. During the *AAYA* interview the author discussed the book, a retelling of the Robin Hood legend from the perspective of the Sheriff of Nottingham which he started twelve years ago. "I did a tremendous amount of research for *In A Dark Wood*," Cadnum recalled, "but I didn't know I was doing research. I thought I was reading about Robin Hood and traveling to Crusader castles in the Middle East and monasteries in France. I was just doing what I loved, and I turned out to know enough after a while to write a novel."

Cadnum summarized the story for *AAYA*: "It takes place as the Sheriff of Nottingham struggles to come to grips with the chaos caused by an uncatchable, mischievous robber some people are calling Robin Hood," he said. Since his version of the Robin Hood tale offers "a gritty, naturalistic view of the Middle Ages," he stressed that *In A Dark Wood* will appeal to sophisticated young adult readers. "The assistant to the Sheriff, Hugh, is a young man, in his early teens," Cadnum stated, "but the novel is best considered a 'crossover' book, not fitting into a typical YA category. It features torture, a boar hunt, a rampaging bear, archery, and bloodshed."

Another forthcoming novel is *Heat*, which features a platform diver who has been injured in an accident. Cadnum told *AAYA* how he developed the character of the swimmer: "As I wrote *Heat*, . . . I kept a Speedo swimsuit pinned to my bulletin board, the exact size and color my character wore," he said. "It was like having the character in the room with me." Further elaborating on his approach, Cadnum explained, "When I write a novel I live in the world of that story. . . . I want to become that character as I write, to smell the chlorine and feel the blood in my scalp."

Later he described his wider purpose in creating fiction: "I want to give a voice to characters who ordinarily never have one. So few people tell the story of a family that never discovers the truth about a missing child, as in *Zero at the Bone*," Cadnum asserted. "Few people have seen the Robin Hood story through the eyes of the Sheriff of Nottingham, as I do in *In A Dark Wood*. I want to tell the secrets that are not told, and to see the world through new eyes." Finally, Cadnum is motivated by the ultimate challenge to a writer: "I want to experience the joys and fears of people whom I never really meet."

■ Works Cited

Blitz, Rachelle M., review of *The Judas Glass, Voice of Youth Advocates*, December, 1996, p. 276.

Block, Marylaine, review of *Ghostwright, Library Journal*, July, 1992, pp. 119-20.

Bryant, Edward, review of *Nightlight, Locus*, June, 1990, p. 23.

Cadnum, Michael, interview with Peggy Saari for *Authors and Artists for Young Adults*, September 9 and 17, 1997.

Campbell, Don G., review of *Saint Peter's Wolf, Los Angeles Times Book Review*, July 21, 1991, p. 6.

Campbell, Patty, review of *Calling Home, Horn Book*, May/June, 1994.

Chamberlain, Amy E., review of *Edge, Horn Book*, July/August, 1997, p. 452.

Chandra, Jane, review of *Calling Home, Voice of Youth Advocates*, August, 1991, p. 168.

Culberson, Delia A., review of *Saint Peter's Wolf, Voice of Youth Advocates*, December, 1991.

Review of *The Horses of the Night, Kirkus Reviews*, June 1, 1993, p. 674.

Johnson, Eric W., review of *Sleepwalker, Library Journal*, February 15, 1991, p. 219.

Jones, Patrick, "People Are Talking about . . . Michael Cadnum," *Horn Book*, March/April, 1994, p. 177.

Knoth, Maeve Visser, review of *Breaking the Fall, Horn Book*, November/December, 1992, p. 726.

Kornman, Becky, review of *Taking It, Voice of Youth Advocates*, February, 1996, pp. 368-69.

MacRae, Cathi Dunn, review of *Calling Home, Wilson Library Journal*, April, 1992, p. 98.

Monks, Merri, review of *Taking It, Booklist*, July, 1995, p. 1879.

Moore, Robert C., review of *Skyscape, Library Journal*, September 1, 1994, p. 213.

Prater, Larry W., review of *Ghostwright, Kliatt*, March, 1994, p. 14.

Roback, Diane, and Elizabeth Devereaux, review of *Taking It, Publishers Weekly*, July 10, 1995, p. 59.

Roback, Diane, and Elizabeth Devereaux, review of *Zero at the Bone, Publishers Weekly*, June 17, 1996, p. 66.

Rogers, Susan L., review of *Breaking the Fall, School Library Journal*, September, 1992, p. 274.

Steinberg, Sybil, review of *Ghostwright, Publishers Weekly*, June 1, 1992.

Steinberg, Sybil, review of *Skyscape, Publishers Weekly*, August 22, 1994, p. 43.

Steinberg, Sybil, review of *The Judas Glass, Publishers Weekly*, January 8, 1996, p. 59.

Stevenson, Deborah, review of *Edge, Bulletin of the Center for Children's Books*, July/August, 1997.

Sutton, Roger, review of *Calling Home, Bulletin of the Children's Center for Books*, May, 1991, p. 212.

Tiernan, Mary Lee, review of *Nightlight, Voice of Youth Advocates*, October, 1990, p. 225.

Tripp, Carla A., review of *Zero at the Bone, Voice of Youth Advocates*, February, 1997, p. 326.

Weiner, Ed, review of *Sleepwalker, New York Times Book Review*, March 31, 1991, p. 16.

Winnett, Scott, review of *Nightlight, Locus*, June, 1990, p. 31.

Winnett, Scott, review of *Horses of the Night, Locus*, July, 1993, p. 33.

■ For More Information See

BOOKS

Something about the Author, Volume 87, Gale, 1996, pp. 32-35.

PERIODICALS

ALAN Review, Spring, 1997.
America, October 28, 1995, p. 27.
Booklist, November 15, 1992, p. 589.

Books for Keeps, July, 1997, p. 27.

Bulletin of the Center for Children's Books, October, 1997, p. 45.

Horn Book, January/February, 1996, p. 77; September/October, 1996.

Junior Bookshelf, October, 1996, p. 198.

Kirkus Reviews, May 15, 1992, p. 625; June 21, 1993, p. 87; September 1, 1997, p. 1386.

Kliatt, November, 1993, p. 4; December 15, 1995, p. 1716.

Library Journal, January, 1990, p. 146; May 15, 1991, p. 106; July, 1993, p. 118; February 15, 1994, p. 216; February 15, 1996, p. 178.

Locus, July, 1992, p. 35.

Publishers Weekly, January 19, 1990, p. 98; May 3, 1991, p. 62; May 10, 1991, p. 284; November 16, 1992, p. 65; June 21, 1993, p. 87; June 17, 1996, p 66; June 2, 1997, p. 72; October 13, 1997, p. 74.

School Librarian, May, 1997, p. 99.

School Library Journal, July, 1991, p. 88; February, 1992, p. 121; August, 1995, p. 154; January 8, 1996, p. 59; February 15, 1996, p. 178; July, 1996, p. 98.

Tribune Books (Chicago), July 18, 1993; September 18, 1994, p. 7.

—Sketch by Peggy Saari

Chris Carter

edy series *Brand New Life,* 1989; Fox Broadcasting Company, creator, executive producer, and occasional director of the drama series *The X-Files,* 1993—, creator and executive producer of the drama series *Millennium,* 1996—.

■ Personal

Born in Bellflower, CA, in 1956; son of William (a construction worker) and Catherine (a homemaker; maiden name, Mulder) Carter; married Dori Pierson (a screenwriter), 1987. *Education:* California State University at Long Beach, graduated in 1979.

■ Addresses

Home—Pacific Palisades, CA. *Office*—Fox Broadcasting Company, 10201 W. Pico Blvd., Los Angeles, CA 90064.

■ Career

Surfing magazine, writer and editor, beginning 1979; Walt Disney Studios, screenwriter for television, including several television movies and pilots for *Cameo by Night* for NBC and *The Nanny* for The Disney Channel; NBC, co-producer of the comedy series *Rags to Riches;* The Disney Channel, creator and executive producer of the com-

■ Awards, Honors

Numerous awards for *The X-Files,* including the Environmental Media Award, Outstanding Episodic Television (Drama), 1994, for "Darkness Falls"; Parent's Choice Honors, 1994, for Best Series; New York Festival for Television Programming and Promotion, Finalist for Best Writing, 1994, for "The Erlenmeyer Flask"; Emmy Award nominations, Outstanding Drama Series and Outstanding Writing in a Dramatic Series, both 1995, both for "Duane Barry"; Golden Globe Award, 1995, for Best Dramatic Series; Television Critics Association Award nominations, 1995, for Best Drama Series and Program of the Year; Viewers for Quality Television Awards nomination, 1995, for Best Drama Series; Saturn Award, Academy of Science Fiction, Fantasy and Horror, 1995, for Outstanding Television Series; Edgar Allan Poe Award nomination, Mystery Writers of America, 1995, for Best Episode in a Television Series, "The Erlenmeyer Flask"; Emmy Award nomination, 1996, for Outstanding Drama Series; Directors' Guild of America Award nominee, Best Direction in a Dramatic Series, 1996, for "The List"; Writers Guild of America Award nominee, Best Writing in a Dramatic Series, 1996, for "Duane Barry"; Golden

Laurel Award nominee, Producers Guild of America, 1996, for Outstanding Series; Saturn Award nominee, Academy of Science Fiction, Fantasy and Horror, 1996, for Best Genre TV Series; New York Festival Awards nominee, 1996, for Best Drama Series; International Monitor Award, Best Director, 1996, for "The List"; Television Critics Association Award nominee, 1996, for Best Drama Series; Golden Globe Award, Best Dramatic Series, 1997.

■ Writings

(With others) *The X-Files* (television drama series), Fox, 1993—.
(With others) *Millennium* (television drama series), Fox, 1996—.

■ Adaptations

The X-Files has been adapted into original full-length adult novels, including *Goblins* and *Whirlwind*, both by Charles Grant, and *Ground Zero* and *Ruins*, both by Kevin J. Anderson, all published by HarperPrism. Episodes from *The X-Files* have been adapted into books for juvenile readers by several authors, including Lee Martin. *The X-Files* has also been adapted into a comic book series, published by Topps Comics, and into interactive adventure CD-ROMs, created by HyperBole Studios and released by Fox Interactive. Two albums including music from the show and music inspired by the show have been released by Warner Bros, *Songs in the Key of X: Music from and Inspired by The X-Files* (Carter wrote the words for the song "If You Never Say Goodbye," recorded by P. M. Dawn) and *The Truth and the Light*. Episodes from *Millennium* have been adapted into a series of books, including *Millennium 2000* and *Gehenna*, both published by Ingram, 1997.

■ Work in Progress

Screenplay for a feature film version of *The X-Files*.

■ Sidelights

Special FBI Agents Dana Scully and Fox Mulder investigate paranormal activity and alien abductions while simultaneously uncovering the govern-

ment conspiracy set in place to hide the very things they seek to expose. Former FBI agent Frank Black, now a member of the secretive Millennium Group, chases down criminals with the help of his psychic vision while working to stop the conspiracy of evil set to peak in the year 2000. "The truth is out there" promises *The X-Files* every week. "I want to believe" declares a poster in Agent Mulder's office, reflecting the very essence of the character himself. His creator, however, does not believe. "I've never had a personal experience with the paranormal," Chris Carter explains in an interview with David Bischoff for *Omni*. "I've never seen a UFO, I've never been contacted by anything or anyone. My personal opinion? Well, I should preface this by saying that I'm a natural skeptic. My tendency is to discount most of the stuff because my personal experience doesn't include it."

And so it was without the help of personal experience that Carter created his critically-acclaimed and popular television dramas *The X-Files* and *Millennium*. Since its debut in 1993, *The X-Files* has slowly built up a following of almost fanatical proportions while also winning the praise of critics and some of the highest ratings on the Fox Broadcasting Company. Because of this success, Carter created *Millennium* in 1996, another dark, apocalyptic drama that boasted the highest-rated premiere of any show in Fox Broadcasting history. "To every generation, there is a televisionary," states a *Time* writer, adding: "Today's seer is Chris Carter, . . . creator of *The X-Files*, a show that takes America's obsession with the occult and coverups, with truths impossible to ignore but too terrible to be told, and transforms that paranoia into a compelling amalgam of hipness and horror—proving it possible to be both cool and unnerved." Terrence Rafferty, writing in *Gentleman's Quarterly*, compares Carter's television accomplishments to the novels of best-selling horror author Stephen King: "Carter's TV shows, like King's novels and stories, rely on meticulous pulp-fiction craftsmanship to tap into an audience's collective fear of dissolution, of encroaching chaos."

The creator of this chaos and paranoia was born and raised in Bellflower, California, a very normal, middle-class suburb of Los Angeles. "I have what a lot of people in this business don't: a very blue-collar background," Carter explains in a *Rolling Stone* interview with David Lipsky. "My mom was a homemaker. My father was a construction

Carter's hit television series, *The X-Files*, which explores paranormal activity and extraterrestrial contact, stars David Duchovny as FBI Agent Fox Mulder and Gillian Anderson as Agent Dana Scully.

worker—the guy people curse as they go down the street because he's one of the men who was tearing up the roads putting in storm drains and sewer lines." Carter's father was also the kind of guy who believed in strict discipline for his sons. Once Carter was punished for coming home late by being forced to eat his dinner outside, on a manhole cover in the middle of the street.

Strange punishments like this one and other factors may have contributed to Carter's later paranoid take on life. He tells Lipsky that he's "very,

very paranoid, in that I'm acutely aware of fear and betrayal. My father had a bad relationship with his mother. She had left his father at an early age, so he was keenly attuned to her betrayal of him. I think that's something that was passed down." Another factor contributing to Carter's early paranoia can be traced back to his mother and her inability to keep a secret. "So if as a kid you go to your mother and you tell her something, and she can't keep a secret, it develops in you, you know, a sense that nothing is safe," Carter reveals in his *Rolling Stone* interview.

While paranoia was becoming a part of Carter's childhood, so was surfing, a sport he discovered at the age of twelve and one in which he remains active today. "Even though we lived inland, I would always find ways to get to the beach," Carter remembers in his interview with Lipsky. "I still surf, though I'm not as nimble as I once was." It was this surfing experience and Carter's journalism major at California State University at Long Beach that led to his first career as a writer. Other college experiences contributed to Carter's

need for perfection and desire to master everything he attempts to accomplish. "I put myself through school working as a production potter," he relates to Lipsky. "When I was a sophomore, I built a house from the ground up with a carpenter. I can build things; I can make things. I know how to take a project and finish it, which is what producing is: seeing a problem, you know, and actually taking the materials and hammering the pieces together."

Anderson, Carter, and Duchovny celebrate backstage at the 54th annual Golden Globe Awards ceremony after receiving honors for their work on *The X-Files*.

Producing television shows was not Carter's first job, though. Following his graduation from college in 1979 he started writing for *Surfing* magazine in San Clemente, California. "I was hired because I was a journalism major in college and had been a surfer all my life," Carter states in a *Sci-Fi Entertainment* interview. "Traveling around the world and surfing, I had one of the best prolonged adolescence a young man could want. It allowed me a lot of freedom to write, develop a voice, read, and see the world . . . and surf, of course." Despite all the writing he did for *Surfing*, Carter didn't consider writing screenplays until he met screenwriter Dori Pierson in 1983; they began dating and were married in 1987. "I had never really had any ambition to be a screenwriter," Carter tells Lipsky. "But I had an idea. I'd go to see movies—I mean, everybody has an idea for a movie. And so I told it to her, she liked it, and she said, 'Well, why don't you write the screenplay?' So I did. And it actually got a lot of attention around town."

This attention never materialized into anything, so Carter wrote another script—a comedy—which was seen by Jeffrey Katzenberg, then the head of production at Disney. Based on this effort, Katzenberg hired Carter to write for television and produce several television movies. "This was at a time when Disney needed product, and they needed writers," Carter explains to Lipsky. "They were doing *The Disney Sunday Movie* every week. These producers would come to my door on the lot, and they'd say, 'You want to do a *Disney Sunday Movie*?' I'd say yes to everybody because, you know, they're asking me to write. That's where I got seduced by television: the pace, the control that I saw that you could have." Among the shows Carter wrote for during his time at Disney were the television pilots for *Cameo by Night* for NBC and *The Nanny* for The Disney Channel.

Taking a break from Disney at the urging of softball pal Brandon Tartikoff, Carter co-produced the second year of the NBC comedy *Rags to Riches*. Back to Disney in 1989, he became the creator and executive producer of *Brand New Life*, a recurring comedy series that ran as part of a rotating schedule on Disney's Sunday night lineup. 1992 saw Carter moving again, this time to Twentieth Century-Fox Television, where he signed an exclusive deal to create and develop television projects for the network.

The X-Files Gets Its Start

The first show Carter pitched to his new network was a scary show like the ones he enjoyed watching as a child, including *Twilight Zone, Night Gallery, The Outer Limits,* and most importantly, *Kolchak: The Night Stalker,* which was the inspiration for *The X-Files.* "He [Kolchak] was a reporter who investigated a monster of the week," describes Carter in his *Rolling Stone* interview. "But what was nice for me is that in the 20 years between *Kolchak* and *The X-Files,* a lot happened in science and technology. And those things—which, you know, became the foundation for *The X-Files*—they didn't really have at the time. . . . What I really wanted was to do a good scary show."

"They are the equal parts of my desire to believe in something and my inability to believe in something. My skepticism and my faith."

—Chris Carter, discussing the characters of Mulder and Scully

With the main premise of the show in place, Carter sketched out the details, which came from a variety of elements. First, he saw an FBI agent on the *Larry King* show whose primary assignment was to investigate satanic cults. "He said that he had found not one ounce of truth in any of those things," Carter relates in his *Rolling Stone* interview, adding: "I found it interesting that they had somebody specifically investigating something like that." Another FBI influence appeared in the form of the movie *Silence of the Lambs;* Carter both admired and studied this film. All of these elements converged into one idea—the show would feature two lead FBI agents who tracked biological and chemical oddities, twists in genetics, and alien sightings and abductions. In addition, Carter wanted to differentiate the series from other horror series by basing it in scientific fact. "It's the idea that shakes up you and your beliefs, not some hideous Frankenstein monster or hand clasping the heroine's shoulder," he explains in an interview for the *San Francisco Chronicle.*

Focusing on his two lead characters, Carter decided to shake up traditional gender stereotypes, making the female (Scully) the skeptical scientist and the male (Mulder) the intuitive believer. And so Mulder and Scully came "right out of my head," Carter explains to Bischoff. "A dichotomy. They are the equal parts of my desire to believe in something and my inability to believe in something. My skepticism and my faith. And the writing of the characters came very easily to me. I want, like a lot of people do, to have the experience of witnessing a paranormal phenomenon. At the same time I want not to accept it, but to question it. I think those characters and those voices came out of that duality." The names of the characters also hold some personal significance for Carter—Mulder is the maiden name of Carter's mother, and Scully is named for Los Angeles Dodgers announcer Vin Scully, who Carter listened to while growing up.

Now that all the pieces were in place, Carter presented his concept to Fox, where it was not well received at first. In between his first pitch to the network and their rejection of the show, Carter made a trip to Martha's Vineyard (which later became the fictional location of Mulder's childhood). While there, he had dinner with a Yale psychology professor and researcher who had been a consultant for the UFO abduction drama *Intruders*. During this dinner Carter was introduced to the statistical survey done by Harvard professor John Mack which shows that three percent of the American public believe they have been abducted by aliens. "Here were two guys—one from Harvard, one from Yale—who were saying, 'There's something here,'" Carter maintains in his interview with Lipsky. "It was all I needed to go back to Fox." And so Carter fought for his idea, eventually winning a chance; filming for *The X-Files* finally began in March of 1993.

Unexpected Success

What followed was something Carter never expected—both critical success and an almost maniacal following. "I had no idea this could happen," Carter states in an *Entertainment Weekly* interview with Dana Kennedy. "I wrote this in my office in my surf trunks, playing with my dog. It never occurred to me that someday there'd be *X-Files* key chains." And *X-Files* conventions, books, comic books, CDs, and thousands of fans visiting hundreds of *X-Files* sites on the Internet on a daily basis. Most importantly, though, *The X-Files* has become the highest rated show on the Fox television network.

From its first season on, *The X-Files* has interwoven episodes concerned with Carter's main conspiracy theory storyline with stand-alone stories of truly bizarre scientific anomalies. "Even in the program's alien-intensive first season, Carter and his writing staff took pains to vary the formula, with episodes whose story lines bypassed the larger conspiracy arc," observes Rafferty. "The inclusion of these self-contained stories is, like everything else about the series' genesis, evidence of Carter's pragmatic intelligence." Rafferty goes on to add that "the stand-alone hours also demonstrated right from the start, the unusual flexibility of the series' concept: The program ranged freely among the distinct genres of fantastic narrative, and Mulder and Scully didn't look out of place in any of them."

The success of the stand-alone episodes is more than matched by the audience's interest in the main conspiracy storyline, which is slowly revealed as each season progresses. These episodes deal with the government's involvement in a convoluted cover-up of extraterrestrial contact, alien abduction of humans (that includes Mulder's sister being abducted when they were children), and genetic experimentation. "The thing that has come through on this show that's really alarming and wonderful for me is that almost everybody feels the government is not acting in their best interests," states Carter in a *Rolling Stone* interview with David Wild. "One survey by the Roper poll said there are 5 million people who believe they've been abducted by aliens. People say, 'Well, then you knew you had an audience.' But that's not my audience, that's my *fuel*."

In addition to its huge public following, *The X-Files* is a critical success and major award-winning show. "By skillfully blending post-Cold War, antigovernment paranoia; old-fashioned conspiracy theory; sly humor; and stories drawn from today's headlines (not to mention little green men and beast-women), *The X-Files* beat out favorites like *NYPD Blue* and *ER* for best drama series at the recent Golden Globes," points out Kennedy in a 1995 *Entertainment Weekly* article. Among the elements that make *The X-Files* an award-winning show are its pervasive atmosphere, its deadpan humor, and its ever-developing and growing main characters. "Each episode is a mood piece—a queasy odyssey," asserts James Wolcott in the *New Yorker.* "It's television's first otherworldly procedural." Wolcott goes on to write that *The X-Files* "takes time to seep into its surroundings," concluding that "what's erotic about the show is its slow progression from reverie to revelation, stopping just short of rapture. It wants to swoon, but swooning would mean shutting its eyes, and there's so much to see."

Also focusing on what can be seen in *The X-Files,* *Entertainment Weekly* writer Ken Tucker describes the show as having "a bland, anonymous look to it that only enhances the show's unsettling atmosphere. Its special effects aren't anything out of the ordinary; instead, Carter, who's also the executive producer, elicits our heebie-jeebies by cre-

ating disturbing moods, and by extracting convincingly rattled performances from the actors." The material the actors have to work with has expanded dramatically since the series beginning, culminating in terminal cancer for the character of Scully. "Carter has turned *The X-Files* into a show about a pair of existential detectives, and in the process he has both expanded and slyly subverted its paranoid premise," points out Rafferty. "Finally, it is not the presence of unidentified flying objects but our increasing identification with *The X-Files'* human protagonists that tells us, beyond dispute, that we are not alone." "Give yourself over to *The X-Files,*" concludes Tucker, "and you'll be in the hands of people who know exactly how to mess with your mind."

The mind of *The X-Files* creator produced an even darker and creepier concept for his second Fox series, *Millennium,* which premiered in 1996 with the highest debut Nielsen rating for any show in Fox history. Based on the premise that violence is not random, *Millennium* instead maintains that it is part of an evil conspiracy, related to the Book of Revelations, that will reach its horrific climax when the year 2000 arrives. Frank Black, an ex-FBI agent who can see into the minds of killers through his psychic ability, is part of the Millennium Group, an undercover Justice Department team which is made up of other former law enforcement officials. At the same time, Black's wife and daughter, as well as the family's huge bright yellow house, seem to represent hope for humanity in the face of all this evil. "For me the whole reason to do the show was that yellow house—a bright center in a dark universe," Carter relates to Ginia Bellafante in *Time.*

Unlike its predecessor, *Millennium* did not have the luxury of developing its dark world slowly; the show was promoted heavily, flooding the media with its numerous promos. Because of the success of *The X-Files,* contends Wolcott, "Carter found himself in the predicament of having to top himself. The pounding promotional hoopla for *Millennium* has prevented it from building slowly, forcing it to come big out of the box." And so the premiere episode of the series was both big and graphically violent. "By most accounts, *Millennium* has scared the living daylights out of quite a few people with its graphic images and horrific tales of serial killers who lop off heads, sew mouths shut, hack bodies, and burn priests at the stake," describes Mark Schwed in *TV Guide.*

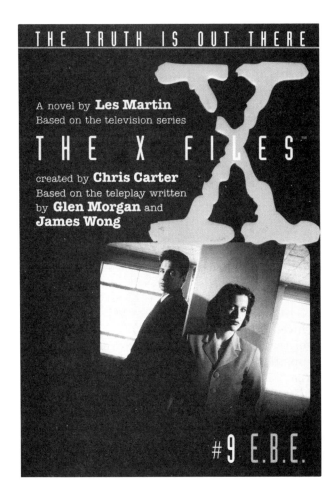

THE TRUTH IS OUT THERE

A novel by **Les Martin**
Based on the television series

THE X FILES™

created by **Chris Carter**
Based on the teleplay written by **Glen Morgan** and **James Wong**

#9 E.B.E.

Mulder and Scully travel across the country to intercept a truck that may be carrying an E. B. E., an Extraterrestrial Biological Entity, in this 1996 novelisation of an episode from the first season of *The X-Files.*

If you enjoy the works of Chris Carter, you may also want to check out the following:

Rod Serling's seminal television series, *The Twilight Zone.*

The Thing, a film produced and co-directed by Howard Hawks, 1951.

The Man Who Fell to Earth, a film starring David Bowie, 1976.

Close Encounters of the Third Kind, a film written and directed by Steven Spielberg, 1977.

This unrelenting horror is exactly what critics cite as the culprit in making *Millennium* too oppressive. "My principal qualm about *Millennium,* the heavy-breathing new series from Chris Carter's crackpot conspiracy canteen," writes John Leonard in *New York,* "is that it's so apocalyptic, we can't even hiccup: It's paranoia without the laughs." While also contending that the show is too depressing, Wolcott does concede that *Millennium* "casts a spell, looking and moving as if it were a prose poem of infernal night, with embers still flickering under the toxic fumes." And Bellafante asserts that "as over the top as *Millennium* can get, the show does succeed at creating a marvelously unrelenting sense of unease."

Having two hour-long drama series running at once finds Carter faced with an unrelenting amount of work, work made much more time-consuming by his perfectionist, controlling tendencies. "Chris has his hands on every single aspect of the show," Gillian Anderson (the actress who plays Scully) tells Lipsky. "He's a controlling maniac, and he's a genius." Lance Henriksen (Frank Black on *Millennium*) similarly states in *TV Guide:* "I can only describe him as the Phantom. He arrives if there is a problem. He disappears right after it's solved. The only thing missing is the outfit." And according to Carter, he is also missing a life outside the work his two series create for him. "I go to work, and I go home," he tells Lipsky. "I had one of those Global Positioning Systems given to me as a gift. It's a little screen in my car that draws a map—drops these little rabbit pellets—to show where you've been. And my map is a very monotonous single track, back and forth to work. I go to Vancouver. I don't do anything else."

Carter's hordes of fanatical fans wouldn't have it any other way. And Carter himself is happy to give them the darkness they crave. "What I've attempted to do was scare you in a smart way that makes you think and question," he states in a *Time* magazine article. "Carter is a storyteller, but one with a unique, sometimes disturbing vision that has slowly seeped into the collective American consciousness," asserts NBC Entertainment president Warren Littlefield in an article in *TV Guide.* "The articulate visual style of his work, coupled with taut, engaging writing, makes for provocative television." "We live in a frightening world," Carter points out to Wild, "and if we can give people a good roller-coaster ride, that's great."

■ **Works Cited**

Bellafante, Ginia, "Mission: Paranormal," *Time,* October 28, 1996, p. 100.

Bischoff, David, "Opening *The X-Files:* Behind the Scenes of TV's Hottest Show," *Omni,* December, 1994, pp. 42-46, 88.

Carter, Chris, in an interview for the *San Francisco Chronicle,* September 5, 1993.

"A Conversation with *The X-Files'* Creator Chris Carter," *Sci Fi Entertainment,* December, 1994.

Kennedy, Dana, "*The X-Files* Exposed," *Entertainment Weekly,* March 10, 1995, pp. 18-24.

Leonard, John, "Doctor Spook," *New York,* October 28, 1996, pp. 132-33.

Lipsky, David, "Chris Carter in The Virtue of Paranoia: The Creator of *The X-Files* Isn't Scared! But He's Nervous," *Rolling Stone,* February 20, 1997, pp. 35-40.

Rafferty, Terrence, "Into the Heart of Darkness," *Gentleman's Quarterly,* April, 1997, pp. 107-13.

Schwed, Mark, "Heart of Darkness" and "Master of the Macabre," *TV Guide,* November 16, 1996, pp. 14-17, 20-21.

"*Time's* 25 Most Influential Americans," *Time,* April 21, 1997, p. 149.

Tucker, Ken, "'X' Marks What's Hot," *Entertainment Weekly,* January 21, 1994, pp. 40-41.

Wild, David, "Television 'X'-Ploitation," *Rolling Stone,* November 30, 1995, p. 79.

Wild, David, "X Files Undercover," *Rolling Stone,* May 16, 1996, pp. 38-42, 74.

Wolcott, James, "'X' Factor," *New Yorker,* April 18, 1994, pp. 98-99.

Wolcott, James, "Too Much Pulp," *New Yorker,* January 6, 1997, pp. 76-77.

■ For More Information See

BOOKS

Lavery, David, editor, *Deny All Knowledge: Reading "The X-Files,"* Syracuse University Press, 1996.

Lavery, David, editor, *Trust No One: Reading "The X-Files,"* Syracuse University Press, 1996.

Lowry, Brian, *The Truth Is Out There: The Official Guide to "The X-Files" Created by Chris Carter,* HarperPrism, 1995.

Schuster, Hal, *The Unauthorized Guide to The X-Files,* Prima Publishing, 1997.

PERIODICALS

Entertainment Weekly, December 1, 1995, pp. 56-57; November 29, 1996, pp. 24-58.

People Weekly, June 19, 1995, pp. 117-19; April 29, 1996, p. 26; September 2, 1996, p. 48.*

—Sketch by Susan Reicha

Cameron Crowe

■ Personal

Born July 13, 1957, in Palm Springs, CA; married Nancy Wilson (a musician), c. 1990. *Education:* Attended California State University.

■ Addresses

Home—Seattle, WA. *Office*—Los Angeles, CA. *Agent*—c/o Creative Artists Agency, 9830 Wilshire Blvd., Beverly Hills, CA 90212.

■ Career

Associated with *Rolling Stone,* San Francisco (now New York City), 1973-82; writer, 1981—; screenwriter, 1982—; director of films, including *Say Anything . . .,* 1989; *Singles,* 1992; and *Jerry Maguire,* 1996.

■ Awards, Honors

Grammy Award nomination, best album notes, Association of Recording Arts and Sciences, 1986, for Bob Dylan's *Biograph;* Academy Award nominations, Best Screenplay Written Directly for the Screen and Best Picture, both 1996, both for *Jerry Maguire.*

■ Writings

BOOKS

Fast Times at Ridgemont High: A True Story, Simon & Schuster, 1981.

SCREENPLAYS

Fast Times at Ridgemont High (adapted from Crowe's book), Universal, 1982.
The Wild Life, Universal, 1984.
Say Anything . . ., Twentieth Century-Fox, 1989.
Singles, Warner Bros., 1992.
Jerry Maguire, TriStar, 1996.

OTHER

Contributor to periodicals, including *Circus, Creem,* and *Rolling Stone.* Author of the album notes for Bob Dylan's *Biograph* and Led Zeppelin's boxed set, 1990.

■ Film Credits

DIRECTOR

Say Anything . . . , Twentieth Century-Fox, 1989.
Singles, Warner Bros., 1992.
Jerry Maguire, TriStar, 1996.

PRODUCER

The Wild Life, Universal, 1984.
Singles, Warner Bros., 1991.
Jerry Maguire, TriStar, 1996.

OTHER

Appeared as delivery boy in *American Hot Wax,* 1978, police officer in *The Wild Life,* Universal, 1984, and club interviewer in *Singles,* Warner Bros., 1991. Creative consultant to television series *Fast Times* (based on *Fast Times at Ridgemont High*), 1986.

■ Sidelights

Although Cameron Crowe has written only five screenplays and has directed just three films, he is considered one of Hollywood's premier filmmakers. Crowe began his cinematic career by penning the screenplay for the wildly popular 1982 film *Fast Times at Ridgemont High* (based on his book of the same name), and he made his directorial debut in 1989 with *Say Anything . . . ,* a sophisticated teen romance. Crowe is perhaps best known, though, for the 1996 film *Jerry Maguire,* which received an Academy Award nomination for Best Picture.

Crowe was born on July 13, 1957, in Palm Springs, California. His father was a real estate agent and his mother was a teacher. He had two older sisters, but one died during childhood. Crowe was a sickly child, suffering from the kidney disease nephritis, but he was also precocious, and skipped kindergarten and two primary grades. For this reason, Crowe never really felt comfortable with his peers. In an interview with Rachel Abramowitz in *Premiere,* Crowe described his high school years in San Diego: "everyone split into two groups: those who had a tan and those who did not have a tan. I could even go to the beach and I would still not have a tan. . . . The girl I asked to the prom laughed hysterically."

One thing that Crowe did enjoy about school was writing for the school newspaper. By the time he was thirteen, he was also writing for the *San Diego Door,* an underground newspaper, and soon after he began submitting articles to the popular-music magazines *Creem* and *Circus.* He graduated from high school at the age of fifteen, and soon

after he began working as a journalist for the magazine *Rolling Stone.* He stayed there for seven years, profiling artists such as the Allman Brothers, the Eagles, Peter Frampton, King Crimson, and Led Zeppelin.

When *Rolling Stone* moved their headquarters to New York, Crowe left his position. He had an idea for a book, though: he would return to high school as a undercover student and write a book about his experiences. He moved back into his parents' house and arranged with the principal of Ridgemont High School to enroll as a senior for the 1979-80 academic year under the name Dave Cameron. In an interview with Richard Harrington of the *Washington Post,* Crowe described his assignment as "the senior year I never had."

Originally, Crowe had planned to be a character in the book that he wrote. But as he became friends with the students, he realized that omitting himself as a character would close the distance between the reader and subjects. He portrayed the students realistically in their own settings—school, the mall where many of the students worked after school, and the beach. "I thought the kids were a lot smarter than they were being given credit for," Crowe said to Harrington. "They're anonymous Joes who are not unwed mothers or angel-dust cases; they're just average kids slugging through life. When I saw the inner trauma in these kids' lives, I started getting excited."

The Inside Stuff

Fast Times at Ridgemont High: A True Story is the book that resulted from Crowe's year in high school in Redondo Beach, California. There are six major characters in the book: an already-jaded sexual sophisticate, a tough guy, a nerd, a surfer, and a middle-class brother and sister. The usual school occasions, such as homecoming, prom, and graduation, are chronicled, as well as several more personal situations, including one student's experience in getting an abortion. Because Crowe left himself out of the book, it reads like fiction, but, as a reviewer noted in *Publishers Weekly,* it contains "some unmistakably real slices of high school life." "Margaret Mead or Robert Coles might have probed more deeply," Harrington added, "but it's doubtful they would have gotten so close to the heart of adolescence."

Sean Penn starred as stoned-out surfer Jeff Spicoli in *Fast Times at Ridgemont High,* a film based on Crowe's book about life in a California high school.

Film rights for *Fast Times at Ridgemont High* were sold even before the book was published. The film was filled with vignettes depicting the rituals, sexual anxieties, and humiliations that high school students face, but it did not have a discernible plot or a famous actor to star in it. For this reason, the studio, Universal, underpromoted the film. Studio executives were pleasantly surprised when *Fast Times at Ridgemont High* emerged as the sleeper of the year, garnering huge audiences by word of mouth and favorable reviews.

Some reviewers found *Fast Times at Ridgemont High* unconvincing, others found it plausible, and most found it entertaining. Writing in the *New Yorker,* Pauline Kael noted "Watching *Fast Times at Ridgemont High,* I was surprised at how not-bad it is. It may fall into the category of youth-exploitation movies, but it isn't assaultive, and it's certainly likable. Directed by a young woman— Amy Heckerling, making her feature-film debut— the movie has an open, generous tone." Janet Maslin, reviewing the film in the *New York Times,* called it "a jumbled but appealing teenage comedy with something of a fresh perspective on the subject."

Fast Times at Ridgemont High launched the careers of several actors, including Sean Penn, who played the partying surfer Jeff Spicoli; Jennifer Jason Leigh, who played Stacy Hamilton, a freshman who is disappointed by her first sexual experience; Nicholas Cage, who made his film debut under his real name, Nicholas Coppola; and Eric Stoltz,

Crowe made his directorial debut with the 1989 romantic comedy *Say Anything . . .*, featuring John Cusack as a non-conformist who falls for the brilliant Ione Skye.

who has appeared in all of Crowe's projects to date.

Next, Crowe wrote the screenplay for *The Wild Life*, which was crafted as a sequel to *Fast Times*. The film depicts teenagers living in a singles apartment complex immediately after high school, and stars Eric Stoltz, Lea Thompson, and Christopher Penn (Sean Penn's younger brother). In a press release from *Universal News,* Crowe explained that *"The Wild Life* is also about the last week of summer. These young people reach the end of this period of time when you are supposed to have a really wild time and . . . they realize they haven't stockpiled enough experiences. . . . The film is about these kids who blow it out a bit more and discover how hard it is getting back to normal."

Unlike its predecessor, *The Wild Life* was not popular with reviewers and it bombed at the box of-

fice. Gene Siskel, writing in the *Chicago Tribune,* commented that the film "is totally preoccupied with sex" and noted that he disliked "the depiction of males exploiting females." David Ansen, reviewing the film in *Newsweek,* wrote that *The Wild Life* is "more interested in flattering its audiences with fantasies of wild partying and romance than telling it like it is. This is one for the kids; had it tried harder, it could have been one for everyone."

Although *The Wild Life* bombed at the box office, it opened a number of doors for Crowe because producer, writer, and director James L. Brooks saw that Crowe had potential. In an interview with Michael Walker of the *New York Times,* Brooks observed that "There are only a handful of people who have a distinctive voice. Cameron has that voice. He really does see the world in a certain way. If he doesn't do a movie, no one else will." Brooks worked with Crowe, meeting frequently to discuss his writing. In an interview with Susan Morgan for *Details*, Crowe remembered that Brooks was "brutally honest." "It was my version of film school," he said.

It was Brooks who mentioned to Crowe that father/daughter relationships are rarely depicted in film. This idea evolved into Crowe's third screenplay and his directorial debut, *Say Anything. . . .* The film depicts a complex triangular relationship between a gifted high school graduate, her doting father, and a likable, underachieving classmate who falls for her. The story concerns a change in the relationship between father (John Mahoney) and daughter Diane (Ione Skye) when the daughter discovers that her father is involved in a nursing home scam. The other important relationship in the film involves Diane and Lloyd (John Cusack), a fledgling kickboxer who feels that he is too much of a misfit to date Diane. In a *Los Angeles Times* review, Sheila Benson noted that

Crowe succeeds in his endeavor "to dig among the slag heaps of an almost mined-out genre—the teen-age movie—and come up with one of the nicest of the species, a film of warmth, insight, humor, and surprising originality." In the *Chicago Tribune*, Dave Kehr called *Say Anything . . .* "a beautiful film, full of wit, freshness and surprise and graced with a vivid, convincing sense of character and place." *People* reviewer Scott Haller described the film as "Frisky, savvy and wonderfully entertaining. . . . As he [Crowe] showed us with his script for *Fast Times at Ridgemont High*, the glorious champion of this inglorious genre, Crowe is a suburban sociologist wise in the tribal ways of youth." David Ansen of *Newsweek* noted that the film is "warm and generous-spirited, and Crowe's dialogue is light-years ahead of most adolescent sagas," and *New Yorker* reviewer Pauline Kael observed, "Crowe . . . keeps faith with teen-agers; he doesn't generalize about them (or about the older generation, either)."

A group of twenty-somethings learn about life and love in the 1992 film *Singles,* starring Matt Dillon, Bridget Fonda, and Kyra Sedgwick.

Moving beyond the Teenage World

After *Say Anything . . .* , Crowe was eager to leave the world of the very young and begin writing about men and women in their mid-twenties. "I just couldn't move on without trying to nail that experience," he explained in an interview with Walker. He wrote, directed, and coproduced *Singles*, a comedy about a group of young adults living in Seattle. There are four main characters in the film. Janet (Bridget Fonda), a waitress in an espresso shop and an aspiring actress, is obsessed with Cliff (Matt Dillon), a not-so-bright and emotionally callow rock musician whose band has a greater following in Belgium than in his hometown of Seattle. Janet's ex-boyfriend Steve (Campbell Scott) is a workaholic transportation planner who gets involved with Linda (Kyra Sedgwick),

an environmentalist who is afraid of commitment. All of the characters live in the same apartment complex; the familial atmosphere provides the characters with emotional connections to each other. In *New York,* David Denby wrote that the characters in *Singles* "are waiting for someone to tell them that it's okay to fall in love—yet no one can tell them such a thing but themselves. That's the gentle point of the picture."

Drawing on his background in rock music, Crowe enlisted Seattle sensations Alice in Chains and Soundgarden to perform live in *Singles.* The soundtrack for the movie, which was scored by Paul Westerberg, was instrumental in getting the film released. Studio executives, skeptical of the Seattle setting of the movie and marketing issues, delayed the film's release several times. However,

"Show me the money!"—Tom Cruise played a frustrated sports agent in Crowe's Academy Award-nominated 1996 film, *Jerry Maguire.*

when the soundtrack for the movie, which was released in June 1992, became a best-seller, no more delays took place.

The film met with mixed reviews. In *New Statesman and Society*, reviewer Jonathan Romney described *Singles* as a "1990s update on that 1980s invention, the lifestyle movie, and [it] inherits that form's inherent complacency. Its characters are self-obsessed, strictly part-time neurotics you'd love to slap. . . . It's nevertheless engaging, thanks to the deft touch of director/writer Cameron Crowe." David Ansen, writing in *Newsweek*, remarked: "Employing an unconventional structure full of funny flashbacks and talking-to-the-camera monologues, *Singles* is brimful of clever bits and likable performances. Why, then, does it feel so weightless?" Denby wrote that "the movie is a hand-holding charmer." Chicago *Sun-Times* reviewer Roger Ebert declared, "*Singles* is not a great cutting edge movie, and parts of it may be too whimsical and disorganized for audiences raised on cause-and-effect plots. But I found myself smiling a lot during the movie, sometimes with amusement, sometimes with recognition. It's easy to like these characters, and care about them." In an interview with Tim Appelo of *Entertainment Weekly*, Crowe himself said of the movie, "The good thing about *Singles* is that it comes from the right place. It's from the heart."

Jerry Maguire

In 1996, Crowe wrote and directed his most acclaimed film, the Academy Award-nominated *Jerry Maguire*. The film, starring Tom Cruise, is the story of a high-powered sports agent who is caught up in the world of deal-making. He views everything as a commodity, from his clients to his NFL-publicist fiancee (Kelly Preston) to his life. But despite his capitalistic success, Jerry feels disconnected. So he writes a mission statement advocating that Sports Management International (SMI), the company he works for, pay more attention to fewer clients (for less revenue). Within days, he is fired by SMI and stumbles upon a new life. He remains a sports agent, albeit a struggling one. He holds on to a single client, the Arizona Cardinals' brash wide receiver Rod Tidwell (Cuba Gooding, Jr.). Jerry dumps his fiancee and abruptly marries Dorothy Boyd (Renee Zellweger), a single mom who is so enamored with Jerry and his mission statement that she quits her

If you enjoy the works of Cameron Crowe, you may also want to check out the following films:

American Graffiti, written and directed by George Lucas, 1973.
Moonstruck, starring Cher and Nicolas Cage, 1987.
An Officer and a Gentleman, starring Richard Gere and Debra Winger, 1982.
Slacker, 1991, and *Dazed and Confused,* 1993 both written and directed by Richard Linklater.

job as a bookkeeper at SMI to work for him. "I love him for the man he almost is," she says at one point during the film. "To be or not to be—a human being, that is. That's the question that courses through nearly every scene of Jerry Maguire," stated Owen Gleiberman of *Entertainment Weekly*. In a review of *Jerry Maguire* in the *Nation*, Stuart Klawans said of Crowe's direction of the film: "Except for one or two point-of-view shots and a handful of disjunctive cutaways, about the flashiest move he [Crowe] makes is to let you hear the sizzle of the ice cubes in a glass of water. . . . To be subtle without demanding that the audience notice one's subtlety—what a marvelous gesture of respect. It's enough to make you believe in the radical premise that Crowe has been testing throughout his film career: that people want to live decently, most of the time, and with some effort can do it."

Although his experience as a director is limited, Crowe has earned a reputation for being able to summon amazingly naturalistic performances from the actors in his films. Sometimes he requires that actors go through more than a dozen takes to achieve this realism. *New Yorker* reviewer Terrence Rafferty noted that in Crowe's latest film, his "delicate touch has a beneficial effect on the star: Cruise looks uncharacteristically relaxed, and in the first half-hour of *Jerry Maguire* he does the best acting of his career." But Crowe is also a director that actors and actresses enjoy working with. As Polly Platt, the producer of *Say Anything . . . ,* explained in an interview with Abramowitz, "Cameron gets his way through being an inherently decent human being."

■ Works Cited

Abramowitz, Rachel, "The Making of the Film *Singles*," *Premiere*, August, 1992, p. 66.

Ansen, David, "Careening Teens," *Newsweek*, October 8, 1984, p. 89.

Ansen, David, "A Crowe's Eye View of Teen Love," *Newsweek*, April 17, 1989, p. 72.

Ansen, David, "The Games People Play," *Newsweek*, September 21, 1992, p. 78.

Appelo, Tim, "Seattle Night Fever," *Entertainment Weekly*, September 18, 1982, pp. 47-49.

Benson, Sheila, review of *Say Anything . . .* , *Los Angeles Times*, April 14, 1989.

Crowe, Cameron, interview with Richard Harrington, *Washington Post*, August 13, 1982.

Crowe, Cameron, interview with Susan Morgan, *Details*, September, 1992.

Crowe, Cameron, interview with Michael Walker, *New York Times*, September 6, 1992.

Denby, David, review of *Singles*, *New York*, October 5, 1992, p. 102.

Ebert, Roger, review of *Singles*, *Sun-Times* (Chicago), September 18, 1992.

Gleiberman, Owen, "Agent of Change," *Entertainment Weekly*, December 13, 1996, pp. 53-54.

Haller, Scott, review of *Say Anything . . .* , *People*, April 24, 1989.

Kael, Pauline, review of *Fast Times at Ridgemont High*, *New Yorker*, November 1, 1982, pp. 146-51.

Kael, Pauline, review of *Say Anything . . .* , *New Yorker*, May 15, 1989, pp. 122-23.

Kehr, Dave, review of *Say Anything . . .* , *Chicago Tribune*, April 14, 1989.

Klawans, Stuart, "Poor Sports," *Nation*, December 30, 1996, pp. 34-36.

Publishers Weekly, July 17, 1981.

Maslin, Janet, review of *Fast Times at Ridgemont High*, *New York Times*, September 3, 1982.

Rafferty, Terrence, review of *Jerry Maguire*, *New Yorker*, December 16, 1996, pp. 118-19.

Romney, Jonathan, "The Grunge Generation," *New Statesman and Society*, January 15, 1993, p. 34.

Siskel, Gene, review of *The Wild Life*, *Chicago Tribune*, October 2, 1984.

Universal News, press release from Press Department of Universal Studios, August 1, 1984.

■ For More Information See

PERIODICALS

America, April 10, 1982, pp. 273-75.

Entertainment Weekly, March 5, 1993, p. 61; January 17, 1997, p. 62.

Interview, November, 1984.

Nation, November 21, 1981, pp. 548-49.

National Review, February 24, 1997, p. 54.

Newsweek, September 20, 1982, pp. 92-93.

New York Times Book Review, May 5, 1989.

People, November 19, 1984; May 22, 1989, p. 62; September 21, 1992, p. 18.

Playboy, September, 1981, p. 116.

Rolling Stone, February 3, 1978, pp. 32-36.

Sports Illustrated, December 23, 1996, p. 20.

Time, September 28, 1992, p. 75; December 16, 1996.

Vogue, September, 1992, p. 330.*

—Sketch by Irene Durham

Salvador Dali

■ Personal

Born Salvador Domenech Felipe Jacinto Dali, May 11, 1904, in Figueras, Spain; son of Salvador (a notary) and Felipe Dome (Domenech) Dali; married Gala Eluard, 1935; died January 23, 1989, of respiratory failure and pneumonia. *Education:* Marist Friars School, Figueras, 1914-18; San Fernando Academy of Fine Arts, Madrid, 1921-26.

■ Career

Artist. Illustrator for books and magazines, Figueras, 1919-21; artist in Sitges, 1925-30, Paris, 1930-40, Pebble Beach, CA, 1940-48, and in Port-Lligat, Spain, from 1948 until his death. Filmmaker, with Luis Bunuel, *Un Chien andalou* (*An Andalusian Dog*), 1929 and *L'Age d'or* (*The Golden Age*), 1930. Ballet designer, Bacchanale, 1939, Labyrinth, 1941, Mad Tristan, Sentimental Colloquy, Cafe de Chinitas, all 1944, and Le Chevalier remaine et la dame espagnole, 1961; member of Andre Breton's Surrealist Group of artists and writers in Paris, 1930-34; Dali museums established in St. Petersburg, FL, and Figueras.

■ Awards, Honors

Huntington Hartford Educational Foundation award, 1957; gold medal of the city of Paris, 1958.

■ Exhibitions

INDIVIDUAL EXHIBITIONS

1925 Galeria Dalmau, Barcelona
1927 Galeria Dalmau, Barcelona
1929 Galeria Goemans, Paris
1931 Galerie Pierre Colle, Paris
1932 Julien Levy Gallery, New York; Galerie Pierre Colle, Paris
1933 Galeria d'Art Catalunya, Barcelona; Julien Levy Gallery, New York; Galerie Pierre Colle, Paris
1934 Julien Levey Gallery, New York; Galeria d'Art Catalunya, Barcelona; Zwemmer Gallery, London; Galerie Quatre Chemins, Paris; Galerie Jacques Bonjean, Paris
1936 Alex Reid and Lefevre Gallery, New York; Julien Levy Gallery, New York
1939 Dali Studio, Paris; Julien Levy Gallery, New York
1941 Museum of Modern Art, New York; Julien Levy Gallery, New York; Julien Levy Gallery, Hollywood, CA
1942 Museum of Modern Art, New York
1943 M. Knoedler and Co., New York
1945 Bignon Gallery, New York
1946 M. Knoedler and Co., New York

1947 Cleveland Museum of Art; Bignon Gallery, New York

1948 Bignon Gallery, New York

1950 Carstairs Gallery, New York

1951 Galerie David Weill, Paris; Alemany and Ertman, New York; Lefevre Gallery, London

1952 Carstairs Gallery, New York; Alemany and Ertman, New York

1953 Santa Barbara Museum of Art, CA

1954 Palazzo Pallaricini-Rospigliosi, Rome; Carstairs Gallery, New York

1955 Philadelphia Museum of Art; Denver Art Museum

1956 Casino Communal, Knokke, Belgium; Carstairs Gallery, New York

1958 M. Knoedler and Co., New York; Carstairs Gallery, New York

1959 French and Co., New York

1960 Musee Galliera, Paris; Finch Gallery, New York; Carstairs Gallery, New York

1963 M. Knoedler and Co., New York

1964 Prince Hotel Gallery, Tokyo (travelled to Prefectural Museum of Art, Nagoya and the Municipal Art Gallery, Kyoto); Los Angeles Municipal Art Gallery

1965 M. Knoedler and Co., New York; Phyllis Lucas Gallery, New York

1966 Gallery of Modern Art, New York

1967 Hotel Meurice, Paris; Galerie D, Prague; Staempfli Gallery, New York

1968 Palais des Beaux-Arts, Charleroi, Belgium; London Graphic Art Gallery; Phyllis Lucas Gallery, New York

1969 Galerie Les Heures Claires, Paris; Hiram College, OH; Galerie Knoedler, Paris; Zachary Walker Gallery, Los Angeles

1970 Museum Boymans-van Beuningen, Rotterdam (retrospective); M. Knoedler and Co., New York; Galleria Guissi, Turin; Musee de l'Athenee, Geneva; Galerie Andre-Francois Petit, Paris; M. Knoedler and Co., New York; Karl-Ernst-Osthaus Museum Hagen, West Germany

1971 *Gemalde, Zeichnungen, Objekte Schmuck,* Staatliche Kunsthalle, Baden-Baden, West Germany; *Art-in-Jewels Exhibition,* Whitechapel Art Gallery, London; Museum Boymans-van Beuningen, Rotterdam

1972 *Holograms Conceived by Dali,* M. Knoedler and Co., New York; Museum Boymans-van Beuningen, Rotterdam; Galerie Isy Brachot, Brussels

1974 Städtisches Galerie/Stadelsches Kunstinstitut, Frankfurt

1977 *Bilder, Gouachen, Zeichnungen, Skulpturen,* Sammlung Levy, Hamburg

1979 *Retrospective 1920-1980,* Centre Georges Pompidou, Paris

1980 Tate Gallery, London

1982 *Obra Grafica,* Caja de Ahorros, Madrid

1984 Galeria Surrealista, Barcelona

1987 Galerie 1900-200, Paris

SELECTED GROUP EXHIBITIONS

1921 *Group Exhibitions,* Galeria Dalmau, Barcelona

1933 *Exposition Surrealiste,* Galerie Pierre Colle, Paris

1936 *Fantastic Art, Dada & Surrealism,* Museum of Modern Art, New York

1940 *Exposicion Internacional del Surrealismo,* Galeria de Arte Mexicano, Mexico City

1951 *Surrealisme en Abstractie,* Stedelijk Museum, Amsterdam

1959 *Exposition Internationale du Surrealisme,* Musee d'Art Moderne, Paris

1965 *Bienal,* Sao Paolo

1968 *Dada, Surrealism and Their Heritage,* Museum of Modern Art, New York

1970 *Surrealism,* Moderna Museet, Stockholm

1982 *A Century of Modern Drawing,* British Museum, London (travelled to the Boston Museum of Fine Arts, and the Cleveland Museum of Art)

MAJOR MUSEUM COLLECTIONS

Teatro Museo Dali, Figueras, Spain; Dali Museum, St. Petersburg, FL

OTHER MUSEUM COLLECTIONS

Museum of Modern Art, New York; Musee National d'Art Moderne, Paris; Metropolitan Museum of Art, New York; Salvador Dali Museum, Cleveland, OH; National Museum, Stockholm; Stedelijk, Amsterdam; Nationalgalerie, Berlin; Tate Gallery, London; Guggenheim Museum, New York; Art Institute of Chicago; Staatsgalerie Moderner Kunst, Munich; Glasgow Art Gallery; National Gallery of Art, Washington, DC; Kunstmuseum, Basel, Switzerland

■ **Writings**

IN ENGLISH TRANSLATION

The Declaration of Independence of the Imagination and of the Rights of Man to His Own Madness, [New York], 1939.

La Vie secrete de Salvador Dali (autobiography), translation by Haakon M. Chevalier published as *The Secret Life of Salvador Dali,* Dial, 1942, new and enlarged edition, 1961, 5th edition, Vision Press, 1976.

Rostros ocultos (novel), translation by Chevalier published as *Hidden Faces,* Dial, 1944, Morrow, 1974.

(Editor and illustrator) Michel Eyquem de Montaigne, *Essays,* translated by Charles Cotton, Doubleday, 1947.

(And illustrator) *Fifty Secrets of Magic Craftsmanship,* translation by Chevalier, Dial, 1948.

(With Philippe Halsman) *Dali's Mustache: A Photographic Interview,* Simon and Schuster, 1954.

Les Cocus du vieil art moderne, Fasquelle, 1956, translation by Chevalier published as *Dali on Modern Art: The Cuckolds of Antiquated Modern Art,* Dial, 1957.

Impressions and Private Memoirs of Salvador Dali, January, 1920, translated by Joaquim Cortada i Perez and edited by A. Reynolds Morse, Morse Foundation, 1962.

Journal d'un genie (autobiography), La Table Ronde, 1964, translation by Richard Howard published as *Diary of a Genius,* Doubleday, 1965.

(With Alain Bosquet) *Entretiens avec Salvador Dali,* Editions Pierre Belfond, 1966, translation by Joachim Heugroschel published as *Conversations With Dali,* Dutton, 1969.

(And illustrator) *Lettre ouverte a Salvador Dali,* A. Michel, 1966, translation by Harold J. Salemson published as *Open Letter to Salvador Dali,* James Heineman, 1968.

(With Luis Bunuel) *L'Age d'or; [and] Un chien andalou* (two screenplays; title of former means "The Golden Age," produced in France by Vicomte de Noailles, 1930; title of latter means "An Andalusian Dog," co-produced in France with Bunuel, 1928), translated by Marianne Alexandre from unpublished French manuscripts, Simon and Schuster, 1968.

Dali par Dali, Draeger, 1970, translation by Eleanor R. Morse published as *Dali by Dali,* Abrams, 1970.

(With Andre Parinaud, and illustrator) *Comment on Devient Dali: Les Aveux inavouables de Salvador Dali* (autobiography), R. Laffont, 1973, translation by Salemson published as *The Unspeakable Confessions of Salvador Dali as Told to Andre Parinaud,* Morrow, 1976.

Les Diners de Gala, Draeger, 1973, translation by J. Peter Moore published under same title by Felicie, 1973.

Explosion of the Swan: Salvador Dali on Frederico Garcia Lorca and Three Poems by Gerard Malanga, Black Sparrow Press, 1975.

(With Max Gerard and Louis Orizet, and illustrator) *Les Vins de Gala,* Draeger, 1977, translation by Olivier Bernier published as *Dali: The Wines of Gala,* Abrams, 1978.

Dali: The Salvador Dali Museum Collection, foreword by A. Reynolds Morse, introduction by Robert S. Lubar, Brown/Bulfinch, 1991.

IN FRENCH

La Femme visible, Editions surrealistes, 1930.

Babaouo, [Paris], 1932, reprinted, Editorial Labor, 1978.

(With Michel Deon, and illustrator) *Histoire d'un grand livre: Don Quichotte,* J. Foret, 1957.

Le Mythe tragique de l'Angelus de Millet, J. J. Pauvert, 1963.

(With Louis Pauwels) *Les Passions selon Dali,* Denoel, 1968.

Dali de Draeger, edited by Gerard, Le Soleil Noir, 1968.

Oui: Methode paranoiaque-critique et autres textes, Denoel-Gonthier, 1971.

(Contributor) *Proces en diffamation, plaide devant la Conference du Stage,* P. Belfond, 1971.

(Contributor) Henri-Francois Rey, *Dali dans son labyrinthe: Essai,* B. Grasset, 1974.

(With Sarane Alexandrian) *Dali et les poetes,* Filipacchi, 1976.

ILLUSTRATOR

Andre Breton, *Second Manifeste du surrealisme,* Kra, 1930.

Breton, *Le Revolver a cheveux blancs,* Cahiers libres, 1932.

Isidore Lucien Ducasse, *Les Chants de Maldoror,* A. Skira, 1934.

Tristan Tzara, *Grains et Issues,* Denoel and Steel, 1935.

Paul Eluard, *Cours naturel,* Sagittaire, 1938.

Maurice Yves Sandoz, *The Maze,* Doubleday, Doran, 1945.

Billy Rose, *Wine, Women, and Words,* Simon and Schuster, 1948.

Sandoz, *La Labyrinthe,* Mermod, 1949.

Sandoz, *La Maison sans fenetres,* P. Seghers, 1949.

Sandoz, *On the Verge,* Doubleday, 1950.

Sandoz, *La Limite,* La Table Ronde, 1951.

Eugenio d'Ors y Rovira, *La Verdadera historia de Lidia de Cadaques,* J. Janes, 1954.

Clair Goll and Yvan Goll, *Nouvelles petites fleurs de Saint Francais d'Assie,* Emile-Paul, 1958.

Pedro Antonio de Alarcon, *Le Tricorne,* Nouveau Cercle Parisien du Livre, 1958.

Dante Alighieri, *La Divine comedie,* Editions d'art Les Heures Claires, 1960.

Gerson D. Cohen, *Aliyah,* introduction by David Ben-Gurion, Sherwood, 1968.

Lewis Carroll, *Alice's Adventures in Wonderland,* Maecenas, 1969.

Alexander Jones, editor, *The Jerusalem Bible,* Doubleday, 1970.

Alfred Laepple, *Bilder zur Bibel,* Pattloch, 1974.

Contributor to magazines, including *Le Surrealisme au service de la revolution, L'Amic des arts, Gaseta de les arts, Le Minotaure, American Weekly,* and *Cahiers d'art.* Also contributor to sound recording "Dali in Venice: 'The Spanish Lady and the Roman Cavalier,'" Richmond, 1962.

■ Sidelights

Even people unfamiliar with Surrealism know Salvador Dali: his name and his wild-eyed look, heightened by that gravity-defying moustache, are almost synonymous with the movement for the general audience. Dali's paintings, distorted images executed in his signature old master technique, are hallmarks of the Surrealist credo, the embrace of the irrational. His unsettling images and dreamscapes affected the arts at every level; echoes of his work can still be seen in many advertisements and music videos, and the technique of juxtaposing familiar images with peculiar settings that seems common today began with Dali. In his lifetime, Dali was as well known for his artwork (which in addition to painting, encompassed filmmaking and theatrical productions, even clothes design) as for his persona. He blazed the trail for the artist as star (setting the scene for much of Pop art and its greatest artist/star, Andy Warhol), eagerly gobbling up every opportunity for self-promotion. Ultimately, even unenthusiastic critics acknowledge that what *Newsweek*'s Scott Sullivan termed the "haunting psychic landscapes, hard-edged and viscous at the same time," have "become a permanent feature of the century's visual consciousness."

Dali was born in 1904 into a prosperous family in Figueras, Catalonia, coincidentally the same Spanish region that produced Pablo Picasso and

Juan Gris. An older brother, also named Salvador, died in infancy exactly nine months and ten days before Dali's birth. The surviving Dali often spoke of an awareness of his older brother's presence. Although they kept a picture of the deceased brother in their bedroom, Dali's parents doted on him as well, this in spite of his frequent temper tantrums and violent tendencies. From early on, Dali was drawn to displays of power, either by authorities or of his own. In his autobiography, *The Secret Life of Salvador Dali,* he described himself as a self-absorbed, often cruel child who enjoyed exhibitionism and voyeurism. In one incident, he recalled kicking his sister in the head when she was a toddler—and his "delirious joy" in doing so.

But along with this unusual behavior, Dali showed an unusual talent for drawing and painting. Before he was ten, Dali concentrated primarily on landscapes; two exceptions are *Portrait of Helen of Troy* and *Joseph Greeting His Brethren,* both of which show the direct influence of nineteenth-century academic Spanish painting. Not only did his parents encourage his interest, they provided space for a studio in an unused part of their house. They also arranged for the adolescent Dali to live with their friend, Ramon Pitchot, an impressionist artist. Pitchot exposed the young artist to ideas beyond the academic paintings he had seen and copied. He began seeing the canvas as more than merely a surface for paint. In one instance, he attached cherry stems and worms to a painting of cherries, favorably impressing his mentor. Pitchot's influence was both direct and indirect. Quite by accident, Pitchot provided a prop that would serve Dali for most of his artistic life, when the young painter came across a crutch during his exploration of Pitchot's attic.

Dali enrolled at the San Fernando Institute of Fine Arts in Madrid in 1921, his days consumed with making his own art and familiarizing himself with the Prado Art Museum collection. Influenced by Juan Gris and Cubism, he left the sunnier colors of his early work behind, concentrating on a darker, more disconcerting palette. Yet he still incorporated the harsh elements of his native Catalonian landscape; impressions left by this dry, rocky terrain remained in his work throughout his career. The ease with which Dali painted and drew allowed him to move freely among various forms of art; he was a meticulous imitator (and ardent admirer) of Raphael and especially Jan

Vermeer, in addition to his more flamboyant flirtations with dadaism and other revisionary artistic movements whose agendas included social upheaval. Dali's embrace of revolutionary ideas and his need to act on them led to his eventual expulsion from the Institute, though not before he befriended the poet Federico Garcia Lorca and filmmaker Luis Bunuel. He later collaborated with Bunuel on two films, *Un Chien andalou* (*An Andalusian Dog*) and *L'age d'or* (*The Golden Age*), deemed "provocative classics" by *Time* art critic Robert Hughes.

Surrealism and Gala: Life Changing Forces

His visit to Pablo Picasso in Paris in 1928 became a seminal event for Dali: his first meeting with Andre Breton and the group of writers and artists that identified themselves as surrealists. Incorporating the controversial writings of Sigmund Freud on the unconscious, dreams, and sexuality, the surrealists aimed to break the constraints of realist representation, to reach the fantasies and dreams that constitute inner life. Surrealism's key spokesman, Breton, the artist Tristan Tzara (the founder of the surrealist movement) and poet Paul Eluard (whose wife, Gala, Dali eventually married) effectively changed the course of Dali's life.

Many critics highlight 1928 through 1938 as the artist's most solidly productive period. It was at this time that he announced the invention of his "paranoiac critical method," a self-hypnosis that he claimed allowed him to hallucinate freely. He said that he served as no more than a conduit for the unconscious images produced in this state, visions he then transferred onto his canvas. He explained these "double images" in his essay *The Stinking Ass*, as "such a representation of an object that it is also, without the slightest physical or anatomical change, the representation of another entirely different object, the second representation being equally devoid of any deformation or abnormality betraying arrangement." Thus, Dali not only emphasized the images in his paintings, but the importance of the process that brought them about.

In *The Imagery of Surrealism*, critic J. H. Matthews noted that the "paranoiac-critical method stands for something of more lasting significance than Daliesque self-advertisement." He added that Dali's "special contribution . . . to the surrealist

concept of the reality of things" is that the theory "vigorously affirmed the polyvalent function of visible forms." In short, it is the effect of seeing one object within another (the shape of a dog in the bark of a tree, for example). Writing of the paranoiac-critical method, Robert Hughes notes that "Dali's art may not tap far into his unconscious, but it reveals a great deal about what he imagined his unconscious to be."

Several well-known works were painted during this time, particularly in 1929, including *The Great Masturbator*, *The Lugubrious Game*, *Illumined Pleasures*, *Accommodations of Desire*, and *The Enigma of Desire*. They introduced viewers to the disturbing combination of highly accomplished realistic representations coupled with nightmarish images that would become Dali's trademark. Vast, uninviting landscapes serve as backdrop for several classically Freudian images: the lion (frequently emblematic of a threatening father), and the locust and the ant (both associated with sexual desire). Dali himself claimed to be surprised at what he saw appear with "fatality" on his canvases; in an article in *Art Digest*, he alluded to "all those manifestations, concrete and irrational, of that sensational and obscure world discovered by Freud, one of the most important discoveries of our epoch, reaching to the most profound and vital roots of the human spirit." That same year, Dali had his first solo exhibition, in Paris. Critical reception was not entirely favorable, but enthusiasts compared his work to the Dutch medieval painter Hieronymous Bosch and sixteenth-century Italian painter Giuseppe Arcimboldo.

Over the next two years, he worked with Bunuel on *An Andalusian Dog* and *The Golden Age*. He would later collaborate on several other films, including work with Walt Disney and Harpo Marx. Of these, his dream sequence for Alfred Hitchcock's 1945 film, *Spellbound*, is the best known. Eager to incorporate a dream that didn't use the cliched hazy images, James Bigwood noted that the director admitted in an interview that he considered Giorgio de Chirico or Max Ernst, artists who worked in a similar, dreamlike vein, "but none as imaginative and wild as Dali."

By 1930, Dali had established himself as a rising art star and was deeply involved with Gala Eluard. Many art historians and critics credit Gala as muse to several of the Surrealists, but her most wide-reaching influence was with Dali. Their love

Dali posing with a portrait of the Madonna, one of several works he painted containing mystical imagery.

affair became serious during the summer of 1929, when Gala and then-husband Paul Eluard visited Dali in Cadaques, Spain. Dressed in ragged clothes, his body smeared with a combination of fish glue and water, Dali managed to lure her away from her first marriage with his willingness to go to any excess. By the time of their own marriage in 1935, Gala had taken full charge of Dali's career, advising him on how to promote his work and himself. Their connection was so integral to his life and work that he often signed both names to his paintings.

Among the important paintings of 1931 are *Slumber, Burning Giraffe,* and his most recognizable work, *The Persistence of Memory.* Describing the erie, abandoned landscape (which includes a distorted face), draped with melting, tongue-like watches, as "vintage" Dali, critic Hughes notes that "we are looking down the wrong end of the telescope at a brilliant, clear, shrunken and poisoned world whose deep mannerist perspective and sharp patches of shadow invite the eye but not the body." Richard Lacayo in *People* noted that this painting "has become one of the touchstone images of the world."

Other important works he produced at this time include *The Enigma of William Tell* (1933) and *Average Atmospherocephalic Bureaucrat in the Act of Milking a Cranial Harp* (1933). Along with *The Persistence of Memory,* they are generally agreed by critics to be replete with symbols of impotence and decay, recurring themes in Dali's work. Dali's work was exhibited in Europe and, beginning in 1932, in the United States. He began to expand from painting to sculpture—including *Lobster Telephone* (1936), which featured a lobster as a receiver—and eventually collaborated with jewelry and clothing designers, including Elsa Schiaparelli and Coco Chanel.

Avida Dollars Appalls the Surrealists

By the mid-1930s, Dali's relationship with the Surrealists and Breton in particular became strained. In part, this had to do with Breton's idea that Surrealism align itself with the Marxist revolution, but more distressing to the Surrealists was Dali's fascination with power, specifically his unabashed early admiration for Adolf Hitler. His unwillingness to choose sides in the Spanish Civil War only alienated his former friends more. Dali had re-

cently finished *Soft Construction with Boiled Beans: Premonitions of Civil War* (1936), which many critics consider an antiwar piece. Writing about this painting, which depicts a human figure pulling itself to bits, William Gaunt observed in *The Surrealists* that "as a memento of a cruel century, the painting is comparable with *Guernica* of Picasso." Dismayed by Dali's political fence-sitting and embrace of brazen consumption, the Surrealists formally dropped him in 1938. A decade later, Breton anagrammed Dali's name to make his famous nickname: Avida Dollars (Greedy Dollars), a pointed reference to Dali's self-admitted devotion to cash.

Meanwhile, Dali continued to show his work and to spark controversy with his appearances. Engaged to lecture in London, he arrived encased in a deep-sea diving suit, to which he had attached an ornamental dagger and a cue stick, two leashed Russian wolfhounds in tow. Explaining himself, he proclaimed, "I just wanted to show that I was plunging deeply into the human mind." He travelled often during this period, especially to Italy where he immersed himself in Renaissance art. As well, he managed to meet Freud, then living in London. Asked for his diagnosis of Dali, Freud is reported to have commented, "I have never seen a more complete example of a Spaniard. What a fanatic."

Over this time, Dali's popular reputation grew in the United States, leading to a commission for the 1939 World's Fair in New York. Titled "Dali's Dream of Venus," the extravaganza was described by Fleur Cowles in her book *The Case of Salvador Dali* as: "Seventeen live mermaids, wearing fins, tails, brassieres, and very little else dived and played inside a tank filled with water. These girls were supposed to represent a 'prenatal chateau,' but among other things they were busy at highly surrealist activities inside the tank. . . . Some milked an underwater cow, some played imaginary music on piano keys painted on the body of a rubber woman (who was chained to a grand piano). Some 'liquid ladies' (as Dali called them) were also busy telephoning and typing." Unhappy with necessary changes to his overall concept decreed by his sponsors, Dali published *The Declaration of Independence of the Imagination and of the Rights of Man to His Own Madness.*

Anxious to capitalize on Dali's recognition in the United States, the New York department store

The bizarre, grotesque imagery which often imbued Dali's work can be seen in *The Face of War.*

Bonwit Teller commissioned a window from him. According to Cowles, Dali's design incorporated "a mannequin whose head was roses (her fingernails ermine, her negligee green feathers)" and "a lobster telephone." A male mannequin "wore Dali's 'aphrodisiac' dinner jacket with eighty-one glasses of *creme de menthe* attached to it. . . . Each glass was complete with a dead fly and a straw." The only furniture was "an old-fashioned bathtub" which Dali "lined in Persian lamb [and] filled with water and floating narcissi—with three wax hands holding mirrors about the edge." Unprepared for Dali's version of a display window, the Bonwit Teller staff took it upon themselves to make changes. As Cowles described, "Dali was so infuriated by [the] changes made without his permission that he stalked into the shop, walked inside the window, tipped the water out of his bath-

tub and smashed his way right through the pane of glass into the street amid a stunned sidewalk audience." Officers who briefly held him but soon let him go chalked up his aberrant behavior to being an artist.

With the onslaught of World War II, Dali and Gala moved to California. There, Helena Rubinstein and Billy Rose, among others, commissioned paintings. In addition to his film work, Dali published *The Secret Life of Salvador Dali* and his first novel, *Hidden Faces*, neither of which were hailed by most critics. One exception was B. D. Wolfe, writing in the *New York Herald Tribune*, who found it "impossible not to admire this painter as writer."

The explosion of the atomic bomb affected Dali deeply with what he termed a "great fear." Characteristic of this new awareness of the power of science and scientific ideas is *Exploding Raphaelesque Head*, which he painted in 1951. After the war, Dali returned to Spain, soon making another unexpected turnaround: he dedicated himself to strict Catholicism and began producing work for the church. Dali took on traditional New Testament subjects in his religious paintings, convinced, according to his own statements, that he had mystical abilities. The best known of his early 1950s paintings, *Christ of St. John of the Cross* (1951) and *Crucifixion* (1954), display a different perspective that hints of this otherworldly element. At the same time, Dali continued to experiment with more hallucinatory material in other canvases of the period.

Dali's obsession with science continued, with works such as *Sistine Madonna* (1958) which shows the double image of a woman and an ear, both composed of particles. A 1963 canvas titled *Portrait of My Dead Brother* shows a grainy image blown-up to form a series of dots. Stereoscopy and holography, both methods for making three-dimensional images, captured his imagination as well. He carried on his experimentation into the next two decades.

The "Mad Dandy" Begins to Fall Apart

By the late 1960s, Parkinson's Disease had begun to hamper Dali's work, but his personality had so thoroughly captured the public's imagination that he continued to exert influence, if only as a source from which to copy ideas. In a catalogue essay for a 1979 Surrealist exhibition at the Cleveland Art Museum, curator Edward B. Henning notes that Dali's "most striking creation remains himself: the mad dandy, leading an ocelot on a leash down Madison Avenue. Far from being mad, however, he attempts to expose the insanity and

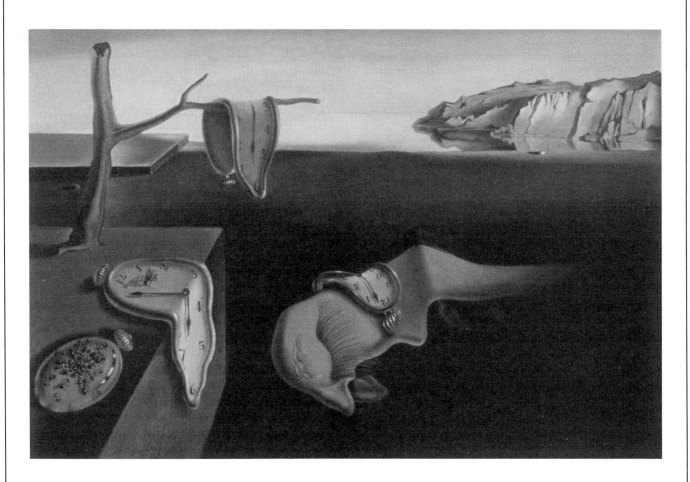

Featuring the now-famous soft, melting watches, *The Persistence of Memory* is Dali's most recognizable work.

If you enjoy the works of Salvador Dali, you may also want to check out the following:

The works of medieval Dutch painter Hieronymus Bosch and seventeenth-century Dutch master Jan Vermeer.
The works of surrealists Rene Magritte, Joan Miro, and Pablo Picasso.
The surrealist films of director Luis Bunuel.

---

stupidity of society by means of his solemn clowning on the one hand, and commands attention and garners rewards for his bizarre and entertaining behavior on the other."

Financial and strategic blunders resulted in many scandals during the late 1970s, the worst of which was his reported signing of thousands of sheets of blank paper, falsely rendering anything later added to the paper a Dali lithograph. It was later estimated that collectors had spent at least $750 million on phony Dali prints between 1980 and 1989.

In 1980, the Pompidou Center in Paris mounted a Dali retrospective which included more than 150 paintings, 200 drawings, 2,000 documents, and 30 other objects (comprised of jewelry, playing cards, and a couch representing Mae West's lips). Some 1.2 million spectators visited the show over its two-month run. In *Newsweek*, Scott Sullivan remarked that the retrospective amounted to "an iconology that is as freakish as it is unforgettable," but that he felt a "certain sadness" about the show, "the clear sense that it marks the end of a long enterprise." Another large retrospective was held in Madrid in 1983 and two museums, one in Figueras, Spain, the other in St. Petersburg, Florida, were constructed to hold permanent collections of Dali's work.

Gala's death in 1982 plummeted Dali into a severe depression; he had to be force-fed through a tube and remained reclusive. In 1984 an electrical fire nearly cost him his own life. Finally, he settled in Torre Galatea, a castle in Figueras, where he was nursed twenty-four hours a day until his death on January 23, 1989. He left his hefty estate to the Catalan government, the Spanish state, and the Dali Museum. Dali's remains, entombed under a glass dome, were embalmed to last 300 years.

In a 1985 interview quoted by *MacLean*'s Pamela Young, Dali hoped to be remembered as a thinker. "Painting," he declared, "is an infinitely minute part of my personality." In his foreword to *Dali: The Salvador Dali Museum Collection*, A. Reynolds Morse, whose collection is housed in the St. Petersburg museum, declared that Dali deserves recognition "as a major factor in twentieth century art." *Artforum*'s Carter Ratcliff acknowledged that Dali was important but perhaps not for the reasons the artist thought: "Dali matters because he doesn't exist, because he is sheer image, and because he inspires the fear that his condition is universal."

In their *Newsweek* obituary, David Gates and Christopher Dickey wrote: "In the 30s and 40s, Dali was top contender for Picasso's title as heavyweight champion of the art world; it's clear today that while Picasso transcended cubism, Dali's gift was more limited. . . . The exacting technique with which he created delirious images made him modern art's ambassador to the philistines. Whatever it *meant*, it sure did take some darned hard work." In his *Dali: A Study of His Life and Work*, Morse takes a more positive view: "With his sheer technical mastery and natural flare for publicity, [Dali] was able to . . . exercise a profound influence on art as a whole because he had freed himself from the shackles of a minor movement and stood as a symbol of freedom from the inertia and lassitude which overtook art after the stimulation of surrealism was lessened by use and familiarity and dissensions." Summing up the long, varied, and often ridiculed career of Dali in his introduction to *Dali: The Salvador Dali Museum Collection*, Robert S. Lubar wrote that the artist "sought nothing less than the liberation of desire through a critique of language and visuality."

■ Works Cited

Bigwood, James, "Salvador Dali: Reluctant Filmmaker," *American Film*, November, 1979, pp. 62-63, 70-71.
Cowles, Fleur, *The Case of Salvador Dali*, Little, Brown, 1959.
Dali, Salvador, "The Stinking Ass" (translated by J. Bronowski), *This Quarter*, September, 1932.

Dali, Salvador, "Dali Proclaims Surrealism a Paranoiac Art," *Art Digest,* February 1, 1935, p. 10.

Dali, Salvador, *Dali: The Salvador Dali Museum Collection,* foreword by A. Reynolds Morse, introduction by Robert S. Lubar, Brown/Bulfinch, 1991.

Dali, Salvador, *The Secret Life of Salvador Dali,* Dial, 1993.

Gates, David, and Christopher Dickey, *Newsweek,* February 6, 1989, p. 77.

Gaunt, William, *The Surrealists,* [New York], 1972.

Henning, Edward B., "Surrealism and the Visual Arts," *The Spirit of Surrealism,* Cleveland Museum of Art, 1979, pp. 62-124.

Hughes, Robert, "The Embarrassing Genius," *Time,* February 6, 1989.

Hughes, Robert, "Baby Dali," *Time,* July 4, 1994, pp. 68-70.

Lacayo, Richard, *People,* February 6, 1989, pp. 105-8.

Matthews, J. H., *The Imagery of Surrealism,* [Syracuse, New York], 1977.

Morse, A. Reynolds, *Dali: A Study of His Life and Work,* [Greenwich, CT], 1957.

Ratcliff, Carter, "Swallowing Dali," *Artforum,* September, 1982, pp. 33-39.

Sullivan, Scott, "Maximum Dali," *Newsweek,* January 21, 1980, p. 87.

Wolfe, B. D., *New York Herald Tribune,* December 27, 1942.

Young, Pamela, "A Surreal Life," *Maclean's,* February 6, 1989, p. 58.

■ For More Information See

BOOKS

Ades, Dawn, *Dali,* London, 1983, revised and updated, [New York], 1995.

Bona, *Dominique,* Gala, Paris, 1995.

Bouguenec, Andre, *Dali: Philosophe et Esoteriste Incompris,* [Paris], 1993.

Brihuega, Jaime, *Miro y Dali: Los Grandes Surrealistas,* [Madrid], 1993.

Carter, David, *Salvador Dali,* [New York], 1995.

Catterall, Lee, *The Great Dali Fraud and Other Deceptions,* [Fort Lee, NJ], 1992.

Crevel, Rene, *Dali, o el anti-oscurantismo,* [Barcelona], 1978.

Del Arco, Manuel, *Dali in the Nude,* [St. Petersburg, FL], 1984.

De la Serna, Gomez, *Dali,* [Madrid], 1977, [London], 1984.

Descharnes, Robert, *The World of Dali,* [London and New York], 1972.

Descharnes, Robert, *Salvador Dali,* [New York], 1993.

Dopagne, Jacques, *Dali,* Paris, 1974; [New York], 1976.

Etherington-Smith, Meredith, *The Persistence of Memory; A Biography of Dali,* [New York], 1995.

Finkelstein, Haim, *Salvador Dali's Art and Writing, 1927-1942,* [Cambridge, England], 1996.

Gerard, Max, editor, *Dali,* [New York], 1968.

Gimenez-Frontin, J. L., *Teatro-Museo Dali, Fundacio Gala-Salvador Dali,* [Madrid], 1994.

Gomez de Liano, Ignacio, *Dali,* [London], 1987.

Guardiola Rovira, Ramon, *Dali y su museo,* [Figueras, Spain], 1984.

Lear, Amanda, *L'amant Dali,* [Paris], 1994.

Livingstone, Linda, editor, *Dali,* [Greenwich, CT], 1959.

Maddox, Conroy, *Dali,* [London and New York], 1979.

Morse, A. Reynolds, *A New Introduction to Dali,* [Cleveland], 1960.

Morse, A. Reynolds, *The Dali Museum,* [Cleveland], 1962.

Morse, A. Reynolds, *A Dali Primer,* [Cleveland], 1970.

Morse, A. Reynolds, *The Draftsmanship of Dali,* [Cleveland], 1970.

Morse, A. Reynolds, *Dali: The Masterworks,* [Cleveland], 1971.

Morse, A. Reynolds, *Dali: A Guide to His Works in Public Museums,* [Cleveland], 1974.

Passeron, Rene, *Dali,* [Paris], 1978.

Rojas, Carlos, *El mundo mitico y magico de Dali,* [Barcelona], 1985.

Romero, Louis, *Dali,* [Secaucus, NJ], 1979.

The Salvador Dali Museum Collection, [New York], 1994.

Secrest, Meryle, *Dali, The Surrealist Jester,* [London], 1986.

Soby, James Thrall, *Dali,* [New York], 1946.

Vilaseca, David, *The Apocryphal Subject: Masochism, Identification, and Paranoia in Salvador Dali's Autobiographical Writings,* [New York], 1995.

Walton, Paul, *Dali, Miro,* [New York], 1967.

PERIODICALS

American Imago, Winter, 1983, pp. 311, 337, 349.

Art in America, October, 1991, p. 56.

ARTnews, May, 1986, p. 28; Summer, 1988, p. 138; May, 1990, p. 89; January, 1991, p. 161.

Bookwatch, June, 1993, p. 9.
Economist, January 26, 1991, p. 86.
Forbes, August 29, 1994, p. 104.
Interview, January, 1990, p. 16.
Los Angeles Times Book Review, December 14, 1986, p. 3.
MacLean's, May 7, 1990, p. 64.
New Republic, October 17, 1994, p. 40.
New Statesman and Society, October 19, 1990, p. 36.
New York, July 18, 1994, p. 54.
New Yorker, December 16, 1991, p. 41.
Omni, February, 1982, p. 68.
Playboy, July, 1994, p. 34.
Publishers Weekly, October 7, 1996, p. 52.
School Arts, April, 1992, p. 33.
Smithsonian, October 1986, p. 62.
Times Literary Supplement, May 20, 1994, p. 16.
Travel and Leisure, April, 1992, p. 66.

EXHIBITION CATALOGUES

Abadie, Daniel, *Dali: Retrospective 1920-1980,* [Paris], 1979.
Dali en los fondos de la Fundacion Gala-Salvador Dali, [Seville], 1993.
Fanes, Felix, and Montserrat Aguer, *Dali: El Pan,* [Barcelona], 1993.
Michler, Ralf, and Lutz W. Löpsinger, editors, *Salvador Dali: A Catalogue Raisonne of Etchings and Mixed-media Prints,* [Munich], 1994.

Morse, A. Reynolds, *Catalogue of Worlds by Dali,* [Cleveland], 1956.
Morse, A. Reynolds, *Dali: Catalogue of a Collection: 93 Oils 1917-1970,* [Cleveland], 1973.
Palau, Robert, *Dali, els anys joves, 1918-1930,* [Barcelona], 1995.
Raeburn, Michael, editor, *Salvador Dali: The Early Years,* [New York], 1994.
Wach, Kenneth, *Salvador Dali: Masterpieces from the Collection of the Salvador Dali Museum,* [New York], 1996.

■ Obituaries

BOOKS

Current Biography, H. W. Wilson, 1989.
Modern Arts Criticism, edited by Joann Prosyniuk, Gale, 1991.

PERIODICALS

Art in America, March, 1989, p. 21.
ARTnews, April, 1989, p. 69.
Chicago Tribune, January 24, 1989.
Detroit News, January 23, 1989.
Forbes, February 20, 1989, p. 139.
Los Angeles Times, January 24, 1989.
New York Times, January 24, 1989.
Times (London), January 24, 1989.*

—Sketch by C. M. Ratner

Charles Dickens

■ Personal

Born February 7, 1812, in Portsmouth, England; died of a paralytic stroke, at Gad's Hill, Kent, England, June 18, 1870; buried in Poet's Corner of Westminster Abbey; son of John (a clerk in the Navy Pay Office) and Elizabeth (Barrow) Dickens; married Catherine Hogarth, April, 1836 (separated, 1858); children: ten. *Education:* Taught at home by mother; attended a Dame School at Chatham for a short time, and Wellington Academy in London; further educated by reading widely in the British Museum.

■ Career

Novelist, journalist, court reporter, editor, amateur actor. Editor of London *Daily News,* 1846; founder and editor of *Household Words,* 1833-35, and of *All the Year Round,* 1859-70; presented public readings of his works, beginning 1858.

■ Writings

The Life and Adventures of Nicholas Nickleby, Chapman & Hall, 1837-39, Buccaneer, 1990.

Sketches of Young Gentlemen, Dedicated to the Young Ladies, Chapman & Hall, 1838.

Sketches of Young Couples, with an Urgent Remonstrance to the Gentle of England (Being Bachelors or Widowers), on the Present Alarming Crisis, Chapman & Hall, 1840.

The Old Curiosity Shop, Chapman & Hall, 1841, published as *Master Humphrey's Clock,* Lea & Blanchard, 1841, Buccaneer, 1990.

Barnaby Rudge: A Tale of the Riots of 'Eighty, Chapman & Hall, 1841.

American Notes for General Circulation, Chapman & Hall, 1842, Harper, 1842, Fromm, 1985.

The Life and Adventures of Martin Chuzzlewit, Chapman & Hall, 1842-44, Harper, 1844, Unwin Hyman, 1985.

A Christmas Carol, in Prose: Being a Ghost Story of Christmas, Chapman & Hall, 1843, Carey & Hart, 1844, Oxford University Press, 1975, original manuscript printed, Dover, 1971.

The Chimes: A Goblin Story of Some Bells That Rang an Old Year Out and a New Year In, Chapman & Hall, 1845.

Pictures from Italy, Bradbury & Evans, 1846, Ecco Press, 1988, published as *Travelling Letters: Written on the Road,* Wiley & Putnam, 1846.

The Cricket on the Hearth: A Fairy Tale of Home, Bradbury & Evans, 1846, Chapman & Hall, 1962.

Dealings with the Firm of Dombey and Son, Wholesale, Retail, and for Exportation, Bradbury &

Evans, 1846-48, Wiley & Putnam, 1846-48, Oxford University Press, 1974.

The Battle of Life: A Love Story, Wiley & Putnam, 1847.

The Haunted Man and the Ghost's Bargain: A Fancy for Christmas-time, Bradbury & Evans, 1848, Dutton, 1907.

The Personal History of David Copperfield, Bradbury & Evans, 1849-50, Lea & Blanchard, 1851, Warner Libraries, 1991.

A Child's History of England, Lea & Blanchard, 1851, Bradbury & Evans, 1852-54.

Bleak House, Bradbury & Evans, 1852-53, Harper, 1853, Buccaneer, 1990.

Hard Times: For These Times, Bradbury & Evans, 1854, McElrath, 1854, Barrons, 1985.

Little Dorrit, Bradbury & Evans, 1855-57, Peterson, 1857, Buccaneer, 1990.

A Tale of Two Cities, Chapman & Hall, 1859, Peterson, 1859, Random House, 1990.

Great Expectations, Chapman & Hall, 1861, Peterson, 1861, Harper, 1861, Buccaneer, 1986.

The Uncommercial Traveller, Chapman & Hall, 1861, Sheldon, 1865.

Our Mutual Friend, Chapman & Hall, 1864-65, Harper, 1865, Buccaneer, 1990.

Hunted Down: A Story with Some Account of Thomas Griffiths Wainewright, The Poisoner, Hotten, 1870, Peterson, 1870.

The Mystery of Edwin Drood, Chapman & Hall, 1870, Fields, Osgood, 1870, concluded by Leon Garfield, Pantheon, 1980.

A Child's Dream of a Star, Fields, Osgood, 1871.

The Life of Our Lord, Simon & Schuster, 1934.

The Speeches of Charles Dickens, Clarendon Press, 1960.

Uncollected Writings from Household Words, 1850-1859, Allen Lane, 1969.

Charles Dickens Book of Memoranda: A Photographic and Typographic Facsimile of the Notebook Begun in January 1855, Astor, Lenox & Tilden Foundation, 1981.

WITH WILKIE COLLINS

Holly Tree Inn, Household Words, 1855.

Wreck of the Golden Mary, Bradbury & Evans, 1856.

Two Apprentices, with a History of Their Lazy Tour, Peterson, 1857.

No Thoroughfare, A Drama in Five Acts, by Collins, Charles Fechter, and Dickens, De Witt, reprinted, Chapman & Hall, 1890.

Under the Management of Mr. Charles Dickens, Cornell University Press, 1966.

COLLECTIONS

Cheap Edition of the Works of Mr. Charles Dickens, Chapman & Hall, 1847-52, Bradbury & Evans, 1858.

The Charles Dickens Edition, Chapman & Hall, 1867-75.

The Works of Charles Dickens, Macmillan, 1892-1925.

The Works of Charles Dickens, Chapman & Hall, 1897-1908, Scribners, 1897-1908.

The Nonesuch Edition, Nonesuch Press, 1937-38.

The New Oxford Illustrated Dickens, Oxford University Press, 1947-58.

The Clarendon Dickens, (5 volumes published), Clarendon Press, 1966.

UNDER PSEUDONYM BOZ

The Village Coquettes: A Comic Opera in Two Acts, Bentley, 1836.

The Posthumous Papers of the Pickwick Club, Edited by "Boz," Chapman & Hall, 1836-37.

Sketches by Boz, Illustrative of Every-Day Life and Every-Day People, Macrone, 1837.

The Strange Gentleman: A Comic Burletta in Two Acts, Chapman & Hall, 1837.

Memoirs of Joseph Grimaldi, Edited by "Boz," Bentley, 1838.

Oliver Twist, or the Parish Boy's Progress, by "Boz," Bentley, 1838, Turney, 1838, Oxford University Press, 1966.

■ Adaptations

Motion pictures based on *A Christmas Carol* have been shown since 1913. Notable among these are the Alistair Sim film, *A Christmas Carol,* made in 1951 and still shown on television today; a musical version starring Albert Finney and Alec Guinness in 1970; the 1972 United Productions of America film with the animated character Mr. Magoo; and "Mickey's Christmas Carol," with the beloved Disney characters, which has appeared on television since the early 1980s. In 1979 NBC aired an animated special called *The Stingiest Man in Town,* featuring the voice of Walter Matthau. George C. Scott appeared in a television special of *A Christmas Carol* which first aired in 1984.

On television *Masterpiece Theatre* has shown "David Copperfield" and "A Tale of Two Cities," *Mobil Showcase* has featured "Nicholas Nickleby" (which was also presented as a nine-hour show on Broadway), and "Great Expectations" was a feature on the Disney Channel.

In 1934 Freddie Bartholomew, W. C. Fields, and Lionel Barrymore starred in the MGM film *David Copperfield*; it was also filmed in 1972, with Susan Hampshire. *A Tale of Two Cities* appeared on the screen in 1935 with Ronald Colman, and again in 1957 starring Dirk Bogarde. There have been many versions of *Oliver Twist*, including the 1933 film starring Dickie Moore; the 1951 version with Alec Guinness; and the musical hit *Oliver!*, which was first a Broadway show and then a movie with Ron Moody and Jack Wild. In 1947 Jean Simmons and John Mills appeared in a film version of *Great Expectations* and an updated version of the book came to the screen in 1997. In 1987 English Sands Films produced *Little Dorrit*. *The Pickwick Papers* was filmed in 1955, with Nigel Patrick and Hermione Gingold.

■ Sidelights

He was only fifty-eight when he died. His horse had been shot, as he had wanted; his body lay in a casket in his home at Gad's Hill, festooned with scarlet geraniums. Tributes poured in from all over his native England and from around the world. Statesmen, commoners, and fellow writers all grieved his passing. As quoted in Peter Ackroyd's monumental study, *Dickens*, the news of Charles Dickens death on June 9, 1870, reverberated across the Atlantic, eliciting the poet Longfellow to say that he had never known "an author's death to cause such general mourning." England's Thomas Carlyle wrote: "It is an event world-wide, a *unique* of talents suddenly extinct." And the day after his death, the newspaper Dickens once edited, the London *Daily News*, reported that Dickens had been "emphatically the novelist of his age. In his pictures of contemporary life posterity will read, more clearly than in contemporary records, the character of nineteenth century life."

It was a judgment that has been proven more than perceptive. Not only was Dickens a popular recorder of the life of his times, but he was also an incredibly successful man of letters. One of the more interesting aspects of Dickens life, in fact, was the degree of popularity which he experienced during his lifetime. There was no *la vie bohème* for Dickens, no artistic squalor or neglect

of his works. From the age of twenty-four, with publication of *The Posthumous Papers of the Pickwick Club*, Dickens was an amazing literary success on both sides of the Atlantic. By the age of thirty he had five immensely popular and immense novels under his belt, including such perennial favorites as *Oliver Twist* and *The Life and Adventures of Nicholas Nickleby*.

His early period of creativity was marked by a proclivity to humor and the picaresque, and early on his readership marveled at his assortment of characters. If a Dickens plot was not always of clockwork fastidiousness, the author more than made up for it with a host of leading and secondary characters that would make a Hollywood casting director envious. It has been reckoned that Dickens created over 2,000 such characters during his relatively short creative life. He wrote fourteen full novels—most over 800 pages in their modern editions—as well as sketches, travel, and Christmas books, and was at work on his fifteenth novel when he died. Dickens grew throughout his career; he was not content to reproduce formulaic successes. He took chances; he dealt with social issues; he was not shy of working with ideas. A popular novelist, he was never so in love with his reputation as to stand still.

His late period was marked by brooding and dark novels that illuminated a part of England most would have been happy to have left in the dark. The somber tone of *Bleak House* and *Hard Times* reflected the harsh social reality of an England besotted with industrial progress at any price. Ironically, many of the societal ills which Dickens wrote about in such novels had already been righted by the time of publication. The 1850s and 1860s in England were decades of hope and prosperity, but Dickens could never forget another age, a time during which he himself was growing up. Throughout his work there is a constant returning to themes of his own childhood: of debtor's prisons—such as the one to which his own father was once sent—and the internal dealings of family. Dickens was a writer of the city and of the country, and both strains were part of his own make-up as well. His depictions of Victorian London have, as was prophesied by the *Daily News*, become historical records of a world now forever lost.

The fame of this enormously inventive author has not diminished over time. He, and his fellow countryman, William Shakespeare, are the most written about authors in the English language. His novels not only bridge cultures, equally popular in many of the world's languages, but they also span generations, appealing to adult and young readers alike. Books such as *Oliver Twist, A Christmas Carol, The Personal History of David Copperfield, A Tale of Two Cities,* and *Great Expectations* have long been part of the canon of literature in high schools, and deservedly so for, as in the case of *A Tale of Two Cities,* their action, and in several others, their depictions of youthful characters facing life with both determination and a sense of humor.

A Childhood on the Move

Charles Dickens was the second of eight children born to John and Elizabeth Barrow Dickens. His father was a descendant of a servant, dead before the arrival of Charles Dickens, but one who always took pains to appear higher than such a station would allow. In his dress, manner, and speech, John Dickens aped the world of aristocracy, and a tendency to live beyond his means ultimately led to one of the tragedies of Dickens's young life. On the mother's side were office workers and bureaucrats, including Elizabeth Barrow's father who had been accused of embezzling funds at his job and had fled prosection. Servants and convicts in flight thus make up part of the family package Charles Dickens was born into on February 7, 1812. His birthplace was Portsmouth, where his father, employed by the Pay Office of the Navy, was then stationed. Dickens grew up mostly in towns on the south coast of England, and the family moved often, if only changing lodgings within one town, residing for a short period even in London. Though he is forever linked with that diverse and populous capital, Dickens in fact lived in London for only about half of his life. The first and last decades of his life were spent in and near the towns of Rochester and Chatham in Kent.

His parents were great talkers, and Dickens immortalized them as characters in his fiction, his father as the loquacious Mr. Micawber, and his mother as the chatterbox Mrs. Nickleby. It was his mother who first instructed Dickens in reading and in Latin. By age six, after the family had finally settled near Chatham, he and his older sister Fanny attended a Dames School, so-called as

such establishments were generally run by older women who had no real training in education, but who were educated themselves. Dickens benefited from such tutelage, but remembered later in life especially the birch rods employed on recalcitrant learners. At about this age, Dickens began his lifelong love affair with books, discovering the works of Tobias Smollet and Henry Fielding, and the illustrations of William Hogarth. Favorite books included *Roderick Random, The Vicar of Wakefield, Don Quixote, Gil Blas, Robinson Crusoe, The Arabian Nights,* and *Tales of the Genii.* Dickens has his autobiographical double, David Copperfield, ruminate about reading, stating that it "was my only and my constant comfort. When I think of it, the picture always rises in my mind, of a summer evening, the boys at play in the churchyard, and I sitting on my bed, reading as if for life." A series of children's nurses also informed these early years, and the stories they told—often quite horrific—at bedtime filled the young child's mind with an alternate vision of the world from the rather benign and tranquil one in which he grew up.

The years spent in Rochester and Chatham were idyllic in many ways, full of a security that Dickens would never experience again in his life, even after he was a feted author. Christmas was an especially happy time for the family, and the first eight years of his life the winters were particularly harsh, with a white Christmas each December. This is particularly interesting in light of the fact that Dickens the author, as Peter Ackroyd noted, "almost single-handedly created the modern idea of Christmas" as a snow-filled world with family gatherings and generosity toward others.

At age nine, Dickens left the Dames School for more formal education at an establishment run by a young man named William Giles where, by all accounts, he did quite well both academically and socially. Dickens himself, however, when looking back on his childhood, always thought of himself as a lonely boy. It was while still a young child also that Dickens first encountered the wonders of drama and the theater, a fascination that stood him in good stead later in life when he became quite famous both in England and the United States for readings of his own works. But such youthful preoccupations came to a sudden end for Dickens. The family moved again to London, where the father's work took him, and to a less

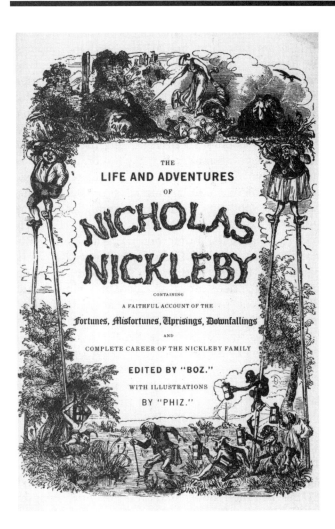

THE
LIFE AND ADVENTURES
OF
NICHOLAS NICKLEBY

CONTAINING

A FAITHFUL ACCOUNT OF THE

Fortunes, Misfortunes, Uprisings, Downfallings

AND

COMPLETE CAREER OF THE NICKLEBY FAMILY

EDITED BY "BOZ."

WITH ILLUSTRATIONS
BY "PHIZ."

Presented in serial form as it was written and first read, this facsimile edition of this Dickens tale from 1838 includes not only all twenty installments but original ads and illustrations as well.

favorable economic situation, one that was only exacerbated by the father's mismanagement. In London the father's debts became insupportable and John Dickens was sent to that peculiar nineteenth-century British institution, debtor's prison, at the Marshalsea Prison in London. At age twelve, Dickens was sent off to work at a blacking warehouse, placing labels on bottles of shoe polish, living alone in cheap lodgings with never enough to eat. No wonder that he later felt utterly abandoned by his family; the year-long experience was one from which he would never fully recover.

Dickens recalled these months in John Forster's *Life of Charles Dickens*, "It is wonderful to me how

I could have been so easily cast off at such an age. . . . No words can express the secret agony of my soul as I sunk into this companionship. . . . My whole nature was so penetrated with grief and humiliation of such considerations, that even now, famous and caressed and happy, I often forget in my dreams that I have a dear wife and children; even that I am a man; and wander desolately back to that time in my life." The experiences of those twelve months would cloud the entire rest of his life. As George H. Ford noted in his entry on Dickens in *Dictionary of Literary Biography*, "That [Dickens's] novels would be full of characters who are orphans is not surprising." The custom of the time allowed for entire families to be housed in such debtor's prisons, and soon the rest of the family, except for Charles, were living at the Marshalsea, where young Charles would visit them after work. Yet even in such circumstances, the active mind of young Dickens was recording impressions and details that would later fill out the pages of his fiction. Visiting the family at the Marshalsea, he heard tales of woe from other inmates and filed them away for later use.

From Poverty to Man of Letters

Finally, John Dickens was released from his debts, rescued his son from the blacking work, and sent him to a school in London where he remained until the age of fifteen. Dickens's mother, however, was in favor of leaving her oldest son at work to help out the family, and Dickens looked upon such an attitude as a further betrayal. Meanwhile, his older sister Fanny had been able to continue her studies at the Royal Academy of Music throughout the debtor's prison period. It must have seemed that the entire family had been conspiring against him, and this year-long period as an adolescent set the tone not only for his life but for his fiction. Dickens was, as Ford commented in *Dictionary of Literary Biography*, "in his energetic pursuit of his goals, the embodiment of his age, the archetypal Victorian." Once out of his miserable job and enrolled at Wellington Academy, Dickens demonstrated a terrific resolve to succeed in the world. He finished head of his class and the winner of a prize for Latin, and at age fifteen left formal schooling for good. Thereafter, what education he achieved was self-delivered, and by age eighteen he had a reading card for the library at the British Museum, an establishment that has provided intellectual nourishment for many other autodidacts, Karl Marx among them. The hours Dickens spent at the library took him into the realms of history and literature—especially Shakespeare—and would furnish a storehouse of knowledge from which Dickens would draw his entire life.

From age fifteen to twenty-two Dickens continued living at home with his family, and took an assortment of jobs from law to journalism. His first two years after school were spent as a law clerk, a position which provided material he later used

This classic 1838 novel of a London orphan who falls into the hands of Fagin, the dean of pickpockets, includes comedy and tragedy and remains a perennial favorite to this day.

in many instances in his fiction. The following four years saw him preparing shorthand reports for lawyers, and his shorthand was so accurate and fast that it won him a job as a news reporter on the *Morning Chronicle*. From 1834 to 1836 he worked as a political reporter, not only recording speeches but also learning the ins and outs of Parliament. Soon his reporting left the realms of straight news and took on the flavor of what is now known as the feature article. He wrote dozens of sketches about members of Parliament, about the political world in general, and about quirky London scenes and characters, all of which had that particular humorous trademark that critics have come to call Dickensian: potty characters caught in the petri dish of the author's fertile imagination, their antics revealed in loving detail. "Jocularity of tone," is how Ford typified these articles in *Dictionary of Literary Biography*. Dickens was always able to see the absurd in any situation, however serious it might be on one level.

In addition to his newspaper work, Dickens also kept up his passion for the theater. He was a deeply involved spectator, but at one point he also applied for an audition as an actor, only to have a severe cold force a cancellation of his try-out. There were romantic liaisons during his late teenage years, as well. At eighteen he was introduced to the Beadnell household and promptly fell in love with the daughter, Mary, two years his senior. For four years the infatuation lasted, only to end in heartbreak for Dickens when Mary's interest in him cooled after being sent to finishing school in Paris. This unsuccessful romance served to convince Dickens that he must work harder and become a success at his chosen profession. This profession more and more was writing. The first of his sketches appeared in print in 1834 when Dickens was still twenty-one.

By 1836 he had collected some sixty such sketches, gathered together in his first publication, the two-volume *Sketches by Boz*. Dickens had assumed this pen name, from a mispronounced pet name for his younger brother, Augustus. Even after the true identity of Boz was revealed, however, many of Dickens's readers continued to think of him affectionately by the name which accompanied his earliest successes. This first book was well received, the reviewer for the *Morning Chronicle* noting Dickens's ability to "look on the bright and sunny side of things," even when picturing the London slums. That same reviewer called Dickens

Oliver!, the 1968 musical adaptation of Dickens's famous novel starring Mark Lester as Oliver Twist, won five Academy Awards including Best Picture.

a "close and acute observer of character and manners, with a strong sense of the ridiculous." The trademark Dickens optimism and humor were well established by the age of twenty-four. This insightful review in the *Morning Chronicle* was written by George Hogarth, soon to become Dickens's father-in-law.

Early Successes

In April 1836, Dickens married Hogarth's eldest daughter, Catherine, whom he called Kate, and the couple lived in a suite of three furnished rooms in Furnival's Inn for the first year of their marriage. It was here his first child was born and his first literary success was created. The publishers Chapman and Hall, impressed with the comic overtones of *Sketches by Boz*, contracted with Dickens to come up with a series of humorous sketches to be illustrated by the popular artist, Robert Seymour. The first of these, describing the adventures of a loopy group of Londoners out for hunting and fishing trips to the country, appeared just days before his marriage. The serialization of *The Posthumous Papers of the Pickwick Club*, better known as simply *The Pickwick Papers*, made Dickens's reputation and fortune. However, the illustrator Seymour killed himself early in the venture, and the project became Dickens's, who was free to call all the artistic shots at the tender age of twenty-four. A new illustrator, Hablot Browne, was found and by the time of the final installment of the book in October 1837, forty thousand copies were printed to meet the growing demand. The invention of two Cockney characters, Sam Weller and his father Tony, midway into the adventures were what turned the book around in public acceptance, amusing readers and building a loyal following for successive installments.

Serial publication thus became a boon for a writer such as Dickens, ever with an ear to his reading public. Throughout his career, Dickens continued to listen to the voice of his audience and rework plots and characterization during the course of publication to better fit public demand. As Ford commented in *Dictionary of Literary Biography*, "The Pickwick Papers ended up as the most sensational triumph in nineteenth-century publishing." The book appealed to all classes, could be read aloud, and avoided any offensive language or compromising sexual incidents. One judge was known to read installments on the bench as jurors were

deliberating, and this first novel by the young writer may well have been his most popular with Victorian readers.

Dickens did not rest on his laurels, and even as *The Pickwick Papers* was being published he launched other writing projects, including an opera libretto and what would become his second novel, *Oliver Twist*. With *Oliver Twist* appears the first of a long line of orphaned protagonists, and with this second novel, Dickens left behind the purely frolicsome world of Pickwick. Young Oliver battles the brutality and cruelty of the world. Born in the workhouse where his mother died in childbirth, Oliver passes his early years in a bleak and forbidding environment, always under the thumb of the beadle, Mr. Bumble. Escaping the horrors of the workhouse, Oliver arrives in London where he falls in with a gang of criminals led by Fagin, a man who has organized young boys into a successful team of pickpockets. Among their number is the irrepressible Artful Dodger. Fagin stokes many illegal fires, receiving stolen goods from the thief, the brutal Bill Sikes. Among a host of other notable characters is Nancy, the archetypal prostitute with a heart of gold with whom Sikes lives. Recruited for a time into Fagin's gang, Oliver ultimately finds protection with a wealthy benefactor. In one of the strongest scenes Dickens would ever write, Sikes murders Nancy, only to be hanged by an outraged crowd. The novel ends with Fagin—part villain, part father-figure to his gang—in his cell at Newgate Prison awaiting his final hours.

Oliver Twist was a stretch for Dickens: a second novel that diverged in content from his fabulously popular first. Drawing on the tradition of crime stories then popular, known as Newgate novels, such a book was still a gamble for a young writer, and some critics have suggested that *Oliver Twist* actually preceded *The Pickwick Papers* in conception. In the event, however, Dickens's gamble paid off, and from the very first of its two-year serialization, the novel found wide readership. Unlike *The Pickwick Papers*, *Oliver Twist* was published not under its own cover, but as installments in a magazine, *Bentley's Miscellany*. It is also much shorter than the first novel, and the illustrations were by George Cruikshank, which marked the beginning of a fruitful collaborative effort.

Critics of the day, such as that at the *Quarterly Review*, were quick to point out that Dickens dealt in hyperbole: "*Oliver Twist* is directed against the poor-law and workhouse system, and in our opinion with much unfairness. The abuses which [Dickens] ridicules are not only exaggerated, but in nineteen cases out of twenty do not exist at all." But that same reviewer also noted that "Boz is regius professor of slang." A reviewer for the *Spectator* concurred that the workhouse scenes were overdone, but commented that Dickens's "powers of pathos, sadly touching rather than tearful, are great, he has a hearty sympathy with humanity." Later critics have pointed out this melodramatic potential in Dickens's work as well, but most are forgiving of this defect in light of Dickens's great talent for creation of character. Jack Lindsay in *Charles Dickens: A Biographical and Critical Study* wrote that "the last word . . . must be given to Dickens's power to draw characters in a method of intense poetic simplification, which makes them simultaneously social emblems, emotional symbols, and visually precise individuals." The English critic and writer, Angus Wilson, noted in *The World of Charles Dickens* that "perhaps more than any other," the novel *Oliver Twist* "has a combination of sensationalism and sentiment that fixes it as one of the masterpieces of pop art." The book is also one of the more enduring classics of the Dickens canon, immortalized both by its 1948 film adaptation and the 1968 musical comedy *Oliver!*

Part of the success of *Oliver Twist*, despite its rather somber theme and content, is that the book is also balanced with typical Dickensian humor. The author avows this technique in chapter seventeen of *Oliver Twist*, where he notes: "It is the custom on the stage, in all good murderous melodramas, to present the tragic and the comic scenes, in as regular alteration, as the layers of red and white in a side of streaky bacon." This "streaky bacon" method can be seen in the characters of both the beadle, Bumble, and the crime master, Fagin, both of whom have their humorous sides. Beadle is the henpecked husband whose wife bosses him around as he does his young charges. Artful Dodger, the young pickpocket, also is a character who provides fun for the reader, especially in one notable court scene in which he demands his "priwileges." This alternation of humor and pathos, comedy and tragedy, also became part of the Dickens recipe book.

Publication of the novel was not an unblemished success, however. Dickens's personal life intervened early on in the serial installments when his beloved sister-in-law, Mary Hogarth, who had been living with the Dickens family, suddenly died on May 7, 1837. Dickens was profoundly affected by this death, and publication of his work was put off for the time. Until his death, Dickens wore the ring Mary had been wearing at the time of her death, and he wished to be buried alongside her—a wish that was not fulfilled. It seems his nearly year-long mourning was stopped only by the simmering of a new literary project. The character of Smike came into his head, and he began the novel *The Life and Adventures of Nicholas Nickleby*, the story of another orphan who makes his way in the world.

This novel also exposes, as did *Oliver Twist*, corrupt institutions of the times. With *Oliver Twist* it had been the workhouses and the New Poor Law of 1834 which established them; with *Nicholas Nickleby* it was schools such as Dotheboys Hall where young Nicholas is sent for a time to teach. These were terrifically prolific years for Dickens, who worked on two or three novels simultaneously. Before he was thirty, he had written *The Pickwick Papers*, *Oliver Twist*, *Nicholas Nickleby*, *The Old Curiosity Shop*, and *Barnaby Rudge*. Only the last of these suffered from some lack of popularity; with all of them Dickens created memorable characters, such as Little Nell of *The Old Curiosity Shop*, whose names have passed into the language as embodiments of certain very human characteristics: big-heartedness, avarice, verbosity. Indeed, the characters are what make the novels of Dickens, according to many reviewers.

Even contemporaneously with Dickens, critics such as his best friend and biographer, John Forster, noted that in *Nicholas Nickleby* a "want of plan is apparent . . . from the first, an absence of design. The plot seems to have grown as the book appeared by numbers, instead of having been mapped out beforehand." Forster, of course, was right. But Dickens made up for any such deficiencies in plot with his "gallery of colorful characters," according to Ford in *Dictionary of Literary Biography*. *The Old Curiosity Shop* returns to the episodic plotting of *The Pickwick Papers* when Little Nell discovers that her grandfather is deeply in debt from gambling. To save the old man, who runs The Old Curiosity Shop, she takes him away from London on travels throughout England. Such a structure allowed for the encounter with a score of colorful characters throughout the pair's trav-

This read-aloud version of Dickens's *A Christmas Carol*, about the skinflint Scrooge and how he changes thanks to three spirits who teach him the real meaning of Christmas, is illustrated by *New Yorker* artist Carter Goodrich.

els. The death scene of Little Nell called up in Dickens all the sorrow he felt at the death of Mary Hogarth and is one of the most memorable of Dickens's tragic creations.

To America and a Renewed Vision

Dickens took a much needed rest with his wife when they sailed for the United States in January of 1842. For the next five months, Dickens wrote only letters and played the role of tourist, logging thousand of miles throughout America. However, what started out as a love affair with the brash new country ended up in antipathy on the part of Dickens. Ultimately he was disappointed in what he saw, in the slavery and the wheeling-dealing in Washington, D.C. With his return to London, Dickens eagerly got back to his desk, writing up his American journals in *American Notes for General Circulation,* and then beginning serial publication of a new novel, *The Life and Adventures of Martin Chuzzlewit,* the first of his novels to be unified by a theme—that of selfishness. Two memorable characters, Mrs. Gamp and Pecksniff, come from that novel, but in general it was not a popular success.

In 1843, Dickens won back legions of his reading public with the first of his Christmas stories, *A Christmas Carol.* He forged this new genre and added to it yearly with such titles as *The Chimes* and *Cricket on the Hearth,* all of which blend fable and fantasy, but it is *A Christmas Carol* which has remained the most popular of all such short books, not only through the novel itself, but through its numerous screen and stage adaptations. The story of miserly Scrooge who has lost the spirit of Christmas and who rediscovers it through the visitation of the ghosts of Christmas past, present, and future, *A Christmas Carol* has more than any other work by Dickens become part of the communal psyche. The very word "Scrooge" has entered the vocabulary to describe an avaricious, mean-spirited person. Though Dickens had earlier painted Christmas vignettes in his *Sketches by Boz* and *The Pickwick Papers,* this was his first full-scale treatment of the season which he so loved as a child. It was cheerfully received by the public and critics alike. The *Dublin University Magazine* concluded its fulsome review with the fervent wish that "this eminent man continue to instruct and benefit while he delights us. It is thus that fiction may lay claim to be called

literature, and its authors earn a niche—more than a niche—a chapel, in the temple of Fame." Modern reviewers have largely agreed with this assessment. Stephen Prickett, in *Victorian Fantasy,* noted that "the strength of *A Christmas Carol* lies quite simply in its psychological credibility."

The success of *A Christmas Carol* helped to put matters right with Dickens's finances, but these were always stretched to the limit. By this time he had five children and a wife to support, as well as another sister-in-law, Georgina Hogarth, who had come to live with the family. The author's father was always in need of financial assistance, as well. To help with finances, the Dickens clan lived in Italy in 1844, where expenses would be about half of what they were in London. Further Christmas books were published as well as an Italian travel book, *Pictures from Italy.* In 1846 the family again moved to the continent, spending a year in Switzerland, and it was there that *Dombey and Son* was begun, a book generally accepted as marking the beginning of Dickens's mature period. Philip Collins noted in *Victorian Fiction: A Second Guide to Research* that *Dombey and Son* is Dickens's "first mature masterpiece."

Novels of Maturity

The later phase of Dickens's creative efforts produced such enduring classics as *The Personal History of David Copperfield, Bleak House, Hard Times, Little Dorrit, A Tale of Two Cities,* and *Great Expectations.* "The best-loved of all Dickens' novels" as well as the "favourite child" of Dickens himself according to the biographer Edgar Johnson in his *Charles Dickens: His Tragedy and Triumph, David Copperfield* is highly autobiographical and features yet another orphaned protagonist. Young David loses his father, and when his mother remarries, he is packed up by his stepfather and sent to a school near London run by the brutal Mr. Creakle. Upon the death of his mother, he is sent out to work, lodging with the Micawber family, always on the brink of financial ruin. Timely help from a relative, Miss Trotwood, helps David to win an education. While lodging at school he encounters the oily Uriah Heep, another classic Dickens creation. Articled to the bar, David makes an unwise marriage to the impractical Dora. When Dora dies, David spends several years traveling, and upon his return Miss Trotwood arranges for him to marry the woman he has always loved, Agnes. He is now free to begin his life as a writer.

From even such a brief plot summary, parallels can be seen in Dickens's own life. Written in the first person, such a connection of David Copperfield to the author is only strengthened in the reader's mind. Reviewers from the time of publication to the present day have labeled this among the best of Dickens's novels. A contemporary reviewer in *Fraser's Magazine* called the book "the best of the author's fictions," and Samuel Phillips wrote in *The Times* in 1851 that "In *David Copperfield* there are more contrasts of character, more varieties of intellect, a more diverse scenery, and more picturesqueness of detail. It is the whole world rather than a bit of it which you see before you."

Part of the reason for the instant and lasting success of *David Copperfield* is, according to some reviewers, the fact that David is a character who grows and changes, unlike, for example, Oliver Twist, who is essentially a "static character," according to Ford in *Dictionary of Literary Biography*. Another factor in its popularity is that it was less a crusading social documentary and more a real novel of character. And, as usual with Dickens, there is humor, some of it grotesque, some simply fun, as with the word-happy Micawber, a character drawn after John Dickens.

Less fun is to be found in the quartet of novels that make up Dickens's so-called Dark Period: *Bleak House, Hard Times, Little Dorrit,* and *Our Mutual Friend.* Of these, *Bleak House* is generally considered to rank among Dickens's masterpieces, inventing in its pages the first detective in crime fiction, Inspector Bucket. Between *David Copperfield* and *Bleak House,* Dickens was also hard at work as owner and editor of his own magazine, *Household Words.* In the 1850s and 1860s, he also made a name for himself as a public speaker, giving dramatic readings of his works on both sides of the Atlantic.

Another major upheaval in Dickens's life was the separation from his wife in 1858 and the relationship he developed with the actress Ellen Ternan, a woman twenty-seven years his junior. By this time, Dickens had already realized a childhood dream of purchasing Gad's Hill Place just outside of Rochester. Upon separation, his wife took the oldest child with her, but Dickens remained at Gad's Hill with the rest of his ten children and with his estranged wife's sister, Georgina, in charge of domestic arrangements. Dickens established the Ternan family at yet another residence, though word of his affair was kept secret during the writer's lifetime, not being revealed until publication of *Dickens and Daughter* in 1939.

A further fallout of the Ellen Ternan liaison was a quarrel with his publishers, Bradbury and Evans, and the inception of yet another magazine, *All Year Round*, published by Chapman and Hall. It was in the pages of this magazine that two further novels popular with both young readers and adults were published: *A Tale of Two Cities* and *Great Expectations.* One of Dickens's two historical novels, *A Tale of Two Cities* is set during the French Revolution, linking the two cities of London and Paris with a select cast of characters. A fast-moving novel filled with action, it has won young readers since the time of its publication in 1859. A London lawyer, Sydney Carton, falls in love with Lucie Manette, a young Frenchwoman. But Carton, something of a drunkard, knows he does not stand a chance with Lucie, and in fact it is a man he much resembles physically, Charles Darnay, whom Lucie marries. But when Darnay, a member of the French aristocracy who has fled to London, returns to Paris on a mission, he is captured and faces the guillotine. Carton rescues his rival, standing in for this look-alike at the guillotine, and utters the famous phrase just before his death: "It is a far, far better thing that I do, than I have ever done."

A popular novel, *A Tale of Two Cities,* perhaps because of its adventure-story format, has never received the same critical attention that other Dickens novels have. One early reviewer from the *Examiner,* however, wrote: "This novel is remarkable for the rare skill with which all the powers of the author's genius are employed upon the conduct of the story. In this respect it is unequalled by any other work from the same hand, and is not excelled by any English work of fiction." Though some modern critics have taken Dickens to task for historical inaccuracy in his novel, others have mentioned that his reduction of history to a mere backdrop was in fact the author's intention. Barton R. Friedman, in *Fabricating History: English Writers on the French Revolution,* noted that the "sole escape from history is, finally, Carton's escape: to a world—perhaps fantasy, perhaps reality—where there is no time, and no trouble."

If you enjoy the works of Charles Dickens, you may also want to check out the following books and films:

Berlie Doherty, *Street Child*, 1994.

The works in Joan Lowery Nixon's *The Orphan Train Quartet*.

Jill Paton Walsh, *A Chance Child*, 1978.

Miracle on 34th Street, a film starring Maureen O'Hara and Natalie Wood, 1947.

The Prince and the Pauper, a film based on the novel by Mark Twain, 1937.

Another popular Dickens novel for young readers is *Great Expectations*, the story of young Philip Pirrip, called Pip, and his adventures from childhood to manhood. Conceived as essentially a comic novel and a bail-out for his magazine which was suffering financially because of the serialization of another author's poorly received novel, *Great Expectations* became instead a book "full of the distilled wisdom of maturity," according to Philip Hobsbaum in his *A Reader's Guide to Charles Dickens*. Indeed, some critics even put this novel among his other Dark Period works. Dickens, Hobsbaum noted, "warns us to put no trust in the surface of illusions or class and caste. Our basic personality is shaped in youth and can never change. . . . Every hope of altering his condition that Pip, the central character, ever entertained is smashed over his head."

One of Dickens's shortest novels, *Great Expectations* tells the story of Pip, another orphan protagonist, who is raised in a small English coastal town by a strict sister and her husband. One day he finds an escaped prisoner in the marshes near his house and helps him. When this man is subsequently caught by the police, he promises to repay the boy's kindness. Pip is also invited to play at the house of the wealthy and eccentric Miss Havisham, and there he falls under the spell of Estella, the adopted daughter of Miss Havisham. Pip receives indenture money from the strange lady to apprentice as a blacksmith, and later when he receives another anonymous bequest that allows him to move to London and set up as a gentleman, he thinks it likewise has come from Miss Havisham. In London, Pip studies, trying to ad-

vance himself, but Estella's arrival and subsequent marriage to a fellow student is a harsh blow for him. Soon Pip learns that his real benefactor has been Abel Magwitch, the escaped convict whom he helped many years earlier. Pip's world comes down around him when he learns that Magwitch is actually Estella's father; neither are Pip's attempts to smuggle Magwitch out of England successful. Miss Havisham dies in a fire and Pip is once again penniless. Eleven years pass as Pip joins a friend in the export business, and then, revisiting his childhood haunts, he discovers Estella, widowed. She has grown because of the difficult events of her life, and in the end, the childhood friends once again cleave to each other, walking away hand in hand.

A reviewer for *Dublin University Magazine* at the time of publication, while noting that Dickens's power as an author seemed to have been faltering of late, concluded a lengthy review of *Great Expectations* by stating that Dickens's "plot, like his characters however improbable, has a kind of artistic unity and clear purpose, enhanced in this case by the absence of much fine-drawn sentiment and the scarcity of surplus details. If the author must keep on writing novels to the last, we shall be quite content to gauge the worth of his future essays by the standard furnished to us in *Great Expectations*." Modern critics, such as G. Robert Stange in *College English*, echo this early assessment. "*Great Expectations* is a peculiarly satisfying and impressive novel," Stange commented. "It is unusual to find in Dickens' work so rigorous a control of detail, so simple and organic a pattern. . . . The simplicity is that of an art form that belongs to an ancient type and concentrates on permanently significant issues."

Final Years

Dickens did, as the reviewer for the *Dublin University Magazine* wrote, "keep on writing novels to the last." But his usual gargantuan production slowed, due in part to the rigors of his speaking schedule. His first tour, for example, booked him for eighty-seven performances, and performances they were, with the author reciting from his works like a true tragedian. The novel *Our Mutual Friend*, one of Dickens's bleakest, appeared in 1865, and then it was another four years before he returned to novel writing. The time in between was taken up with numerous smaller writing projects and touring, both in America and England. His American tour was a towering success, but it cost him physically. Pushing himself even when sick, he returned to England in 1868 exhausted. Then back in England he began another series of one hundred scheduled readings. Simultaneously he began work on his last novel, *The Mystery of Edwin Drood*, planned for publication in twelve installments. However Dickens never finished this pioneering mystery story. On the evening of June 8, 1870, after a long day of writing at Gad's Hill, Dickens suffered a stroke and died the following day.

His wishes about being buried in the Rochester area or near his beloved sister-in-law were one of the few wishes denied him. The nation demanded a more honored place of interment, and on June 14, the nation got its wish. Dickens was interred in Poet's Corner of Westminster Abbey in a private ceremony. His grave at Westminster Abbey was left open for two days so that the crowds of admirers could see his final resting place. At the end of the first day, more than a thousand persons were still waiting to pay their respects when the Abbey closed its doors. Dickens continues to be revered to this day. His books remain in print, well over a century after publication; his words continue to delight and inform. As Johnson commented in his *Charles Dickens: His Tragedy and Triumph*, "The world he created shines with undying life, and the hearts of men still vibrate to his indignant anger, his love, his glorious laughter, and his triumphant faith in the dignity of man."

■ **Works Cited**

Ackroyd, Peter, *Dickens*, Sinclair-Stevenson, 1990.

Review of *A Christmas Carol, Dublin University Magazine*, April, 1844.

Collins, Philip, "Charles Dickens," *Victorian Fiction: A Second Guide to Research*, edited by George H. Ford, Modern Language Association, 1978, pp. 34-114.

Review of *David Copperfield, Fraser's Magazine*, December, 1850, pp. 698-710.

Dickens, Charles, *Oliver Twist*, Carey, Lea & Blanchard, 1839.

Dickens, Charles, *David Copperfield*, Lea & Blanchard, 1851.

Dickens, Charles, *A Tale of Two Cities*, Chapman & Hall, 1859.

Ford, George H., "Charles Dickens," *Dictionary of Literary Biography*, Volume 21: *Victorian Novelists Before 1885*, Gale, 1983, pp. 89-124.

Forster, John, *Life of Charles Dickens*, 2 volumes, Scribners, 1905.

Friedman, Barton R., "Antihistory: Dickens' *A Tale of Two Cities*," *Fabricating History: English Writers on the French Revolution*, Princeton University Press, 1988, pp. 145-71.

Review of *Great Expectations, Dublin University Magazine*, December, 1861, pp. 685-93.

Hobsbaum, Philip, *A Reader's Guide to Charles Dickens*, Farrar, Straus and Giroux, 1972, pp. 221-42.

Johnson, Edgar, *Charles Dickens: His Tragedy and Triumph*, Viking, 1977.

Lindsay, Jack, "At Closer Grips," *Charles Dickens: A Biographical and Critical Study*, Philosophical Library, 1950, pp. 167-72.

Review of *Oliver Twist, Quarterly Review*, June, 1839, pp. 83-102.

Review of *Oliver Twist, Spectator*, November 24, 1838, pp. 1114-16.

Phillips, Samuel, "David Copperfield and Arthur Pendennis," *The Times*, June 11, 1851, p. 8.

Prickett, Stephen, "Christmas at Scrooge's," *Victorian Fantasy*, Indiana University Press, 1979, pp. 54-64.

Review of *Sketches by Boz, Morning Chronicle*, February 11, 1836.

Stange, G. Robert, "Expectations Well Lost: Dickens's Fable for the Times," *College English*, Volume XVI, 1954-55, pp. 9-17.

Review of *A Tale of Two Cities, Examiner*, December 10, 1859, pp. 788-89.

Wilson, Angus, *The World of Charles Dickens*, Viking, 1970.

■ **For More Information See**

BOOKS

Bloom, Harold, editor, *Charles Dickens*, Chelsea House, 1987.

Characters in Young Adult Literature, Gale, 1997.

Dictionary of Literary Biography, Gale, Volume 55: *Victorian Prose Writers Before 1867*, 1987, Volume 70: *British Mystery Writers, 1860-1919*, 1988.

Ford, George H., and Lauriat Lane, Jr., editors, *The Dickens Critics*, Cornell University Press, 1961.

MacKenzie, Norman, and Jeanne MacKenzie, *Dickens: A Life*, Oxford University Press, 1979.

Marcus, Stephen, *Dickens from Pickwick to Dombey*, Simon & Schuster, 1965.

Murray, Brian, *Charles Dickens*, Continuum, 1994.

Priestley, J. B., *Charles Dickens*, Viking, 1962.

Slater, Michael, *Dickens and Women*, Dent, 1983.

Something about the Author, Volume 15, Gale, 1979.

Trilling, Lionel, *The Opposing Self: Nine Essays in Criticism*, Viking, 1955, pp. 50-65.

Who's Who of Children's Literature, Schocken Books, 1968.

Writers for Children, Charles Scribners Sons, 1988.

PERIODICALS

American Health, December, 1988, p. 14.

American History Illustrated, December, 1987.

American Scholar, Winter, 1990.

Booklist, December 15, 1995, p. 401; July, 1996, p. 1838; March 15, 1997, p. 1252.

History Today, July, 1987; December, 1993.

Horn Book, January-February, 1996, p. 73.

Insight on the News, March 4, 1991.

Library Journal, June 15, 1995, p. 66; March 1, 1996, p. 126; February 15, 1997, p. 174.

Modern Maturity, December-January, 1991.

National Review, August 3, 1992.

New Republic, September 14, 1987.

New Yorker, August 31, 1992; October 11, 1993; September 25, 1995, p. 40.

New York Review of Books, October 2, 1988; January 19, 1989.

New York Times Book Review, May 15, 1988; October 2, 1988; January 22, 1995, p. 22.

Publishers Weekly, March 7, 1995, p. 36; September 18, 1995, p. 96.

School Library Journal, October, 1995, p. 37.

Utne Reader, January-February, 1990.

Variety, December 5, 1994, p. 80.

Washington Monthly, December, 1988.

Yankee, January, 1992.*

—*Sketch by J. Sydney Jones*

Greg Evans

■ Personal

Born November 13, 1947, in Los Angeles, CA; son of Herman (an electrical inspector) and Virginia (a homemaker; maiden name, Horner) Evans; married Betty Ransom (a teacher and city councilmember), December, 1970; children: Gary, Karen. *Education:* California State University at Northridge, B.A., 1970. *Hobbies and other interests:* Movies, plays, writing music, golf.

■ Addresses

Office—c/o United Media, 200 Madison Ave., New York, NY 10016.

■ Career

High school art teacher in California and Australia, 1970-74; radio and television station promotion manager in Colorado Springs, CO, 1975-80; author and artist of comic strip *Luann*, 1985—.

■ Writings

Meet Luann, Berkeley, 1986.
Why Me?, Berkeley, 1986.
Is It Friday Yet?, Berkeley, 1987.
Who Invented Brothers Anyway?, Tor, 1989.
School and Other Problems, Tor, 1989.
Homework Is Ruining My Life, Tor, 1989.
So Many Malls, So Little Money, Tor, 1990.
Pizza Isn't Everything but It Comes Close, Tor, 1991.
Dear Diary: The Following Is Top Secret, Tor, 1991.
Will We Be Tested on This?, Tor, 1992.
There's Nothing Worse than First Period P.E., Tor, 1992.
If Confusion Were a Class I'd Get an A, Tor, 1992.
School's OK if You Can Stand the Food, Tor, 1992.
I'm Not Always Confused, I Just Look That Way, Tor, 1993.
My Bedroom and Other Environmental Hazards, Tor, 1993.

■ Adaptations

Eleanor Harder wrote a musical play entitled *Luann*, which was based on Evans's comic strip characters. The vocal score was published by Pioneer Drama Service of Denver, Colorado, in 1985.

■ Work in Progress

More "Luann" collections; a gift book entitled *Sometimes You Just Have to Make Your OWN Rules*, for Rutledge Hill Press.

■ Sidelights

"Greg Evans," says Dennis Wepman in *100 Years of American Newspaper Comics*, "taught junior and senior high school art in his native California, worked as promotion manager and graphic artist for a TV station in Colorado, and entertained with a robot at trade shows and fairs before he sold *Luann* to News America Syndicate in 1984." Evans's heroine, the thirteen-year-old Luann DeGroot, deals with the trials and tribulations of her adolescence in her own inimitable fashion—finding answers to common teenage problems like dating, lack of money, school, and older brothers. "*Luann* neither sentimentalizes nor demonizes the period of life it features," declares Wepman: "rather, its sometimes poignant humor derives from its honest portrayal of the sibling hostility, academic tedium, and adolescent angst of its characters."

Evans's ambition to be a professional cartoonist dates back as far as he can remember. It was "probably in my chromosomes or something. I'm one of those people who was born with this cartoon disease," the artist tells Deborah Stanley in an interview for *Something about the Author* (*SATA*). "I was a big fan of all the Disney characters. I grew up in Burbank, near the Disney studios, and always wanted to work at Disney. I used to draw pictures of Mickey Mouse and Donald Duck; in school I'd doodle when I should have been listening to the teacher." He explains that he first sent his work to a professional magazine when he was only eleven. "My first submission was to *Playboy*, because they paid a lot of money. Of course my cartoon was rejected. But that's how I got started. I kept submitting cartoons to magazines all through my youth and through college. I never sold anything. I started trying to create ideas for comic strips and again I didn't have any success. Finally I had the idea for *Luann* in 1985, and that was the right one."

After graduating from high school, Evans attended the University of California's Northridge campus. He received his bachelor's degree there in 1970, qualifying to teach high school art. The same year he married Betty Ransom, a fellow teacher. Evans taught art in California for two years before moving to Australia to teach. At the time, the artist explains to *Authors and Artists for Young Adults* (*AAYA*), the Australians "had a shortage of teachers and were recruiting Americans. We lived there for two years and returned for a visit two years ago. It hasn't influenced my work, but I really love the country and the people."

Professional Identity

Finding the right idea, however, was only part of the long hard process of becoming a professional cartoonist. "The first strip I ever tried to do was back in the seventies," he tells Stanley. "I was going to do a strip called *Founding Fathers*, about the colonial period. Mr. Fogarty from *Luann* was in it, and he was just the same as he is now—a grumpy school teacher, because I was teaching at the time. I think early on I knew I wasn't going to like teaching. It was not my thing, and I was always pretty grumpy. Mr. Fogarty has a lot of

Luann, Evan's popular comic strip featuring thirteen-year-old Luann DeGroot and her family, deals with such familiar teen issues as dating, school, and, in this case, fashion trends.

that feeling in his character." Ms. Phelps, the school counselor, had her origins in the same strip. "I wanted a foil for him, so I had this stuffy, prim character (I think she was a school teacher at that time, too). You know cartoonists never throw away a good character, so I brought her into *Luann* and cast her as the counselor."

When he returned to the United States in 1974, Evans was still unable to sell his cartoon strips. He worked for years as a graphic artist for a television station in Colorado before finally selling the concept for *Luann* to King Features Syndicate. "Get a real job. Cartooning is an iffy career," he advises in his *SATA* interview. "There's thousands and thousands if not millions of people who want to be cartoonists. There's lots of talent out there but very few make it." "You have to be lucky and you have to have the right idea at the right time, and lightning has to strike," he tells Stanley. "In the meantime, you know, you've got to be doing something. I got my teaching credentials and I taught for a while, and I did other jobs. I was about thirty-eight before I got going with *Luann* and made a dime on my cartooning."

The strip was finally successful, Evans explains to Stanley, probably from "a combination of a couple of things. It was probably the right idea at the right time because it filled a niche, I think. There weren't many strips with female characters and strips aimed at teenagers, so it seemed to be the right combination of ideas." His own maturity was also a factor. "I firmly believe that sometimes you are trying before you're ready. In the creative world, you'll hear about somebody who has written seven books and none of them did anything, and all of a sudden their eighth book is a huge smash. I think you reach a certain level of personal development, or you're suddenly working on the right thing that taps into the right creative flow inside."

Adolescent Angst

The right thing, in this case, was the story of a rather gawky, unsure, blonde girl who confides in her friends and fights with her older brother. Evans originally thought that he might base the story on his daughter, who was about five at the time. "I was playing with the idea of a strip about a saucy little five-year-old," he tells Stanley. "You know how little girls are at that age. They like to put on lipstick, Mom's big old high heel shoes, and clop around the house. As I think back now I should have given her an imaginary tiger and then. . . . But I thought, five is so young; you don't really have any life experiences. So I kept aging the character a little bit, and finally I said, 'Oh, I'll make her a teenager because I can remember being a teenager. From my school teaching experience I'll have something to draw upon.'"

Evans drew on his own experiences growing up and his observations of his son and daughter, as well as his memories of teaching in creating Luann DeGroot. "Luann is like me in the sense that she's so ordinary," he tells *AAYA*. "I was an ultra-typical teen; not class president, not class nerd. Just one of the mass of ordinary kids, struggling to make it through adolescence." "I was sort of a wallflower and, you know, I wasn't the high school anything—football captain or class president or anything like that. I just drifted through school and that's how Luann is," he tells Stanley. But, he adds, "the relationship between Luann and her brother is very much based upon the relationship I see between my own kids." "My family has always had a great influence on my strip," Evans continues in his *AAYA* interview. "My daughter and son moved through those ages (thirteen and seventeen) a few years ago and, yes, there was lots of inspiration. The basic relationship between Luann and Brad is based on that of my own kids and that hasn't changed as they've grown."

As the title character, Luann is most often the subject of the strip's gently ironic look at life. Her companions and confidantes include the counselor Ms. Phelps, her dog Puddles, and her girlfriends Bernice and Delta. Both of them seem to have more control over their lives than does their friend. Delta in particular is a self-confident African American entrepreneur who juggles her school life, her personal life, and her work with equal aplomb. In contrast, Luann has a long-term crush on Aaron Hill, her unattainable schoolmate, but she is so shy she can't approach him without embarrassing herself. She feels that she suffers by comparison with the beautiful but shallow Tiffany. She also had to wear braces for a long period, which made her sensitive about her appearance. But Luann is not a "loser," Evans says in his *AAYA* interview. "She's a victim, like all of us, of the vagaries of life. But no one's singled her out to yank the football away. Her woes are typical of a girl her age."

Luann relationship with her main antagonist, her older brother Brad, is based in part on the relationship between Evans's own children when they were teenagers.

Although Luann is the primary focus of the strip, her older brother Brad is a well-developed character in his own right. He is most often depicted as an unkempt, slovenly lout—the kind of older brother girls have nightmares about—who serves as Luann's primary foil. But Brad, on rare occasions, demonstrates the same kind of sensitivity that characterizes his sister. In one strip sequence, he finally gets a date with Diane, the beautiful girl next door. They go to the movies and, as he pays for the tickets, a condom drops out of his pocket. Diane gets very angry with him, but Brad explains that he is motivated by respect rather than lust. "I wouldn't even put my arm around you without asking," he says. "And I respect you way too much to even think of doing more than that. . . . To you, I guess it's a sign of what I want, but it's really a sign of what I don't want." "It was almost out of character for Brad," Evans explained to Stanley, "but I had to present that point of view, and he was the one who had to say it."

Brad's condom incident is only one of several serious issues Evans confronts in Luann. Evans has confronted drug abuse, ear-piercing, and—in 1991—menstruation. Drug abuse "wasn't really difficult or controversial," Evans says in his SATA interview, "because everyone agrees that drugs are a bad thing. Then I decided that with Luann being thirteen, she was right at the age when she was going to have her first period. I thought real long and hard about doing a story about it. I got mixed reactions—mostly favorable, but there were those who thought it was inappropriate for the

comic page." But "it's important to me that my strip NOT just be about hair and clothes and make-up and puppy love," Evans tells AAYA. "Being a teen today is serious business and I want to reflect that in Luann. My goal has always been to entertain AND enlighten."

Because Luann is primarily about young people, the strip partly follows the model of past comic strips featuring teenagers. But Evans's strip looks at young people as people facing serious issues—as opposed to earlier strips, which largely depicted teenagers as boy-, girl-, or clothes-crazy. One of the earliest newspaper strips dealing with the trials and tribulations of the teenage years was Carl Ed's Harold Teen, which was introduced in 1919. Harold Teen captured the imagination of teenagers during the 1920s with its use of the latest slang (footnoted for readers unfamiliar with teen culture). The strip was adapted into a 1928 movie by Warner Bros. and into a radio program. Unlike Luann, Harold Teen focused almost exclusively on the love life of the title character. At times, the strip approached soap-opera in its treatment of its characters. Artist Don Flowers began Oh, Diana, a self-described "bobby-soxer" newspaper strip, in 1940, and it continued until 1957. Again, the focus was on teenage culture as a separate and amusing artifact. Teena (1941-1964), Penny (1943-1970), and The Jackson Twins (1950-1979) all found situational humor in the teen years.

Perhaps the most famous of the teen strips is Archie, which began as a newspaper feature in 1947 (the comic book in which the title character first appeared came out in 1943) and continues to this day. *Archie* is perhaps the best-known of all comic features, and it has sometimes worked through serious issues. However, *Archie,* unlike *Luann,* in many ways resembles earlier comic strips about teenagers. It usually has very little domestic conflict—Archie is almost never at odds with his parents, and (like the earlier *Harold Teen*) the strip focusses mainly on Archie's pursuit of love in the form of wealthy sub-debutante Veronica Lodge and girl-next-door Betty Cooper. "*Archie,*" Evans tells Stanley, "isn't really about being a teenager."

If there is one comic strip that *Luann* most resembles, says Evans, it is Charles Schulz's *Peanuts.* When *Peanuts* first appeared in 1950, it broke new ground because of its philosophic depiction of childhood. "*Peanuts* is such a brilliantly simple strip in its concept and its execution," Evans tells Stanley. "It's deceptively simple." Schulz once described his strip as being about the ways in which children are cruel to one another, and *Luann* echoes this with its conflict between the title character and her brother, as well as her arch-rival Tiffany. In addition, Evans echoes the unrequited love that Charlie Brown has for the little red-haired girl with Luann's love for Aaron Hill. "A lot of people don't realize what Charles Schulz did to comics," Evans states in his *SATA* interview. "He really revolutionized comics. Before he came along they featured corny humor, with lots of people slipping on banana peels—slapstick stuff, not introspective. He introduced concepts like the security blanket and these philosophic musings,

If you enjoy the works of Greg Evans, you may also want to check out the following:

The comic strips *Fox Trot* by Bill Amend and *For Better or For Worse* by Lynn Johnston.
Ellen Conford, *The Alfred G. Graebner Memorial High School Handbook of Rules and Regulations,* 1976.
Caroline B. Cooney, *The Girl Who Invented Romance,* 1988.
Peter D. Sieruta, *Heartbeats and Other Stories,* 1989.

taking these little things of life and finding humor in them. Nobody had done that before. He's influenced every cartoonist since."

Evans acknowledges that *Luann* has become more complex graphically as the strip has matured. "In the beginning," he tells Stanley, "Luann was a little more cartoony and a little simpler—almost a caricature of a teenager. Now she is much more an authentic teenager to me. In the past few years I've been tackling more serious subject matter and more issues that teens have to deal with. That's probably the biggest difference between what I'm doing now and what I did in the beginning of the strip." Other, more cosmetic, changes arose from story ideas. Shortly before Evans ran a story in which Luann had her ears pierced, he redesigned the character to make her ears visible.

Beautiful Tiffany, Luann's chief competitor for the affections of heartthrob Aaron Hill, gets her comeuppance during gym class in this 1996 strip.

"She's had ears ever since," he said to Stanley, "and it makes her look different—a little cuter, I think." "Luann will also get a new hair style sometime," he tells *AAYA*. "Whether it's in three months or three years, I'm not sure."

At bottom, *Luann* presents an honest, if comic, realization of life in the teen years. "Simplistically drawn," states Wepman, ". . . *Luann* remains a sympathetic record of the changing lifestyles of contemporary youth. Teenagers of both sexes find in the strip much that is familiar and the reassurance that they are not alone." *Luann*'s philosophy, says Evans, could be summed up as "It's tough being a teenager, but you will survive. Billions of people have survived it. Just try to have a sense of humor. And don't let anyone tell you these are the best years of your life."

■ Works Cited

Evans, Greg, interview with Deborah Stanley, *Something about the Author,* Volume 73, Gale, 1992, pp. 53-56.

Evans, Greg, e-mail interview with Kenneth R. Shepherd for *Authors and Artists for Young Adults,* October 14-20, 1997.

Wepman, Dennis, "Luann," *100 Years of American Newspaper Comics,* edited by Maurice Horn, Random House, 1996, pp. 189-90.

■ For More Information See

PERIODICALS

Voice of Youth Advocates, August, 1997, p. 159.

—*Sketch by Kenneth R. Shepherd*

Cynthia D. Grant

1991, and Author Day Award, Detroit Public Library, 1992, all for *Phoenix Rising;* some of the author's works have been chosen as Best Books for Young Adults by the American Library Association, and as Children's Books of Distinction by *Hungry Mind Review.*

■ Personal

Born November 23, 1950, in Brockton, MA; daughter of Robert C. and Jacqueline (Ford) Grant; married Daniel Heatley (marriage ended); married Erik Neel, 1988; children: (first marriage) Morgan; (second marriage) Forest. *Education:* Attended high school in Palo Alto, CA.

■ Addresses

Home—Box 95, Cloverdale, CA 95425.

■ Career

Writer, 1974—.

■ Awards, Honors

Annual book award from Woodward Park School, 1981, for *Joshua Fortune;* Best Book of the Year award, Michigan Library Association's Young Adult Caucus, 1990, PEN/Norma Klein award,

■ Writings

JUVENILE

Joshua Fortune, Atheneum, 1980.
Summer Home, Atheneum, 1981.

YOUNG ADULT

Big Time, Atheneum, 1982.
Hard Love, Atheneum, 1983.
Kumquat May, I'll Always Love You, Atheneum, 1986.
Phoenix Rising; or, How to Survive Your Life, Atheneum, 1989.
Keep Laughing, Atheneum, 1991.
Shadow Man, Atheneum, 1992.
Uncle Vampire, Atheneum, 1993.
Mary Wolf, Atheneum, 1995.

■ Sidelights

Cynthia D. Grant is a popular American author who writes novels about growing up. Her books appeal to young adults who want to read stories about life in the real world. As Grant commented in an interview with *Authors and Artists for Young Adults,* "Since 1980 I have published ten books for children and young adults, primarily for the young adult category, which is considered age twelve and up. I don't ever sit down and write 'for' children. I'm an adult; I write what sounds good to me." In her novels, Grant tackles difficult social problems such as alcoholism, child abuse, and homelessness. Grant is not afraid to portray violence and other graphic situations. However, the overall message she conveys is that, no matter what the problem, young adults can survive adolescence. After all, Grant said, "Most of us who write for children or young adults know that they read books not only to be entertained, but to be enlightened and encouraged." Her characters are heroes who triumph over tragedy. They are realistic young people who overcome a variety of obstacles, and stand for the winning qualities of righteousness, maturity, humor, and independence. Grant has received important awards for her work, including the PEN/ Norma Klein Award in 1991.

Born on November 23, 1950, in Brockton, Massachusetts, Grant began writing poems and stories when she was only eight years old. Despite her young age, however, she did manage to get published. Grant said, "My grandmother was a stringer for our town newspaper, the *Brockton Enterprise,* and she was able to sneak my efforts into print." Grant loved the attention she received from such an achievement, but there were other things that she liked about being a young author. Grant said one of the reasons she started writing was because she "loved to play with the sounds of words." Ultimately, she wrote because she felt compelled to: "It was something I did automatically, like breathing."

Along with being an enthusiastic writer, Grant was also a voracious reader. She told *AAYA,* "I loved to read. I devoured books. Especially the biographies of famous women. Amelia Earhart. Harriet Tubman. Marie Curie. Eleanor Roosevelt. I too wanted to do something huge and noble and important one day." Though Grant pays homage to these great historical women, she admits that her main interest was Nancy Drew, a fictional character in a series of mysteries written by Carolyn Keene. Grant said, "I owned almost a complete set of the Nancy Drew mysteries; the ones with the blue cloth covers published in the

1930s." Grant liked the stories because they were inspirational, and because Nancy Drew had so much freedom. Nancy was allowed to go speeding around in her roadster solving mysteries with her best friends Bess and George, and her boyfriend Ned Nickerson. "Nancy lived a life of independence and glamour unheard of in the world I inhabited in Brockton, Massachusetts . . . ," Grant remarked. "There was no one to tell Nancy what to do, or trim her bangs too short." The most appealing thing about Nancy Drew was that she was a great role model and a source of strength for Grant when she was a young woman: "Nancy's courage, self-confidence and skill, not to mention her slim, blonde good looks, were enormously appealing to someone who was redhaired, frightened and freckled."

Understands Teens' Emotions

As a writer, Grant is particularly tuned in to adolescent pain. She feels strongly about the social struggle that all young adults must endure while growing up, and it has become an important theme in her work. Grant experienced great difficulty when she was in junior high school. She said, "Junior high school was the worst time in my life. I have never felt so ugly, so awkward or so hopelessly flawed as I did in the seventh grade." In a particularly poignant illustration of her childhood struggle for survival, Grant said, "The kids were so mean to each other! If you stuck out in any way, by being especially smart, or handicapped, or even handicapped with an especially hideous home permanent, you were picked on until you bled to death of a thousand tiny cuts. Kids who were picked on took it out on smaller kids. Hurt people hurt people—and themselves. Is this a system?"

Luckily, Grant survived junior high school and went on to become highly motivated. The obstacles she encountered as a child did not keep her from dreaming about the future. She told *AAYA,* "By the time I entered high school, I knew what I wanted to be when I grew up: famous. Significant lives seemed to be lived onstage. Important people always had an audience." Thus, Grant began her ambitious struggle for fame, during which she bypassed college and went straight into the real world. She wanted "to be a great actress, director and writer," and she followed the traditional formula for success by moving, as she

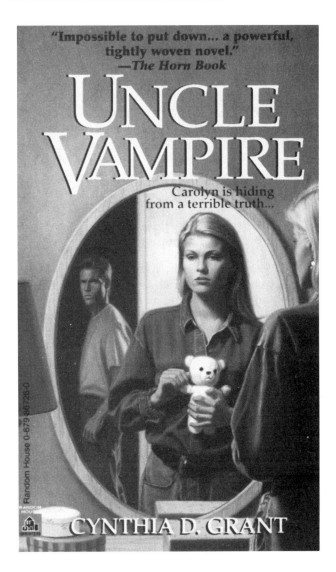

"Impossible to put down... a powerful, tightly woven novel."
—*The Horn Book*

UNCLE VAMPIRE

Carolyn is hiding from a terrible truth...

CYNTHIA D. GRANT

Carolyn and her twin sister, Honey, share a terrible secret about their uncle in this 1993 novel.

said, "into my own glamorous studio apartment, with its glamorous sunken shower, sunken floor and sunken bed, and waited for success to knock at my door."

Unfortunately, success did not arrive immediately, much to Grant's dismay. In order to make a living she first took a job as an insurance file clerk, and then later she became a waitress. However, she never stopped writing and submitting material to publications such as the *New Yorker* and the *Atlantic Monthly*. Finally, she had a story published in a feminist journal. Throughout her struggle to get published, Grant was persistent. As she recalled in the *AAYA* interview, when people asked her why she continued writing despite rejection, she answered, "Birds gotta fly, and I gotta write. Why this is so for me I cannot say."

Literary Success

Grant wrote her one of her first books for young adults, titled *Hard Love*, in 1983. *Hard Love* is narrated by Stephen, a high school senior who is coping with some difficult problems. He is worried that his friend Paulie is losing his grip on reality, and he is trying to convince Paulie's father of this fact. Stephen is also in love with an older woman named Molly. When she finds out that he is only seventeen, she decides they should just be friends. Finally, Paulie's father becomes convinced that his son does indeed have problems. The subject matter of this novel reaches beyond the sphere of adolescence and into the realm of adulthood, and critics praised the work for its realism. Zena Sutherland wrote in *Bulletin of the Center for Children's Books,* "The elements of the story are nicely knit together into a smooth narrative that has depth and intelligence." In *Children's Book Review Service,* Lucy Marx observed that *Hard Love* will prove popular with the young reader who is "trying to find a place in the world."

Grant's next book, *Kumquat May, I'll Always Love You,* poses an intriguing question for young adults: What would happen if my parents suddenly disappeared? Grant offers some interesting answers in a book that Barbara Chatton of *School Library Journal* called "an engaging and unusual survival story." The main character, Livvy, is a high school senior who has lived alone for two years since her widowed mother went out one night and never returned. Livvy is able to fend for herself, though, through a small income, the use of a car, and a spacious home. The challenge for Livvy and her friend Rosella is to convince the rest of the town that Livvy's mother has not disappeared. Livvy's independence becomes threatened when she falls in love with Raymond Mooney, upon whom she reluctantly becomes dependent. Chatton noted that *Kumquat May, I'll Always Love You* "will hold the interest of young readers who have wondered if they could make it on their own."

But Grant also realizes that tragedy is not so easy to endure, that the death of a family member or a friend can be particularly difficult. Grant her-

If you enjoy the works of Cynthia D. Grant, you may also want to check out the following books and films:

Jean Ferris, *Signs of Life*, 1995.
Hadley Irwin, *Abby, My Love*, 1985.
Kathryn Jensen, *Pocket Change*, 1989.
Kathryn Lasky, *Memoirs of a Bookbat*, 1994
Ruth White, *Weeping Willow*, 1992.
Gas Food Lodging, a film starring Ione Skye and Fairuza Balk, 1992.

self has survived such an experience, and her grief inspired her next novel, *Phoenix Rising: Or How to Survive Your Life*. The book is about seventeen-year-old Jessie, who has just lost her older sister, Helen, to cancer. The character Helen is based on Grant's friend, Harriet, who died of cancer in 1978 when she was just nineteen. Commenting on her desire to immortalize Harriet by writing about her, Grant told *AAYA*, "I did not want to let her go. I wanted to capture her on paper."

The plot of the novel focuses on Jessie's struggle to accept the loss of her sister. Her family, who is traumatized as well, wants to help, but Jessie continually escapes into isolation. Finally, Jessie discovers the diary that Helen wrote in before she died. Helen's reflections on life give Jessie what she needs to go on. Critics praised *Phoenix Rising* as a valuable book for young adults. Mary Helen Smith wrote in *Voices of Youth Advocates* that the work "will appeal to YA's because it is about a real problem that many of them face, how to deal with the death of a close friend or sibling." Fran Lantz reported in *Kliatt*, "Grant has written a moving, unflinching portrait of two sisters, one facing death, the other struggling to face life on her own."

Grant's next novel, *Keep Laughing*, is more light-hearted than her previous work. However, as Carol Shama of *Voice of Youth Advocates* stated, "*Keep Laughing* is not a funny book." It is the story of Shep, a fifteen-year-old boy whose parents are divorced. He has lived with his mother for years, and until recently he has gotten along well with her. Shep worries about his relationship with his father, Joey Young, a successful comedian, and is afraid that his father does not care about

him. Unfortunately, after he goes to live with Joey for a while, his suspicions are confirmed. Shep's mother, who seemed overprotective at first, emerges as a rational figure who was merely trying to protect her son from his irresponsible father. According to Shama, Grant makes a definitive statement with this book: "*Keep Laughing* posits that it is important to uncover the illusions with which we live and to move beyond them with a clearer sense of what is real in our relationships."

Tackles Challenging Subjects

Grant's 1992 novel, *Shadow Man,* is unique because the main character, Gabriel, is dead—killed when he crashed his pickup truck into a tree. The Gabriel seen by readers is a composite sketch, a portrait drawn by the townspeople who all express different reactions to the tragedy. Everyone misses Gabriel for different reasons, and many believe Gabriel could have led a successful life if it had not been for family problems such as alcoholism and abuse. Describing the narrative structure of the book, a critic in *Kirkus Reviews* observed, "The events unfold in orderly fashion, each chapter featuring the distinctive first-person reflections of one of many characters." *Shadow Man* exemplifies Grant's ability to create imperfect heroes. In *Booklist,* Gary Young stated, "Gabriel makes a great symbol of fulfillment in the midst of tragedy."

Grant's next book, *Uncle Vampire,* is a brutally honest story about child molestation. It portrays the victimization of sixteen-year-old Carolyn, who is sexually abused by her Uncle Toddy. Carolyn forms a delusional response to her predicament: she convinces herself that Uncle Toddy is a vampire who visits her nightly to drink her blood. She is too afraid to tell anyone except her sister Honey about these terrible events. Uncle Toddy is not a vampire, however, and Honey is just an imaginary friend. As the abuse continues, Carolyn withdraws further from life, loses friends, and does poorly in school. Finally, Carolyn gets help from a school counselor and begins to put her life back together again. Critic Beverly Youree of *Voice of Youth Advocates* stated, "This is a terrific novel about a very serious and all too prevalent problem within our society." Maeve Visser Knoth, reviewing the work in *Horn Book*, noted, "Grant's plot and character development are flawless; she never loses the limited perspective of a young woman struggling with a terrifying and damaging situation."

Addressing the modern problem of homelessness in *Mary Wolf*, Grant offers a story full of tension and violence. According to Deborah Stevenson in *Bulletin of the Center for Children's Books*, "Grant portrays convincingly the desperate self-delusion of a family fallen on hard times from which they can't extricate themselves." The father of sixteen-year-old Mary Wolf cannot hold a job, so he decides to pack up the RV and take the family on the road. They arrive at a campsite in California where other homeless families live, but soon afterwards they are threatened with eviction. After Mary's father suffers an emotional breakdown, he lashes out violently by shooting her mother and taking her siblings hostage. Finally, with an action that asserts her courage and superiority, Mary confronts her father with a gun. Critics praised *Mary Wolf* for its depiction of the painful nomadic lifestyle of homeless families. Stevenson stated, "This is a compelling story, and kids who find *The Grapes of Wrath* too dry and distant will relate to a strong young heroine undergoing more contemporary difficult times."

Overall, Grant's work shows that as a writer she walks a fine line between optimism and despair. She told *AAYA*, "I'm trying to write honest books for and about real people." In her novels, a happy ending is not as important as what the characters had to endure to get there. Her books are realistic because they are not falsely optimistic. However, Grant is not just another writer dealing in despair. As she suggests, Grant does not write just to entertain and enlighten readers, but to nurture them as well: "Through my writing, I want to reach out to readers and let them know that they are not alone; that, unique as each of us is, we all feel lonely and scared and confused sometimes. And to say, in the words of an anonymous author: Be kind; everyone you meet is fighting a hard battle."

■ Works Cited

Chatton, Barbara, review of *Kumquat May, I'll Always Love You, School Library Journal*, May, 1986, p. 103-4.

Knoth, Maeve Visser, review of *Uncle Vampire, Horn Book*, January, 1994.

Lantz, Fran, review of *Phoenix Rising: Or How to Survive Your Life, Kliatt*, September, 1991, p. 8.

Marx, Lucy, review of *Hard Love, Children's Book Review Service*, January, 1984, p. 52.

Review of *Shadow Man, Kirkus Reviews*, November 1, 1992, p. 1375.

Shama, Carol, review of *Keep Laughing, Voice of Youth Advocates*, February, 1992, pp. 370-71.

Smith, Mary Helen, review of *Phoenix Rising: Or How to Survive Your Life, Voice of Youth Advocates*, June, 1989, p. 101.

Stevenson, Deborah, review of *Mary Wolf, Bulletin of the Center for Children's Books*, November, 1995, p. 91.

Sutherland, Zena, review of *Hard Love, Bulletin of the Center for Children's Books*, December, 1983, p. 67.

Young, Gary, review of *Shadow Man, Booklist*, November 1, 1992, p. 504.

Youree, Beverly, review of *Uncle Vampire, Voice of Youth Advocates*, February, 1994, p. 381.

■ For More Information See

BOOKS

Twentieth-Century Young Adult Writers, 1st edition, St. James Press, 1994.

PERIODICALS

Booklist, August, 1983, p. 1457; October 1, 1995, p. 303.

Bulletin of the Center for Children's Books, April, 1982, p. 148; February, 1989, p. 147.

Horn Book, December, 1980, p. 641; July-August, 1989, p. 488; March-April, 1996, p. 206.

Kirkus Reviews, November 1, 1991, p. 1402.

Kliatt, winter, 1985, p. 10.

Publishers Weekly, June 27, 1986, p. 95; February 10, 1989, p. 73; October 11, 1991, p. 64; November 1, 1991, p. 1402; October 16, 1995, p. 62.

School Library Journal, September, 1981, p. 125; April, 1982, p. 82; October, 1983, p. 168; February, 1989, p. 100; October, 1992, p. 140; November, 1993, p. 122.

Voice of Youth Advocates, April, 1982, p. 34; August/October, 1986, pp. 142, 144; December, 1992, p. 278; December, 1995, p. 300.

Wilson Library Bulletin, November, 1989.

—Sketch by Stephen Allison

Mary Downing Hahn

Navy Federal Credit Union, 1963-65; homemaker and writer, 1965-70; Prince George's County Memorial Library System, Laurel Branch, Laurel, MD, children's librarian associate, 1975-91; full-time writer, 1991—. Freelance artist for "Cover to Cover," on WETA-TV, 1973-75. *Member:* Society of Children's Book Writers and Illustrators, Washington Children's Book Guild (president, 1997-98).

■ Personal

Born December 9, 1937, in Washington, DC; daughter of Kenneth Ernest (an automobile mechanic) and Anna Elisabeth (a teacher; maiden name, Sherwood) Downing; married William E. Hahn, October 7, 1961 (divorced, 1977); married Norman Pearce Jacob (a librarian), April 23, 1982; children: (first marriage) Katherine Sherwood, Margaret Elizabeth. *Education:* University of Maryland at College Park, B.A., 1960, M.A., 1969, doctoral study, 1970-74. *Politics:* Democrat. *Hobbies and other interests:* Travel, cooking, history.

■ Addresses

Office—c/o Clarion Books, 215 Park Avenue South, New York, NY 10003.

■ Career

Art teacher at junior high school in Greenbelt, MD, 1960-61; Hutzler's Department Store, Baltimore, MD, clerk, 1963; correspondence clerk for

■ Awards, Honors

American Library Association (ALA) Reviewer's Choice, Library of Congress Children's Books, and *School Library Journal's* Best Book citations, all 1983, Child Study Association of America Children's Books of the Year, and National Council of Teachers of English Teacher's Choice citations, both 1984, and William Allen White Children's Choice Award, William Allen White Library, 1986, all for *Daphne's Book;* Dorothy Canfield Fisher Award, 1988, and children's choice awards from ten other states, all for *Wait Till Helen Comes: A Ghost Story;* Child Study Association Book Award, 1989, Jane Addams Children's Book Award Honor Book, 1990, and California Young Reader's Medal, 1991, all for *December Stillness;* ALA Books for Reluctant Reader citation, 1990, and children's choice awards from five states, all for *The Dead Man in Indian Creek;* children's choice awards from seven states, all for *The Doll in the Garden;* ALA Notable Book Citation, Scott O'Dell Award for Historical Fiction, and Joan G. Sugarman Award, all 1992, Hedda Seisler Mason Award, 1993, and children's choice awards from three states, all for *Stepping on the Cracks*; Best Books for Young Adults citation, Young Adult Library Services Association, 1993, and New York Public Library Books for the Teen Age citation, 1994, both for *The Wind Blows Backward*; William Allen White Children's Book Award, 1997, for *Time for Andrew: A Ghost Story.*

■ Writings

The Sara Summer, Clarion, 1979.
The Time of the Witch, Clarion, 1982.
Daphne's Book, Clarion, 1983.
The Jellyfish Season, Clarion, 1985.
Wait Till Helen Comes: A Ghost Story, Clarion, 1986.
Tallahassee Higgins, Clarion, 1987.
December Stillness, Clarion, 1988.
Following the Mystery Man, Clarion, 1988.
The Doll in the Garden, Clarion, 1989.
The Dead Man in Indian Creek, Clarion, 1990.
The Spanish Kidnapping Disaster, Clarion, 1991.
Stepping on the Cracks, Clarion, 1991.
The Wind Blows Backward (young adult), Clarion, 1993.
Time for Andrew: A Ghost Story, Clarion, 1994.
A Visit with Mary Downing Hahn (video), Kit Morse Productions, 1994.
Look for Me by Moonlight (young adult), Clarion, 1995.
The Gentleman Outlaw and Me—Eli, Clarion, 1996.
Following My Own Footsteps, Clarion, 1996.
As Ever, Gordy, Clarion, 1998.

Hahn's books have been translated into Danish, Swedish, Italian, German, Japanese, and French. Contributor to anthologies, including *Don't Give up the Ghost,* 1993, *Bruce Coville's Book of Ghost Stories,* 1994, and *Bruce Coville's Book of Nightmares,* 1995.

■ Work in Progress

Anna All Year Round, a chapter book for Clarion based on the reminiscences of the author's mother growing up in Baltimore in 1914; an untitled Civil War story for young teens, set in Maryland.

■ Sidelights

Mary Downing Hahn has taken the old dictum of writing what you know and has turned it into a body of work that encompasses some twenty novels for young teens and young adults. Mining her own childhood as well as that of her parents and children, Hahn writes closely detailed stories that explore family issues such as loss of a parent or loved one, the struggle for identity and acceptance, and the blending of families. Many of her novels are set in rural and suburban Maryland where Hahn herself grew up and still resides.

Critics often note that Hahn mixes such stories with a subtle and compassionate humor and with insightful character sketches. The results have proved successful, winning not only awards for novels such as *Daphne's Book, Wait Till Helen Comes: A Ghost Story, The Jellyfish Season, December Stillness, Time for Andrew: A Ghost Story, Stepping on the Cracks,* and *The Wind Blows Backward,* but also a large and loyal readership whom Hahn regularly visits on her school speaking tours. Most of her books are told from the point of view of a young female protagonist, a girl caught in the flux of development, often awkward, often insecure, a mixture of frailties. Hahn once told *Something about the Author* (*SATA*) that she strives to create "real life" in her novels. "Like the people I know, I want my characters to be a mixture of strengths and weaknesses, to have good and bad qualities, to be a little confused and unsure of themselves." Neither are happy endings always a guarantee in a Hahn novel, for life does not always provide such endings. "At the same time, however," Hahn remarked, "I try to leave room for hope."

"But not all my work is of this serious nature," Hahn reported in an interview for *Authors and Artists for Young Adults* (*AAYA*). "Some of my books I call entertainments, and they are often among my most popular. In those I use elements of fantasy and the supernatural, elements I can't employ in the serious fiction. You can't simply have a ghost come along in real life and change the course of a story. Or have the main character time travel out of trouble. But with my entertainments, that is not only possible but demanded." Happy endings *are* possible in such books, as well as time travel, witches, and even a vampire. Among such entertainments, Hahn places *The Time of the Witch, Wait Till Helen Comes, The Doll in the Garden, Time for Andrew,* and *Look for Me by Moonlight.* Other entertainments include a popular book for male readers, *The Dead Man in Indian Creek,* and a western adventure, *The Gentleman Outlaw and Me—Eli,* in which Hahn was finally able to

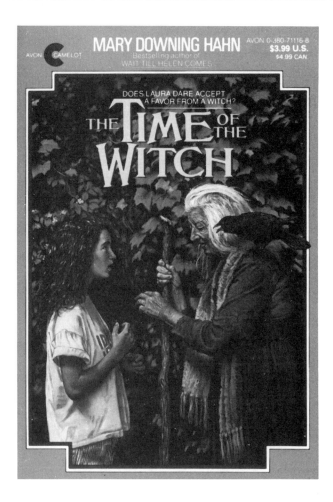

DOES LAURA DARE ACCEPT A FAVOR FROM A WITCH?

MARY DOWNING HAHN

THE TIME OF THE WITCH

In a wild effort to stop her parents' divorce, Laura engages the help of a witch who has her own malicious reasons to intervene in this 1982 work.

indulge her own childhood fantasies of running off to the Wild West.

A Childhood in Maryland

Hahn was born on December 9, 1937, in Washington, D.C., the first child of Anna Elisabeth Sherwood Downing and Kenneth Ernest Downing. She spent most of her childhood in College Park, Maryland, "a wonderful place to grow up," as she typified it in her *AAYA* interview. "The University of Maryland is located there, so the town was a mix of working class people and professionals. It was the sort of place where kids could go off on their own in complete safety. There were few cars then, especially during and just after the Second World War. The only worry for us kids then

was wondering if your mother's friends would see you doing things you didn't want your mother to know about. Since my mother was a local teacher, I was well known. It was hard for me to get in trouble."

Hahn's parents both had childhoods marred by loss. In her mother's case, it was the beloved father—Hahn's maternal grandfather—who died when his daughter was thirteen. His death left his family "almost penniless," as she noted in an essay for *Something about the Author Autobiography Series* (*SAAS*). "Her father's death ended my mother's childhood and her happiness. . . . She was left in the hands of a cold and unloving mother who claimed she could not support a daughter." Hahn's mother grew up with relatives, graduated from high school, took a teacher's training course, and began teaching at College Park Elementary School when she was nineteen. Later she met Kenneth Downing, whose early life was also marked by loss, of nationality and family wealth. "My father was first and foremost an English citizen," Hahn recalled in *SAAS*. At age ten, his family left a comfortable life in England to seek their fortune in America, whereupon they lost all their money in a failed farming venture. "Thanks to my grandfather's neglect, my father's life in America was full of hardship," Hahn wrote in *SAAS*. "Looking back, he must have seen England as the lost Eden of his childhood, a place to which he longed to return but could not."

Hahn's father kept both his accent and his English citizenship until his death in 1963, working as an auto mechanic all the while. Hahn's parents met at a dance and were married in 1935. The honeymoon was barely over when the mother's mother moved in with the couple. "Unfortunately," Hahn recalled, "my grandmother's presence did not contribute to the happiness of my parents' marriage. She disliked my father." Hahn was born two years later, and the following year, her mother returned to teaching, leaving her daughter in the care of the grandmother. It was an arrangement born out of financial necessity, but not an optimum situation. "Already suffering from arteriosclerosis, Nanny was a strange and frightening person," Hahn noted in *SAAS*. " Given to morbid ramblings about sin and death, she made my early childhood less than happy." By the time she was three, Hahn was already spending as much time as possible out of doors, away from her grandmother.

Growing up during World War Two, Hahn was also influenced by the flavor of those times, of the blackout laws and the possibility of air raids and the sounds of sirens. She began her education at a Catholic school, but soon transferred to the public school. Yet her months at Catholic school had gotten her on the way to reading; she now could entertain herself with her favorite tales: *The Little Engine That Could*, the Raggedy Ann and Andy books, and above all, A. A. Milne's Pooh stories. One of Hahn's first artistic efforts, in fact, involved the enhancement of Ernest Shepherd's black-and-white illustrations for Pooh: One rainy day she colored in all the line drawings. Discovering the book, Hahn's mother thenceforth made sure her daughter had plenty of drawing paper to work on.

A sister was born in 1943, but once again Hahn's grandmother tainted the event, convincing Hahn that both her mother and the newborn were dead. The following year, Hahn's favorite uncle, Dudley, her father's brother, was killed in the war, an event that stayed with her, only to be purged years later in her novel, *Stepping on the Cracks*. A self-proclaimed "fearful child," such a loss did nothing to make Hahn feel more secure in her early years. Life in College Park, however, did. There were friends on the block, and an understanding teacher at school, Mrs. Schindler, who initiated a book club for some of her precocious first graders. There were also the tracks of the Baltimore and Ohio Railroads only a block from Hahn's house, and the lonely sound of the trains at night that beckoned her to the romance of travel and adventure. Encouraged at school to draw and read—two of her favorite activities—Hahn began to find a place in her childhood world, and she was even able to finally read all the way through the events in the tale of Hansel and Gretel, a story that had frightened her for years.

The eventual death of her grandmother came as a relief to the young Hahn. "My tormentor was gone for good," she wrote in *SAAS*, but then guilt feelings arose at such a reaction and when only a week later her beloved paternal grandmother died, it was like a punishment. But such events were quickly forgotten with the birth of a baby brother not long after. The postwar world sent the family on a further roller coaster ride when they had to vacate their rented house so that the owner's son, a returning veteran, could take it.

Hahn and her family were forced for a time to share the small house belonging to her father's family. Squeezed into insufficient space, there were animosities and rivalries. Hahn's cousin did not want to share her space with her relatives, and squabbles ensued. Hahn was sent off to summer camps, and when she returned, her family had finally been able to buy a house in College Park in her old neighborhood and just next door to her best friend.

Books and friends informed Hahn's world for the next years. During the days she played games with her friends, and at night she read into the late hours. Nancy Drew and the Hardy Boys set her and her friends up in business as self-appointed spy chasers in the early years of the Cold

Hahn's award-winning 1983 book tells about two seventh-grade girls who become friends working on a school project together until one learns a deep secret about the other which poses a moral dilemma.

War. Dog books soon replaced mysteries, with *Lassie Come Home, Call of the Wild,* and *Greyfriar's Bobby* topping that list. Hahn was also addicted to stories about orphans: *The Secret Garden, Anne of Green Gables, Oliver Twist,* and *Kidnapped* being early favorites. "Obviously books played an important part in my life," she recalled in *SAAS.* "I didn't just read them, I *lived* them." Radio shows were also an important influence in Hahn's budding sense of storytelling, and soon she was busy writing stories and illustrating them. In the seventh grade she began keeping a diary, and one of her first entries foretold a future career: "What I want to be when I grow up—a writer and illustrator." She began work on her first book, "Small Town Life," about the daily adventures of an awkward twelve-year-old who vaguely resembled the author: self-conscious and different from everyone else. Yet by high school, Hahn had determined to turn her life around, to leave behind her tomboy stage and conform. She became, along with other bobby-soxers of her generation, boy crazy. She was, as she described it in *SAAS,* "a teenager, fifties style." Throughout high school she was friends with a clique of seven or eight girls, and had adventures at the local drugstore and at the seashore—where Hahn fell in love, from a distance, with a sailor.

From Mother to Author

Upon graduation from high school, Hahn attended the University of Maryland, just a mile from her family house in College Park. She majored in studio art and English, two subjects she dearly loved. By the time she was a senior she had met and fallen in love with the man whom she would marry, though no date had been set. After college, Hahn took an art position at a junior high school, but left after a year, despising the role of authority figure she was cast in. After a summer in Europe, Hahn married and started graduate school in English. When her husband decided upon law school, she left her own studies behind to support the family with a variety of low-paying jobs. Her first daughter was born in 1965, and then a second in 1967. Living in College Park, Hahn was a full-time mom for some time, loving the task of reading to her children. It was then she rediscovered her own dream of writing and illustrating books, but her children's tastes were not the same as the publishers, it seemed. She sent off several manuscripts only to have them rejected.

Despite her aversion to her whiny stepsister, Molly realizes it's up to her to rescue the little one from a malevolent ghost-child in this 1986 novel.

In 1971, as her first marriage began to fall apart, Hahn returned to school to try for a Ph.D in English, a single mother at age thirty-four. Toward the end of the four-year program, Hahn became a freelance illustrator for a children's reading series on PBS, "Cover to Cover." Through this work her knowledge of children's literature broadened, and eventually she took a job as a children's librarian. Her intention was to continue writing her dissertation in her spare time, but in the event what she wrote was her first novel, *The Sara Summer.* Begun in 1975, that first novel was finally published in 1979. The initial writing took a year, but it was not until a friendly editor at Clarion Books, James Giblin, sent back a rejection with some suggestions for revision that Hahn began her real apprenticeship in children's writing. What ensued were two years and seven revisions until finally in 1978 Giblin took the book on. Hahn has been with Clarion and her editor, Giblin, ever since. "I can't believe how lucky I have been to have the same editor all these years," Hahn said in her interview with *AAYA*. "When I hear the horror stories of other writers, how their editors leave or their publishing houses die, I realize how fortunate I have been."

Similar to her first efforts at juvenile writing with "Small Town Life," *The Sara Summer* takes place in a suburb of Washington, D.C., and draws on Hahn's memories of what it is like to be a twelve-year-old, the tallest in school and unsure of one-self. Coltish Emily Sherwood, deserted by her only friend, happily takes on the newcomer in town, Sara Slater, a rough-hewn gem of a girl whose mouth manages to make adults uneasy. Sara is even taller than Emily and exhibits the same dis-interest in boys and clothes—the perfect friend, it seems. But Emily must learn to find herself in the relationship, and this is partly accomplished by her saving Sara's little sister from almost certain death on the train tracks. Emily must learn to speak up for herself, to call her new friend on the cruel manner in which she treats her little sis-ter whom she dubs "Hairball." Most critics com-mented on the episodic quality of the book, a hazard of first novels. Richard Ashford, writing in *Horn Book*, noted that despite some sketchy characterization of minor characters, "the vivid characterizations of the two girls make the author's first novel a worthwhile venture." Cyrisse Jaffee in *School Library Journal* also commented on some "one-dimensional characters (especially the adults)," but concluded that Hahn "convincingly portrays the ups and downs of a friendship that kids will find easy to read and relate to." *Pub-lishers Weekly* critic Jean F. Mercier also noted that Hahn exhibited an "intimate knowledge of sub-teens and a well-tuned ear." It was these quali-ties which distinguished Hahn's work from the outset and has kept readers coming back for more.

Hahn's second book, *The Time of the Witch*, opened the door to fantasy, with a blending of both a realistic domestic situation and an element of magic. The first of her "entertainments," *The Time of the Witch* tells the story of sulky young Laura who tries to stop her parents' impending divorce. The story was partly inspired by Hahn's own daughters who had trouble accepting Hahn's di-vorce. But Laura, in her quest, seeks help from the local witch in the mountains of West Virginia where she lives. The witch, however, has a sepa-

In this 1988 work, a social studies project to inter-view a Vietnam vet turns into tragedy as fifteen-year-old Kelly and her family raise disturbing questions.

rate agenda: She wants to get even with Laura's family for an old grudge. "One editor at Clarion actually wanted the witch to turn out to be just a regular person, misunderstood by the local chil-dren," Hahn told *AAYA*. "But Jim [Giblin] wouldn't go along with that. He didn't want her to be just an old lady with problems. I'm grate-ful we made that decision, as I was always dis-appointed in stories that explained away the magic when I was a kid." Critics concurred, in-cluding Karen Stang Hanley in *School Library Jour-nal* who noted that "elements of suspense and the occult are expertly balanced against the realistic dimensions" of the story. Such fantasy stories involving witches and ghosts are among Hahn's most popular with children. "People are always asking me when I'm going to write another ghost story," she told *AAYA*, "and I can only tell them I'll write one when it comes to me. I cannot write to order, even if I know sales are assured."

Hahn's third novel, *Daphne's Book*, returned to the serious theme of the outsider and also won awards on both the state and national level. Jessica is none too happy being stuck with "Daffy" Daphne as a partner on a class project, yet eventually the two girls form a friendship. Jessica, however, soon discovers a secret about Daphne that challenges their friendship. Daphne and her small sister are living with a senile grandparent after the death of their parents. When Jessica discovers this secret, Daphne swears her to silence, but ultimately Jessica feels she must tell the authorities to save her friend. In the construction of this third novel, Hahn had learned her lessons. According to Audrey B. Eaglen in *School Library Journal*, the characters, "even secondary ones, are completely believable and very likable." Nancy C. Hammond, writing in *Horn Book*, while noting that Hahn was "perceptive" in her depiction of pre-adolescents, commented that each girl "learns that the issues of betrayal and loyalty, hurting and helping, can be perplexingly unclear; the ending . . . is hopeful rather than happy." Writing in the *New York Times Book Review*, Barbara Cutler Helfgott noted that the book's vitality "derives from a convincing respect for hopeful beginnings and hard choices—two conditions for growth, no matter what your age." And *Publishers Weekly* critic Mercier summed up the book by calling it a "gently humorous novel about characters the author endows with humanity."

The realistic approach was also employed in Hahn's fourth book, *The Jellyfish Season*, "a sensitive, moving story that focuses on a family in crisis," according to a critic in *Kirkus Reviews*. Using personal material from the uncomfortable summer when her family had to share housing with her father's relatives, Hahn tells the story of Kathleen, whose family is forced into similar circumstances when the father loses his job at a steel mill. The family must leave Baltimore and move in with an uncle and a spoiled cousin on Chesapeake Bay. Kathleen is on the outs at the new house, a sworn enemy of her cousin Fay until she discovers her cousin's secret—a sailor-boyfriend who thinks Fay is eighteen. Kathleen develops a crush on the sailor herself, and ultimately the two cousins call a truce, though Kathleen's relationship with her mother—pregnant again—takes more work to reestablish their former intimacy. Some family order is restored when the father finds another job, but their former life in Baltimore is gone forever. A contributor in *Kirkus Reviews* noted that Hahn "has drawn an evocative portrait of the struggling American family of our times," and concluded that "Readers who come from similar backgrounds will find it easy to identify with" the characters. Nelda Mohr in *Children's Book Review Service* felt that the book was a "very realistic story of a young teen who has all the usual problems of growing up with the additional burden of her parents' economic and marital problems," and observed that the book "should be popular."

Set during World War II, two patriotic girls who have brothers fighting in Europe become involved with a conscientious objector in this winner of the Scott O'Dell award for historical fiction.

Marjorie Lewis in *School Library Journal* echoed this sentiment, concluding in her review that *The Jellyfish Season* "should be a favorite among young teens." Zena Sutherland in *Bulletin of the Center for Children's Books* noted that though she felt the pacing was off, the "characters, dialogue, and interpersonal dynamics are extremely well handled . . . and there's plenty for early adolescents to identify with here. Above all, it's honest." *Horn Book*'s Mary M. Burns also commented on a typical Hahn quality—"the frequently humorous touch" which does not, however, diminish "the difficulties."

Blending the Supernatural with the Realistic

Hahn typically does not work from a plot outline; rather she begins with a character and situation and writes until the voice of that character—or others in the story—begin to take over. "Sometimes my characters are reticent," Hahn told *AAYA*. "Then I find other things to do, go for a walk, do the laundry, talk on the phone, doodle. Anything to let the book simmer on the unconscious level. Sometimes I work on more than one project at a time, especially when I've just sent a book off to my editor and am waiting for revisions. I have to admit that I have had the most fun writing my entertainments, involving elements of fantasy in the brew. The serious books take much longer to develop. Not only does the action have to be more consistent, but the resolutions need to be worked out in a realistic manner. Also, since I write in the first person, characterization can be tricky. I need to show the real character behind the facade not by simply telling, but by showing in their actions and interactions with other characters."

Hahn blended supernatural and realistic elements once again in her popular work *Wait Till Helen Comes*, the story of Molly and her brother Michael who move into a converted church with their mother and new stepfather and his daughter, Heather. This daughter makes life miserable for the family, especially Molly and Michael, but soon there is more in the air than just whining. Heather, Molly comes to understand, has been possessed by a ghost named Helen, buried in the graveyard attached to the converted church. As Roger Sutton noted in *Bulletin of the Center for Children's Books*, "This junior gothic is genuinely scary, complete with dark secrets from the past,

unsettled graves, and a very real ghost." Sutton commented also that the realistic portion of the book, the strained family relations, were "heightened and intensified by the supernatural goings-on." Judy Greenfield, writing in *School Library Journal*, concluded that *Wait Till Helen Comes* "is a powerful, convincing, and frightening tale," and should create "a heavy demand from readers who are not 'faint at heart.'" Hahn herself is one of those faint at heart. "The book is scary," she told *AAYA*. "I don't think I would have been able to read it when I was ten. It has remained one of my most popular titles and was one of the quickest and easiest I've written. I have no idea why some books are so hard and some so easy."

Hahn has written several other titles employing elements of fantasy and even dark possession. Among these are *The Doll in the Garden, Time for Andrew,* and *Look for Me by Moonlight*. While Hahn mixes both the realistic with the fantastical in these titles, a lighter touch is employed with *The Doll in the Garden,* which follows Ashley and her mother as they move into a new flat following the death of Ashley's father. Ashley and a new friend soon uncover a doll buried in the garden, and this doll leads the pair back in time to a dying child, and the unearthing of further secrets involving a crusty landlady. Comforting the child in her time travels, Ashley also helps to heal her own pain at her father's death. Ethel Twichell, writing in *Horn Book,* noted that Hahn's "story line is well worked out, and the shift from past to present offers its own enchantment." Other reviewers noted that the book was not as scary as *Wait Till Helen Comes,* and Sutton in *Bulletin of the Center for Children's Books* felt that the book benefited from a "direct style and smooth storytelling." Hahn further explored the possibilities of time travel with *Time for Andrew: A Ghost Story,* which features a young male protagonist in 1910 who is dying of diphtheria. He falls through a hole in time to the present into the room now occupied by his great-great nephew, Drew. By changing places, Drew is able to save his relative with modern medicine, and then the two try to switch roles—with less than perfect results. Noting the humorous sections in the book, Virginia Golodetz concluded in *School Library Journal* that "there is enough tension to keep readers engaged." *Booklist*'s Stephanie Zvirin observed that "There's plenty to enjoy in this delightful time-slip fantasy: a fascinating premise, a dastardly cousin, some good suspense, and a roundup of characters to care about." Sutton, in *Bulletin of the Center for Children's Books*, summed up the book neatly, calling it "an assured work from a deservedly popular writer, who, while gifted with the instincts of a storyteller, doesn't let her narrative get away from her characters."

Quite different in tone is another novel involving the supernatural, this time for older readers and involving a vampire. Set at an inn in a remote part of Maine, *Look for Me by Moonlight* involves the usual Hahn mix of family relations—this time a new stepmother for the sixteen-year-old protagonist, Cynda, to get used to. Cynda soon finds some solace in her new friend, Vincent Morthanos. Vincent has more on his mind than friendship, however, and naive Cynda only slowly realizes that he is a vampire. While Ilene Cooper noted in *Booklist* that the story "both terrorizes and tantalizes," Hahn herself was less pleased with the book. "Of all my books it's my least favorite," she told *AAYA* in her interview. "It has always made me uncomfortable; there is little light in that book. It makes me wonder what part of me that story came from."

A Full-Time Writer

Hahn remarried in 1982, and by 1991 her writing and publishing were steady enough that she could leave her library work and devote herself full time to her novels. "Now that I have all this time, I find lots of ways to use it up," Hahn told *AAYA*. "In ways I was more disciplined when I had to squeeze my writing in between my job and my house." But Hahn has continued to publish a new title almost yearly. Other popular works in her serious vein include *Tallahassee Higgins* and *December Stillness*. With the former title, Hahn revisited the time her family had to share housing with relatives, but in this treatment she has the female protagonist face the situation alone. When Tally's flighty mother takes off to become a star in Hollywood, she parks her daughter with an aunt and uncle. *December Stillness* looks at the Vietnam war and its effects on one veteran. Kelly interviews the homeless vet for a school project. Inspired by a man who used to spend long hours at the library where Hahn worked, *December Stillness* is, according to several reviewers, more didactic in tone than other Hahn titles. Sutton, in *Bulletin of the Center for Children's Books*, while commenting on the "message-driven" nature of the book, also remarked that "Hahn's practiced handling of suspense serves her well here."

Quite different in theme and style are adventure stories Hahn has written for young readers, including *The Dead Man in Indian Creek*, *The Spanish Kidnapping Disaster*, and *The Gentleman Outlaw and Me—Eli*. The first title tells the story of two boys who find a body in a local creek and appoint themselves detectives to track down the killer. Suspicion falls on an antique dealer in this "entertaining mystery with a lot of action and plenty of tension," according to Jean Kaufman in *Voice*

"HANDS DOWN, THE GIRL BOOK OF THE YEAR!"
The Bulletin of the Center for Children's Books

THE WIND BLOWS BACKWARD
Award-winning author
MARY DOWNING HAHN

Haunted by his father's suicide, Spencer leans on Lauren, his best friend in junior high and now a high school senior, burdening her with his moods and miseries in this melodramatic 1993 romance.

If you enjoy the works of Mary Downing Hahn, you may also want to check out the following books and films:

Lois Duncan, *Locked in Time*, 1985.
Margaret Mahy, *The Changeover*, 1984
Norma Fox Mazer, *Heartbeat*, 1989.
Richard Peck, *The Dreadful Future of Blossom Culp*, 1983.
The Lady in White, a film about a boy who is visited by a ghost, 1988.

---

of Youth Advocates. The story grew out of an incident in Hahn's past as well as the cajoling of young male readers who demanded an action book from the author. It remains one of her most popular titles. Carolyn Noah remarked in *School Library Journal* that "There's more than enough action, and Hahn's effortless mastery of kids' dialogue makes this an easy read." With *The Gentleman Outlaw and Me—Eli*, Hahn was able to indulge a childhood fantasy of running off with cowboys. "Growing up in College Park, there was not much opportunity for such high adventure," she told *AAYA*. Orphaned Eliza cuts off her hair and passes as a boy in a grab-bag of adventures. Susan Dove Lempke noted in *Booklist* that "Hahn's writing crackles like gunshot in the Ol' West."

New Literary Territory

Hahn also broke new ground with her young adult novel, *The Wind Blows Backward*, a romantic novel about Lauren and Spencer, who revive a junior high crush during their senior year in high school. But Spencer is haunted now by his father's suicide, and it seems to Lauren that he may be preparing to follow his father's example. Diane Roback commented in *Publishers Weekly* that the novel was a "taut and emotionally driven story that manages to be romantic without romanticizing the fierceness of teenage love," while *Booklist*'s Zvirin noted the "sensitively drawn" characters and concluded that "Hahn evokes a fantasy love gone awry and shows clearly that while loving deeply and truly may be wonderful, it's not always enough."

Hahn returned to the more familiar audience of young teen readers with a trio of books set dur-

ing and after the Second World War. The first book, *Stepping on the Cracks*, tells the story of two girls who become involved with a conscientious objector and incorporates some of Hahn's own experiences from the time, including her sadness at the loss of her Uncle Dudley. The bully, Gordy, from that book, is the protagonist for two further related titles, *Following My Own Footsteps* and *As Ever, Gordy*. Reviewing *Stepping on the Cracks* in *Horn Book*, Maeve Visser Knoth concluded that the "engrossing story handles the wide range of issues with grace and skill." With the war over in *Following My Own Footsteps*, Gordy goes to North Carolina to escape his abusive father in a story that provides a "terrific rendering of day-to-day life in the mid-1940s," according to *Booklist*'s Lempke. *Horn Book*'s Knoth concurred, adding that Hahn "brings many issues, including alcoholism, abuse, and definitions of courage, into her story and handles them deftly." Gordy makes a further appearance in *As Ever, Gordy*, when he returns to College Hill where the action in *Stepping on the Cracks* began. In the eighth grade now, he has learned some lessons from his time in North Carolina. "This book had a very complex structure," Hahn reported in her *AAYA* interview, "and took me a couple of years to write."

Hahn has also written her first chapter book, and has, as she says, "dozens more ideas." Throughout all of her books, she manages to cast a spell of verisimilitude with her attention to detail and use of personal experience. Her goal in writing is straightforward, as she concluded in her interview with *AAYA*: "I want to tell a good story, first and foremost. I don't think about theme. If it comes, great. But that is not my focus. I want readers to come away from my books feeling that they have read a story that sticks with them, with characters that linger on the mind. They might also gain a bit more understanding about people and realize that everyone has a story inside of them."

■ Works Cited

Ashford, Richard, review of *The Sara Summer*, *Horn Book*, October, 1979, p. 534.

Burns, Mary M., review of *The Jellyfish Season*, *Horn Book*, March-April, 1986, p. 201.

Cooper, Ilene, review of *Look for Me by Moonlight*, *Booklist*, March 15, 1995, pp. 1322-33.

Eaglen, Audrey B., review of *Daphne's Book*, *School Library Journal*, October, 1983, p. 168.

Golodetz, Virginia, review of *Time for Andrew: A Ghost Story, School Library Journal,* May, 1994, p. 114.

Greenfield, Judy, review of *Wait Till Helen Comes, School Library Journal,* October, 1986, p. 176.

Hahn, Mary Downing, comments in *Something about the Author,* Volume 50, Gale, 1988, pp. 88-90.

Hahn, Mary Downing, essay in *Something about the Author Autobiography Series,* Volume 12, Gale, 1991, pp. 125-40.

Hahn, Mary Downing, interview with J. Sydney Jones for *Authors and Artists for Young Adults,* conducted September, 1997.

Hammond, Nancy C., review of *Daphne's Book, Horn Book,* December, 1983, p. 708.

Hanley, Karen Stang, review of *The Time of the Witch, School Library Journal,* November, 1982, p. 84.

Helfgott, Barbara Cutler, review of *Daphne's Book, New York Times Book Review,* October 23, 1983, p. 34.

Jaffee, Cyrisse, review of *The Sara Summer, School Library Journal,* December, 1979, p. 86.

Review of *The Jellyfish Season, Kirkus Reviews,* October 1, 1985, p. 1088.

Kaufman, Jean, review of *The Dead Man in Indian Creek, Voice of Youth Advocates,* August, 1990, p. 160.

Knoth, Maeve Visser, review of *Stepping on the Cracks, Horn Book,* November, 1991, p. 736.

Knoth, Maeve Visser, review of *Following My Own Footsteps, Horn Book,* September, 1996, pp. 595-96.

Lempke, Susan Dove, review of *The Gentleman Outlaw and Me—Eli, Booklist,* April 1, 1996, p. 1364.

Lempke, Susan Dove, review of *Following My Own Footsteps, Booklist,* September 15, 1996, p. 240.

Lewis, Marjorie, review of *The Jellyfish Season, School Library Journal,* October, 1985, p. 172.

Mercier, Jean F., review of *The Sara Summer, Publishers Weekly,* November 19, 1979, p. 79.

Mercier, Jean F., review of *Daphne's Book, Publishers Weekly,* August 5, 1983, p. 92.

Mohr, Nelda, review of *The Jellyfish Season, Children's Book Review Service,* February, 1986, p. 78.

Noah, Carolyn, review of *The Dead Man in Indian Creek, School Library Journal,* April, 1990, p. 118.

Roback, Diane, review of *The Wind Blows Backward, Publishers Weekly,* August 26, 1993, pp. 80-81.

Sutherland, Zena, review of *The Jellyfish Season, Bulletin of the Center for Children's Books,* February, 1986, p. 108.

Sutton, Roger, review of *Wait Till Helen Comes, Bulletin of the Center for Children's Books,* October, 1986, p. 27.

Sutton, Roger, review of *December Stillness, Bulletin of the Center for Children's Books,* September, 1988, pp. 9-10.

Sutton, Roger, review of *The Doll in the Garden, Bulletin of the Center for Children's Books,* March, 1989, p. 171.

Sutton, Roger, review of *Time for Andrew: A Ghost Story, Bulletin of the Center for Children's Books,* April, 1994, pp. 259-60.

Twichell, Ethel, review of *The Doll in the Garden, Horn Book,* May, 1989, p. 370.

Zvirin, Stephanie, review of *The Wind Blows Backward, Booklist,* May 1, 1993, pp. 1581-82.

Zvirin, Stephanie, review of *Time for Andrew: A Ghost Story, Booklist,* April 1, 1994, pp. 1446-47.

■ For More Information See

BOOKS

Contemporary Authors, New Revision Series, Volume 48, Gale, 1995.

Sixth Book of Junior Authors and Illustrators, edited by Sally Holmes Holtze, H. W. Wilson, 1989.

Something about the Author, Volume 81, Gale, 1995.

PERIODICALS

Bulletin of the Center for Children's Books, February, 1980, pp. 109-10; April, 1987, p. 146.

Horn Book, May, 1990, pp. 334-35; September, 1996, p. 595.

School Library Journal, May, 1993, p. 124.

Voice of Youth Advocates, June, 1987, p. 78; June, 1988, p. 86; April, 1989, p. 28; June, 1991, p. 96; August, 1993, p. 152; August, 1995, pp. 147, 171; June, 1996, p. 95.

Wilson Library Bulletin, June, 1987, p. 64; June, 1995, p. 135.*

—Sketch by J. Sydney Jones

M. E. Kerr

■ Personal

Real name, Marijane Meaker; also writes as Ann Aldrich, M. J. Meaker, Vin Packer, and Mary James; born May 27, 1927, in Auburn, NY; daughter of Ellis R. (a mayonnaise manufacturer) and Ida T. Kerr. *Education:* Attended Vermont Junior College and New School for Social Research; University of Missouri, B.A., 1949.

■ Addresses

Home—12 Deep Six Dr., East Hampton, NY 11937. *Agent*—Julia Fallowfield, McIntosh & Otis, Inc., 475 Fifth Ave., New York, NY 10017.

■ Career

Writer. Worked at several jobs, including assistant file clerk for E. P. Dutton (publisher), 1949-50; freelance writer, 1949—. Founder of Ashawagh Hall Writers' Workshop. *Member:* PEN, Authors League of America, Society of Children's Book Writers and Illustrators.

■ Awards, Honors

American Library Association (ALA) Notable Book, one of *School Library Journal*'s Best Books of the Year, both 1972, and winner of the Media and Methods Maxi Awards, 1974, all for *Dinky Hocker Shoots Smack! Book World*'s Children's Spring Book Festival Honor book, one of Child Study Association's Children's Books of the Year, and one of *New York Times*' Outstanding Books of the Year, all 1973, all for *If I Love You, Am I Trapped Forever?;* one of *School Library Journal*'s Best Books of the Year, 1974, for *The Son of Someone Famous;* ALA Notable Book, one of ALA's Best Books for Young Adults, and one of *New York Times*' Outstanding Books of the Year, all 1975, all for *Is That You, Miss Blue?;* one of *School Library Journal*'s Best Books of the Year, 1977, for *I'll Love You When You're More Like Me;* Christopher Award, The Christophers, *School Library Journal*'s Book of the Year Award, one of *New York Times*' Outstanding Books of the Year, all 1978, and one of New York Public Library's Best Books for the Teenage, 1980 and 1981, all for *Gentlehands;* Golden Kite Award, Society of Children's Book Writers, one of *School Library Journal*'s Best Books of the Year, both 1981, and one of New York Public Library's Books for the Teenage, 1982, all for *Little Little;* one of *School Library Journal*'s Best Books of the Year, 1982, for *What I Really Think of You;* one of ALA Best Books for Young Adults, 1983, for *Me, Me, Me, Me, Me: Not a Novel;* one of ALA Best Books for Young Adults, 1985, for *I Stay Near You;* one of ALA recommended books for the reluctant young adult reader, 1986, and California Young Reader Medal, 1991, both for *Night Kites*; Margaret A. Edwards award, *School Library Journal/ALA*, 1993, for body of work.

■ **Writings**

YOUNG ADULT FICTION; UNDER PSEUDONYM M. E. KERR

Dinky Hocker Shoots Smack! Harper, 1972.
If I Love You, Am I Trapped Forever?, Harper, 1973.
The Son of Someone Famous, Harper, 1974.
Is That You, Miss Blue? Harper, 1975.
Love is a Missing Person, Harper, 1975.
I'll Love You When You're More Like Me, Harper, 1977.
Gentlehands, Harper, 1978.
Little, Little, Harper, 1981.
What I Really Think of You, Harper, 1982.
Him She Loves?, Harper, 1984.
I Stay Near You, Harper, 1985.
Night Kites, Harper, 1986.
Fell, Harper, 1987.
Fell Back, Harper, 1989.
Fell Down, Harper, 1991.
Linger, HarperCollins, 1993.
Deliver Us from Evie, HarperCollins, 1994.
"Hello," I Lied, HarperCollins, 1997.

Contributor to *Sixteen*, edited by Donald R. Gallo, Delacorte, 1984.

FICTION

(Under name M. J. Meaker) *Hometown*, Doubleday, 1967.
Game of Survival, New American Library, 1968.
Shockproof Sydney Skate, Little, Brown, 1972.

UNDER PSEUDONYM MARY JAMES

Shoebag, Scholastic, 1990.
The Shuteyes, Scholastic, 1993.
Frankenlouse, Scholastic, 1994.
Shoebag Returns, Scholastic, 1996.

NONFICTION

(Under pseudonym Ann Aldrich) *We Walk Alone*, Gold Medal Books, 1955.
(Under pseudonym Ann Aldrich) *We Too Must Love*, Gold Medal Books, 1958.

(Under pseudonym Ann Aldrich) *Carol, in a Thousand Cities*, Gold Medal Books, 1960.
(Under pseudonym Ann Aldrich) *We Two Won't Last*, Gold Medal Books, 1963.
(Under name M. J. Meaker) *Sudden Endings*, Doubleday, 1964, paperback edition published under pseudonym Vin Packer, Fawcett, 1964.
Take a Lesbian to Lunch, MacFadden-Bartell, 1972.
(Under pseudonym M. E. Kerr) *Me, Me, Me, Me, Me: Not a Novel* (autobiography), Harper, 1983.

FICTION; UNDER PSEUDONYM VIN PACKER

Dark Intruder, Gold Medal Books, 1952.
Spring Fire, Gold Medal Books, 1952.
Look Back to Love, Gold Medal Books, 1953.
Come Destroy Me, Gold Medal Books, 1954.
Whisper His Sin, Gold Medal Books, 1954.
The Thrill Kids, Gold Medal Books, 1955.
Dark Don't Catch Me, Gold Medal Books, 1956.
The Young and Violent, Gold Medal Books, 1956.
Three-Day Terror, Gold Medal Books, 1957.
The Evil Friendship, Gold Medal Books, 1958.
5:45 to Suburbia, Gold Medal Books, 1958.
The Twisted Ones, Gold Medal Books, 1959.
The Damnation of Adam Blessing, 1961.
The Girl on the Best Seller List, Gold Medal Books, 1961.
Something in the Shadows, Gold Medal Books, 1961.
Intimate Victims, Gold Medal Books, 1962.
Alone at Night, Gold Medal Books, 1963.
The Hare in March, New American Library, 1967.
Don't Rely on Gemini, Delacorte Press, 1969.

■ **Adaptations**

Dinky Hocker Shoots Smack! was adapted into a television film starring Wendie Jo Sperba and released by the Learning Corporation of America; *If I Love You, Am I Trapped Forever?* was released as an audio cassette by Random House, 1979.

■ **Overview**

M. E. Kerr has written books under many different pseudonyms (in fact, M. E. Kerr is a pseudonym based on the author's real name, Marijane Meaker), however, since she discovered writing for young adults, her fictional aim has been true—she has become known as an award-winning "problem" novelist for adolescents. With her seminal *Dinky Hocker Shoots Smack*, which detailed the life of the daughter of a do-gooder who must do something outrageous to get her mother's attention, Kerr captured the imagination of teens from all over. With equal aplomb, she has tackled such varied topics as Nazis and homosexuality, proving herself to be versatile as well as popular. In 1993, she was awarded the fifth Margaret A. Edwards Award by the American Library Association, which put her in the company of S. E. Hinton, Richard Peck, and Lois Duncan.

Kerr was born in Auburn, an upstate New York town where her father owned a food manufacturing plant and her grandfather was the proprietor of many local grocery stores. But it was her father's love of books that most influenced Kerr. "I grew up always wanting to be a writer," Kerr told *Something about the Author Autobiography Series (SAAS)*. "My father was a mayonnaise manufacturer, with a strange habit, for a mayonnaise manufacturer, of reading everything from the Harvard Classics, to all of Dickens, Emerson, Poe, Thoreau, Kipling, and John O'Hara, Sinclair Lewis, John Steinbeck, all the Book-of-the-Month Club selections, plus magazines like *Time, Life, Look,* and *Fortune,* and all the New York City newspapers, along with the local Auburn, New York *Citizen Advertiser.*"

Kerr's other strong writing influence was her mother, but the influence was an unusual one. Her mother's primary love in life was local gossip, and she was unusually good at finding out and distributing information. "One of the most vivid memories of my childhood is of my mother making a phone call," Kerr told *SAAS*. "First, she'd tell me to go out and play. I'd pretend to do that, letting the back door slam, hiding right around the corner of the living room, in the hall. She'd have her pack of Kools and the ashtray on the desk, as she gave the number of one of her girlfriends to the operator. . . . My Mother would begin nearly every conversation the same way: 'Wait till you hear this!'" Later, as a writer, Kerr was able to see how her spy sessions had a positive effect on her career. Kerr told *SAAS* that: "Even today, when I'm finished with a book and sifting through ideas for a new one, I ask myself: Is the idea a 'wait till you hear this?'"

Kerr and her mother also went on informal reconnaissance missions into the heart of their small hometown. They would take their car to the local park, survey the parking lot of the pub, and look over the visitors to the Women's Union, a building where many single women kept an apartment. "Then home . . . ," related Kerr in her autobiographical work *Me, Me, Me, Me, Me: Not a Novel,* "and a lesson from my mother on the importance of fiction. Fiction, I learned early on, spins off grandly from fact. Our trip downtown would be related over the phone, beginning, 'Wait till you hear this! Carl Otter sent poor little Polly off to see "Brother Rat" so he could have a night on the town, that dear little woman with her face down to her shoes, standing in line by herself

In this 1972 work, overweight Dinky pretends she's on drugs to win some attention from her parents, especially her neglectful mother who is out to reform drug-abusers.

while he treats Ellie Budd to old-fashioneds down at Boysen's.'"

Teachers who knew Kerr recognized her ability to spin a tale. "So did . . . librarians who had to pull me out of the stacks at closing time. And there were my favorite writers like Thomas Wolfe, Sherwood Anderson, the Brontes, and our hometown hero, Samuel Hopkins Adams. (I'd pedal past his big house on Owasco Lake, just to see where a real writer lived!)," Kerr related in *SAAS*. However, she concluded that it was her mother who really gave her the skills she needed to be a writer.

When Kerr was twelve, her younger brother was born. That, along with the fact that her older brother had just entered military school, created upheaval for her. She was jealous of the attention her younger brother was getting and confused by the rapid change in her older brother's personality. "I was suddenly the nothing, sandwiched between two stars," she wrote in her autobiography. She became morose and depressed, admitting in her autobiography that: "Locked in my room, I wrote stories about murder and suicide, tried on clothes, daydreamed about boys, and listened to records like 'Blues in the Night' and 'Let's Get Away from It all.'"

Her mother thought dancing school would cheer her up, which it didn't. Then her parents took more drastic measures. They sent her to an Episcopalian boarding school in Virginia, far from her New York home. Kerr's rebellious and mischievous nature, however, caused her to get into trouble in the staid academy. Once, she was caught throwing darts at photos of the faculty. She was expelled from the school, but her mother stepped in so that she would be able to graduate.

During her summers at home from the boarding school, Kerr had a chance to let her creativity grow. Her parents had moved to an isolated lot on a local lake, and she was far away from any other adolescents her age. "The summer of 1944 I became Eric Rantham McKay. . . .," Kerr wrote in *Me, Me, Me, Me, Me*. "The pseudonym was chosen because my father's initials were E. R. M. After I wrote a story, I mailed it off to a magazine with a letter written on my father's stationery, engraved with his initials and our home address." With this pen name, she composed stories by a mythical military man about the war. They were all rejected by publishers, but she cherished the notes they sometimes wrote across the stock rejection letters.

After finishing high school, Kerr went to Vermont Junior College where she enjoyed the freedom of wearing jeans to class and skiing after school. She had decided that she wanted to be a journalist and eventually went to the University of Missouri, despite her father's warnings that if she went to school there she would end up marrying someone from Missouri and they would never be able to visit her. There, she had a new realization about her writing. "I switched my major from Journalism to English . . . partly because I failed Economics, which one had to pass to get into J-School, and partly because I realized I didn't want anything to do with writing fact. I wanted to make up my own facts. I wanted to do creative writing," she wrote in *SAAS*.

While in college, she participated in sorority life, even though she felt it was elitist. She also dated a man who was very involved with the Communist party. She considered marrying him, but he got involved in a nasty F.B.I. investigation that Kerr believed was spurred by her mother.

After she graduated, Kerr decided to move to New York City with several of her sorority sisters. "In those days, New York City was still a place where you could take a subway at night and not fear getting mugged. You could also find a two-bedroom apartment for $150 a month," she told *SAAS*. While her apartment mates got good jobs as secretaries, Kerr took a low-paid file clerk job. Even then, her mind was still on her writing. "I wasn't worth the thirty-two dollars Dutton paid me to file letters and answer phones and carry things from one floor to another," she wrote in her autobiography. "My own work came first with me. I was always sitting there scratching out short stories and poems. I think the only time I looked up was when an author came into the area to discuss the artwork on his/her cover. I was in awe of all the authors."

With her nose to the grindstone, Kerr continued to send out her stories. "I couldn't get an agent, so I began sending out manuscripts under my roommates' names," she confessed in *Me, Me, Me, Me, Me*. "I wanted a variety of names, and I wanted to be sure the manuscripts were safely

In one traumatic summer, Buddy Boyle falls in love with an upper-class girl, comes to know his aristocratic grandfather, and discovers a terrible secret from the past that threatens them all.

returned to our mailbox." At that time, she hadn't found a writing niche. "I wrote anything and everything in an effort to get published. I wrote confession stories, articles, 'slick' stories for the women's magazines, poetry and fillers," she recalled in her autobiography.

"Meanwhile, I'd found a way to get an agent: I'd become my own agent, print up stationery with my name on it and 'Literary Agent,' and send out stories under pseudonyms," she wrote in *Me, Me, Me, Me, Me*. During this time, she had a series of jobs in which she participated in a lackluster fash-

ion and was often fired. At one job, she took two and three hour lunch breaks where she went out and tried to sell her works to publishers. Tiring of this, she worked out a deal with her roommates where she would cook and clean for them in order to get food money. This freed her up to write full-time.

In 1951, Kerr received her first acceptance letter. She was so excited that she thought she was going to be paid $75 for the work. When her roommates returned, they informed her that the letter actually said it was going to pay her $750! This was the impetus she needed to never work at a "regular" job again. In 1952, she published a novel entitled *Spring Fire* which sold over a million copies, eclipsing the works of many famous authors of the day. "Long out of print now, *Spring Fire* enabled me to become a full-time free-lance novelist, enjoy a trip to Europe, and get my first apartment, sans roommates," she remembered in *SAAS*.

Kerr also turned to different pen names to write a series of thrillers and suspense stories. She was fairly successful with this, getting national notice and critical attention. However, her friend Louise Fitzhugh, who had written the young adult novel *Harriet the Spy,* encouraged her to try a different audience. "'You'd be a good young adult writer,' Louise would tell me, 'since you're always writing about kids,'" Kerr told *SAAS*. In 1967, she published *Shockproof Sydney Skate* under her own name. "It became a Literary Guild alternate, and a selection of the Book Find Club, and the paperback money was exceptional, enough eventually to buy me the house I live in today, in East Hampton, New York," she related in *SAAS*.

Because the protagonist in that story was a teenager, Fitzhugh again encouraged Kerr to write for young adults. The idea didn't appeal to Kerr until she read Paul Zindel's novel *The Pigman*. Then she realized that writing for young adults could be exciting *and* original. Around that time, Kerr was also volunteering as a teacher with a writers in schools project. "I'd been assigned to some classes at Central Commercial High School, in New York City. . . . These kids worked half a day and went to school half a day. They were wild, unruly, wonderful kids who didn't give a fig for reading, but who responded to writing assignments with great vigor and originality," she told *SAAS*.

An obese girl in the class who was nicknamed Tiny gave Kerr the idea for her first wildly successful young adult novel. Tiny's mother continually left her alone when she would go out and do her church work. Tiny entertained herself by eating and inventing wild stories. "That was the birth of my first book for young adults. Tiny translated into 'Dinky,' and since I knew that this story could be told about any family, black or white, rich or poor, I decided to stick close to home. I'd just moved to Brooklyn Heights, which abounded with lawyers because the courts were right nearby. I set my story there, and made Dinky's mother a middle-class lawyer's wife who was involved in rehabilitating dope addicts. . . . The result was *Dinky Hocker Shoots Smack*," Kerr recalled in *SAAS*.

Pamela D. Pollack, writing in *School Library Journal*, claimed that Kerr's "funny/sad first novel shoots straight from the hip." She praised the development of the novel, claiming that "the characters are sympathetic and engaging, and the whole is a totally affecting literary experience." Dale Carlson, writing in the *New York Times Book Review*, added that "The pages rush by in this superb first novel by M. E. Kerr, who has an ear for catching the sound of real people talking and a heart for finding the center of real people's problems." Carlson concluded: "this is a brilliantly funny book that will make you cry."

In Kerr's 1978 novel *Gentlehands*, she focuses on a sixteen-year-old protagonist, Buddy Boyle. Buddy comes from a middle-income family but he falls for the rich and privileged Skye Pennington. Their romance seems unlikely, but Buddy is good looking, and soon he and Skye are going out together. Buddy takes her to meet his grandfather, Frank Trenker, a cultured millionaire with excellent tastes, in the hopes that his grandfather will help him appear classier. Buddy's admiration for his grandfather turns to horror when a reporter prints an article in a local newspaper accusing Trenker of being a former Nazi tormentor, nicknamed "Gentlehands," during the Holocaust.

"Miss Kerr's book is important and useful as an introduction to the grotesque character of the Nazi period, as well as to the paradoxes that exist in the heart of man," related Richard Bradford in the *New York Times Book Review*. Geraldine DeLuca, writing in the *Lion and the Unicorn*, believed that "Adolescents can handle more complexity than she

brings to her subject," even though she found that the author's "treatment is strong and honest, supported by direct accounts of torture written into newspaper articles."

Me, Me, Me, Me, Me: Not a Novel (1983) is Kerr's autobiographical memoir that covers her life until the year 1951 when her first work was published. Kerr chronicles the ups and downs of her life, from listening to gossip at her mother's side to joining the Communist party. In one episode, she writes to a Communist party official while in prep school to tell him that many of the boarders are

This challenging 1994 tale concerns Parr Burrman, a young man who faces the consequences when his older sister Evie, a lesbian, leaves the family farm to move in with a banker's daughter.

interested in joining, prompting a flood of return mail. Paul A. Caron, writing in *Best Sellers*, believed that Kerr's fans would enjoy the work: "The author's style and technique are very effective. She presents these autobiographical chapters in such a way that the reader enters into stories without realizing it." Joyce Milton claimed in the *New York Times Book Review* that "this book offers a satisfying if brief encounter with a humorist whose delight in poking fun at the trappings of authority is unmarred by either self-hatred or pettiness toward others."

■ Update

"I like to write about the underdog, the outsider, the person who is different," Kerr told *Children's Books and Their Creators*. "I've seldom met a kid who didn't feel he was different in one way or another. Kids are so vulnerable, so sure they're alone in whatever it is they're struggling with. I like to tell them they're not alone." After establishing herself with books like *Dinky Hocker Shoots Smack*, Kerr continued to write provocative books about young adults.

Many of Kerr's books take place in one of two settings that are based on her life experience. After earning money from some of her best-selling novels, Kerr moved to East Hampton, New York, a beautiful resort town on Long Island. This place "would eventually become Seaview, New York, in many of my novels," she told *SAAS*. "My old hometown, Auburn, would appear from time to time as Cayuta, New York."

Kerr's "Fell" trilogy takes place in Seaview. In *Fell* (1987), *Fell Back* (1989), and *Fell Down* (1991), Kerr chronicles the life of a normal adolescent who finds himself in difficult and mysterious situations. In the first book, Fell is paid to impersonate a rich boy who doesn't want to attend an exclusive school. He finds out more about the elite there than he ever thought he would know. In addition, Fell, the son of a policeman, finds himself wrapped up in a prep school mystery. "Fell is sensitive, funny, sexy, and a gourmet cook," commented Hazel Rochman in *Booklist* about Kerr's memorably-drawn character. In *Voice of Youth Advocates*, Christy Tyson remarked that "Kerr manages an almost perfect balance of dry wit and suspense, with Fell standing squarely as a likable, well-balanced hero."

In *Fell Back*, Fell and his policeman father decide to investigate the murder of a student at Fell's exclusive prep school. After some sleuthing, Fell finds a drug ring in operation in this moneyed setting. A *Publishers Weekly* reviewer was disappointed with this sequel, writing that "the spark that ignited [*Fell*] seems to have fizzled out." *Voice of Youth Advocates* contributor Christy Tyson believed that the novel "offers too many characters insufficiently developed . . . too little humor . . . and too much introspection" from its main character to sustain a mystery novel.

Kerr's third book in the series, *Fell Down*, finds that main character has dropped out of his exclusive prep school. In this book, Fell once again needs to solve a mystery, this time, one that has happened in the past. The present-day narrative is interwoven with a storyline detailing the events of years before. Tyson, writing in the *Voice of Youth Advocates*, found fault with the novel, believing that Kerr's writing is excellent but the plot is farfetched: "*Fell Down*, even more than its prequels, promises much but fails to deliver." Rochman, on the other hand, called the work "a brilliant mystery, one that will have genre fans fitting the pieces together for days." She continued, "There's a strangeness uncovered beneath the surface, a nervy sense of dislocation in family, community, and individual personality."

Battle of the Haves and Have-Nots

Many of Kerr's books have the disparities of socioeconomic status as a focal point. The author stated that this was a significant issue for her while growing up. In an interview with Roger Sutton in *School Library Journal*, she related that "I was aware of class ever since I was a little hick from Auburn, New York, who went off to boarding school thinking I was rich, never realizing that I wasn't rich at all; I was just an average middle-class kid. My father owned a factory in our town and my grandfather owned all the grocery stores, but when I got to boarding school and met children of heads of international corporations, and found out differences, I was very, very surprised. Since then I've always paid attention to haves and have-nots."

In *Linger* (1993), Kerr looks at another clash between rich and poor, this time in Pennsylvania during the Gulf War. Gary, a waiter at the posh restaurant Linger, falls in love with the proprietor's daughter. However, she is in love with a local teacher who begins to reciprocate her advances. The teacher is also a strong anti-war activist. Because of his attraction to the young woman, and his politics, he is eventually run out of town. Hazel Rochman praised the work in *Booklist*, claiming that "Kerr is one of the few YA writers who can dramatize politics and ideas without haranguing the reader." Diane Roback and Elizabeth Devereaux wrote in *Publishers Weekly* that the book is "complex and challenging."

Another theme that Kerr often writes about is the idea of fitting in. "I think my sympathies are usually with the underdog, the outlaw character, the misfit," she related to Sutton. "I've always identified more with those people. It's funny. We never know what's going on behind a kid's little face in school. I don't think there are any kids in high school who don't in some way feel that they don't measure up, because that's the time when they first go out and start comparing themselves with other kids."

Deliver Us From Evie (1994) combines several of Kerr's common themes. Kerr, a lesbian, has written several books about homosexual teens and their struggles. In *Deliver Us From Evie* she chronicles the story of a lesbian youth who must conquer class struggles to be with the young woman she loves. Evie lives on a farm in Missouri where she looks, dresses, and behaves "like a man." She is able to fix farm equipment and do as much physical work as many of the male workers. Evie's mother encourages her to be more feminine, but she will have none of it. Meanwhile, Evie is falling deeply in love with the daughter of the local banker, Patty. The narration by her younger brother, Parr, focuses on the changes in the family as Evie and Patty run away to New York City.

"It's a story that challenges stereotypes, not only about love, but also about farmers and families and religion and responsibility—about all our definitions of 'normal,'" observed Hazel Rochman in *Booklist*. Maeve Visser Knoth, writing in *Horn Book*, claimed that "the strong, multi-dimensional, well-plotted story addresses current issues with sensitivity, thoughtfulness, and a touch of humor." In the *New York Times Book Review*, Lois Metzger praised the book, claiming that it "is so original, fresh and fiery, you'd think that M. E. Kerr, one

If you enjoy the works of M. E. Kerr, you may also want to check out the following books:

Jay Bennett, *The Pigeon*, 1981.
Nancy Garden, *Lark in the Morning*, 1991.
Ron Koertge, *The Arizona Kid*, 1988.
Susan Beth Pfeffer, *Family of Strangers*, 1992.

of the grand masters of young-adult fiction, was just now getting started."

Explores Controversial Themes

Lang, Kerr's openly homosexual character in *"Hello," I Lied*, is a male counterpart of Evie. Lang has a boyfriend and is becoming happy and comfortable with being gay. During the summer of his seventeenth year, he moves with his mother to Long Island to work for a retired rock star named Ben Nevada. Nevada also invites Hugette, his daughter from a previous liaison, to join them after her mother dies. Lang and Hugette are reluctant friends at first, because Lang feels like she has been dumped on him. Eventually, however, Lang finds himself attracted to her, despite the fact that he is in love with another man, and he is confused at his newfound feelings.

In general, critics were impressed with Kerr's sensitive handling of a gay youth who has unanswered questions about the nature of love. "This book successfully challenges readers' assumptions, breaking them down to offer more hopeful, affirming ideas about love and truth," a *Publishers Weekly* reviewer concluded. Mary B. McCarthy, writing in *Voice of Youth Advocates*, believed that the book does credit to its subject: "the author has again crafted a story that forces readers to examine their own ideas of contentment, attraction, and love."

"I've never married nor had children, and I've lately thought this has been a great asset," related Kerr in *SAAS*. "If I'd had children, I'm sure I would have been tempted to keep them tied to something in an upstairs room, so no harm would come to them. I think the youngster in me remains vivid because I've never raised any children to compete with her, or compare with her, and I have not had to pace the floor nights worrying where they are or with whom, and what has happened to the family car." In addition, remaining childless gives Kerr a different advantage: "I have only one childhood to keep track of and that's mine. I think that gives you a clearer picture," she told Sutton. "If I had three kids and had to keep in my mind all their childhoods and everything that happened to them, it would seem to me a bit fogged over. It's hard to forget yourself when you don't have children."

In addition, in order to keep up with her audience, Kerr has cultivated adolescent tastes. "One great advantage in writing for kids is keeping up with the times," she wrote in *SAAS*. "I've developed a very enthusiastic interest in today's music. I listen faithfully to the top ten, and I follow all the groups from pop to rock to heavy metal. I'm an MTV watcher. . . . Some of the videos I love, and some I really hate, but all of them teach me about kids today. It's a whole new world for me, one I probably wouldn't have investigated if I wasn't a Y.A. writer."

A factor she contends with in her resort town is isolation. "When I first moved to East Hampton, I missed New York City a lot," she claimed in *SAAS*. "Three months of the year our little village jumps with tourists and summer people . . . but the rest of the year we are a sleepy little place without an industry or very much going on." Kerr decided to see if she could get a writer's group started "by putting an ad in the paper to see what interest there was out there. I would lead this workshop. It would be a non-profit undertaking, benefiting the Springs Scholarship Fund—'Springs' being the section of East Hampton where I live. . . . The response was quick and most enthusiastic."

Keeping tabs on teens tastes and staying involved in her writing community help to keep Kerr's writing fresh and interesting to youth. In *SAAS*, Kerr concluded about her career: "I love writing, and I particularly love writing for young adults. I know other young adult writers who claim that their books are just slotted into that category, and claim there's no difference between an adult novel and a young adult one . . . I beg to disagree. When I write for young adults I know they're still wrestling with very important problems like winning and losing, not feeling accepted or accept-

ing, prejudice, love—all the things adults ultimately get hardened to, and forgetful of. I know my audience hasn't yet made up their minds about everything. . . . Give me that kind of an audience any day!"

■ Works Cited

Bradford, Richard, review of *Gentlehands, New York Times Book Review,* April 30, 1978, p. 30.

Carlson, Dale, "Smack," *New York Times Book Review,* Part I, February 11, 1973, p. 8.

Caron, Paul A., review of *Me, Me, Me, Me, Me: Not a Novel, Best Sellers,* June, 1983, p. 110.

DeLuca, Geraldine, review of *Gentlehands, Lion and the Unicorn,* Winter, 1979-80, pp. 125-48.

Review of *Fell Back, Publishers Weekly,* September 29, 1989, p. 70.

Review of *"Hello," I Lied, Publishers Weekly,* March 31, 1997, p. 75.

Kerr, M. E., *Me, Me, Me, Me, Me: Not a Novel,* Harper, 1983.

Kerr, M. E., essay in *Something about the Author Autobiography Series,* Volume 1, Gale, 1986, pp. 141-54.

Kerr, M. E., interview with Roger Sutton in *School Library Journal,* June, 1993, pp. 24-29.

Kerr, M. E., comments in *Children's Books and Their Creators,* edited by Anita Silvey, Houghton, 1995, p. 369.

Knoth, Maeve Visser, review of *Deliver Us from Evie, Horn Book,* January, 1995.

McCarthy, Mary B., review of *"Hello," I Lied, Voice of Youth Advocates,* June, 1997, p. 110.

Metzger, Lois, review of *Deliver Us from Evie, New York Times Book Review,* April 9, 1995, p. 25.

Milton, Joyce, review of *Me, Me, Me, Me, Me: Not a Novel, New York Times Book Review,* May 22, 1983, p. 39.

Pollack, Pamela D., review of *Dinky Hocker Shoots Smack!, School Library Journal,* December, 1972, p. 67.

Roback, Diane, and Elizabeth Devereaux, review of *Linger, Publishers Weekly,* June 21, 1993, p. 105.

Rochman, Hazel, review of *Fell, Booklist,* June 1, 1987, pp. 1515-16.

Rochman, Hazel, "To Be Continued: *Fell Down* and Other Sequels," *Booklist,* September 15, 1991, p. 135.

Rochman, Hazel, review of *Linger, Booklist,* June 1 and 15, 1993, p. 1814.

Rochman, Hazel, review of *Deliver Us from Evie, Booklist,* September 15, 1994, p. 125.

Tyson, Christy, review of *Fell, Voice of Youth Advocates*, October, 1987, p. 202.

Tyson, Christy, review of *Fell Back, Voice of Youth Advocates*, December, 1989, pp. 277-78.

Tyson, Christy, review of *Fell Down, Voice of Youth Advocates*, December, 1991, pp. 313-14.

■ **For More Information See**

BOOKS

Authors and Artists for Young Adults, Volume 2, Gale, 1989.

Children's Literature Review, Volume 29, Gale, 1993.

Contemporary Literary Criticism, Gale, Volume 12, 1980, Volume 35, 1985.

Fourth Book of Junior Authors and Illustrators, edited by Doris De Montreville and Elizabeth D. Crawford, H. W. Wilson, 1978.

Literature for Today's Young Adults, 2nd edition, Scott, Foresman, 1985.

Nilsen, Alleen Pace, *Presenting M. E. Kerr*, Twayne, 1986.

Speaking for Ourselves, compiled and edited by Donald R. Gallo, National Council of Teachers of English, 1990.

Twentieth-Century Children's Writers, 3rd edition, St. Martin's, 1989.

Twentieth-Century Young Adult Writers, 1st edition, St. James Press, 1994.

PERIODICALS

Books for Keeps, May, 1997, p. 5.

Bulletin of the Center for Children's Books, June, 1997, p. 363.

English Journal, December, 1975; February, 1986, p. 26.

Horn Book, February 1973, p. 56; August, 1975, p. 365; June, 1977, p. 288; July/August, 1997, pp. 457-58.

New York Post, July 8, 1978.

Times Literary Supplement, November 23, 1973; September 19, 1975; December 1, 1978.

Voice of Youth Advocates, February, 1985, p. 307.

Washington Post Book World, May 19, 1974; May 10, 1981, p. 15; July 11, 1982.

Wilson Library Bulletin, December, 1993, p. 117; September, 1994, pp. 116-17.*

—Sketch by Nancy Rampson

Daniel Keyes

■ Personal

Born August 9, 1927, in Brooklyn, NY; son of William and Betty (Alicke) Keyes; married Aurea Vazquez (a fashion stylist, photographer, and artist), October 14, 1952; children: Hillary Ann, Leslie Joan. *Education:* Brooklyn College (now Brooklyn College of the City of New York), A.B., 1950, A.M., 1961.

■ Addresses

Office—Department of English, Ohio University, Athens, OH 45701. *Agent*—Marcy Posner, William Morris Agency, 1325 Avenue of the Americas, New York, NY 10019. *Electronic mail*—dankeyes@usa.net.

■ Career

Novelist and nonfiction writer. Stadium Publishing Co., New York City, associate fiction editor, 1951-52; Fenko & Keyes Photography, Inc., New York City, co-owner, 1953; high school teacher of English, Brooklyn, NY, 1954-55, 1957-62; Wayne State University, Detroit, MI, instructor in English, 1962-66; Ohio University, Athens, lecturer, 1966-72, professor of English, 1972—, director of creative writing center, 1973-74, 1977-78. Supervising producer of television movie *The Mad Housers,* 1990. *Military service:* U.S. Maritime Service, senior assistant purser, 1945-47. *Member:* PEN, Societe des Auteurs et Compositeurs Dramatiques, Authors Guild, Authors League of America, Dramatists Guild (full voting member), Mystery Writers of America, MacDowell Colony Fellows.

■ Awards, Honors

Hugo Award, World Science Fiction Convention, 1959, for "Flowers for Algernon" (short story); Nebula Award, Science Fiction Writers of America, 1966, for *Flowers for Algernon* (novel); fellow, Yaddo artist colony, 1967; fellow, MacDowell artist colony, 1967; special award, Mystery Writers of America, 1981, for *The Minds of Billy Milligan;* Kurd Lasswitz Award for best book by a foreign author, 1986, for *Die Leben des Billy Milligan,* the German translation of *The Minds of Billy Milligan;* Edgar Allan Poe Award nomination, Mystery Writers of America, 1986, for *Unveiling Claudia: A True Story of a Serial Murder;* Baker Fund Award, Ohio University, 1986; individual artists fellowship, Ohio Arts Council, 1986-87; Award of Honor, Distinguished Alumnus Brooklyn College, 1988.

■ Writings

FICTION

Flowers for Algernon (novel), Harcourt, 1966.

The Touch (novel), Harcourt, 1968, published in England as *The Contaminated Man*, Mayflower, 1973.

The Fifth Sally, Houghton Mifflin, 1980.

Daniel Keyes Collected Stories, Hayakawa (Tokyo, Japan), 1993.

Daniel Keyes Reader, Hayakawa, 1994.

NONFICTION

The Minds of Billy Milligan, Random House, 1981, revised edition, with afterword, Bantam, 1982.

Unveiling Claudia: A True Story of a Serial Murder, Bantam, 1986.

The Milligan Wars (sequel to *The Minds of Billy Milligan*), Hayakawa, 1993, Bantam, 1996.

OTHER

Contributor to numerous anthologies, including *Ten Top Stories*, edited by David A. Sohn, Bantam, 1964. Contributor of fiction to periodicals. Associate editor, *Marvel Science Fiction*, 1951.

Keyes's works have been translated into numerous foreign languages, including Danish, Dutch, French, German, Italian, Swedish, and Spanish. "The Daniel Keyes Collection," a repository of papers and manuscripts, is housed at the Alden Library, Ohio University, Athens, OH.

■ Adaptations

The television play *The Two Worlds of Charlie Gordon*, based on the short story "Flowers for Algernon," was broadcast on CBS Playhouse, February 22, 1961; the feature film *Charly* starring Cliff Robertson (winner of an Academy Award for his role), based on the novel *Flowers for Algernon*, was produced by Cinerama, 1968; a two-act play *Flowers for Algernon* was adapted by David Rogers, Dramatic Publishing, 1969; a dramatic musical *Charlie and Algernon* was first produced at Citadel Theater, Alberta, Canada, December 21, 1978, produced at Queens Theater, London, England, June 14, 1979, first produced in the United States at Terrace Theater, Kennedy Center, Washington, DC, March 8, 1980, produced on Broadway at Helen Hayes Theater, September 4, 1980. Other stage adaptations of *Flowers for Algernon* have been produced in France, Australia, Poland, and Japan, and a radio play has been produced in Ireland and the former Czechoslovakia.

■ Sidelights

What if you could volunteer to take part in an experiment that would triple your intelligence level? How would your new ability affect your relationships to other people and your feelings about yourself? Those are the questions posed by Daniel Keyes in *Flowers for Algernon*, the 1966 novel for which he is best known. In the story, a mentally retarded man in his early thirties agrees to an experimental neurological operation that bolsters his below-average intelligence to the genius level—but only temporarily, as the impermanently enlightened character realizes to his distress. Categorized as science fiction, the novel supersedes such easy classification, its concerns, as Mark R. Hillegas noted in *Saturday Review*, "moral, social, psychological, theological, or philosophical problems imagined as resulting from inventions, discoveries or scientific hypotheses." *Flowers for Algernon* was the first of Keyes's three novels and three nonfiction works that grappled with the mysterious world of mental processes, particularly those at a remove from the average person's thinking. Keyes has received science fiction and mystery awards for his work, including the prestigious Hugo and Nebula awards. *Flowers for Algernon* remains his calling card, termed by Joseph McLellan of the *Washington Post Book World* "one of the most memorable novels of the 1960s."

Keyes is a Brooklyn native, born August 9, 1927. After a public school education, he joined the U.S. Maritime Service, where he worked as ship's purser on oil tankers. In 1947, he enrolled in Brooklyn College, earning a B.A. in psychology in 1950. For a short period, Keyes worked in magazine publishing in New York. As he reported in *Something About the Author* (SATA), "here I began to learn the craft of writing." He tried fashion photography for a while, but eventually wound up in academia. In *SATA*, he said he found himself "coming full circle to teach at the high school from which I had graduated ten years earlier." In addition to his daytime job, Keyes earned a Master's degree in English and American literature at night. He used the weekends to write.

One of Keyes's first stories was the original version of *Flowers for Algernon*, which was published in 1959 in the *Magazine of Fantasy and Science Fiction*. The story won a Hugo Award and was adapted for television in 1961 before Keyes decided to expand it into a novel. The story is told through journal entries ("Progress Reports") by Charlie Gordon, a 32-year-old janitor with an IQ of 68. Despite his low intellectual capacity, Charlie is an eager learner who attends night school. At the suggestion of his teacher, Charlie volunteers to take part in experimental neurosurgery that increases his intelligence to genius level. Only a laboratory mouse, Algernon, has undergone a similar operation. The "Progress Reports" reflect Charlie's growing sophistication, his intelligence eventually outstripping that of the scientists who performed the operation. More intelligence leads to a more complex social life for Charlie—in particular, an affair with one of his teachers—and he very quickly grasps that knowledge can't always compensate for a lack of emotional experience. Even more disturbing is his discovery, through Algernon, that the operation has no permanent effect. In the end, he reverts to his mentally retarded state, burdened with a new awareness of all that he's missing.

A Sci Fi Classic

Although primarily categorized as science fiction, the award-winning *Flowers for Algernon* addressed such a wide range of psychological, social, and moral themes that most critics did not bind it to a strict genre classification. The sociological elements of the story were not lost on critics; *Saturday Review* writer Hillegas, for instance, praised *Flowers for Algernon* for its "compassionate insight into the situation of the mentally retarded: how they feel, how they are treated by parents, friends, institutions."

A reviewer in the *Times Literary Supplement* remarked on the inevitable conclusion of the novel, understood by Charlie and the reader simultaneously: "Charlie's hopeless knowledge that he is destined to end in a home for the feeble-minded, a moron who knows that he is a moron, is painful, and Mr. Keyes has the technical equipment to prevent us from shrugging off the pain." In his *New York Times* review, Eliot Fremont-Smith criticized aspects of the story as sentimental, faulting it for psychological pretensions and an overall predictability. Nonetheless, alluding to the original short story, Fremont-Smith concluded that the fact that *Flowers for Algernon* "works at all as a novel is proof of Mr. Keyes's deftness. And it is really quite a performance. He has taken the obvious, treated it in a most obvious fashion, and

succeeded in creating a tale that is convincing, suspenseful and touching. . . ."

Addressing the transition of *Flowers for Algernon* from a science fiction short story to a novel, Robert Scholes, in his book *Structural Fabulation: An Essay on Fiction of the Future,* complimented Keyes on the "great skill" with which the author amplified his short story into a full-length novel, deeming the work "beautifully problematic." For Scholes, however, its appearance in both short story and novel formats ultimately rendered *Flowers for Algernon* "deficient in artistic integrity." In

This 1966 work, which details the changes in a mentally impaired man, Charlie Gordon, after he undergoes a daring neurological experiment, received the Nebula Award for best novel.

Trillion Year Spree: The History of Science Fiction, Brian W. Aldiss took up the same theme, declaring: "This moving story lost something of its power when expanded to novel length." In *Understanding Contemporary American Science Fiction,* Thomas D. Clareson credited Keyes for having "revitalized the myth of Frankenstein by introducing a fresh narrative perspective" and fusing "Mary Shelley's nameless creature and the crazed scientist into the single figure of Charlie." Clareson also noted *Flowers for Algernon's* "narrative perspective" as "unique in the science fiction pantheon."

In addition to numerous radio and stage productions (including a dramatic Broadway musical), *Flowers for Algernon* was adapted for television and, in 1968, made into a movie titled *Charly.* Cliff Robertson, who had also starred in the television production, won an Academy Award for Best Actor for his portrayal of Charlie Gordon. Many readers have been introduced to the novel through their English classes, as *Flowers for Algernon* has become a favorite for young adult readers.

Keyes had been at Ohio University in Athens a few years by the time he published his second novel, *The Touch.* Barney and Karen Stark are a young couple, eager to become parents. When Barney is accidentally contaminated with radioactive dust at his job, he unknowingly infects Karen, too, who has just learned that she is finally pregnant. In her mixed review, *Publishers Weekly's* Alice P. Hackett described the work as "an all too believable could-happen. . . ." However, she continued that Keyes shouldn't have "saved his one unerring jab to the heart" for the end.

From Fiction to Nonfiction

Retaining his focus on psychological problems, Keyes centered his next novel, *The Fifth Sally,* on multiple-personality disorder. This was the first fictional treatment of this disturbing subject. Within Sally Porter live four distinct personalities: artistic Nola; tomboyish Derry; promiscuous Bella; and Jinx, who is lethally violent. Working with her psychiatrist, Sally tries to meld these discrete personalities into one integrated whole. Reviewers were not especially complimentary; in *Publishers Weekly,* Barbara A. Bannon faulted Keyes for "formula writing" and his effort to add social significance by having the psychiatrist comment that the

recent rise in dissociative disorders may brand them as the hallmark of this century. Bannon wrote that Keyes's "desire to please a mass audience will not attract discriminating readers." Mel Gilden of the *Los Angeles Times* was gentler, finding *The Fifth Sally* "an intriguing story" if a little emotionally uninvolving. Ultimately, he found that "despite the intellectual distance maintained between Sally and the reader, the book will reward almost anyone who reads it."

Keyes's 1982 book, *The Minds of Billy Milligan,* chronicled the first case in United States history of a legal acquittal based on multiple personality. Billy Milligan was arrested on three rape charges in 1977 in Ohio; psychological tests revealed twenty-four personalities (three female), some children, some adolescents, and a few in their early twenties. The dominant personalities were Arthur, an Englishman who oversaw everyone else; Ragen, a protector who was given to violence and who could also read and write Serbo-Croatian fluently; and Adalana, the nineteen-year-old lesbian who ultimately admitted to goading Billy into raping three times. Keyes wrote that these personalities, along with the other twenty-one, took turns occupying "the spot" (Milligan's consciousness), one of them dominating the others according to circumstances.

Only after several of Milligan's personalities read *Flowers for Algernon* would he agree to work with Keyes. In the book, Keyes devotes considerable attention to "The Teacher," the personality most able to tap into Milligan's memories. The Teacher gives most of the background, which Keyes then fills in with reports from other personalities. Gradually, a chronicle of repeated abuse emerges, torturous behavior that Milligan tried to dodge by retreating into himself, seeking out the many people living within him. Finally, Milligan was arrested and sentenced to a correctional institution. His case sparked controversy in the legal and medical fields. Writing in the *New York Times Book Review,* Robert Coles cited other accounts of multiple personality disorder, noting that "the historical tensions within the [medical] profession have yet to be resolved, and have, in fact, been given new expression in this instance." The prosecuting attorneys called for Milligan's imprisonment even as doctors and psychologists in Ohio tried to determine the best way to treat Milligan. As Coles noted further, "when he was found 'insane,' . . . the arguments did not by any means abate. Was

Cliff Robertson won an Academy Award for his portrayal of Charlie Gordon in *Charly,* the 1968 film adaptation of Keyes's novel *Flowers for Algernon.*

he a 'sociopath'—a liar, an impostor? . . . Was he a severely disturbed and dangerous 'psychotic' who required careful watching, lots of medication, maybe a course or two of electric shock treatment?"

Coles praised Keyes for his rendition of this confusing story, commenting that "it reads like a play: Billy's 'personalities' come onstage, leave to be replaced by others and then reappear." For Peter Gorner, writing in the *Chicago Tribune,* Keyes's inclusive method worked against the story, annoying rather than enlightening the reader. Gorner noted that Keyes "interviews everybody, reconstructs, flashes back, and confuses the story in a chatty, conversational style. The alter egos seem to dance before our eyes like a stroboscope." Re-

viewing the work in the *Los Angeles Times,* David Johnston stated, "telling the stories of twenty-four different personalities would be a difficult task for any writer. To tell of two dozen personalities in one human body is an extremely complex task. Keyes, on balance, carries it off quite well. While it shortchanges the reader by limiting explanation of motives almost exclusively to Milligan's personalities, [*The Minds of Billy Milligan*] is nonetheless a fascinating work." Making special mention of the "warmth and empathy" that Keyes showed, reviewer McLellan found that "complexity is the keynote of the Billy phenomenon and equally of its treatment by Daniel Keyes. The challenge of first unearthing this story . . . and then telling it intelligibly is a daunting one. He has carried it off brilliantly. . . ."

If you enjoy the works of Daniel Keyes, you may also want to check out the following books and films:

Harper Lee, *To Kill A Mockingbird*, 1960.
Colby Rodowsky, *What About Me?*, 1989.
John Steinbeck, *Of Mice and Men*, 1940.
Theodore Sturgeon, *More than Human*, 1953.
Rainman, a film starring Tom Cruise and Dustin Hoffman, 1988.

Turning once again to nonfiction, Keyes delved more deeply into the violent side of disturbed thinking with *Unveiling Claudia: A True Story of a Serial Murder*. Claudia Elaine Yasko convinced herself that she was the murderer in three Ohio killings in the 1970s. Her acquaintance with the victims and the killers led to her to believe herself culpable and to confess. Only after the real murderers were accidentally found out were the charges against her dropped. In his portrayal, Keyes traced the events that led to the killings (culled over the course of two years of interviews with the self-alleged serial murderer) in an attempt to demonstrate how Yasko came to know so much. *Library Journal* reviewer Gregor A. Preston deemed this effort "not as intriguing" as *The Minds of Billy Milligan* but found that "this is a masterfully told, absorbing story."

The work Keyes produced subsequent to *Flowers for Algernon* earned him a dedicated following in the United States as well as an enormous readership in Japan. *The Daniel Keyes Collected Stories* and *The Daniel Keyes Reader* both appeared in Japan only. Largely in response to readers eager to hear news of Billy Milligan, Keyes published *The Milligan Wars*, a sequel, in Japan in 1994 and in the United States in 1996. In the decade since Keyes had completed the first book, Billy had been moved from one maximum security hospital to another all over Ohio. It wasn't until 1991 that medical authorities deemed Billy "fused," that is, no longer suffering from a mental disorder, and capable of living independently.

In his nonfiction, short stories, and novels, Keyes has shown himself to be endlessly "fascinated by the complexities of the human mind," he commented in *SATA*. Critics and readers have found Keyes's fascination to be tempered with compassion. By sympathetically revealing the world of the mentally retarded and the mentally disordered, Keyes allows his readers to better understand the emotional similarities shared by humans, no matter how different their mental processes may be.

■ Works Cited

Aldiss, Brian W., *Trillion Year Spree: The History of Science Fiction*, Gollancz, 1986.

Bannon, Barbara A., review of *The Fifth Sally*, *Publishers Weekly*, July 25, 1980, p. 45.

Clareson, Thomas D., *Understanding Contemporary American Science Fiction: The Formative Period, 1926-1970*, University of South Carolina Press, 1990.

Coles, Robert, "Arthur, Ragen, Allen et Al," *New York Times Book Review*, November 15, 1981, pp. 9, 30.

Fremont-Smith, Eliot, review of *Flowers for Algernon*, *New York Times*, March 7, 1966, p. 25.

Review of *Flowers for Algernon*, *Times Literary Supplement*, July 21, 1966.

Gilden, Mel, review of *The Fifth Sally*, *Los Angeles Times*, December 12, 1980.

Gorner, Peter, review of *The Minds of Billy Milligan*, *Chicago Tribune*, November 11, 1981.

Hackett, Alice P., review of *The Touch*, *Publishers Weekly*, August 12, 1968, pp. 46-47.

Hillegas, Mark R., review of *Flowers for Algernon*, *Saturday Review*, March 26, 1966.

Johnston, David, review of *The Minds of Billy Milligan*, *Los Angeles Times Book Review*, January 3, 1982.

Keyes, Daniel, comments in *Something About the Author*, Volume 37, Gale, 1986.

McLellan, Joseph, review of *The Minds of Billy Milligan*, *Washington Post Book World*, November 29, 1981.

Preston, Gregor A., review of *Unveiling Claudia: A True Story of a Serial Murder*, *Library Journal*, July, 1986.

Scholes, Robert, "Structural Fabulation," *Structural Fabulation: An Essay on Fiction of the Future*, University of Notre Dame Press, 1975.

■ For More Information See

BOOKS

Perkins, George, Barbara Perkins, and Phillip Leininger, editors, *Benet's Reader's Encyclopedia of American Literature*, HarperCollins, 1991.

Seymour-Smith, Martin, editor, *Novels and Novelists: A Guide to the World of Fiction*, St. Martin's Press, 1980.

Watson, Noelle, and Paul E. Schellinger, editors, *Twentieth-Century Science-Fiction Writers*, St. James Press, 1991.

PERIODICALS

Booklist, June 1, 1966, p. 948; January 1, 1969, p. 482; September 1, 1980, p. 31; October 15, 1981, p. 274; July, 1985, p. 1546; May 1, 1986, p. 1259; May 15, 1988, p. 1597; February 1, 1991, p. 1123.

Cosmopolitan, January, 1982, p. 52.

Library Journal, February 15, 1966, p. 965.

New Yorker, September 22, 1980; February 15, 1982, p. 57.

New York Times Book Review, February 25, 1968, p. 20; December 19, 1982, p. 27; August 24, 1986, p. 19.

Observer, August 7, 1966, p. 21.

Punch, July 20, 1966, p. 125.

Whole Earth Review, March, 1985, p. 49.*

—Sketch by C. M. Ratner

■ Personal

Born September 10, 1927, in New York, NY; daughter of Max (a lawyer) and Eleanor (a musician; maiden name, Mack) Lowenthal; married Alvin Levin (a lawyer), August 3, 1947; children: Katherine, Bara, Jennifer. *Education:* University of Rochester, A.B. (high honors), 1949; Radcliffe College, M.A., 1951; Harvard University, A.M.T., 1951.

■ Addresses

Agent—Dorothy Markinko, McIntosh and Otis Inc., 310 Madison Ave., New York, New York 10017. *Home*—Old Winter St., Lincoln, MA 01773.

■ Career

Museum of Fine Arts, Boston, MA, assistant in research, 1951-52; part-time teaching fellow, Harvard Graduate School of Education, Cambridge, MA, 1953; creative writing fellow, Radcliffe Institute, 1968-70; Massachusetts coordinator, McCarthy Historical Archive, 1969; Pine Manor Open College, Chestnut Hill, MA, instructor in literature, 1970-75; Minute Man Publications, Lexington, MA, feature writer, 1972; Center for the Study of Children's Literature, Simmons College, Boston, special instructor in children's literature, 1975-77, adjunct professor of children's literature, 1977-87; instructor at Emmanuel College, Boston, 1975, and at Radcliffe College, Cambridge, MA, 1976—. Member of the steering committee, Children's Literature New England. Sheep farmer. *Member:* Authors Guild, Authors League of America, Children's Books Authors (Boston), Masterworks Chorale, Middlesex Sheep Breeders Association.

■ Awards, Honors

Judy Lopez Memorial Award, 1989, for *The Trouble with Gramary*; Best Book for Young Adults citation, American Library Association, 1990, for *Brother Moose*; New York Public Library Books for the Teen Age list, 1993, for *Mercy's Mill*; *Parents' Choice* Story Book Award, 1994, for *Away to Me, Moss!*

■ Writings

JUVENILE NOVELS

The Zoo Conspiracy, illustrated by Marian Parry, Hastings House, 1973.

The Sword of Culann, Macmillan, 1973.

A Griffon's Nest (sequel to *The Sword of Culann*), Macmillan, 1975.

The Forespoken (sequel to *A Griffon's Nest*), Macmillan, 1976.

Landfall, Atheneum, 1979.

The Beast on the Brink, illustrated by Parry, Avon, 1980.

The Keeping-Room, Greenwillow, 1981.

A Binding Spell, Lodestar/Dutton, 1984.

Put on My Crown, Lodestar/Dutton, 1985.

The Ice Bear, Greenwillow, 1986, MacRae (London), 1987.

The Trouble with Gramary, Greenwillow, 1988.

Brother Moose, Greenwillow, 1990.

Mercy's Mill, Greenwillow, 1992.

Starshine and Sunglow, illustrated by Joseph A. Smith, Greenwillow, 1994.

Away to Me, Moss!, Greenwillow, 1994.

Fire in the Wind, Greenwillow, 1995.

Gift Horse, Greenwillow, 1996.

Island Bound, Greenwillow, 1997.

Look Back, Moss, Greenwillow, 1998.

OTHER

Contributor to books, including *Innocence and Experience: Essays and Conversations on Children's Literature,* compiled and edited by Barbara Harrison and Gregory Maguire, Lothrop, 1987; and *Proceedings for Travelers in Time,* Green Bay Press, 1990. Also contributor of articles to periodicals, including *Harvard Educational Review, Horn Book,* and *Children's Literature in Education.* Levin's manuscripts are housed in the Kerlan Collection, University of Minnesota, Minneapolis.

■ Sidelights

An award-winning author of novels for children and young adults, Betty Levin places her stories in both realistic and fantasy settings. Frequently she uses a modern-day location as a point from which to move her characters back in time to the world of ancient myths or actual historical events. Levin is also an animal lover, a fact that influences her tales, which often feature animals. The writer is noted for complicated plots involving young people who embark on a strange adventure only to find themselves in the middle of a mystery. As they try to find a solution they learn lessons about life, in the end reaching a new level of maturity.

Similarly, Levin's novels have taken on new dimensions since she published her first book in 1973. Adele M. Fasick observed in *Twentieth-Century Children's Writers* that "Levin's work grows in strength and scope with each book. . . ." Fasick pointed out that although the novelist is "not an easy writer," readers who remain patient with numerous plot twists and turns "will find themselves embarking on an enriching experience." Levin's fiction has been recognized with honors from the American Library Association, the New York Public Library, and *Parents' Choice* magazine, among other organizations.

Reflecting on her own childhood in *Something About the Author Autobiography Series (SAAS),* Levin recalled events and relationships that formed her as an adult. "Early memories are like scraps of trash set loose by a space capsule," she observed. "Detached fragments continue in orbit, but outside the scheme that spawned them. They are so unfixed that it is often impossible to date them. Yet they float across our consciousness. When we recognize the truth of them, we suspect that in some way they are still part of us." Her family's permanent home was in New York City, where Levin attended school until she was thirteen or fourteen. During her early years, however, she spent summers on a farm near Bridgewater, Connecticut, with her parents, Max and Eleanor Lowenthal, and her two brothers, David and John. The extended family also included Kitty Healy, who came from Ireland as a young girl to live with the Lowenthals, and Robby, who had grown up on a farm in Virginia. Levin formed a close friendship with Kitty, a "born storyteller," whose tales about Ireland sparked the writer's later interest in the Celtic myths that were the basis for three of her first books. Almost a second mother to Levin, Kitty stayed with the family until she was married and had her first child, Katherine, who died of pneumonia at age two. Levin dedicated *The Sword of Culann* to Kitty and named her own first child Katherine in memory of her friend's baby.

In *SAAS* Levin said that growing up on the farm with older brothers and neighborhood playmates helped her learn about herself. In particular she remembered a winter day when she missed out on ice skating with David, John, and their friend Buddy. As her cold-numbed fingers struggled to tie the laces on her skates, the boys would not wait for her and instead rushed ahead to the pond. Another time a girl named Sally, who was the sister of Levin's best friend, pinned her down and sat on her. Levin asked John to beat up on Sally but he refused, saying Sally would win because she was bigger. Writing in *SAAS*, Levin concluded, "My brothers were not mean. They were just older and taller and stronger and smarter than I was." The memory of the day she did not get to skate, she said, only "confirms certain facts about myself that were confirmed over and over again when I grew up. On the day I didn't get to skate I only knew that I could never quite catch up, no matter how much I wanted to."

"Early memories are like scraps of trash set loose by a space capsule. Detached fragments continue in orbit, but outside the scheme that spawned them. They are so unfixed that it is often impossible to date them. Yet they float across our consciousness. When we recognize the truth of them, we suspect that in some way they are still part of us."

—Betty Levin

Living on the farm had another lasting effect on Levin: she discovered her love for animals. She had always enjoyed books about animals that her mother and Kitty read to her. In her autobiographical essay for *SAAS* she recalled that when she was eight she was given her first pet, a puppy, which the rest of her family "barely tolerated." Levin noted, "I was the only animal lover in our family." Soon her "animal family" included a puppy, a pony, a cat, a rabbit, and another dog. Then, during a visit to a sheep farm when she was eleven, she met two border collies that herded the sheep. "The working partnership between a human and a dog," Levin wrote, "was one of the great discoveries of my life." She continued this partnership as an adult, when she and her husband, Alvin, bought a sheep farm. Their first dogs were the offspring of the two border collies she had met when she was a child. Today Levin still raises sheep and enters her dogs in competitive sheep dog trials.

Levin's father worked as a lawyer for government agencies, and frequent traveling kept him away their home in New York City for long periods of time. Sometimes the family went with him to places such as Montana and New Mexico. In 1940, when Levin was in junior high school, the Lowenthals finally moved to Chevy Chase, Maryland, a suburb of Washington, D.C. In Washington, Levin witnessed racism and bigotry for the first time. This experience was especially shocking because she had grown up with friends from a variety of backgrounds in New York and she had never been aware of racial differences. The incident with Sally gained significance when Levin encountered racism for the first time in the eighth grade: "When I was very young and my best friend's sister proved that she was a bully," Levin stated in *SAAS*, "I experienced in a small way, and briefly, the helplessness that victims feel when overpowered by the strong and arrogant." Her awareness was further heightened during World War II when her mother worked with a U.S. War Department agency that helped refugees fleeing from Nazism in Europe.

Eventually her mother enrolled her at the National Cathedral School, where she became active in choral groups and met new friends. Levin also began volunteer work as a junior nurse's aide at a hospital. Once she even delivered a baby by herself because there was a shortage of doctors and nurses. In 1944, near the end of World War II, Levin's parents left their government jobs and returned to New York. She completed her senior year at Lincoln High School with her old friends. The summer after Levin graduated from high school she worked at office jobs on Madison Avenue. Although she was offered a permanent position at an advertising agency, she decided to go to college instead. In her *SAAS* essay Levin commented, "That brought to a close my New York careers." She enrolled at the University of Rochester, planning to major in voice at the Eastman School of Music. By the end of the first semester, however, she realized she did not want to pursue a professional singing career. When Levin changed her major to history and literature, her life took two important turns: she met her future husband, Alvin Levin, and she set in motion an eventual writing career. Alvin had just returned from the war in Europe, still wearing fatigues, the day she first saw him. He also became an English major, and soon they were inseparable. They were married shortly before starting their junior year. Living in a one-room apartment, they worked at part-time jobs until they finished college and joined Betty's parents at the farm.

Develops Interest in Children's Literature

In 1949 the Levins moved to Boston and Alvin entered the Harvard University Law School. The following year Betty enrolled in graduate school at Radcliffe College. While writing a seminar paper on literature about New York City, she discovered children's books and thus became interested in the history of children's literature, a subject she has taught for many years. During this time Levin held several part-time jobs, among them a position in the library of the Museum of Fine Arts, where she was introduced to Celtic studies. After the birth of Katherine, Alvin graduated from law school and Levin used a small inheritance to finance a family trip to rural regions in Scotland and England.

A time-travel story, this 1992 novel revolves around Sarah, who is rescued by a mysterious boy who may or may not be a runaway slave.

Upon returning home the Levins built a small farm near Lincoln, Massachusetts, and the following summer their second daughter, Bara, was born. A year later, in 1955, both Levin and her husband contracted polio during an epidemic that struck Boston. Levin, who was pregnant again, recovered from the disease, but she lost the child. Alvin became totally paralyzed, however, and spent two years in an iron lung. Eventually he was able to go home, but he was confined to a wheelchair for the rest of his life. Nevertheless he was able to work, and Levin and the children adapted their daily lives to his condition. Soon things were back to normal and the Levins had a third daughter, Jennifer. Yet, as Levin observed in *SAAS*, they had to "learn new ways of living and being parents." The family spent summers on a sailboat that was outfitted for Alvin's wheelchair, exploring the coast of Maine, which became the setting for several of Levin's books.

Just as the farm was once again thriving with new sheep, puppies, stray cats, and a pony, the Levins' land was taken by the government as part of the Minute Man National Historical Park. Forced to sell their home, they finally found another farm in Lincoln that they shared with neighbors who were also being displaced. During the 1960s and 1970s Levin became increasingly involved in civil rights and the anti-Vietnam War movement. She also continued to raise sheep and sheep dogs.

History and Myth

Levin's writing career began in the early 1970s. She held a creative writing fellowship at the Bunting Institute from 1968 to 1970, then published *The Zoo Conspiracy* in 1973. She had written the story several years earlier for her children, and Bara had suggested the title. In the mid-seventies Levin gained critical recognition for the trilogy *The Sword of Culann*, *A Griffon's Nest*, and *The Forespoken*. All three books feature Claudia, who lives on an island off the coast of Maine and is led back in time by an ancient bronze sword hilt belonging to an eccentric hermit. In the first two novels Claudia is accompanied by her step-brother Evan. During their adventures in *The Sword of Culann* they find themselves in Iron Age Ireland, witnessing the feats of Cuchulain (the Hound of Culann), a hero of ancient Irish myth. Cuchulain earns his status as a warrior, defeats the army of Queen Medb in the Cattle Raid of

Cooley (Táin Bó Culaigne), and then succumbs to the powers of witchcraft. Many reviewers found the plot to be confusing and the dialogue sometimes too modern for ancient characters, yet they praised Levin's use of Irish legends. For instance, Helen Gregory noted in *Library Journal* that "the story of Medb's bloody war is fast moving, suspense filled and would encourage more reading of Celtic myth."

In *A Griffon's Nest* Evan and Claudia travel back in time to the Orkney Islands off the coast of Scotland during the seventh and tenth centuries. Still guided by the sword hilt, Claudia and Evan meet a Pictish mute, Viking raiders, an Irish slave, and a Christian monk. The story ends in Ireland, where they become involved with an Irish princess and her Viking court. They witness the Battle of Clontarf, an actual event in which the Irish defeated the Vikings and regained control of their country. Although Jean Mercier stated in *Publishers Weekly* that "Ms. Levin has created another spell binder," other critics thought the action was too slow and the plot too complex. Cynthia Adams also noted in *School Library Journal* that readers would need a knowledge of Celtic myth in order to appreciate the fantasy.

Transported again by the magic sword hilt, this time to the nineteenth century, Claudia returns to the Orkneys alone in *The Forespoken*. She meets the boy Thomas, who is known as "the forespoken" because he was named before his christening and therefore shunned by a curse as unnatural. Thomas mistakes Claudia for a selkie, a half-human and half-sea creature that is destined to be his wife. When Thomas discovers the sword, which he thinks is a "bronze man," he wants to give it to an archaeologist. Claudia persuades him to keep it, however, and the sword draws them into an encounter with Greenland Vikings. After going back to twentieth-century Maine she sees Thomas for the last time and tries to tell him he has suffered from neglect as the result of superstition. *Horn Book* reviewer Ann A. Flowers praised Levin's realistic depiction of the Orkneys in *The Forespoken*. But, she added, "awkward transitions of time and place, as well as the complexity of the plot, will make the book fairly inaccessible to most children."

Setting her eighth novel, *A Binding Spell*, in present-day rural Maine, Levin tells the story of Wren, who is unhappy about her family's move

If you enjoy the works of Betty Levin, you may also want to check out the following books:

Chester Aaron, *Lackawanna*, 1986.
Avi, *Something Upstairs: A Tale of Ghosts*, 1988.
Margaret Mahy, *Memory*, 1988.
Patricia Pendergraft, *As Far as Mill Springs*, 1991.

to a farm. Excluded by her two brothers and a neighbor boy, Larry Pederson, who are rebuilding an old wagon they found in a barn, Wren explores the rest of the cluttered building on her own. She finds pieces of horse equipment and entertains herself with visions of a horse called Jake, which the boys cannot see. Wren also visits Axel Pederson, Larry's uncle, a recluse who lives in a dilapidated house nearby. Convinced that Axel is somehow connected with Jake, Wren enlists Larry's aid in helping the old man. They become involved in a series of mysteries, and Wren gains self-confidence as she discovers the meaning of past and present events. Reviewing the novel in *Horn Book*, Ethel R. Twichell questioned the presence of a phantom horse, which "might seem more appropriate in a setting of Celtic mythology." However, she concluded, "The growing suspense and puzzling questions about the Pederson family should . . . hold the reader's attention up to the final pages." A reviewer for *People* recommended *A Binding Spell* as a "smart, unsentimental book with a true eye for character and a strong sense of place."

Levin sets *The Ice Bear* in the imaginary northern Kingdom of Thyrne, where the evil Lord of Urris tries to assume power during the king's absence. The hero of the story is Wat, a baker's helper in the town of Oldstone, where a gigantic ice bear, a gift to the king, has been hanged in the square and its keeper killed. Seizing one of the bear's cubs, Wat flees with Kalia, the apparently retarded daughter of the bear keeper. Wat plans to win the king's favor later by returning the cub, while Kalia wants to take it to her homeland in the far north. Although Wat is too young to comprehend the significance of his act, he struggles with the conflicting needs of freedom and bondage. As Wat and Kalia encounter danger and adventure on

their journey, he discovers she is highly resource-
ful in spite of being an "idiot," and he comes to
appreciate her as a human being. By the end of
the tale Wat and Kalia have learned that each
decision has its consequences and that compromise
is often necessary. Reviewers responded positively
to *The Ice Bear*. Among them was Zena Sutherland,
who wrote in *Bulletin of the Center for Children's
Books*: "The story has a good pace and sweep; the
characters change and grow; the setting is roundly
conceived."

Revealing American History

In *The Trouble with Gramary* Levin returns to
Maine, this time placing the story in contemporary times. The main character is Merkka, who
lives in the small town of Ledgeport, where her
parents work in the fishing industry. They share
a house with Merkka's grandmother, Mary Weir,
the Gramary of the title. Gramary is an artist who
collects old machine parts for her metal sculptures
in the back yard, and neighbors consider the scrap
heap to be unsightly. Worse, it is a deterrent to
tourism. As the story opens, Gramary is being
pressured by a real-estate developer to sell her
harbor-front property. But she will not yield, and
her stubbornness causes conflicting emotions in
Merrka. Although she has a close bond with
Gramary, she is embarrassed by her grandmother's
behavior, especially when school friends say
Gramary is actually "Mary Weird," a witch with
mysterious powers. At the end of the novel, when
Gramary dies of a stroke, Merkka realizes that she
admires the elderly woman's courage and commitment to her convictions.

Reviewers greeted *The Trouble with Gramary* enthu-
siastically. Frances Bradburn observed in *Wilson
Library Bulletin* that Levin "has given a very special gift to her middle readers. In *The Trouble with
Gramary* she, like Mary Weir, conveys the confidence that her readers are bright enough, strong
enough, and loving enough to handle a very realistic portrait of the aging, inevitable decline, and
death of a very special older adult." Bradburn also
commended Levin's portrayal of Merkka's arrival
at a new level of maturity, stating that young
readers "will see Merkka draw from her grandmother's strength and acceptance of the courage
to live life to its fullest in spite of its perils, both
real and imagined." Nancy Vasilakis wrote an
equally positive response in *Horn Book*. Noting that

In the midst of the terrible wildfires in Maine, Meg
witnesses her "backward" cousin involved in an act
she can neither tell about or forget.

Merkka's family would be moving out of the
house after Gramary's death, Vasilakis points out
that "the author has made it clear to her readers
that the narrow confines of the conventional world
are no more likely to restrict the vision of her
young heroine than they did her grandmother."

The Trouble with Gramary was followed by *Brother
Moose*, which depicts a shocking event in American history. During the nineteenth century thousands of orphaned and poor children were sent
to live with families in rural areas. Instead of
experiencing a better life, as well-meaning adop-
tion agencies had intended, the children were often mistreated and exploited. Drawing on these
facts, Levin tells the story of Nell and her "almost sister" Louisa, Canadian orphans who are

placed with families in northern Maine. The girls eventually become lost in the wilderness and meet Joe, a Native American, and his grandson, who promise to take them back to Nell's new family. It is wintertime, and their arduous journey through the woods is plagued by hardship and danger. The characters also have personal conflicts. Although Nell suspects Joe may have murdered someone, she comes to respect his customs and survival skills. A critic for the *New York Times Book Review* found *Brother Moose* to be a "chilling historical tale well told." Nancy Vasilakis wrote in a *Horn Book* review that "For those readers up to the challenge, [the novel is] an uncompromising unconventional survival story." *Brother Moose* was chosen as a Best Book for Young Adults by the American Library Association in 1990.

During the 1990s Levin was honored for two other books, *Mercy's Mill,* and a work for younger readers, *Away To Me, Moss!* Selected for the New York Public Library Books for the Teen Age list, *Mercy's Mill* is a time-travel story set in nineteenth-century Massachusetts. The main character, Sarah, moves from the city to an old house in the country with her mother, stepfather, baby brother, and foster sister. Bored and unhappy with her new home, Sarah wanders off while her parents are remodeling an old mill they plan to use as an antiques shop. She falls into the mill pond, then plunges headlong into a complex mystery when she is saved by Jethro. He claims to be a runaway slave who has entered the twentieth century through the mill. Jethro is looking for Mercy, an abused child from colonial New England who had time-traveled into the nineteenth century. Sarah helps Jethro find Mercy, at the same time protecting him from authorities who will charge him with truancy.

Through her friendship with Jethro and the search for Mercy, Sarah gains a new understanding of her family, especially her foster sister. However, she and the reader must decide the truth about Jethro: is he a time traveler, or is he actually an abused boy who has created the story to mask his own harsh reality? In a review for *Publishers Weekly* Diane Roback and Richard Donahue wrote that "Levin masterfully explores the concept of time, in an illuminating blend of history and fantasy." Deborah Abbott was equally impressed with the book, observing in *Booklist* that "Levin, who has written many fine novels for this age [young adults], includes many fascinating items about the

history of the mill, a stop on the Underground Railroad, and tantalizes the reader with details about witchcraft in early American history."

"The themes I'm drawn to and the situations I explore through fiction reflect not only the places and people and ways of life I love, but also the baffling aspects of the human condition—human traits that sadden and trouble me."

—Betty Levin

Levin continued to portray complex family relationships in her next book, *Fire in the Wind.* It is the story of Meg, who lives in Maine with her extended family in 1947 when wildfires threatened homes in the backwoods. Although Meg wants to protect her "backward" cousin Orin, she must cope with the consequences of his destructive behavior. Meg sees Orin set a fire that burns down her house, but she keeps his secret when he rescues her and her brother. Finally she tells her family about Orin's act, only to discover he was really a hero because he had set a backfire that saved the barn. Meg comes to realize that Orin does not need her protection, and she and her family undergo other changes as they struggle with wildfires. In a review for *Horn Book,* Maeve Visser Knoth commended Levin's depiction of a period in Maine history: "The book's vivid setting and details of life during and after a terrifying fire are memorable, and the balance of the tense plot with strong characterization makes this a powerful read." Although Carol A. Edwards also called *Fire in the Wind* "an appealing combination of history and adventure" in a review for *School Library Journal,* she concluded that the book "just doesn't quite live up to the promise of the first few paragraphs."

A more recent novel is *Island Bound.* The main character is Chris, a boy who is staying alone for a week on deserted Fowlers Island, which is supposedly haunted. But Chris is determined to prove he can brave any potential danger. Soon he meets Joellen, who is accompanying her father as he studies puffins that have been recently reintroduced to their natural habitat. The two young people then attempt to solve a series of mysteries, including the sighting of a ghost and the discovery of a journal that suggests one of Chris's ancestors may have committed a murder. A *Kirkus Reviews* contributor termed *Island Bound* "an ambitious undertaking," yet pointed out that the plot is so "disorienting" that the reader will not be able to determine whether there actually was a ghost or even if Joellen "somehow controlled events . . . , or if she was just the victim of uncanny circumstances."

Since the late 1980s, when her husband Alvin died of complications from a respiratory infection, Levin has lived alone on their sheep farm. Characterizing this new stage in her life, she wrote in the *SAAS* essay: "In one sense that is the end of my story as well as his, because we were so much a part of each other. But my life continues, full of farming and writing and teaching, enlivened by my beloved family and friends and my dear, indispensable dogs. And if that is true, which it is, then I suppose his life continues along with mine."

■ Works Cited

Abbott, Deborah, review of *Mercy's Mill, Booklist,* December 1, 1992, pp. 670-71.

Adams, Cynthia, review of *A Griffon's Nest, School Library Journal,* September 1975, pp. 121-22.

Review of *A Binding Spell, People,* December 17, 1984.

Bradburn, Frances, review of *The Trouble with Gramary, Wilson Library Bulletin,* October, 1988.

Review of *Brother Moose, New York Times Book Review,* July 29, 1990, p. 33.

Edwards, Carol A., review of *Fire in the Wind, School Library Journal,* October, 1995, p. 136.

Fasick, Adele M., *Twentieth-Century Children's Writers,* 4th edition, St. James Press, 1995.

Flowers, Ann A., review of *The Forespoken, Horn Book,* February, 1977, p. 58.

Gregory, Helen, review of *The Sword of Culann, Library Journal,* October 15, 1973, p. 3156.

Review of *Island Bound, Kirkus Reviews,* June 15, 1997, pp. 951-52.

Knoth, Maeve Visser, review of *Fire in the Wind, Horn Book,* March, 1996.

Levin, Betty, essay in *Something About the Author Autobiography Series,* Volume 11, Gale, 1991, pp. 197-211.

Mercier, Jean, review of *A Griffon's Nest, Publishers Weekly,* August 18, 1975, p. 68.

Roback, Diane, and Richard Donahue, review of *Mercy's Mill,* September 21, 1992, p. 95.

Sutherland, Zena, review of *The Ice Bear, Bulletin of the Center for Children's Books,* January, 1987, p. 91.

Twichell, Ethel R., review of *A Binding Spell, Horn Book,* November 12, 1984, p. 759.

Vasilakis, Nancy, review of *The Trouble with Gramary, Horn Book,* May/June, 1988, pp. 352-53.

Vasilakis, Nancy, review of *Brother Moose, Horn Book,* September/October, 1990, pp. 605-6.

■ For More Information See

BOOKS

Contemporary Authors, New Revision Series, Volume 50, Gale, 1996.

Sixth Book of Junior Authors and Illustrators, edited by Sally Holmes Holtze, H. W. Wilson, 1989.

PERIODICALS

Booklist, November 15, 1984, p. 449; May 1, 1990, p. 1598; December 1, 1992, p. 670.

Booktalker, January, 1991, p. 4.

Bulletin of the Center for Children's Books, January, 1975, p. 81; January, 1976, p. 81; April, 1981, p. 155; July/August, 1985; May, 1990, p. 219.

Fantasy Review, January, 1987, p. 45.

Five Owls, February, 1995, pp. 63-64.

Horn Book, January/February, 1977; November/December, 1979, pp. 669-70; January/February, 1993, p. 92; September/October, 1994, pp. 587-88.

Kirkus Reviews, November 1, 1973, pp. 1212-13; April 15, 1975, p. 465; July 15, 1976, p. 799; August 15, 1992, p. 1064; May 15, 1994, p. 702.

Library Journal, December, 1984, p. 101.

Publishers Weekly, June 18, 1973, p. 70; September 17, 1973, p. 57; May 13, 1988, pp. 277-78; September 21, 1992, p. 95.

Quill & Quire, February, 1991, p. 25.

School Library Journal, September, 1973, p. 71; October, 1973, p. 126; October, 1976, p. 118; November, 1979, pp. 89-90; October, 1986, p. 192; April, 1988, p. 102; July, 1990, p. 77; September, 1992, p. 278.

Times Educational Supplement, June 5, 1987.

Times Literary Supplement, July 24, 1987, p. 804.

Voice of Youth Advocates, August, 1981, pp. 29-30; December, 1986, p. 220; August, 1988, p. 132.

Wilson Library Bulletin, October, 1988, p. 78; January, 1991, p. 4.*

—Sketch by Peggy Saari

George Lucas

Agency. Founder of American Zoetrope, with Francis Ford Coppola, 1969; founder of Industrial Light and Magic (a special effects company), San Rafael, CA, 1976; founder of Lucasfilm Ltd., San Anselmo, CA, and of Sprocket Systems, 1980. *Member:* Writers Guild of America, Academy of Motion Picture Arts and Sciences, Screen Directors Guild.

■ Personal

Born George Walton Lucas Jr., May 14, 1944, in Modesto, CA; son of George (a retail merchant) and Dorothy Lucas; married Marcia Griffin (a film editor), February 22, 1969 (divorced, 1984); children: Amanda. *Education:* Modesto Junior College, A.A., 1964; University of Southern California, B.A., 1966.

■ Addresses

Home—San Anselmo, CA. *Office*—c/o Lucasfilm Ltd., P.O. Box 2009, San Rafael, CA 94912.

■ Career

Director of motion pictures and writer, 1971—; executive producer of films, 1979—. Assistant to Francis Ford Coppola for films *Finian's Rainbow* (editor and cameraman), 1967, and *The Rain People* (assistant art editor and assistant cameraman), 1969; worked as a cameraman for director Saul Bass and as a film editor for U.S. Information

■ Awards, Honors

Received Third National Student Film Festival Award, 1967-68, for *THX 1138;* Golden Globe Award, Best Screenplay Award from New York Film Critics, and from the National Society of Film Critics, and nominations from the Academy of Motion Picture Arts and Sciences for Best Screenplay, Best Director, and Best Film, all 1973, all for *American Graffiti;* Best Film Award from the Los Angeles Film Critics, Oscars for art direction, sound, score, costume design, visual effects, editing, and sound effects editing, and nominations from the Academy of Motion Picture Arts and Sciences, for Best Director and Best Film, all 1977, and British Fantasy Award nomination, 1979, all for *Star Wars;* recipient of numerous other film awards.

■ Writings

American Graffiti, Grove, 1974.
(With Alan Dean Foster; published under Lucas's name alone) *Star Wars,* Ballantine, 1976.

(With Chris Claremont) *Shadow Moon*, Bantam, 1995.

Also author of original stories for films *More American Graffiti*, 1979, *The Empire Strikes Back*, 1980, (with Philip Kaufman) *Raiders of the Lost Ark*, 1981, *Return of the Jedi*, 1983, *Indiana Jones and the Temple of Doom*, 1984, *Indiana Jones and the Last Crusade*, 1989, and *Radioland Murders*, 1994; author of original stories for television movies, including *The Ewok Adventure*, 1985, and *Ewoks: The Battle for Endor*, 1986.

SCREENPLAYS

(With Walter Murch; and director) *THX 1138*, Warner Bros., 1971.

(With Gloria Katz and Willard Huyck; and director) *American Graffiti*, Universal, 1973.

(And director) *Star Wars*, starring Mark Hamill, Harrison Ford, and Carrie Fisher, Twentieth Century-Fox, 1977, twentieth anniversary re-release, 1997.

(And executive producer) *The Empire Strikes Back* (sequel to *Star Wars*), Twentieth Century-Fox, 1980, twentieth anniversary re-release, 1997.

(And executive producer) *Raiders of the Lost Ark*, Lucasfilm, 1981.

(With Lawrence Kasdan; and producer) *Return of the Jedi* (third film in the *Star Wars* trilogy), Twentieth Century-Fox, 1983, twentieth anniversary re-release, 1997.

(And executive producer) *Star Wars Ewoks and Droids Adventure Hour* (weekly television show), ABC-TV, 1985.

Also author of three alternate *Star Wars* scripts; developer of unproduced script, *Apocalypse Now*.

■ Additional Film Credits

PRODUCER

More American Graffiti, Lucasfilm, 1979.
The Ewok Adventure (television film), ABC-TV, 1984.

Also producer of video game *The Dig*.

EXECUTIVE PRODUCER

(With Akira Kurosawa) *Kagemusha* (also known as *The Double*), Fox, 1980.
Body Heat, Warner Bros., 1981.

Twice Upon a Time, Warner Bros., 1983.
Indiana Jones and the Temple of Doom (sequel to *Raiders of the Lost Ark*), Paramount, 1984.
(With Francis Ford Coppola) *Mishima*, Warner Bros., 1985.
Labyrinth, starring David Bowie, Tri-Star, 1986.
Howard the Duck, Universal, 1986.
(Author of original story; collaborator on screenplay with Ron Howard and Bob Dolman) *Willow*, Lucasfilm, 1988.
Tucker: The Man and His Dream, starring Jeff Bridges, Zoetrope Studios, 1988.
(With Steven Spielberg) *The Land Before Time*, Universal, 1988.
Indiana Jones and the Last Crusade (sequel to *Indiana Jones and the Temple of Doom*), Paramount, 1989.
Radioland Murders, Universal, 1994.

Also executive producer for *Captain Eo*, Walt Disney, and for *Wow!*, 1990.

OTHER

Film editor for *Herbie*, 1966, and *Jurassic Park*, 1993; received screen credit for *Return to Oz*, 1985.

Appeared in films in the roles of Supervisor at Spaceport, *Star Tours*, 1987, in *The Magical World of Chuck Jones*, Warner Bros., 1992, and as Disappointed Man, *Beverly Hills Cop III*, 1994.

■ Work In Progress

Lucas plans to produce and direct the first of three "prequels" to the original Star Wars films that he has written.

■ Adaptations

In 1978, Ballantine publishers released *Splinter of the Mind's Eye* by Alan Dean Foster, a novel featuring George Lucas's characters from *Star Wars*. Numerous works in the series have since been published by such authors as Kevin J. Anderson and Timothy Zahn.

■ Overview

George Lucas is one of the best-known names in American filmmaking. His two trilogies of films, the "Star Wars" and the "Indiana Jones" epics, revolutionized the making of movies in America during the 1970s and 1980s. They are among the highest-grossing films of all time. They also introduced a new generation of American children to unadulterated excitement, adventure, and optimism. Lucas's films typically mix archetypal figures, familiar (but universal) themes, and the eternal conflict between good heroes and evil villains. In films such as *The Empire Strikes Back* and *Indiana Jones and the Last Crusade,* Lucas evokes mythic qualities in his characters. "I want 'Star Wars' to give people a faraway, exotic environment for their imagination to run free," Lucas tells Jean Vallely in a *Rolling Stone* interview. "I want them to get beyond their basic stupidities of the moment and think about colonizing Venus and Mars. And the only way it's going to happen is to have some kid fantasize about getting his ray gun, jumping in his spaceship and flying off into outer space."

Both the "Star Wars" and the "Indiana Jones" films grew out of Lucas's own childhood in Modesto, California. He was influenced during his 1950s childhood by trips to Disneyland, reading comic books, and watching television. "I read Tommy Tomorrow and, of course, lots of (other) comics," he tells Kerry O'Quinn in *Starlog* magazine. "Mostly DC comics—Batman and Superman. But I was also real keen on Donald Duck and Scrooge McDuck." "I loved Disneyland," he confides to Dale Pollack in the biography *Skywalking: The Life and Films of George Lucas.* "I wandered around, I'd go on the rides and bumper cars, the steamboats, the shooting galleries, the jungle rides. I was in heaven." But perhaps the greatest influence on his later filmmaking career was television. "My favorite things were Republic serials and things like Flash Gordon," he tells O'Quinn. "There was a television program called 'Adventure Theater' at 6:00 every night. We didn't have a TV set, so I used to go over to a friend's house and we watched it religiously. It was a twenty-minute serial chapter, and the left over minutes of the half hour was filled with 'Crusader Rabbit.' I loved it."

By the early 1960s, Lucas had moved into a different sphere. "That was my period when I hung out with a real bad element," he tells Pollack. "The only way to keep from getting the s—— pounded out of you was to hang out with some really tough guys who happened to be your friends. . . . They'd send me in and wait until somebody would try to pick a fight with me. Then they would come in and pound 'em. I was the bait. I was always afraid that I was gonna get pounded myself." An early fascination with cars and automobile racing led to a serious accident in 1962. "I spent some time in the hospital," he tells O'Quinn in *Starlog,* "and I realized that it probably wouldn't be smart for me to be a race driver." Lucas nearly died in the crash. His life was saved when his seat belt broke, throwing him free of the car. "You can't have that kind of experience and not feel that there must be a reason why you're here," he explains to Pollack. "I realized that I should be spending my time trying to figure out what that reason is and trying to fulfill it. The fact is, there is no way I would have survived that accident if I'd been wrapped around that tree. Actually, that seat belt never should have broken, under any circumstances."

Later that year, Lucas enrolled in Modesto Junior College, intending to study social sciences and concentrating in psychology, sociology, and anthropology. He completed the program and, following a friend's suggestion, enrolled in the film school at the University of Southern California in 1964. "I suddenly discovered how exciting films were," he says in an article in the *American Film Institute Report.* "I was fascinated by all the technical aspects of it. I never got over the magic of it all." "When I finally decided that I was going to be a filmmaker," Lucas states in an interview with Stephen Farber in *Film Quarterly,* ". . . I lost a lot of face because for hot rodders the idea of going into film was really a goofy idea. And that was in the early sixties. Nobody went into film at that time. At USC the girls from the dorms all gave a wide berth to the film students because they were supposed to be weird."

"There was a small group of us that were making films," Lucas tells O'Quinn, "while the rest of the class sat around and said, 'Gee, we can't make movies—the teacher won't let us do this, or I can't do that, or you never get a break around here.' While they were complaining about why they never got to make movies I made *eight* movies." Other members of Lucas's group included writer/directors Matthew Robbins, John Milius, Willard Huyck, and Robert Zemeckis; writers David S. Ward and Dan O'Bannon; producer Howard Kazanjian; editor Walter Murch; and directors Randal Kleiser and John Carpenter. "We were like foreigners living in a strange country and all speaking the same language," Lucas remembers in an interview with Audie Bock in *Take One*, "all of us banding together to beat on the doors of Hollywood. We would share resources— if you needed something a friend would tell you where to get it from. And we all looked at each other's work, mostly at student film festivals. That's how Steve Spielberg got to be a member of the group. . . . He was at Long Beach State, but we met through film festivals."

One of the eight films Lucas made as a student was *Electronic Labyrinth: THX 1138: 4EB*. It was a science fiction film that presented a stark vision of a grim future, and traces every movement of a man on the run through the point of view of cameras and monitor screens placed along a blind-

ing white corridor. It won the Best Film Award at the 3rd National Student Film Festival in 1967-68. It also won Lucas the attention of Hollywood powers and the esteem of his peers. "I won a couple of scholarships at the end of that semester—one to watch Carl Foreman make 'McKenna's Gold' out in the desert and make a little behind the scenes movie, and the other was a Warner's scholarship where you observe movie-making for six months," he tells O'Quinn. "Well, it takes about a week of watching for you to get bored. After that you've seen all that you could possibly see about making a movie."

In July 1967, Lucas began an apprenticeship at Warner Brothers, working with Francis Ford Coppola. "I had already been through all of this

Lucas's first big-screen success was the 1973 film *American Graffiti*, starring Ron Howard and Cindy Williams, which looked at one night in the life of a group of California teenagers in the early 1960s.

on another scholarship, the Carl Foreman grant, so what I wanted to do was get into the animation department, steal some footage or whatever and start making a film," he says in his interview with Bock. "About three weeks into the picture I told Francis I was bored, but he said, 'Look, kid, stick with me and I'll give you things to do.' He did and it turned out that we complimented each other very well. I was essentially an editor and cameraman, while Francis is a writer and director—more into actors and acting." In 1967 and 1968, Lucas worked with Coppola on *Finian's Rainbow* and *The Rain People*. Later Coppola supported Lucas during the making of Lucas's first feature film, an expanded version of his student film *THX 1138*.

THX 1138 proved to have a rough trip to its release. Coppola and Lucas jointly formed a production company, American Zoetrope, with Lucas's film as one of its first productions. On November 21, 1969, Warner Brothers cancelled its deal with Zoetrope and took *THX 1138* away from Lucas to re-cut themselves. "Francis had borrowed all this money from Warner Bros. to set this thing up," he tells Vallely, "and when the studio saw a rough cut of 'THX' and the scripts of the movie we wanted to make, they said, 'This is all junk. You have to pay back all the money you owe us.' Which is why Francis did 'Godfather.' He was so much in debt he didn't have any choice." *THX 1138* was finally released in 1971 to a lukewarm reception. "I realized after 'THX' that people don't care about how the country's being ruined," Lucas says to Farber. "I would make a more optimistic film that makes people feel positive about their fellow human beings. It's too easy to be optimistic when everything tells you to be pessimistic and cynical. I'm a very bad cynic." "Maybe kids will walk out of the film and for a second they'll feel, 'We could really make something out of this country, or we could really make something out of our lives,'" he concludes. "It's all that hokey stuff about being a good neighbor, and the American spirit and all that crap. There *is* something in it."

The Big Break

Lucas's next film won him a reputation as a major American filmmaker. It was a nostalgic look at teenage life in 1962 entitled *American Graffiti*. Lucas directed the film with the help of friends Gary Kurtz and Coppola on a shoestring budget of $780,000. Universal executives disliked the loosely-plotted movie, but nonetheless decided to release it in 1973. Two years later it had grossed $50 million and had won a Golden Globe award for best comedy, New York Film Critics and National Society of Film Critics awards for best screenplay, and five Oscar nominations. "The film is about change," Lucas tells Farber. "It's about the change in rock and roll, it's about the change in a young person's life at 18 when he leaves home and goes off to college; and it's about the cultural change that took place when the fifties turned into the sixties—when we went from a country of apathy and non-involvement to a country of radical involvement. The film is saying that you have to go forward."

American Graffiti gave Lucas the political and economic clout in Hollywood to make his next film. "I expected 'American Graffiti' to be a semi-successful film and make maybe $10 million—which would be classified in Hollywood as a success—and then I went through the roof when it became this big, huge blockbuster," he states in an interview with Paul Scanlon in *Rolling Stone*. "And they said, well, gee, how are you going to top that? And I said, yeah, it was a one-shot and I was really lucky. I never really expected that to happen again." "I was thinking about quitting directing," he says to Vallely, "but I had this huge draft of a screenplay and I had sort of fallen in love with it." The script was very large—far larger than Lucas could use for a single film. "I wanted to make a fairy tale epic, but this was like *War and Peace*," he continues in his interview with Vallely. "So I took that script and cut it in half, put the first half aside and decided to write the screenplay from the second." The second half also expanded beyond the limits of a single film, so it in turn was cut into three parts—and they became the genesis of the *Star Wars* films: *Star Wars*, *The Empire Strikes Back*, and *Return of the Jedi*.

Space Operas and Fantastic Adventures

Lucas began filming *Star Wars* in 1976, on location in Tunisia and in London. So complex were the special effects that Lucas had to form his own company, Industrial Light and Magic, to handle them. Despite the efforts that went into the production, Lucas invited no comparisons with other science-fiction films, such as Stanley Kubrick's *2001: A Space Odyssey*. Lucas insists in his inter-

Indiana Jones, Lucas's intrepid archaeologist, explorer, and treasure hunter played by Harrison Ford, made his debut in the rollicking 1984 film, *Raiders of the Lost Ark*.

view with Scanlon that *Star Wars* is primarily "a space fantasy that was more in the genre of Edgar Rice Burroughs; that whole other end of space fantasy that was there before science took it over in the fifties. Once the atomic bomb came, everybody got into monsters and science. . . . I think speculative fiction is very valid but they forgot the fairy tales and the dragons and Tolkien and all the *real* heroes." Drawing on his experience in anthropology and psychology, Lucas hoped that *Star Wars* would provide a modern fairy tale for younger generations.

Critics were strongly divided on the merits of *Star Wars*, despite the fact that it won seven Oscars for art direction, sound, score, costume design, visual effects, editing, and sound effects editing. Robert G. Collins declared in the *Journal of Popular Culture* that the film "functions as magic. With incredible audacity, it combines the stereotypes of modern pop literature and cinema with the Arthurian Romance." *America* critic Richard A. Blake called the film "original and surprising. It

is witty, not only in its comic dialogue, but in its ability to spoof itself and the science-fiction genre without going for the cheap laugh." On the other hand, *New Republic* reviewer Stanley Kauffman stated that "the only way that *Star Wars* could have been interesting was through its visual imagination and special effects. Both are unexceptional." And Arthur Lubow, writing in *Film Comment*, compared elements of the film to the Nazi propaganda movies of Leni Riefenstahl. "*Star Wars* is a paean to mysticism and an attack on modern science," he stated. "That message has a powerful appeal. It was the essence of the Nazi myth, and that's worth pointing out—not because the analogy makes *Star Wars* a 'fascist movie' (its good humor and lack of rancor insure that it's not), but because it explains some of the buzz of excitement from the audiences leaving the movie theater."

Despite critical misgivings about the themes and presentation of *Star Wars*, the financial returns on the movie and the sales of its tie-in merchandise gave Lucas the funds he needed to create his own production company, Lucasfilm. He also was able to build Industrial Light and Magic into a leading producer of motion picture special effects. In 1980 and 1983, he produced two more episodes in the *Star Wars* saga: *The Empire Strikes Back* and *Return of the Jedi*. He also produced several straight adventure films in conjunction with Stephen Spielberg: *Raiders of the Lost Ark* (1981), *Indiana Jones and the Temple of Doom* (1984), and *Indiana Jones and the Last Crusade* (1989). All three were based on action-adventure stories like the serials Lucas had grown up watching on television. They also drew on Lucas's background in anthropology: the protagonist, Indiana Jones, is an itinerant archaeologist who travels around the world on his swashbuckling adventures.

Raiders of the Lost Ark was a great commercial success, grossing almost as highly as the lucrative *Star Wars* had done. Lucas recruited friend and director Steven Spielberg to direct the film, and critics recognized Spielberg's influence on the final product. Reviewers praised the way Lucas and Spielberg evoked the feeling and the pace of the great Saturday morning movie serials. Vincent Canby, writing in the *New York Times*, explained that from the very beginning of the film, "'Raiders of the Lost Ark' is off and running at a breakneck pace that simply won't stop until the final shot, an ironic epilogue that recalls nothing less than 'Citizen Kane.' That, however, is the only high-toned reference in a movie that otherwise devotes itself exclusively to the glorious days of the B-picture." Canby praised the film extravagantly, calling it "one of the most deliriously funny, ingenious and stylish American adventure movies ever made." "It is an homage to old-time movie serials and back-lot cheapies that transcends its inspirations," the reviewer concluded, "to become, in effect, the movie we saw in our imaginations as we watched, say, Buster Crabbe in 'Flash Gordon's Trip to Mars' or in Sam Katzman's 'Jungle Jim' movies." *Raiders*, in which Indy chased around the world—from a trap-filled cave in the highlands of South America to the snow-encrusted mountains of Tibet to the burning desert of lower Egypt—to keep the lost Ark of the Covenant out of the hands of Nazi troopers, set the tone for its two sequels, *Indiana Jones and the Temple of Doom* and *Indiana Jones and the Last Crusade.*

Lucas served as executive producer for the 1988 film *Tucker: A Man and His Dream*, **which follows the life of Preston Tucker, an industrialist who in 1946 designed the car of the future.**

Indiana Jones and the Temple of Doom echoed the commercial success of *Raiders of the Lost Ark,* but several reviewers felt overall that the sequel lacked the drive and thought of the first film. Its images repeated those of *Raiders:* it begins with a break-neck chase scene (this time in a sleazy Hong Kong nightclub), and continued with a bumpy plane ride over the Himalayas and a sudden drop into the jungles of India. Accompanied by an unhappy nightclub singer and a young boy named Short Round, Indy sets out to recover a rare gem from the hands of a renegade bloody priest of Kali and (at the same time) to rescue the children of a remote Indian village from slavery. Several critics felt that the film substituted shock for plot—at one point, the heroine reaches into a crevice and brings her hand out covered with insects and worms. Nonetheless, the film was very popular with audiences, and its most famous scene, a wild bullet-strewn chase through a mining tunnel, has entered into film history as one of the most harrowing adventure scenes in the history of the motion pictures.

Indiana Jones and the Last Crusade was the final chapter in the Indiana Jones trilogy, and it continued the patterns set by the previous two. "When 'Raiders of the Lost Ark' appeared," writes critic Roger Ebert in the Chicago *Sun-Times,* "it defined a new energy level for adventure movies; it was a delirious breakthrough." However, the critic concludes, in this final chapter the series appeared to be winding down. "The Jones movies by now have defined a familiar world of death-defying stunts, virtuoso chases, dry humor and the quest for impossible goals in unthinkable places," Ebert states. "But there was no way for Spielberg to top himself, and perhaps it is just as well that 'Last Crusade' will indeed be Indy's last film." *Last Crusade* introduces Professor Henry Jones, Indy's father (played by Sean Connery), and sends him and his son on a chase through 1930s Europe searching for the cup that Jesus Christ used in the Last Supper. Despite his disappointment in the lack of innovation in *Indiana Jones and the Last Crusade,* Ebert praised the film as a good piece of escapist adventure fiction. "'Raiders of the Lost Ark,' now more than ever, seems a turning point in the cinema of escapist entertainment," Ebert concludes, "and there was really no way Spielberg could make it new all over again. What he has done is to take many of the same elements, and apply all of his craft and sense of fun to make them work yet once again. And they do."

The space operas and fantasy adventures of Luke Skywalker and Indiana Jones were Lucas's most popular films. However, he was also involved in the production of *Labyrinth* (1986) and the surprise fantasy hit *Willow* (1988). Several of his other efforts, however—most notably *Howard the Duck* (1986)—were financial and critical failures. Between productions, Lucas completed the building of Skywalker Ranch, his home near San Rafael, California, and expanded Lucasfilm to include separate animation, theater operations, post-production, retailing, and computer gaming facilities. "Ever since I was in film school in the '60s," he tells *Time*'s Gerald Clarke, "I've been on a train. Back then I was pushing a 147-car train up a very steep slope—push, push, push: I pushed it all the way up, and when 'Star Wars' came along in 1977, I reached the top. I jumped on board, and then it started going down the other side of the hill. I've had the brakes on ever since."

■ Update

Lucas's career—which had been quiet since the release of his last Indiana Jones movie in 1989—picked up again in the mid-1990s with the rerelease of *Star Wars, The Empire Strikes Back,* and *Return of the Jedi.* Lucas took the opportunity to clean old prints of the films, augment the sound tracks, and add new scenes and characters using enhanced computer graphics and imaging that were not available when the movies were originally released. "I wanted to preserve ('Star Wars' and its subsequent two sequels) so that it would continue to be a viable piece of entertainment into the 21st century," Lucas declared in an article published in *CNN Online.* The three films were released at approximately three-week intervals during January, February, and March of 1997. Lucasfilm and Twentieth Century-Fox called the revamped films the *Star Wars Trilogy Special Edition* and hoped that they would prove as popular with audiences of the 1990s as they had with audiences twenty years earlier. Their hopes were more than realized. By mid-February, *Star Wars* had passed *E.T.—The Extraterrestrial* as the highest grossing film of all time.

Lucas had recognized that the films had fallen short of his original vision even as he released them. "It's not that I didn't like the movies," he said in a *Rolling Stone* interview with Scanlon, "but if I look at them now, each one falls a bit

"The Force" was with moviegoers again in 1997 as Lucas celebrated the twentieth anniversary of *Star Wars* by rereleasing restored and updated versions of the the films in the *Star Wars* trilogy starring Mark Hamill as Luke Skywalker, Carrie Fisher as Princess Leia, and Harrison Ford as Han Solo.

short of what I had hoped it to be—because I guess I either set my sights a little bit lower, or we actually do get a little bit better." The sequel films, Lucas explained, got closer to his vision as he proceeded, in part because of increased funding and in part because of improved special effects made possible by new computer technology. "So a lot of these things I have finally worked out," he told Scanlon. "I finally got the end battle the way I wanted it, I got the ground battle that I wanted, I got the monsters the way I wanted them."

Speculation was rife among fans of the films about the changes Lucas had made. "[On] *Star Wars*, you know, we had this kind of low-budget,

young director, and all these problems that we had to cope with, which made the picture less than what it could be," Lucas says in his 1997 Mr. Showbiz interview. Some of the new technology was used simply to clean up and restore the twenty-year-old picture, but Lucas also took the opportunity to introduce new creatures (dewbacks and rontos, added by means of digital matting and computer animation) and to increase the visibility of the explosions and other special effects. He added a scene that had been cut from the original film—a scene in which Han Solo confronted Jabba the Hutt, who reappeared in *Return of the Jedi*. In the final version released to theaters in January of 1997, almost five minutes had been added to the length of *Star Wars*. "Basically, he's

If you enjoy the works of George Lucas, you may also want to check out the following books and films:

The works of Lois McMaster Bujold, including *The Warrior's Apprentice*, 1986, *Shards of Honor*, 1991, and *Barraryar*, 1991.

Clive Cussler's "Dirk Pitt" novels, including *Raise the Titanic*, 1976, and *Treasure*, 1988.

The *"Star Trek"* films, including *Star Trek 2: The Wrath of Khan*, 1982.

Swashbuckling films like *The Adventures of Robin Hood*, 1938, and *The Three Musketeers*, 1974.

stretched the film like an old T-shirt to fit a much broader audience," states reviewer Paul Tatara in a *CNN Online* article. "The result is an extremely pleasant diversion—instant nostalgia for the old folks, and just a hell of a lot of fun for anyone, regardless of their age, who loves the thrill of a good old-fashioned popcorn movie."

The other two films had smaller additions. In *The Empire Strikes Back,* the wampa (the snow creature that seizes Luke and the animal he is riding, the tauntaun, at the beginning of the film) is seen for the first time clearly. In his Mr. Showbiz interview, Lucas explains the problems confronting himself and the director Irvin Kershner when the movie was originally made: "We built a snow monster; it just looked terrible. It was Kershner who said, 'We can't let this stay in here.' And I said, 'You're right, it's terrible.' So we cut it out. We had someone else do another little tiny puppet that we used just marginally to give you the impression of a monster. But we all wanted to have that monster." Other changes include an improved vision of Cloud City and of bounty hunter Boba Fett's ship *Slave I*. In *Return of the Jedi,* new aliens have been added to the scene at Jabba the Hutt's palace and some of the previous creatures have been replaced by computer-generated graphical versions. "A lot of these things are things you want on the set that you have to make compromises for," Lucas concludes. "And you say, 'Now we are going to do it the way we wanted to do it then.'"

New Versions Meet With Success

Although film purists objected to the proposed changes, most critics celebrated the films on their rerelease. "In spite of its status as an icon, 'Star Wars' does still hold its own," wrote Marshall Fine in *Florida Today Space Online*. "There's a reason this film is so beloved and so influential—and the reason is that it is still a great movie." "If the last time you saw 'Star Wars' on a big screen was the late 1970s—or if you've never seen it in a theater—you owe it to yourself not to miss this opportunity to view one of the watershed films of movie history the way it was meant to be seen," he concluded. Roger Ebert, in a review published in the Chicago *Sun-Times* online, explained that "To see 'Star Wars' again after 20 years is to revisit a place in the mind. George Lucas' space epic has colonized our imaginations, and it is hard to stand back and see it simply as a motion picture, because it has so completely become part of our memories. It's as goofy as a children's tale, as shallow as an old Saturday afternoon serial, as corny as Kansas in August—and a masterpiece."

At the same time that the twentieth-anniversary versions of the *Star Wars* trilogy were released, Lucas announced his intention of creating a series of three "prequels" to the films. He explained that he would produce and direct the first in the series, just as he had done with the original *Star Wars* films. "I can tell another story about what happened to Luke after this trilogy ends," Lucas said in his *Rolling Stone* interview with Scanlon. "All the prequel stories exist: where Darth Vader came from, the whole story about Darth Vader and Ben Kenobi, and it all takes place before Luke was born." Lucas had enough story outlines and plots for a total of six films—which explains why the original *Star Wars* begins with the onscreen title "Episode IV: A New Hope." "After the first film came out, and suddenly it was a giant hit," he says in his Mr. Showbiz interview, "I said, 'Oh, I get to do these two movies.' Everyone said, 'What [else] are you going to do?' I said, 'Gee, I could do these back stories too. That would be interesting.' That's where the [idea of] starting in episode four came [from], because I said, 'Well, maybe I could make three out of this back story.' That evolved right around the time the film was released, after I knew it was a success."

Lucas has also considered taking the *Star Wars* saga beyond the conclusion of *Return of the Jedi,* but these stories are currently not organized. "What happens to Luke afterward," he said in his 1983 *Rolling Stone* interview, "is much more ethereal." "The only notion on that one," he continues in the Mr. Showbiz interview, "is wouldn't it be fun to get all the actors to come back when they're like sixty or seventy years old, and make three more that are about them as old people." "The first six will get finished and will be the film," he concludes. "Whether I go and do a sequel of this—because I'll also be seventy—I'm not sure whether that's going to happen."

■ Works Cited

Blake, Richard A., "Two Histories of Film," *America*, June 25, 1977, pp. 568-89.

Bock, Audie, "George Lucas: An Interview," *Take One*, May 15, 1979.

Canby, Vincent, review of *Raiders of the Lost Ark*, *New York Times*, June 12, 1981.

Clarke, Gerald, "I've Got to Get My Life Back Again," *Time*, May 23, 1983.

Collins, Robert G., "'Star Wars': The Pastiche of Myth and the Yearning for a Past Future," *Journal of Popular Culture*, summer, 1977, pp. 1-10.

Ebert, Roger, review of *Indiana Jones and the Last Crusade*, *Sun-Times* (Chicago), May 24, 1989.

Ebert, Roger, "*Star Wars* Special Edition," *Sun-Times* (Chicago) online. Available at http://www.suntimes.com/ebert/old_movies/star_wars.html.

Farber, Stephen, "George Lucas: The Stinky Kid Hits the Big Time," *Film Quarterly*, spring, 1974.

Fine, Marshall, "20 Years Later, 'Star Wars' Still Packs a Wallop," *Florida Today Space Online*, January 31, 1997. Available at http://www.flatoday.com/space/explore/stories/1997/013197a.htm.

Kauffman, Stanley, "Films: 'Star Wars,'" *New Republic*, June 18, 1977, pp. 22-23.

Lubow, Arthur, "A Space 'Iliad'—The 'Star Wars' War: I," *Film Comment*, July-August, 1977.

Lucas, George, "Young Directors, New Films," *American Film Institute Report*, winter, 1977.

"The Mr. Showbiz Interview: George Lucas, January 31, 1997," http:\\www.mrshowbiz.com/features/interviews/plus/lucas.html.

O'Quinn, Kerry, "The George Lucas Saga—Chapter One: A New View," *Starlog*, July, 1981.

O'Quinn, Kerry, "The George Lucas Saga—Chapter Two: The Cold Fish Strikes Back," *Starlog*, August, 1981.

O'Quinn, Kerry, "The George Lucas Saga—Chapter Three: The Revenge of the Box Office," *Starlog*, September, 1981.

Pollack, Dale, *Skywalking: The Life and Films of George Lucas*, Harmony Books, 1983.

Scanlon, Paul, "The Force behind George Lucas," *Rolling Stone*, August 25, 1977.

Scanlon, Paul, "George Lucas Wants to Play Guitar," *Rolling Stone*, July 21/August 4, 1983.

"Spit-and-Polished 'Star Wars' Returns to the Big Screen," *CNN Online*, January 30, 1997. Available at http://www.cnn.com/EVENTS/1997/star.wars.anniversary.

Tatara, Paul, "Long, Long Ago, in Movie Era Far, Far Away . . . " *CNN Online*, February 3, 1997. Available at http://www.cnn.com/SHOWBIZ/9702/03/starwars.review/index.html.

Vallely, Jean, "The Empire Strikes Back," *Rolling Stone*, June 12, 1980.

■ For More Information See

BOOKS

Contemporary Literary Criticism, Volume 16, Gale, 1981.

Pye, Michael, and Lynda Miles, *The Movie Brats: How the Film Generation Took Over Hollywood*, Holt, 1977.

Twentieth-Century Science Fiction Writers, 3rd edition, St. James, 1989.

PERIODICALS

Analog: Science Fiction/Science Fact, May, 1990, pp. 63-64.

Daily News (New York City), October 23, 1984.

Film Quarterly, fall, 1973.

Forbes, March 11, 1996, pp. 122-29.

Journal of Popular Film, Volume 4, number 1, 1975.

Maclean's March 2, 1992, p. 54.

Nation, June 25, 1977.

New Republic, April 10, 1971; September 15, 1973.

Newsday, June 15, 1987.

Newsweek, May 31, 1993, p. 45; January 20, 1997, pp. 52-57.

New York, March 9, 1992, p. 74.

New Yorker, October 29, 1973; May 30, 1977; September 26, 1977; January 6, 1997, pp. 40-54.

New York Post, May 15, 1984.

Observer (London), June 10, 1984.

People, March 26, 1984; March 16, 1992, p. 11; February 26, 1996, p. 35.

Publishers Weekly, October 25, 1985.

Rolling Stone, December 1, 1994, p. 134.

Time, May 30, 1977; October 24, 1994, p. 78; September 30, 1996, p. 68; February 10, 1997, pp. 68-74.

Variety, June 22, 1983; June 3, 1987.

Voice of Youth Advocates, February, 1996, p. 384; April, 1996, p. 40.*

—Sketch by Kenneth R. Shepherd

Geraldine McCaughrean

Personal

Also writes as Geraldine Jones; surname is pronounced "Mc-*cork*-ran"; born June 6, 1951, in Enfield, London, England; daughter of Leslie Arthur (a fireman) and Ethel (a teacher; maiden name, Thomas) Jones; married John McCaughrean. *Education:* Attended Southgate Technical College, Middlesex, 1969-70; Christ Church College, Oxford, B.A. (honors), 1977. *Religion:* "Almost Catholic." *Hobbies and other interests:* Playing the concertina; "I have a dilapidated cabin cruiser on the local canal."

Addresses

Home—3 Melton Dr., Didcot, Oxfordshire OX11 7JP, England. *Agent*—Giles Gordon, Anthony Sheil Associates Ltd., 43 Doughty St., London WC1N 2LF, England.

Career

Thames Television, London, England, secretary, 1970-73; Marshall Cavendish Ltd., London, assistant editor, 1977-80, subeditor, 1978-79, staff writer, 1982, 1983-88; Carreras-Rothman Ltd., Aylesbury, England, editorial assistant, 1980-81; writer, 1981—. *Member:* National Union of Journalists, Journalists Against Nuclear Extermination.

Awards, Honors

Winner in short story category, All-London Literary Competition, Wandsworth Borough Council, 1979, for "The Pike"; Whitbread Award, 1987, for *A Little Lower Than the Angels*; Carnegie Medal, British Library Association, and *Guardian* Award, both 1989, both for *A Pack of Lies*; *Gold Dust* was shortlisted for the Smarties Book Prize and received the Beefeater's Children's Book of the Year Award, 1994.

Writings

YOUNG ADULT FICTION

A Little Lower Than the Angels, Oxford University Press, 1987.
A Pack of Lies, Oxford University Press, 1988.
Gold Dust, Oxford University Press, 1993.
Plundering Paradise, Oxford University Press, 1996.

RETELLINGS

One Thousand and One Arabian Nights, illustrated by Stephen Lavis, Oxford University Press, 1982.
The Canterbury Tales, illustrated by Victor Ambrus, Oxford University Press, 1984, Rand McNally, 1985.

The Story of Noah and the Ark, illustrated by Helen Ward, Templar, 1987.

The Story of Christmas, illustrated by Ward, Templar, 1988.

Saint George and the Dragon, illustrated by Nicki Palin, Doubleday, 1989.

El Cid, Oxford University Press, 1989.

The Orchard Book of Greek Myths, Orchard, 1992.

Greek Myths, illustrated by Emma Chichester Clark, Margaret K. McElderry Books, 1993.

The Odyssey, illustrated by Ambrus, Oxford University Press, 1993.

Stories from Shakespeare, illustrated by Antony Maitland, Orion Children's, 1994.

The Orchard Book of Stories from the Ballet, illustrated by Angela Barrett, Orchard, 1994, published as *The Random House Book of Stories from the Ballet,* Random House, 1995.

The Golden Hoard: Myths and Legends of the World, illustrated by Bee Willey, Simon & Schuster/ Margaret K. McElderry, 1996.

Moby Dick, illustrated by Ambrus, Oxford University Press, 1996.

FOR CHILDREN

Seaside Adventure, illustrated by Chrissie Wells, Hamlyn, 1986.

(With Wells) *Tell the Time,* illustrated by Wells, Hamlyn, 1986.

(Translator) Michel Tilde, *Who's That Knocking on My Door?,* Oxford University Press, 1986.

My First Space Pop-Up Book, illustrated by Mike Peterkin, Little Simon, 1989.

My First Earth Pop-up Book, illustrated by Peterkin, Little Simon, 1990.

(Translator) *The Snow Country Prince,* Knopf, 1991.

(Translator) Daisaku Ikeda, *The Princess and the Moon,* Oxford University Press, 1991, Knopf, 1991.

(Translator) Ikeda, *The Cherry Tree,* illustrated by Brian Wildsmith, Knopf, 1992.

(Translator) Ikeda, *Over the Deep Blue Sea,* illustrated by Wildsmith, Knopf, 1993.

Blue Moon Mountain, illustrated by Palin, Golden, 1994.

Blue Moo, illustrated by Colin Smithson, Longman, 1994.

How the Reindeer Got Their Antlers, illustrated by Debi Gliori, Orchard, 1995.

On the Day the World Began, illustrated by Norman Bancroft-Hunt, Longman, 1995.

The Quest of Isis, illustrated by David Sim, Longman, 1995.

Wizziwig and the Crazy Cooker, Orchard, 1995.

Wizziwig and the Singing Chair, Orchard, 1995.

Wizziwig and the Sweet Machine, Orchard, 1995.

Wizziwig and the Wacky Weather Machine, Orchard, 1995.

OTHER

(Under name Geraldine Jones) *Adventure in New York* (textbook), illustrated by Cynthia Back, Oxford University Press, 1979.

(Under name Geraldine Jones) *Raise the Titanic* (textbook) Oxford University Press, 1980.

(Under name Geraldine Jones) *Modesty Blaise* (textbook), Oxford University Press, 1981.

The Maypole (adult novel), 1989.

Fires' Astonishment, Minerva, 1991.

Vainglory (adult novel), Cape, 1991.

Also author of *Heart's Blood* (adult novel), 1994. Editor, *Banbury Focus,* 1981-82; subeditor and writer of stories for *Storyteller* and *Great Composers.*

■ Sidelights

Geraldine McCaughrean is a notable author of fiction and retellings for young adults. Because of the variety of her works, it is almost impossible to characterize her as a writer. While McCaughrean has written popular original fiction novels, she has also produced many retellings of classic stories. Mc-Caughrean rewrites complex texts such as *One Thousand and One Arabian Nights, The Canterbury Tales,* and *The Odyssey* in language that young readers can enjoy and understand. Critics have praised the author's ability to create rich imagery and prose, as well as her frequent use of simile and metaphor. Commenting on her use of stylistic technique, McCaughrean once stated, "[Likening] things to other things gives a spurious unity to the world. . . . It adds a network of connections that don't actually exist but give a sense of structure." McCaughrean has received important awards as a result of her work, including the Carnegie Medal in 1988 and the *Guardian* Award in 1989. She also received the Beefeater's Children's Book of the Year award in 1994.

McCaughrean was born in London, England. As a young woman, she was not a successful student. After leaving school, McCaughrean became a secretary at Thames Television. Then her boss sent her to college at Christ Church, Canterbury. McCaughrean knew that she did not want to be a teacher, so she began to study theater instead. She was particularly interested in Shakespeare, a passion that would someday lead her to write original versions of his plays.

Long before rewriting Shakespeare, however, McCaughrean wrote her own version of *One Thousand and One Arabian Nights*. According to Neil Philip of the *Times Educational Supplement*, it "remains probably the best ever attempt [at retelling the tales]. Its lush, exuberant language revels in the imaginative luxuriance of the stories." *One Thousand and One Arabian Nights* is a series of tales told by the legendary queen Shahrazad to her husband so that he will postpone her execution. McCaughrean gives her audience an account of only thirty-five nights and twenty-four stories that include such favorites as Sinbad, Ali Baba, and Aladdin. The original *One Thousand and One Arabian Nights* can be difficult to read, even for adults. Anne Wilson of *Signal* observed that McCaughrean's version is much more palatable for young readers, stating that the author "has given us a re-creation in miniature for Western children."

Other critics praised McCaughrean's version of *One Thousand and One Arabian Nights* for its narrative structure, strong imagery, and the author's use of language. According to Ralph Lavender in *School Librarian*, "the imagery is brilliantly handled, illuminating each layer of meaning precisely when needed and with a diamond-sharp image." Aidan Chambers, writing in *Horn Book*, added that McCaughrean "manages to capture the flavor of another time and place while also making the stories sound modern and close to us." Wilson concluded that, as evidenced by *One Thousand and One Arabian Nights*, "McCaughrean's arts show limitless versatility in the undertaking of a variety of narrative."

McCaughrean also attempted a retelling of Geoffrey Chaucer's fourteenth-century poem *The Canterbury Tales*, and according to critics, the outcome was successful. Marcus Crouch, a reviewer in *Junior Bookshelf*, stated, "this must be acknowledged as one of the finest interpretations of Chaucer for the young." *The Canterbury Tales* is about a group of pilgrims traveling to Canterbury who tell stories along the way in order to pass the time. For her book, McCaughrean rewrote thir-

McCaughrean's version of Chaucer's *Canterbury Tales*, illustrated by Victor G. Ambrus, is the story of a pilgrimage, complete with the high spirits and countryside smells of medieval England, rather than portraits of each narrator.

teen of these stories, including some of the more bawdy tales like "The Reeve's Tale" and "The Miller's Tale." She also simplified Chaucer's poetic language and omitted obscenities. The result is a more appropriate version of Chaucer's poem for young readers.

In general, critics believe that young students and teachers alike will enjoy McCaughrean's version of *The Canterbury Tales*. In the *Times Educational Supplement*, Terry Jones declared: "there is so much fun and rich detail in these pages that it would be churlish to find the book anything but delightful." McCaughrean's work could also be considered a useful tool for educators, as critics suggested that students who would not normally read

Chaucer will be won over by McCaughrean's work. Ruth M. McConnell, a reviewer for *School Library Journal*, remarked, "This attractive volume is a good introduction to medieval stories for reluctant but able junior high readers."

Young Adult Novels

In addition to her successful retellings, McCaughrean has also written original fiction for young adults. Her first novel was *A Little Lower than the Angels*. Jessica Yates, a reviewer for *British Book News Children's Books* wrote that McCaughrean "has triumphed in her first novel in presenting the lives of ordinary people of the past, in direct, present-day language." *A Little Lower than the Angels* takes place in late medieval England during the era of Mystery Plays, which were put on by traveling performers. It is the story of Gabriel, a young stone mason's apprentice who runs away from his cruel master and joins a traveling group of players. Gabriel becomes part of a moneymaking scheme enacted by the players, and for a short time he actually believes that he is a faith-healer. Critics praised McCaughrean's novel for its compelling narrative, historical detail, and exciting plot. Nigel Andrew of the *Listener* cited the "convincingly recreated" medieval setting, and Margery Fisher, reviewing the work in *Growing Point*, concluded, "This skillfully planned and powerful tale contains a memorable panorama of a world where the tedium of poverty is alleviated by shows and wonders."

McCaughrean's next young adult novel was *A Pack of Lies*. According to Valerie Caless, a reviewer for *School Librarian, A Pack of Lies* "is a highly entertaining book, light-hearted but thought provoking, written with skill and confidence." The main characters in the work are Ailsa Povery and her mother, who owns an antique shop. One day, Ailsa meets a young man named MCC Berkshire who wants to work in the antique shop. The young man turns out to be good at selling things; he weaves fanciful stories about the items in the store, making them irresistible to customers. These stories comprise McCaughrean's novel. Critics praised *A Pack of Lies*. John Clute, reviewing the work in the *Times Literary Supplement*, found each of Berkshire's tales to be a "deft and glowing invention. . . . Each of them is delightful, well shaped, humorous and packed." In *Books for Keeps*, Stephanie Nettell called the work "an exuberant

If you enjoy the works of Geraldine McCaughrean, you may also want to check out the following books:

Leon Garfield and Edward Blishen, *The God Beneath the Sea* (illustrated by Charles Keeping), 1970.
Alan Garner, *The Owl Service*, 1967, and *Red Shift*, 1973.
Rosemary Sutcliff, *Beowulf*, 1984, and *The Shining Company*, 1990.
The Princess Bride, a film directed by Rob Reiner, 1987.
The Thief of Baghad, a film based on the tales of the Arabian Nights, 1940.

celebration of fiction's spell, a smiling surrender to the grip of the unruly imagination, a playful introduction to the riches of style and lie waiting in books."

Other retellings include McCaughrean's version of *Saint George and the Dragon*, the legend that describes how St. George became the patron saint of England when he defeated an evil dragon. Betsy Hearne, writing in *Bulletin of the Center for Children's Books* suggested that the retelling "could serve elementary, junior high, and high school students as an introduction to England's patron saint." McCaughrean also wrote her own version of the twelfth-century Spanish epic poem *El Cid*. It is the tale of Don Rodrigo Diaz, known as El Cid, a Spanish soldier of fortune who battled Christians and Moors. He ended up as the powerful ruler of Valencia, which he had captured from the Moors in 1094. A contributor to *Kirkus Reviews* remarked that McCaughrean produced "a lively narrative sparked with humor, drama, and her hero's daring trickery."

McCaughrean also rewrote a collection of Greek myths and her own version of *The Odyssey* by Homer; McCaughrean uses modern language and simplified plots to retell the ancient Greek stories. *The Orchard Book of Greek Myths* was well-received by critics. Nicholas Tucker, a reviewer for the *Times Educational Supplement*, called the work "a rich meal for the imagination in contrast to much of the junk-food offered to children on television." McCaughrean's version of *The Odyssey* also drew praise; According to Janet Tayler, a critic for *School*

Librarian, the author uses a "lively . . . tongue-in-cheek manner" to bring the adventure to life.

Returning to original fiction, McCaughrean wrote *Gold Dust,* a novel for young adults. It is a story about a small town in Brazil called Serra Vazia. One day, locals start excavating for gold in the middle of a downtown street. Soon, people start flocking to Serra Vazia, and the town consequently becomes corrupted by greed. At the end of the story, Serra Vazia is heroically restored to its former self. With this novel, McCaughrean again demonstrated her ironic humor and broad perspective. Reviewing *Gold Dust* in the *Times Educational Supplement,* Brian Slough stated, "Sharp observations on a kaleidoscope of topics enliven every page," and *Junior Bookshelf* contributor Marcus Crouch deemed it "an engrossing, funny, tragic blockbuster of a story."

Return to the Classics

McCaughrean later rewrote ten well-known Shakespearean plays and titled the collection *Stories From Shakespeare.* Reviewing the work, Maxine Kumin of the *New York Times Book Review* declared that *Stories From Shakespeare* is "useful and enjoyable. . . ." Furthermore, Crouch, in a review for *Junior Bookshelf,* explained that McCaughrean uses an accessible writing style and a solid understanding of Shakespeare to produce a work that children can comprehend and appreciate. Above all, he stated, McCaughrean "aims her book at children who are only just coming to Shakespeare, and she gives them an excellent start, showing that the plays are great entertainment and hinting at the depths to which they can in time be explored."

McCaughrean also wrote her own version of the classic novel *Moby Dick* by Herman Melville. Considered one of the greatest works in the canon of American literature, *Moby Dick* follows the vengeful Captain Ahab's pursuit of a great white whale. Elaine Moss, in an article in *Books for Keeps,* stated her belief that young readers should wait until they are old enough to take on the classics in their original form. However, she made an exception for McCaughrean, remarking, "despite my misgivings about the retellings of the classics I must go on record as saying that if anyone is to retell *Moby Dick* (and I still think nobody should) that person is Geraldine McCaughrean." Moss

cited McCaughrean's skill as a writer as her saving grace, believing that the author had captured the excitement of Melville's novel. Hazel Townson wrote in *School Librarian* that McCaughrean's *Moby Dick* "combines power and beauty with a clarity" which would prove appealing to adolescent readers.

McCaughrean's fourth original work of fiction is a novel titled *Plundering Paradise.* Set in the eighteenth century, *Plundering Paradise* is the story of Nathan Gull, who leaves school after his father dies. Nathan and his sister Maud follow Taco, the son of a pirate, to Madagascar where each young adventurer discovers his own destiny. Mandy Cheetham, a reviewer for *Magpies,* called the novel "vibrant in language, inventive in plot and brilliantly suggestive of time and place. . . ." Cheetham added, "It is refreshing to find a novel about young adults which is not concerned with the grim vicissitudes of life in the dysfunctional fast lane of modern times."

It is clear that McCaughrean has a gift for writing literature for children. The author once commented: "I have now found that my true talent lies in writing for children. In doing so, I have cleaned up a previously elaborate and overwritten style into one that is both more valid and of more use to publishers. This pure luck of being in the right place at the right time has led to the remarkable good fortune of making a living from the thing I like doing best."

■ Works Cited

Andrew, Nigel, "Raining Cats and Dogs," *Listener,* November 19, 1987, pp. 39-40.

Caless, Valerie, review of *A Pack of Lies, School Librarian,* February, 1989, p. 31.

Chambers, Aidan, "Letter from England: Ever After," *Horn Book,* June, 1983, pp. 339-43.

Cheetham, Mandy, "Extending Readers," *Magpies,* September, 1996, p. 36.

Clute, John, "Telling the Tale," *Times Literary Supplement,* November 24-December 1, 1988, p. 1322.

Crouch, Marcus, review of *The Canterbury Tales, Junior Bookshelf,* February, 1985, pp. 41-42.

Crouch, Marcus, review of *Gold Dust, Junior Bookshelf,* February, 1994, pp. 34-35.

Crouch, Marcus, review of *Stories from Shakespeare, Junior Bookshelf,* February, 1995, pp. 38-39.

Review of *El Cid, Kirkus Reviews,* October 15, 1989, p. 1532.

Fisher, Margery, review of *A Little Lower Than the Angels, Growing Point,* July, 1987, pp. 4824-26.

Hearne, Betsy, review of *Saint George and the Dragon, Bulletin of the Center for Children's Books,* December, 1989, pp. 88-89.

Jones, Terry, "Pilgrims' Way," *Times Educational Supplement,* February 1, 1985, p. 27.

Kumin, Maxine, review of *Stories from Shakespeare, New York Times Book Review,* April 23, 1995, p. 27.

Lavender, Ralph, review of *One Thousand and One Arabian Nights, School Librarian,* December, 1982, pp. 339-40.

McConnell, Ruth M., review of *The Canterbury Tales, School Library Journal,* February, 1986, p. 82.

Moss, Elaine, "Classic Cuts," *Books for Keeps,* July, 1997, pp. 4-5.

Nettell, Stephanie, review of *A Pack of Lies, Books for Keeps,* May, 1989, p. 25.

Philip, Neil, "Mining a Rich Seam," *Times Educational Supplement,* February 3, 1995, p. 14.

Slough, Brian, "Gold Fever," *Times Educational Supplement,* November 12, 1993, p. 3.

Tayler, Janet, review of *The Odyssey, School Librarian,* May, 1994, p. 62.

Townson, Hazel, review of *Moby Dick, School Librarian,* May, 1997, p. 89.

Tucker, Nicholas, review of *The Orchard Book of Greek Myths, Times Educational Supplement,* October 30, 1992, p. 7.

Wilson, Anne, "A New Arabian Night," *Signal,* January, 1983, pp. 26-29.

Yates, Jessica, review of *A Little Lower Than the Angels, British Book News Children's Books,* June, 1987, p. 30.

■ For More Information See

BOOKS

Children's Literature Review, Volume 38, Gale, 1996, pp. 131-52.

Twentieth-Century Children's Writers, 3rd edition, St. James Press, 1989, pp. 653-54.

Twentieth-Century Young Adult Writers, 1st edition, St. James Press, 1994, pp. 434-36.

PERIODICALS

Booklist, March 15, 1986, p. 1079; October 15, 1989, p. 461; December 15, 1989, p. 834; February 1, 1993, p. 982; July, 1995, p. 1873.

Books for Keeps, July, 1996, pp. 12-13.

Bulletin of the Center for Children's Books, April, 1988, pp. 161-62.

Junior Bookshelf, February, 1983, p. 44; June, 1987, p. 135; August, 1989, pp. 159-60; February, 1990, p. 47.

Kirkus Reviews, November 1, 1987, p. 1577; September 15, 1989, p. 1406; April 1, 1992, p. 466; May 15, 1993; August 1, 1997, p. 1225.

Listener, April 19, 1990, p. 26.

Publishers Weekly, April 28, 1989, p. 82; August 25, 1997, p. 71.

School Librarian, September, 1985, p. 239; February, 1993, p. 22; May, 1995, 71.

School Library Journal, April, 1988, p. 102; March, 1990, p. 209; April, 1993, pp. 136-37.

Times Educational Supplement, January 14, 1983, p. 33; March 10, 1989, p. B13; June 9, 1989, p. B12; November 10, 1989, p. 58.

Times Literary Supplement, April 13-19, 1990, p. 403.

Voice of Youth Advocates, August, 1997, p. 204.*

—Sketch by Stephen Allison

Margaret Mitchell

■ Personal

Full name, Margaret Munnerlyn Mitchell (also wrote under the bylines Peggy Mitchell, Margaret Mitchell Upshaw, and Elizabeth Bennett, a pseudonym); born November 8, 1900, in Atlanta, GA; died from brain injuries sustained when struck by an automobile, August 16, 1949, in Atlanta, GA; buried in Oakland Cemetery, Atlanta, GA; daughter of Eugene Muse (an attorney) and Maybelle (a women's suffrage activist; maiden name, Stephens) Mitchell; married Berrien ("Red") Kinnard Upshaw, September 2, 1922 (annulled, October 16, 1924; died January 10, 1949); married John Robert Marsh (in public relations), July 4, 1925 (died May 5, 1952). *Education:* Attended Smith College, 1918-1919.

■ Career

Atlanta Journal, Atlanta, GA, feature writer, 1922-26; freelance columnist, 1926; novelist, 1926-36; homemaker, 1936-49. Volunteer selling war bonds during World War II; volunteer for the American Red Cross in the 1940s.

■ Awards, Honors

Pulitzer Prize, 1937, for *Gone With the Wind;* M.A. from Smith College, 1939; named honorary citizen of Vimoutiers, France, 1949, for helping the city obtain American aid after World War II.

■ Writings

Gone With the Wind, Macmillan, 1936.
Margaret Mitchell's "Gone With the Wind" Letters, edited by Richard Harwell, Macmillan, 1976.
A Dynamo Going to Waste: Letters to Allen Edee, 1919-1921, edited by Jane Bonner Peacock, Peachtree Publications, 1985.
Lost Laysen (novella published with photos and letters), Scribner, 1996.

OTHER

Collections of Mitchell's papers are held at the University of Georgia, Athens, and the Atlanta Public Library.

■ Adaptations

Gone With the Wind was adapted for film by Metro-Goldwyn-Mayer, 1939, starring Clark Gable and Vivien Leigh. The film won eight Academy Awards, including Best Picture.

■ Sidelights

You do not have to have read Margaret Mitchell's Civil War epic *Gone With the Wind* (all 1,037 pages of it) to know of Rhett Butler and Scarlett O'Hara. You do not even have to have seen *Gone With the Wind* (all four hours of it) to be able to picture them, for in our collective mind, Clark Gable *is* the gentleman-rogue Rhett and Vivien Leigh *is* Scarlett, that unsinkable southern belle with an Irish fighting streak. And, without having seen either one, you might still be able to recite their most famous lines: "After all, tomorrow is another day"; and "My dear, I don't give a damn" (changed to "Frankly, my dear . . . " in the movie). Such is the cultural phenomenon of *Gone With the Wind*, grown out of an American book classic into something larger than itself, which a caricature in the *New York Review* captured cleverly: In it, a swarthy Gable-as-Butler plants a kiss on the painted lips of the woman he holds in his arms—not Scarlett, mind you, but Margaret Mitchell herself.

Gone With the Wind is a phenomenon built on contradictions. It has been disparaged by critics over time as artistically flimsy, strong on emotion yet weak in morality, factual but not necessarily historical, mythic but not literary, good but not great. Yet it won the Pulitzer Prize for fiction. Although it was the product of a first-time novelist who never wrote another book (and a woman at that, something critics often noted), it broke the publishing records of its day and has become the most popular American novel of all time, with 28 million copies sold to date, second only to the Bible in hardcover sales. James Boatwright, writing in the *New Republic*, called *Gone With the Wind* "not so much a book as a literary Act of God, unexplainable but cataclysmically there. . . ."

Atlanta, Through and Through

It is no wonder that Margaret Mitchell wrote the book that she did. She was born in Atlanta almost 100 years ago, in 1900, and lived her whole life there, in a city and a region immersed in the historical, economic, political, and racial legacies of America's then-not-too-distant Civil War. Mitchell's was an affluent family of conservative Southern Democrats, replete with the kinds of characters and conflicts that would eventually find their way into her novel. In fact, Mitchell's

storytelling experience came not out of any formal literary study as an adult, but rather, out of the accounts she heard as a child from family history and the Civil War. "I heard so much when I was little about the fighting and the hard times after the war that I firmly believed Mother and Father had been through it all," Mitchell once said, according to Patricia Storace in a review of *Southern Daughter*, a Mitchell biography by Darden Asbury Pyron, in the *New York Review of Books*. "In fact I heard everything except that the Confederates lost the war. When I was ten years old, it was a violent shock to hear that General Lee had been licked." It was a fact that Mitchell learned from the black field hands working on a family member's farm.

Mitchell's father Eugene was a lawyer, president of the Atlanta Historical Society, and a descendent of businessmen who were wrapped up in Atlanta's political and civic affairs even before there was an Atlanta (the city grew out of a village called Marthasville). Her mother, Maybelle Stephens Mitchell, was an Irish Catholic (a minority in the South) and an activist for women's suffrage. Maybelle Mitchell's family owned a 3,000-acre farm, worked by slaves, in Clayton County, Georgia, which well may have been her daughter's pattern for Tara, the O'Hara family plantation that is as much a character in *Gone With the Wind* as Scarlett herself.

As a child, Mitchell is said to have been a tomboy who enjoyed sports and wore boys' clothes. She was not a good student, and since she found it hard to make friends, she immersed herself in romance and adventure novels and loved to tell stories to her older brother Stephens. She also wrote plays with titles like "Phil Kelly: Detective," "A Darktown Tragedy," and "The Fall of Roger Rover." She graduated in 1918 from Washington Seminary, an Atlanta private school for girls. That summer, before leaving home to attend Smith College in Northampton, Massachusetts, Mitchell met and became engaged to Lieutenant Clifford Henry. Though World War I was in its final year, it didn't end soon enough for the marriage to take place: Henry was wounded in battle in France and died that fall.

At Smith College, Mitchell was more popular, but her academic struggles thwarted her aspirations of becoming a psychiatrist; English composition was the only subject at which she excelled. When her mother died during an influenza epidemic a year later, she left college and went home to Atlanta to keep house for her brother and father, who had also been ill and was shaken by Mrs. Mitchell's death.

In 1922, Mitchell became a reporter and feature writer for the *Atlanta Journal and Constitution,* covering news topics of the day and even taking part in them, to a degree, by becoming a "flapper," a 1920s term for young women who did bold, unconventional things like dress immodestly, smoke cigarettes, and dance to jazz music. That same year, she married Berrien K. ("Red") Upshaw. It was a tumultuous relationship that ended scandalously in divorce only two years later.

In the summer of 1925, Mitchell married again, this time happily, to John Robert Marsh, a public relations executive. When Mitchell suffered a serious ankle injury in 1926 and had to quit her job, Marsh encouraged her to start writing a novel as a way to pass the time while she recuperated. So, she began researching and writing "Tomorrow is Another Day," a Civil War tale featuring a heroine named Pansy. Biographers say that she finished the novel by 1929, but continued working on it off and on over the next seven years. It was not until 1935 that Mitchell succumbed to pressure by friends and reluctantly showed her work to Harold S. Latham, a Macmillan editor who was in town looking for manuscripts to publish. Hers was reportedly a disorganized heap, nearly five feet high, but Latham fell for her story as soon as he delved into it and purchased it for publication. "I just couldn't believe that a Northern publisher would accept a novel about the War Between the States from the Southern point of view," Mitchell said, according to Earl F. Bargainnier in the *Dictionary of Literary Biography.*

Mitchell spent another year doing extensive revisions to the text, which included changing Pansy's name to Scarlett and the book's title to a phrase from "Cynara," a poem by Ernest Dowson. *Gone With the Wind,* which Mitchell dedicated to her husband, was publicly launched on June 30, 1936, fueled by a then-large $10,000 national advertising campaign that, according to a 1936 *Publishers Weekly* announcement, put special emphasis on heavy publicity in the South, an effort that Macmillan described by using the *Atlanta Journal's* motto, saying that it intended its advertising to "cover Dixie like the dew."

And The Rest Is History

Publishing records were shattered when 50,000 copies—at $3 each—were sold in one day; two million copies in a year's time. Wrote Bargainnier, "The entire nation seemed entranced with the gigantic novel . . . much to the bewilderment of Mitchell, [who wrote in a letter to reviewer Herschel Brickell]: 'it is basically just a simple yarn of fairly simple people. There's no fine writing, there are no grandiose thoughts, there are no hidden meanings, no symbolism, nothing sensational. . . .'" Her "simple yarn" won the 1937 Pulitzer Prize for fiction, edging out heavyweight novels like William Faulkner's *Absalom, Absalom!,* John Dos Passos' *Big Money,* and George Santayana's *The Last Puritan,* a situation that some critics found baffling.

In 1936, movie producer David O. Selznick of Metro-Goldwyn-Mayer bought the film rights to it for $50,000—the most money Hollywood had yet paid for rights to a novel. With Gable and Leigh starring in the lead roles, and Leslie Howard and Olivia De Havilland cast as Ashley Wilkes and his wife Melanie, the movie premiered in Atlanta in 1939. It went on to win ten Academy Awards, Best Picture among them.

Gone With the Wind has been described variously as epic, myth, and folklore, as "an encyclopedia of the plantation legend" by Malcolm Cowley, writing in the *New Republic,* and as "a rogue's-eye view of the Civil War and Reconstruction," a sort of picaresque with a twist, since the "rascal" in this case is "a Georgia lady," according to John Peale Bishop, also in the *New Republic.* It is essentially a romance, but it is also a survival story that, with equal measures of historical detail and melodrama, tries to personalize the sweep of social and economic change brought upon the Old South's traditional society by the Civil War and its aftermath. It does this through the intersected lives of its four main characters (supported by a huge cast of relatives, neighbors, slaves, and soldiers). Ashley and Melanie represent a traditional, pre-war way of life that cannot endure; Scarlett and Rhett are the denizens of change, survivors in an altered world. "I don't know of any other [Civil War novel by a woman] in which the interest is so consistently centered, not upon the armies and the battles, the flags and the famous names, but upon that other world of women who heard the storm, waited it out, succumbed to it or rebuilt after it, according to their natures," wrote Stephen Vincent Benét in the *Saturday Review of Literature*. Though Mitchell avoids "battle-pieces," Benét continued, "the grind of the war is there, the patriotic fairs and the slow killing of friend and acquaintance, the false news and the true, the hope deferred and the end and the strangeness after the end."

Gone With the Wind opens in April 1861 in Clayton County, Georgia. It is a countryside abuzz with talk of war, General Beauregard having recently shelled the Yankees out of Fort Sumter. Already bored by the subject, sixteen-year-old Scarlett O'Hara, with her seventeen-inch waist—"the smallest in three counties"—sits at home in a new hooped gown and matching morocco slippers, doing what she does best: charming two of her many beaus. "Scarlett was not beautiful, but men seldom realized it when caught by her charm as the Tarleton twins were," the story begins. Scarlett adores her father Gerald—a high-spirited, self-made Irishman who won Tara in a poker game—but she worships her calm, stoic mother Ellen, a "Coast aristocrat of French descent." As for Scarlett, Mitchell tells us, "At sixteen, thanks to Mammy and Ellen, she looked sweet, charming and giddy, but she was, in reality, self-willed, vain and obstinate. She had the easily stirred passions of her Irish father and nothing except the thinnest veneer of her mother's unselfish and forbearing nature."

At a barbecue, Scarlett gets a first foreshadowing look at Rhett Butler, "a tall man, powerfully built . . . dark of face, swarthy as a pirate" with eyes "as bold and black as any pirate's appraising a galleon to be scuttled or a maiden to be ravished." She also learns that her beloved Ashley Wilkes ("born of a line of men who used their leisure for thinking, not doing") is engaged to marry his cousin, the frail, saintly Melanie Hamilton. Scarlett fails in an impassioned attempt to win Ashley back, and then is further humiliated to learn that a mocking Rhett has witnessed the rebuff. Out of spite, Scarlett agrees to marry Melanie's brother Charles. Within two weeks she is a wife, and within two months more, a widow, when Charles gets sick and dies in an army camp before ever seeing battle. She bears his son, Wade, but feels as little affection for the baby as she did for his father. Her family interprets her regret and boredom as grief and sends her off, with Wade and a slave girl, Prissy, to visit Melanie and Aunt

Pittypat Hamilton in Atlanta, where she will spend the duration of the war.

"Humming Like a Beehive"

It is by this time the summer of 1862, and the city is "humming like a beehive," its railroads and factories vital to the Confederacy's war efforts. Scarlett joins the other women in volunteer nursing at the "sweltering, stinking" hospital, and later, creates a scandal at a fund-raising bazaar when she breaks the protocol of widowhood by dancing with Rhett Butler, now a blockade runner.

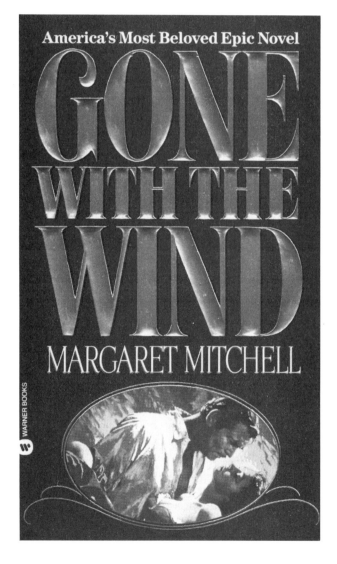

Mitchell's enduring 1936 work has become one of the most popular American novels of all time.

The war drags on, and people have stopped saying it will end with the next battle. Despite harder times, with Confederate money dropping in value, prices going up, and goods growing harder and harder to come by, Scarlett enjoys the informality of war-time society and doesn't care if it lasts forever. Ashley, home from war on a Christmas furlough, makes Scarlett promise to look after Melanie. Ashley is later reported missing in action and assumed dead, intensifying Scarlett's secret pining for him. By 1864, with the Confederate cause nearly lost, Atlanta hears the sound of battle for the first time. Scarlett wants to go home to Tara, but a pregnant Melanie cannot travel and says she will die if Scarlett abandons her. News arrives that the Yankees have reached Jonesboro near Tara, and that Scarlett's mother and sisters Suellen and Carreen have typhoid fever. Still, Scarlett finds time for some barb-filled love-making with Rhett, in which he admits that he wants her like he has wanted no other woman.

Then, on the day that Atlanta is evacuated, Melanie goes into a difficult labor, and Scarlett must search the chaotic streets, filled with wounded soldiers, for the doctor: "Lying in the pitiless sun, shoulder to shoulder, head to feet, were hundreds of wounded men, lining the tracks, the sidewalks, stretched out in endless rows under the car shed. Some lay stiff and still but many writhed under the hot sun, moaning. Everywhere, swarms of flies hovered over the men, crawling and buzzing in their faces, everywhere was blood, dirty bandages, groans, screamed curses of pain as stretcher bearers lifted men." The doctor is too busy to bother with a birth, and Scarlett and Prissy must deliver the baby boy, Beau, and care for Melanie, who is near death.

You Can Go Home Again

Rhett procures a rickety wagon and horse and helps the household set off for Tara, even though Yankee danger lurks around every bend. Once into the countryside, he announces his plan to join the Confederates (though he has scorned their cause in the past), and deserts the women. Scarlett gets them home to a darkened Tara. It is still standing, but has been looted of all food and supplies by the Yankees and has been abandoned by all but a few of its now-free slaves. Scarlett's mother is dead, her sisters still seriously ill, and her father a broken, befuddled old man. Scarlett takes

charge. She finds and gathers withered vegetables from an abandoned garden, but sick with hunger and grief, she collapses. When she rises, head held high, "something that was youth and beauty and potential tenderness had gone out of her face forever. What was past was past. Those who were dead were dead. The lazy luxury of the old days was gone, never to return. . . . There was no going back and she was going forward. . . .

. . . 'As God is my witness, as God is my witness, the Yankees aren't going to lick me. . . . If I have to steal or kill—as God is my witness, I'm never going to be hungry again.'"

The days that follow are filled with back-breaking work. There is never enough to eat. Scarlett's recovering sisters are spoiled and useless. Troubles come to a violent climax when a Yankee cavalryman wanders in and threatens Scarlett. She shoots and kills him with Charles' pistol. She then sees Melanie at the top of the stairs with her grandfather's sword, prepared to do what Scarlett has already done. The moment unites the two in a new way, strengthening their action later when faced with more Yankees, who set Scarlett's meager cotton harvest on fire, as well as Tara's kitchen, and make off with most of what is left of the family valuables.

The following April, in 1865, General Johnston surrenders and the war is over. The news spreads slowly into the countryside and seems almost anticlimactic to Scarlett. Soldiers and exiled neighbors begin their return, and Tara's isolation lessens. News arrives that Ashley is alive after all and, released from an Illinois jail, he eventually makes his way to Tara. With the help of Will Banteen, an injured young war veteran nursed back to health at Tara, Scarlett manages to keep the remnants of her extended family fed. But by early 1866, Georgia is virtually under martial law, and speculators push up property taxes, hoping to force out now-penniless plantation owners like the O'Haras. Having heard that Rhett Butler has made a fortune in illicit war-time dealings and desperate for cash, Scarlett decides to seduce him into giving her the tax money. She has a new dress made out of her mother's draperies, travels to Atlanta, and finds Rhett in a Yankee jail. Rhett goes along with her charade, making her go so far as to offer herself to him as collateral, then refuses her. Sunk only briefly, she learns that sister Suellen's fiancé Frank Kennedy is making money in Atlanta's reconstruction boom. She seduces him instead by lying about Suellen's marriage intentions and marries Frank two weeks later.

"All Flame and Jewel"

Scarlett gets a look at Frank's store records and realizes she would be better at running the business than he is: "With the idea that she was as capable as a man came a sudden rush of pride and a violent longing to prove it, to make money for herself as men made money." Rhett shows up, having blackmailed his way out of jail, and he agrees to loan her money to buy sawmills. She sets Atlanta talking with her unwomanly activities, but a distressed Frank lets Scarlett have her way in order to keep the peace at home: "Sometimes Frank sighed, thinking he had caught a tropic bird, all flame and jewel color, when a wren would have served him just as well. In fact, much better."

By the spring of 1886, political and racial tensions are heightening. Believing that money is the only security in such times, a now-pregnant Scarlett spends her days running her lumber business. That summer she returns to Tara for her father's funeral and learns from Will that Suellen is responsible for Gerald's death, having gotten him drunk and tried to convince him to sign a Union sympathy oath that would win the family compensation money for their war-time losses. Gerald comes to his senses long enough to refuse such betrayal of the Confederacy, rides off in a rage and breaks his neck while trying to jump a fence. Will saves Suellen's reputation and secures his future at Tara by asking to marry her.

Ashley, disillusioned by war, inept at farming, and embarrassed at having to live off of Scarlett's charity, plans to take a banking job in New York. To keep him nearby, Scarlett throws a fit in front of Melanie, who, already homesick for Atlanta, musters up a surprising ire at Ashley. He gives in, taking a mill-management job from Scarlett. The Wilkeses take a house in Atlanta, and the popular Melanie soon becomes head of numerous social committees. Scarlett spends sleepless nights worrying about the mill, since Ashley proves to be just as bad at business as he was at farming. But daughter Ella Lorena is at last born, freeing Scarlett from her confinement.

While riding out alone to inspect one of her mills, Scarlett is attacked by two men, one black and one white. Unbeknownst to Scarlett, both Ashley and Frank have become Ku Klux Klansmen, and that night, Frank gets killed during the Klan murder of Scarlett's black attacker. Scarlett feels responsible for Frank's death, yet in the midst of her battle with her guilty conscience, Rhett proposes. Neither believes that they are in love, but they marry as soon as Rhett returns from one of his mysterious business trips abroad. Scarlett builds a mansion next to that of the hated new Republican governor, whom Rhett has supported, and takes up with a checkered society made up of Atlanta's newcomers. Melanie remains Scarlett's loyal advocate, even though old Atlanta shuns Scarlett for her scandalous behavior. She has another baby, Bonnie, whom she favors and Rhett adores.

The happiness of her new paradise begins to be lost, however, when Scarlett declares she wants no more children and banishes Rhett from her bedroom. Soon after, several of Scarlett's detractors spy Scarlett and Ashley in a friendly embrace and blow the matter into a scandal. Melanie refuses to believe they have done anything wrong, but Rhett, having known of Scarlett's feelings for Ashley all along, comes home in a drunken rage, fights with Scarlett, then carries her off to a passionate night in bed. He is gone in the morning, and Scarlett, believing he loves her after all, is crushed to have him return with plans to take Bonnie away with him indefinitely. While Rhett is away, Scarlett discovers she is pregnant again, and realizing what a poor mother she has been to Wade and Ella, looks forward to a fresh chance with a new baby.

Rhett returns with Bonnie three months later and mocks Scarlett's pregnancy. They argue, and Scarlett falls down a staircase and has a miscarriage. Rhett sends her home to Tara for a rest, then, under the guise that he wants Scarlett to stop working so hard, he gets Melanie to agree to a scheme in which she will convince Ashley to buy Scarlett's store and mills with money sent anonymously by Rhett. Scarlett agrees to sell, though she regrets it almost immediately, since her business is a tangible sign of what she has accomplished for herself.

Things go from bad to worse when Bonnie is killed in a horse-riding accident. Scarlett blames

Winner of ten Academy Awards, the film version of *Gone with the Wind*, starring Clark Gable as Rhett Butler and Vivien Leigh as Scarlett O'Hara, is a classic of American cinema.

Rhett for encouraging Bonnie's reckless behavior and Rhett, overtaken with grief for Bonnie and bitterness toward Scarlett, goes mad for a time, keeping Bonnie's body in his room and refusing a funeral. It takes Melanie to make him come to his senses. Scarlett finds herself afraid and alone. Then Melanie, forbidden by doctors to have another child but secretly pregnant, miscarries and dies. She uses her last breath to make Scarlett promise that she will look after Ashley and little Beau. Scarlett suddenly realizes that her love for Ashley has always been a fantasy, and that it is Rhett whom she really loves. She races home to him, but it is too late. His love for her is dead. When she refuses his offer of divorce, he leaves her anyway, saying he will visit often enough to keep up appearances. She comforts herself with plans to go home to Tara: "With the spirit of her people who would not know defeat, even when it stared them in the face, she raised her chin. She could get Rhett back. She knew she could. There had never been a man she couldn't get, once she set her mind upon him. 'I'll think of it all tomorrow, at Tara. I can stand it then. Tomorrow, I'll think of some way to get him back. After all, tomorrow is another day.'" It is a tantalizing, open ending which Mitchell refused to close, either with surmisings about her characters' futures or plans for a sequel.

Critics Do and Don't Give a Damn

Gone With the Wind debuted to a share of favorable reviews, including Benét's and one in the *New York Times Book Review*, in which a critic called the work "a bounteous feast of excellent story telling." Though *Gone With the Wind* was never a favorite among literary critics and historians, they nonetheless continue to write about it to this day. From the early text-based criticism written largely by men of letters for periodicals to the more recent academic work that incorporates psychological, sexual, and feminist perspectives, the body of writing about *Gone With the Wind* catalogues the shifts in literary criticism over the past sixty years. Much of it is contradictory, with critics conceding certain strengths—vivid characterization, good storytelling, breadth of scope—but eventually finding those overwhelmed by even stronger weaknesses.

Some complain of Mitchell's inexperience as a novelist. "She writes with a splendid recklessness, blundering into big scenes that a more experienced novelist would hesitate to handle for fear of being compared unfavorably with Dickens or Dostoevsky. Miss Mitchell is afraid of no comparison and no emotion . . . ," stated Cowley. Others find the novel has shaky moral underpinnings. W. J. Stuckey, in his book *The Pulitzer Prize Novels: A Critical Backward Look*, wrote, "Miss Mitchell goes to great lengths to justify Scarlett, but her justification is just a vast transparency of rationalization invented to excuse and glamorize piracy, coldly calculated self-interest, and violent disregard for basic human decency, all in the name of historical necessity and survival." Stuckey continued, "Some daily reviewers attempted to place *Gone With the Wind* in the 'older' tradition of the English novel; but while one can hear distant echoes of Fielding, Thackeray (especially), and Emily Brontë in *Gone With the Wind*, Miss Mitchell's art most noisily proclaims its indebtedness to the literature of wish fulfillment—the bosomy and sub-pornographic historical romance, the sentimental novel, and the Hollywood extravaganza."

Still others, like Boatwright in the *New Republic*, admired Mitchell's "energy of conception and organization" but found that overshadowed by sentimentality, a problem of "narrowness of perception and sensibility that inevitably affect everything: dialogue, characterization, incident, meaning. MM may have believed with some justice that she had pictured the South more realistically than most earlier *romancers* (her journalistic training gave her a healthy respect for solid fact, and she is good with *things*—houses, dresses, guns, towns), but the figures in her landscape, their emotions

If you enjoy the works of Margaret Mitchell, you may also want to check out the following books and films:

John Jakes, *Love and War*, 1984.
Ann Rinaldi, *The Last Silk Dress*, 1988.
Filmmaker Ken Burns's nine-part television mini-series, *The Civil War*, 1990.

and inner lives, their motives and actions are preposterous and unintentionally comic—the fantasies of a fatally genteel and superficial imagination."

Historians especially seem to dislike *Gone With the Wind*, for the way it romanticizes a racist culture—particularly for its portrayal of "darkies" as dumbly loyal, comic, stupid, lazy, dishonest, or dangerous—and for the way it oversimplifies and glosses over important aspects of historical events. "Mere dramatization or fictionalizing of history may be a service to history—if it is accurate enough—but it is a disservice to literature," wrote Floyd C. Watkins, a professor at Emory University, writing in the *Southern Literary Journal*. "Obsessive interest in archetypes and mythology ruins the brew, and the contemporary and the humanity in the work are obscured. When a novel is false to historical fact and also false to the human heart in the contemporary age, then it must be simply a poor novel. Despite an immediate popularity which excelled that of all other books, that is the category of *Gone With the Wind*—a bad novel. It creates myth which seems to ease the hunger of all extravagantly Southern and little romantic souls, but it propagandizes history, fails to grasp the complexities of human evil and the significances of those who prevail." And, as Storace noted in the *New York Review of Books*, *Gone With the Wind* "exemplifies the ongoing arguments over which story of the Civil War South is the true story."

A People's Classic

Perhaps the hardest thing for critics to swallow has been *Gone With the Wind*'s popularity, which feeds the notion of the "super-aesthete" that, as Edward Wagenknecht explained in an essay in his *Cavalcade of the American Novel*, "any work which exerts a very wide appeal must necessarily be second-rate." Edward P. J. Corbett, in *America*, stated that *Gone With the Wind*'s weaknesses "did not become stumbling blocks for most readers" and that it appealed "to men and to women, to old and to young, to the romantic and to the realist, to sophisticated readers and to uninitiated readers. . . . [G]reat or not, *Gone With the Wind* may very well be one of the few books from the 20th century that the great mass of readers will assure of survival into the next age. It would not be the first time that the people had made a 'classic' in spite of the critics and the academicians."

For her part, Mitchell is said to have remained humble in spite of *Gone With the Wind*'s success and the fame that it brought her. Mitchell was besieged with fan mail, which she tried to answer herself. False rumors spread about her health and her personal life. Women tried to gain personal profit by impersonating her. There were lawsuits filed by and against Mitchell over plagiarism, copyrights, and commercial spin-offs. But the public's fascination with Mitchell waned once the movie version of *Gone With the Wind* came out. Mitchell did not return to writing, but instead got involved in charitable projects, like fund-raising to build an Atlanta "paying hospital" for black citizens, who at that time were only admitted to charity hospitals. Once World War II was underway, she worked as a Red Cross volunteer and helped sell war bonds. She also spent time caring for her husband John, who had suffered a debilitating heart attack in 1945.

It all came to an end in August 1949, when a speeding car with a drunk driver at the wheel swerved into Mitchell while she and John were crossing a street. She never regained consciousness, and died a few days later. She was forty-eight. Mitchell was buried in Oakland Cemetery in Atlanta, and, according to her brother Stephens' account, "There was a crowd there for two or three days. She had said something to her people and they had answered."

How to explain *Gone With the Wind*'s immediate and then enduring appeal? Numerous writers point to the parallels between the world of *Gone With the Wind* and Americans' experiences at the time the book was published. Undergoing the economic hardships of the Great Depression and sandwiched between two World Wars, 1930s readers could easily identify with war-time sacrifice and with characters who, having lost everything,

either succumb in despair or fight to survive and rebuild their lives. The identification and escape the novel offered had an international appeal, too. By 1949, Wagenknecht wrote, 6 million copies of *Gone With the Wind* had been sold in thirty different languages. During World War II, the Nazis banned the work, though Hitler himself is reported to have insisted on seeing the movie version.

Gone With the Wind's ongoing appeal seems also to have to do with self-identification and adolescence itself, both on national and individual scales. "It's my contention that the Civil War is in our subconscious, the way it would be if something happened to you in your adolescence. You would not be thinking of it all the time, but it would be called up by events," historian Shelby Foote told Renee Loth in the *Boston Globe*. It is an idea that, taken a step further, goes a length toward explaining *Gone With the Wind*'s appeal to young readers, considering its size and the fact that it was written long before there was a young adult fiction genre. It features the coming of age of a vivid young heroine—a central component of most young adult fiction—so that for all her well-discussed moral failings and disagreeable personal traits, Scarlett O'Hara is someone many young readers can identify with. Though her experiences are highly dramatic and often overblown, she still goes through much of what young people in any era do: the experience of strong emotions, a search for and discovery of self-identity, misbehavior and mistakes and their consequences, the passion and pain of illusory first love, chafing under societal and family restrictions and the thrill of rebellion, longing for the security and comforts of childhood yet seeking and savoring independence, leaving home in order to make one's way in the world: it is a long list, and Scarlett takes readers through it with her. She comes out a woman in the end.

Going, Going, Still Not Gone

Gone With the Wind, like Scarlett herself, seems to undergo a rebirth every so many years, so that new generations of readers get exposed to it afresh. In 1986, when the novel turned fifty, there was a "flurry of festivities," as reported by Jean Seligmann in *Newsweek*, that included the release of a reproduction of the original edition of *Gone With the Wind* and a commemorative postage stamp honoring Mitchell. Then, in 1994, the son of one of Mitchell's early boyfriends handed over a packet of old photographs and letters to the Road to Tara Museum in Atlanta. It also contained a novella, titled *Lost Laysen*, that Mitchell had written as a teenager. *Lost Laysen*—published by Scribner in 1996 to coincide with *Gone With the Wind*'s sixtieth anniversary—"is a curio, a slight and puerile story of unrequited love and honor defended" in the South Pacific, according to a contributor in the *New York Times Book Review*.

Lost Laysen followed romance fiction writer Alexandra Ripley's 1991 *Gone With the Wind* sequel, authorized by the Mitchell estate, the rights for which Warner Books paid $5 million. Titled *Scarlett*, it immediately topped the *New York Times* best-seller list, and renewed interest in the original story made *Gone With the Wind* a best-seller again for a time. *Scarlett* received decisively negative reviews all around, and its sales success seems to have had more to do with Warner's huge pre-publication publicity campaign (including an enticing advance excerpt printed in *Life* magazine involving a passionate kissing scene between a reunited Scarlett and Rhett). "Margaret Mitchell refused to write a sequel. She felt she'd said it all, and that subsequent events were better left to the reader's imagination. Unfortunately, some readers don't have any. They need to have it spelled out for them. It's too bad *Scarlett* is spelled out so poorly," concluded Diane White in the *Boston Globe*. A southerner herself, Ripley first read *Gone With the Wind* as a teen, and "wanted to be Melanie," according to Charles E. Claffey, also writing in the *Boston Globe*. He reported that she carefully analyzed Mitchell's style before she began writing her sequel. "Then, in a line worthy of Scarlett, she added: 'Yes, Margaret Mitchell writes better than I do—but she's dead,'" Claffey reported. J. O. Tate, reviewing *Scarlett* in the *National Review*, wondered, "What's the fuss about, anyway? Alexandra Ripley, who word-processed this sequel, has only demonstrated the power of the original, for the result of her efforts is a *tour de faiblesse* of ineptitude, incoherence, and unimaginative droning. Margaret Mitchell, by contrast, never looked so good."

It is criticism that brings things full circle, for if style alone cannot carry a bad story, then it seems that Mitchell was right all along when she said that it was *not* her style but her story that mattered. Belle Rosenbaum, writing in *Scribner's Magazine*, concurred with Mitchell's view, stating that the popularity of *Gone with the Wind* is due to "a chunk of people yearning for a tale well told, for the sake of its telling, by a teller who loves the tale and the art of telling it."

■ **Works Cited**

Bargainnier, Earl F., "Margaret Mitchell," *Dictionary of Literary Biography*, Volume 9: *American Novelists, 1910-1945*, Part 2: Fitzgerald-Rolvaag, Gale, 1981, pp. 224-25.

Benét, Stephen Vincent, "Georgia Marches Through," *Saturday Review of Literature*, July 4, 1936, p. 5.

Bishop, John Peale, "War and No Peace," *New Republic*, July 15, 1936, reprinted in *The Collected Essays of John Peale Bishop*, edited by Edmund Wilson, Charles Scribner's Sons, 1948, p. 253.

Boatwright, James, "Totin' de Weery Load," *New Republic*, September 1, 1973, pp. 29, 31-32.

Claffey, Charles E., "Frankly, My Dear, It's A Novel Obsession," *Boston Globe*, June 20, 1991, p. 69.

Corbett, Edward P. J., "Gone With the Wind Revisited," *America*, August 24, 1957, pp. 525-26.

Cowley, Malcolm, "Going With the Wind," *New Republic*, September 16, 1936, pp. 161-62.

Review of *Lost Laysen*, *New York Times Book Review*, June 23, 1996, p. 23.

Loth, Renee, "Scarlett Fever, GWTW and Its Fiery Young Heroine are 55 But Are Going Like 60," *Boston Globe*, October 13, 1991, p. 77.

Mitchell, Margaret, *Gone With the Wind*, Macmillan, 1936.

Rosenbaum, Belle, "Why Do They Read It?," *Scribner's Magazine*, August, 1937, p. 70.

Seligmann, Jean, "Scarlett Lives On," *Newsweek*, June 30, 1986, p. 65.

Storace, Patricia, "Look Away, Dixie Land," *New York Review of Books*, December 19, 1991, pp. 24-25.

Stuckey, W. J., *The Pulitzer Prize Novels: A Critical Backward Look*, University of Oklahoma Press, 1966, pp. 109-11.

"A Study in Scarlett," review of *Gone With the Wind* in *New York Times Book Review*, July 5, 1936, reprinted in *New York Times Book Review*, October 6, 1996, p. 43.

Tate, J. O., "She Done Her Wrong," *National Review*, March 16, 1992, p. 46.

"They Did Give a Damn," reprint of June 27, 1936, article about *Gone With the Wind* in *Publishers Weekly*, July, 1991, p. 11.

Wagenknecht, Edward, *Cavalcade of the American Novel: From the Birth of the Nation to the Middle Twentieth Century,* Holt, Rinehart and Winston, 1952, p. 426.

Watkins, Floyd C., "*Gone With the Wind* As Vulgar Literature," *Southern Literary Journal,* Spring, 1970, p. 89.

White, Diane, "*Scarlett* Suffers, and So Do Readers," *Boston Globe,* August 14, 1991, p. 57.

■ **For More Information See**

BOOKS

Edwards, Anne, *Road to Tara: The Life of Margaret Mitchell,* Ticknor and Fields, 1983.

Farr, Finis, *Margaret Mitchell of Atlanta: The Author of Gone With the Wind,* Morrow, 1965.

Fiedler, Leslie A., *The Inadvertent Epic: From "Uncle Tom's Cabin" to "Roots,"* Simon & Schuster, 1979.

Harwell, Richard, editor, *Gone With the Wind as Book and Film,* University of South Carolina Press, 1983.

Mott, Frank Luther, *Golden Multitudes: The Story of Best Sellers in the United States,* Macmillan, 1947, pp. 253-61.

Pyron, Darden Asbury, *Southern Daughter: The Life of Margaret Mitchell,* Oxford University Press, 1992.

PERIODICALS

Georgia Review, Summer, 1958, pp. 142-50; Spring, 1974, pp. 9-18.

Proteus, Spring, 1989.

Southern Literary Journal, Fall, 1980, pp. 3-31.*

—Sketch by Tracy J. Sukraw

Walter Dean Myers

tory on a part-time basis in New York City, 1974-75; worked variously as a post-office clerk, inter-office messenger, and a interviewer at a factory. *Military service:* U.S. Army, 1954-57. *Member:* PEN, Harlem Writers Guild.

■ Personal

Given name Walter Milton Myers; born August 12, 1937, in Martinsburg, WV; son of George Ambrose and Mary (Green) Myers; raised from age three by Herbert Julius (a shipping clerk) and Florence (a factory worker) Dean; married second wife, Constance Brendel, June 19, 1973; children: (first marriage) Karen, Michael Dean; (second marriage) Christopher. *Education:* Attended City College of the City University of New York; Empire State College, B.A., 1984.

■ Addresses

Home—2543 Kennedy Blvd., Jersey City, NJ 07304.

■ Career

New York State Department of Labor, New York City, employment supervisor, 1966-70; Bobbs-Merrill Co., Inc. (publisher), New York City, senior trade books editor, 1970-77; full-time writer, 1977—. Teacher of creative writing and black his-

■ Awards, Honors

Council on Interracial Books for Children Award, 1968, for the manuscript of *Where Does the Day Go?; The Dancers* was selected one of Child Study Association of America's children's books of the year, 1972; American Library Association (ALA) notable book citation, 1975, for *Fast Sam, Cool Clyde, and Stuff,* 1978, for *It Ain't All for Nothin',* 1979, for *The Young Landlords,* and 1988, for *Scorpions* and *Me, Mop, and the Moondance Kid;* Woodward Park School Annual Book Award, 1976, for *Fast Sam, Cool Clyde, and Stuff;* ALA best books for young adults citation, 1978, for *It Ain't All for Nothin',* 1979, for *The Young Landlords,* 1981, for *The Legend of Tarik,* 1982, for *Hoops,* and 1988, for *Fallen Angels* and *Scorpions;* Coretta Scott King Award, 1980, for *The Young Landlords,* 1985, for *Motown and Didi: A Love Story,* and 1989, for *Fallen Angels;* Notable Children's Trade Book in the Field of Social Studies from the National Council for Social Studies and the Children's Book Council, 1982, for *The Legend of Tarik;* Edgar Allan Poe Award runner-up, 1982, for *Hoops; Parents' Choice* Award from the Parents' Choice Foundation, 1982, for *Won't Know Till I Get There,* 1984, for *The Outside Shot,* and 1988, for *Fallen Angels;* New Jersey Institute of Technology Authors Award, 1983, for *Tales of a Dead King; Adventure in Granada* was selected one of Child Study Association of America's children's books of the year, 1987; Newbery Honor Book, 1989, for *Scorpions;* Jeremiah Ludington Award, Educational Paperback Association, 1993, for creating "18 Pine St." series; Coretta Scott King Award for *Slam!,* 1997; *Boston Globe-Horn Book* Honor Book, 1997, for *Harlem.*

■ Writings

PICTURE BOOKS

(Under name Walter M. Myers) *Where Does the Day Go?,* illustrated by Leo Carty, Parents Magazine Press, 1969.

The Dragon Takes a Wife, illustrated by Ann Grifalconi, Bobbs-Merrill, 1972, illustrated by Fiona French, Scholastic, 1995.

The Dancers, illustrated by Anne Rockwell, Parents Magazine Press, 1972.

Fly, Jimmy, Fly!, illustrated by Moneta Barnett, Putnam, 1974.

The Black Pearl and the Ghost; or, One Mystery after Another, illustrated by Robert Quackenbush, Viking, 1980.

Mr. Monkey and the Gotcha Bird, illustrated by Leslie Morrill, Delacorte, 1984.

Glorious Angels: A Celebration of Children, HarperCollins, 1995.

The Story of the Three Kingdoms, illustrated by Ashley Bryon, HarperCollins, 1995.

How Mr. Monkey Saw the Whole World, illustrated by Synthia Saint James, Bantam, 1996.

NOVELS; FOR CHILDREN AND YOUNG ADULTS

Fast Sam, Cool Clyde, and Stuff, Viking, 1975, Peter Smith, 1995.

Brainstorm, photographs by Chuck Freedman, F. Watts, 1977.

Mojo and the Russians, Viking, 1977.

Victory for Jamie, Scholastic, 1977.

It Ain't All for Nothin', Viking, 1978.

The Young Landlords, Viking, 1979.

The Golden Serpent, illustrated by Alice Provensen and Martin Provensen, Viking, 1980.

Hoops, Delacorte, 1981.

The Legend of Tarik, Viking, 1981.

Won't Know Till I Get There, Viking, 1982.

The Nicholas Factor, Viking, 1983.

Tales of a Dead King, Morrow, 1983.

Motown and Didi: A Love Story, Viking, 1984.

The Outside Shot, Delacorte, 1984.

Sweet Illusions, Teachers & Writers Collaborative, 1986.

Crystal, Viking, 1987.

Scorpions, Harper, 1988.

Me, Mop, and the Moondance Kid, illustrated by Rodney Pate, Delacorte, 1988.

Fallen Angels, Scholastic, 1988.

The Mouse Rap, HarperCollins, 1990.

Somewhere in the Darkness, Scholastic, 1992.

Mop, Moondance, and the Nagasaki Knights, Delacorte, 1992.

The Righteous Revenge of Artemis Bonner, HarperCollins, 1992.

The Glory Field, Scholastic, 1994.

Darnell Rock Reporting, Delacorte, 1994.

The Shadow of the Red Moon, illustrated by Christopher Myers, Scholastic, 1995.

Smiffy Blue: Ace Crime Detective: The Case of the Missing Ruby and Other Stories, illustrated by David Sims, Scholastic, 1996.

Slam!, Scholastic, 1996.

Also creator and editor of the "18 Pine Street" series of young adult novels featuring African American characters, Bantam, 1992—.

"THE ARROW" SERIES

Adventure in Granada, Viking, 1985.

The Hidden Shrine, Viking, 1985.

Duel in the Desert, Viking, 1986.

Ambush in the Amazon, Viking, 1986.

OTHER

The World of Work: A Guide to Choosing a Career (nonfiction), Bobbs-Merrill, 1975.

Social Welfare (nonfiction), F. Watts, 1976.

Now Is Your Time: The African-American Struggle for Freedom, HarperCollins, 1992.

A Place Called Heartbreak: A Story of Vietnam (nonfiction), Raintree, 1992.

Young Martin's Promise, illustrated by Barbara H. Bond, Raintree, 1992.

Brown Angels: An Album of Pictures and Verse, HarperCollins, 1993.

Remember Us Well: An Album of Pictures and Verse, Harper, 1993.

Malcolm X: By Any Means Necessary, Scholastic, 1993.

Turning Points: When Everything Changes, Troll Communications, 1996.

Toussaint L'Ouverture: The Fight for Haiti's Freedom, illustrated by Jacob Lawrence, Simon & Schuster, 1996.

One More River to Cross: An African American Photograph Album, Harcourt Brace, 1996.

Harlem (poems), Scholastic, 1997.

Work represented in anthologies, including *What We Must See: Young Black Storytellers,* Dodd, 1971; *We Be Word Sorcerers: Twenty-five Stories by Black Americans; On the Wings of Peace: Writers and Illustrators Speak Out for Peace, In Memory of Hiroshima and Nagasaki,* Houghton Mifflin, 1995. Contributor of articles and fiction to periodicals, including *Black Creation, Black World, Scholastic, McCall's, Espionage, Alfred Hitchcock Mystery Magazine, Essence, Ebony, Jr.!,* and *Boy's Life.*

■ Adaptations

The Young Landlords was adapted as a film by Topol Productions.

■ Overview

Walter Dean Myers is regarded as one of the most influential African American writers of juvenile fiction. At a young age Myers perceived a lack of children's books that deal with the concerns and realities of minority children. So he took it upon himself to rectify the problem, going on to publish over sixty-five works, including children's picture books, novels for children and young adults, poetry, and nonfiction.

Frequently facing prejudice, adversity, and general ignorance during his writing career, Myers refused to compromise the subject matter and characters he used in books. His importance lies, however, in his passion and commitment to helping children in a positive way—by not only encouraging them to read, but giving minority children books to read that will speak to their realities, not a European world that is as alien as a fairy tale. The subjects Myers writes about provoke thought and emotions in his readers, and his works speak directly to children, not down at them.

The author was born Walter Milton Myers in Martinsburg, West Virginia, to George Ambrose and Mary Green Myers. His mother died giving birth to his little sister Imogene, and Myers moved to Harlem to be raised by his foster parents, Herbert Julius and Florence Dean. Living in Harlem, a predominantly African American community in New York City, has had the greatest effect on Myers's writing than any other event in his life. Most of his books are set in Harlem or deal with characters who are from Harlem. This fact has given his books credibility and power, earning him a multitude of honors from such prestigious institutions as the Council on Interracial Books for Children and the American Library Association.

In Harlem, Myers learned the values and ideals that would later affect his writing. As he wrote in *Something about the Author Autobiography Series* (*SAAS*), "When I was a child there were two conditions that defined being poor. Were you hungry? Were you cold? With the Deans I was never cold or hungry." Warm and fed under his foster father's roof, Myers had the seeds of storytelling planted in him. When his mother would leave the house, he would be put on his father's knee and told a multitude of scary stories that both frightened and fascinated him. When his mother returned, she would tell him nice stories about princesses and Shirley Temple. Myers's early life was alive with positive affirmation. Remembering life in Harlem as a child, he continued in the *SAAS* essay: "The excitement of city living exploded in the teeming streets. If there was a notion that as a black child I was to be denied easy access to other worlds, it mattered little to me if I could have this much life in the place I found myself."

Myers soon found that the comfort he had in his home and neighborhood could not shelter him from the harsh realities of the outside world. Friends he had played with as a young child began to distance themselves from him because of the difference in skin color. With one particular friend, Myers was forced to make a decision. "For me it meant either accepting my role as his 'colored' friend or rejection of his friendship altogether," he recalled in *SAAS*. This, coupled with a severe speech disability, caused Myers to act out in school. "As a result I found myself suspended from school a great deal. Although I enjoyed school, I found that I didn't always fit in." Embarrassed by the way children laughed at his speech, Myers began to withdraw more and more in the classroom. Had it not been for his fifth grade teacher, Mrs. Conway, Myers may have never found the confidence or desire to become a writer. After she found him reading a comic book in class, she did what many other teachers would have done—she tore it up. The next day, however, she handed him the book *East of the Sun, West of the Moon*, telling him that if he was going to read in the back of the class, he might as well read something good. "Reading took on a new dimension for me" he wrote in *SAAS*. This, coupled with Mrs. Conway's pushing students to write their own stories to read in class, sparked a light in Myers.

Intimidated by the prospect of having to read in front of the class, Myers began writing poetry to reduce the number of words he was unable to pronounce. He found that he loved writing, and he became a changed person. Myers told Roger Sutton in a *School Library Journal* interview that "[Kids] are very moral. They want to be very moral, but they need to find ways. . . . They adopt other things—toughness and gangsterism—in the search for values. . . . [If] given any kind of an opportunity to lead a moral life, they will."

Begins Literary Career

Realizing that he would be unable to attend college due to the high financial costs, Myers entered the military at seventeen. After he was discharged he began working at several magazines and newspapers writing articles and poetry. His first opportunity to showcase his writing talent came when the Council on Interracial Books for Children sponsored a contest for minority writers. Myers wrote his first book, *Where Does the Day Go?*, which was chosen for publication. The story depicts an African American father who leads a group of minority children on a walk, explaining to them the difference between night and day and the uniqueness of each.

From 1970 to 1977 Myers worked as a book editor for the Bobbs-Merrill publishing house. He commented in *SAAS* that he was hired merely because the company "wanted a Black editor." During that time he wrote his second children's book, *The Dancers*. Myers had already experienced a publisher's trying to force him to introduce white characters into his stories. With *The Dancers*, he saw firsthand the control that publishers have over their writers' books. He recalled in *Interracial Books for Children Bulletin*, "The publisher introduced a white character for me. He's not in

the story, but he appears in as many pictures as possible and seems to be in the story. This being a Black writer was not going to be an easy task."

Along with other writers, such as Tom Feelings and Moneta Barnett, who were creating for the audience of minority children, Myers was hopeful that a revolution of children's literature would begin. This belief was wrong, as he observed in *SAAS*: "By the time President Ford left office the 'Days of Rage' had ended and the temper of the time was lukewarm. Blacks were no longer a hot political issue. The librarians were the major markets for black children's books, and when they began to suffer cutbacks it was books on the black experience that were affected most."

When Myers was fired from his job, he and his second wife (his first marriage did not last) decided he should dedicate himself to full-time writing. Myers followed up *The Dancers* with two more children's books, which he published under the name Walter Dean Myers, in honor of his foster parents. The book that finally brought him critical attention, however, was *Fast Sam, Cool Clyde, and Stuff*, which was originally a short story. Myers was persuaded by an editor to expand the story into a full-length book, and it became his first novel for juvenile readers.

Fast Sam is narrated by eighteen-year-old Stuff, who looks back on experiences he had when he was thirteen and living in Harlem. Hanging out with the other title characters, Fast Sam and Cool Clyde, he forms a gang called the Good People. As a close-knit group of good friends they deal with problems confronting teenagers, such as broken homes, welfare, love, drugs, street brawls, encounters with the police, and even death. Reviewers were enthusiastic about the book, especially Myers's use of "street talk" and his portrayal of the characters' tender feelings for one another. In the *New York Times Book Review*, Robert Lipsyte praised Myers's "gentle and humorous touch," and Aleen Pace Nilsen, writing in in *English Journal*, noted that one of the "nicest things" was that the members of the Good People gang "try to communicate rather than to exploit each other. . . ."

After writing *Fast Sam*, Myers recognized the importance of stories minority children can relate to, stories that portray situations and settings that are truer to their realities than European-influenced

The heat is on.

This 1989 Newbery Honor book about twelve-year-old Jamal, pressured to join the gang his imprisoned older brother used to lead, reveals the frightening conditions in which he lives.

juvenile fiction. The author found inspiration from the great African American writers of the past. Referring to one mentor, Myers was quoted by Rudine Sims Bishop in *Presenting Walter Dean Myers* as saying, "I had learned from Langston Hughes that being a black writer meant more than having one's characters brown skinned, or having them live in what publishers insist on describing on book jackets as a 'ghetto.'" One of the most important influences Myers found was not a work by an African American writer, however, but James Joyce, the famous Irish author. Myers had serious doubts about his own ability to become a writer, and he questioned his worth constantly. His validation came, he continued, "When I discovered *Portrait of the Artist as a Young Man* I knew that I was not alone. If Joyce had these doubts,

too, and he was a writer, well—I would also become a writer" he told *SAAS*. This realization inspired Myers to write some of the most powerful children's books addressed to, but not exclusively for, minority children.

Myers's appeal comes with the diversity of his writing, for he has the ability to create both light-hearted and serious fiction. One of the earliest examples of his literary power is *It Ain't All For Nothing'*, which features twelve-year-old Tippy, who is living with his dying grandmother but is forced to move in with his father. A professional criminal, his father is abusive and Tippy is forced to turn him over to the police. The book is painful in its accounts of Tippy's abuse by his father, yet extremely uplifting during the moments when the community comes to Tippy's aid. *School Library Journal* reviewer Steven Matthews stated that the novel gives readers "a vivid slice of New York City life," recommending it as a "first-rate read." According to a *Kirkus Reviews* contributor, "Myers gives us people" in *It Ain't All for Nothin'*, which the critic termed "a winner." Ashley Jane Pennington observed in *Interracial Books for Children* that the novel "deals frankly with the stark realities of ghetto life," and that it is "a devastating book which needed to be written."

Writing for African Americans

While Myers was establishing his career, he encountered many obstacles as an African American writer. First, publishers and libraries were hesitant to carry any of his books, not seeing the need or the audience for them. On the flip side, when Myers attempted to write about things other than African American life, he was faced with questions such as "Why did you decided to write about this?" or "With such a need for Black literature why would you want to write about anything else?" In the interview with Sutton, Myers observed, "Every black writer who's been writing for any length of time has heard this. I remember Langston Hughes saying the same thing." While Myers has seen it as his goal to provide minority children with a canon of literature that speaks to them, doing so has not been an easy task for him. "[People] are very often not looking at the writer simply as a writer. They're jumping over the concept that maybe, as a writer, what I want to do is something entirely different," he told Sutton.

Despite his troubles with publishers and libraries, Myers continued writing. He returned to a more humorous depiction of urban life in *The Young Landlords*, which features the experiences of the narrator, Paul Williams. Like Stuff in *Fast Sam*, Paul has a circle of friends who look out for one another. As the story opens Paul and his buddies have become the owners of a slum building, which they call The Joint. The plot revolves around their zany but frequently dangerous attempts to meet their responsibilities as landlords. *Bulletin of the Center of Children's Books* reviewer Zena Sutherland found "an attractive picture of a black urban neighborhood" in *The Young Landlords*. *Horn Book* contributor Kate M. Flanagan praised the novel for its "masterful blend of humor and realism," adding that Myers "has once again demonstrated his keen sensitivity to the joys and frustrations of adolescence. . . ." Reflecting another view, Pennington cited "certain drawbacks," among them an unbelievable story line, in *Interracial Books for Children Bulletin*. Nevertheless, she commended Myers for offering "a balanced picture" that shows "there are at least two sides in most situations" such as "tenant-landlord relationships, male-female relationships, people-to-people situations."

By 1980 Myers had published four picture books for children, two nonfiction works, and six novels for young adults. The decade of the 1980s was an even more prolific period, during which he produced two other picture books, "The Arrow" series of four adventure tales for juvenile readers, and seventeen other young adult novels. In most of the novels he continues to portray the lives of Harlem teenagers, touching on contemporary social problems.

Hoops is the story of eighteen-year-old Lonnie Jackson, a talented basketball player who has been abandoned by his parents. He befriends Cal Jones, a troubled former basketball pro, when Cal starts coaching the youth team. Soon Cal becomes a father figure to Lonnie in a relationship that *Voice of Youth Advocates* contributor Patricia Berry considered "the best part of the book." Cal eventually reveals that his career ended because he was involved in betting on sports. Other important plot elements are Lonnie's love for his girlfriend Mary-Ann, teen friendship problems, and gangster influences in the neighborhood. In a review for *Best Sellers* Ruth Martin concluded that "*Hoops* is hopeful and sensitive," an examination of Lonnie's "de-

cision to become a young black adult person. . . ." Berry predicted that young adult basketball enthusiasts "will enjoy this one."

In *Won't Know Till I Get There* the story is told through journal entries by Steve, a teenager whose middle-class parents have taken in thirteen-year-old Earl as a foster child. After the boys and two of their friends get into trouble, they end up in juvenile court and are ordered to spend the summer working in an old people's home. As the plot progresses Steve and Earl slowly but painfully become friends. Hazel Rochman stated in *School Li-*

A compelling war story about the Vietnam War, this novel has been favorably compared to Stephen Crane's *The Red Badge of Courage*.

brary Journal that readers will love "the fierce and funny repartee and the grotesque insults" as well as "bantering [that] explodes into violent hostility," shifts from "slapstick to pathos," and "sudden stabs of psychological insight." *Booklist* reviewer Denise M. Wilms singled out Myers's "special knack" at making his teenage characters "seem real flesh-and-blood figures." Diane Gersoni Edelman noted in the *New York Times Book Review* that Myers "ably integrates his dual themes of complex family relationships and senior citizens' problems."

Myers has also written several adventure novels, including the works in "The Arrow" series and *The Nicholas Factor* and *Tales of a Dead King. The Nicholas Factor* features Gerald, a college student, who is invited to join the exclusive Crusade Society. Soon afterward he is asked by a government agent to spy on the group. Gerald travels with the Crusaders on a humanitarian mission to Peru, where they work with an Inca tribe. Gerald and a fellow Crusader, Jennifer, become increasingly suspicious of the group's motives. After the mission is unexpectedly called off and the society leaves Peru, Gerald and Jennifer discover that many Indians are dying as a result of the coercive efforts of the Crusaders, which had once been a religious organization. The action heats up as Crusader leaders pursue Gerald and Jennifer. A *Publishers Weekly* reviewer called *The Nicholas Factor* a "disturbing, powerful work" that makes the reader consider the consequences of "implementing one's vision of the world." Becky Johnson Xavier observed in *Voice of Youth Advocates* that although the plot seems "farfetched," the story works well and readers will be "hooked until the end."

Tales of a Dead King takes place at an archaeological dig in Aswan, Egypt, where John Robie and Karen Lacey become involved in a mystery. Archaeologist Dr. Erich Leonhardt, who is John's great uncle, has left a note saying he was called away. But John and Karen wonder if he may have been kidnapped. Thus ensues a series of adventures as the two teenagers try to find Leonhardt. While most reviewers found plot and characterization to be weak, they noted that Myers tells a good story and acquaints the reader with Egypt. *ALAN Review* contributor Alan McLeod predicted that "The intrigue will entice youthful readers," a few of whom "may develop an interest in archaeology."

Myers also wrote *Motown and Didi: A Love Story* and *The Outside Shot,* which are sequels to novels he wrote in the 1970s. Two minor characters from *It Ain't All for Nothin'* reappear in *Motown and Didi,* a sensitive, moving love story. Didi wants to leave Harlem and go to college, but she is trapped by family problems, which include her brother Tony's heroin habit. Determined not to live in any more foster homes, Motown has settled in an abandoned building and works at odd jobs. The teenagers meet when Motown rescues Didi from thugs who accuse her of trying to turn in their drug-pusher boss to the police. Soon Didi falls in love with Motown, although he does not fit into her dream of leaving Harlem. C. Anne Webb wrote in the *ALAN Review* that *Motown and Didi* was Myers's "best written novel yet," and *Interracial Books for Children Bulletin* reviewer Judy Rogers called *Motown and Didi* "admirable heroes." Nancy C. Hammond, writing in *Horn Book,* praised the "potent anti-drug statement" Myers makes through the character of Tony. In 1985 *Motown and Didi* earned the author the first of three Coretta Scott King awards, which are presented annually by the American Library Association to African American authors and illustrators who make an outstanding contribution to literature.

The main character in *Hoops,* Lonnie Jackson, returns in *The Outside Shot.* Now enrolled at a small Midwestern college on a basketball scholarship, Lonnie has managed to leave Harlem. However, he is not prepared for the world outside his old neighborhood, where he is one of only a few blacks on campus. The novel traces Lonnie's efforts to fit in as he meets people who help him learn about himself. Among them are an autistic child, a female track star, a white roommate, a history professor, and a former college athlete. In a review for *School Library Journal,* Carolyn Caywood praised the novel as a "deeply moving, believable story of a very American rite of passage into adulthood."

One of Myers's more unusual novels is *Sweet Illusions,* a workbook about pregnancy for teenagers. Each of the fourteen chapters focuses on a fictional character who describes the experience of unexpected parenthood. Representing a social and racial cross-section of society, there are five unwed mothers, five fathers, and four family members or friends. At the end of each chapter are blank pages on which readers can write responses

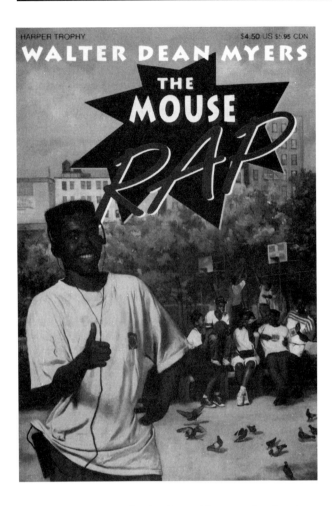

HARPER TROPHY $4.50 US $5.95 CDN

WALTER DEAN MYERS

THE MOUSE RAP

With every chapter beginning with a rap by fourteen-year-old Mouse, this 1990 work details how he avoids his dad, enters a dance contest, and searches for a mobster's loot one busy, exciting summer.

to what they have read. Reviewers welcomed Myers's book. Stephanie Zvirin commented in *Booklist* that "the book is an astute, realistic consideration of some of the problems associated with teenage pregnancy," providing a perspective on teenage fathers, who are "too often neglected." A *Kirkus Reviews* contributor pointed out, however, that "these tales are . . . very scary, and adolescent readers will find them involving and disturbing."

In 1988 Myers published *Scorpions* and *Fallen Angels*, novels he described to Kimberly Olson Fakih in *Publishers Weekly* as "a departure" in his career—"very serious, probing work," he said. "Not that the others didn't address serious issues, too," he continued, "but the new ones were more diffi-

cult to write." *Scorpions* is the story of two boys who join a Harlem gang and become involved in the narcotics trade. As Myers elaborated for *Publishers Weekly*, "The members [of the gang] are young because when they are arrested, there is no penalty. . . . These things are real, and they're happening more than we talk about. You can buy a gun in an hour or so. And a kid needs a reason not to have a gun." The author told *New York Times* interviewer Shirley Horner, "I am writing [in *Scorpions*]. . . about a family like so many I grew up with—low-income families, headed by a single parent, a hard-working woman who leaves her young children every morning and carries around with her all day long a fear that they may go wrong."

Scorpions was followed by *Fallen Angels*, which Myers wrote as a tribute to his brother, who was killed in Vietnam. Featuring a seventeen-year-old boy from Harlem who joins the Army, the novel is based on Myers's own experiences, which he recalled for Fakih: "No one really joined up because they wanted to fight or kill. . . . To me, the pivotal point was when they change from naive young people to understanding what war is about, that the currency of war is death, not ideals." Myers told Horner of the *New York Times* that *Fallen Angels* "also highlights the ironic fact that a generation ago black kids with no place to go were welcome in the Army. These days that's often closed to them, too, because they can't pass the tests."

Fallen Angels was favorably reviewed. Mel Watkins observed in the *New York Times Book Review* that it is "a candid young adult novel that engages the Vietnam experience squarely. It deals with violence and death as well as compassion and love, with deception and hypocrisy as well as honesty and virtue. It is a tale that is as thought-provoking as it is entertaining, touching and, on occasion, humorous." *Fallen Angels* won several awards, among them the Coretta Scott King Award, making Myers a two-time recipient of the honor.

■ **Update**

During the 1990s Myers continued his prolific output, writing the kind of novels that brought him recognition earlier in his career. Among his most popular books is *Darnell Rock Reporting*, published

If you enjoy the works of Walter Dean Myers, you may also want to check out the following books and films:

Frank Bonham, *Durango Street,* 1965.
Alex Haley, *Roots: The Saga of an American Family,* 1976.
Virginia Hamilton, *A Little Love,* 1984.
Will Hobbs, *The Big Wander,* 1992.
Boyz N the Hood, written and directed by John Singleton, 1991.
Sounder, a film based on the novel by William Armstrong, 1972.

in 1994, which features the title character, a thirteen-year-old middle school student. Darnell joins the school newspaper in a final effort to keep the principal from calling his parents and possibly expelling him from school. He finds that his assignments are exciting, but it is not until he interviews a homeless Vietnam veteran that he finds the power of his own voice. He then writes in his article that an abandoned parking lot should be converted into a garden to be used by the homeless to grow food. A local newspaper picks up the story, and Darnell is thrown into the spotlight.

Darnell Rock Reporting tackles issues such as poverty and homelessness. But as Janice Del Negro reported in *Booklist,* "[the] story is not issue driven. It is the development of Darnell's character that moves things forward: we watch as Darnell takes his first tentative steps toward thinking and acting on his own." The book was also praised by Sybil Steinberg of *Publishers Weekly,* who said *Darnell Rock Reporting* is an "optimistic—and realistic— portrayal of a boy learning to live by his convictions."

The Glory Field, also released in 1994, is an epic tale that traces the evolution of the African American experience: from the slave ships to the streets of Harlem. *The Glory Field* received mixed reviews. Hazel Rochman of *Booklist* praised the slavery accounts as "powerful, but afterwards this becomes a sprawling docu-novel, with little of the taut intensity of Myer's great family quest story, *Somewhere in the Darkness.*" Yet Linda Perkins noted in *Wilson Library Bulletin*: "In an era when

other authors would have published a series of books . . . Myers has ambitiously taken the opposite approach. By telescoping generations into one book, he has produced an engrossing fast-forward look at African American history, underscoring the strength and importance of the black family." Kenneth C. Davis of the *New York Times Book Review* took the opposite position. "[S]uch a big bite may be more than can be chewed in one book. The worthy effort proves perhaps too ambitious." Most critics agreed, however, that the best episode deals with Tommy Lewis, a promising young basketball player in the 1960s who rejects a token scholarship offer at a white university. Rochman pointed out in *Booklist* that "instead, he takes part in a civil rights demonstration and chooses a stunning way to expose the official violence that has always kept the races apart." The basic contention of most critics was summed up by Davis: "There are interesting people here. But it is sometimes difficult to know enough to feel an emotional link to them."

Collaborates with Son

Myers's next book, *Shadow of the Red Moon,* marks his first collaborative effort with his son Christopher, who did the illustrations. Myers weaves a tale of survival and fantasy centering around a group of young children, led by Jon, who escape from Crystal City to make their way through the Wilderness and past their enemies to the Ancient Land, where a new start awaits them. The story follows the usual fantasy encounters with unicorns, traps, packs of wild blind dogs, and the inevitable group bonding. As Hazel Rochman wrote in *Booklist,* "The surprise is that they also bond with the enemy. . . ." *Shadow of the Red Moon* also received mixed reviews. Tim Rausch, writing for *School Library Journal,* reported that young adults "will enjoy the fantasy and adventure, while mature readers will recognize the story's vivid parallels with modern society." Rochman complained, however, that "The problem is that the very vagueness of the characters, both friend and foe . . . makes it hard to care about the conflict. . . ."

Myers has also received recognition for *Slam!,* a basketball story that features the eponymous title character as a teenager who is in control on the court, yet his personal life is rife with difficulties. Slam's grades are low, he cannot fit in with the predominately white students at his school, his grandmother is dying, and his best friend Ice is dealing crack. *Booklist* reviewer Bill Ott wrote, ". . . Myers does a good job of rescuing his characters from stereotype. . . . [He also uses] crisp details, not flowery language to achieve muscular poetry." The ending of the novel pits Slam and Ice against one another in a symbolic basketball game that mirrors the problems in their friendship. Maeve Visser Knoth of *Horn Book* observed that "readers will appreciate *Slam!* for the honesty with which Myers portrays the dreams of one Harlem teenager." In 1997 *Slam!* earned Myers his third Coretta Scott King Award.

In 1997 Myers and his son collaborated again, this time on a children's book titled *Harlem*. Through Walter Dean Myers's poem and Christopher Myers's illustrations, the work celebrates both the promise and problems that Harlem gives to the African American community as well as its connection to Africa. *Booklist* contributor Michael Cart praised the work, calling the text "as much song as poem" while adding that "it is Harlem as a visual experience that YAs will return to again and again." Diane Roback and Elizabeth Devereaux of *Publishers Weekly* observed that *Harlem's* "artistic integrity is unmistakable. . . ."

At the end of the 1990s Myers remained one of the foremost African American authors of books for children and young adults. Nearly a decade earlier he had written in *SAAS*: "As a Black writer I want to talk about my people. I want to tell the reader about an old Black man I knew who told me he was God. I want to tell a reader how a blind man feels when he hears that he is not wanted because he is Black. I want to tell Black children about their humanity and about their history and how to grease their legs so the ash won't show and how to braid their hair so it's easy to comb on frosty winter mornings."

"The books come," Myers continued. "They pour from me at a great rate. I can't see how any writer can ever stop. There is always one more story to tell, one more person whose life needs to be held up to the sun." In an essay for *Children's Books and Their Creators* in 1995, Myers further elaborated on his role as a writer: "What I do with my books is to create windows to my world that all may peer into. I share the images, the feelings and thoughts, and, I hope, the delight."

■ Works Cited

Berry, Patricia, review of *Hoops, Voices of Youth Advocates*, April, 1982, p. 36.

Bishop, Rudine Sims, *Presenting Walter Dean Myers*, Twayne, 1991, 123 p.

Cart, Michael, review of *Harlem, Booklist*, February 15, 1997, p. 1021.

Caywood, Carolyn, review of *The Outside Shot*, *School Library Journal*, November, 1984, pp. 135-36.

Davis, Kenneth C., review of *The Glory Field*, *New York Times Book Review*, November 13, 1994.

Del Negro, Janice, review of *Darnell Rock Reporting, Booklist*, August, 1994, p. 2044.

Edelman, Diane Gersoni, review of *Won't Know Till I Get There*, *New York Times Book Review*, June 13, 1982, pp. 26-27.

Fakih, Kimberly Olson, "Walter Dean Myers," *Publishers Weekly*, February 26, 1988, p. 117.

Flanagan, Kate M., review of *The Young Landlords, Horn Book*, October, 1979, p. 535.

Hammond, Nancy C., review of *Motown and Didi: A Love Story, Horn Book*, March-April, 1985, pp. 186-87.

Horner, Shirley, "Author Seeks to Inspire Black Youth," *New York Times*, Section 22, August 21, 1988, p. 10.

Review of *It Ain't All for Nothin', Kirkus Reviews*, October 15, 1978, p. 1143.

Knoth, Maeve Visser, review of *Slam!, Horn Book*, January/February, 1997, pp. 63-64.

Lipsyte, Robert, review of *Fast Sam, Cool Clyde, and Stuff*, *New York Times Book Review*, May 4, 1975, p. 30.

Martin, Ruth, review of *Hoops, Best Sellers*, February, 1982, pp. 442-43.

Matthews, Steven, "Junior High Up: *It Ain't All for Nothin'*," *School Library Journal*, October, 1978, p. 158.

McLeod, Alan, review of *Tales of a Dead King*, *ALAN Review*, Winter, 1984, p. 29.

Myers, Walter Dean, "The Black Experience in Children's Books: One Step Forward, Two Steps Back," *Interracial Books for Children Bulletin*, Volume 10, number 6, 1979, pp. 14-15.

Myers, Walter Dean, essay in *Something about the Author, Autobiography Series*, Volume 2, Gale, 1986, pp. 143-56.

Myers, Walter Dean, interview with Roger Sutton in *School Library Journal*, June, 1994, pp. 24-28.

Myers, Walter Dean, essay in *Children's Books and Their Creators*, edited by Anita Silvey, Houghton Mifflin, 1995, p. 475.

Review of *The Nicholas Factor, Publishers Weekly,* March 18, 1983, p. 70.

Nilsen, Alleen Pace, review of *Fast Sam, Cool Clyde, and Stuff, English Journal,* March, 1976.

Ott, Bill, review of *Slam!, Booklist,* November 15, 1996, p. 579.

Pennington, Ashley Jane, review of *It Ain't All for Nothin', Interracial Books for Children Bulletin,* Volume 10, Number 4, 1979, p. 18.

Pennington, Ashley Jane, review of *The Young Landlords, Interracial Books for Children Bulletin,* Volume 12, Number 1, 1981, p. 15.

Perkins, Linda, review of *The Glory Field, Wilson Library Bulletin,* November, 1994, p. 121.

Rausch, Tim, review of *Shadow of the Red Moon, School Library Journal,* December, 1995, p. 106.

Roback, Diane, and Elizabeth Devereaux, review of *Harlem, Publishers Weekly,* January 13, 1997, p. 76.

Rochman, Hazel, review of *Won't Know Till I Get There, School Library Journal,* May, 1982, pp. 72-73.

Rochman, Hazel, review of *The Glory Field, Booklist,* October 1, 1994, p. 319.

Rochman, Hazel, review of *Shadow of the Red Moon, Booklist,* November 15, 1995, p. 549.

Rogers, Judy, *Motown and Didi: A Love Story, Interracial Books for Children Bulletin,* November-December, 1985, p. 19.

Steinberg, Sybil, review of *Darnell Rock Reporting, Publishers Weekly,* July 4, 1994, p. 65.

Sutherland, Zena, review of *The Young Landlords, Bulletin of the Center for Children's Books,* November, 1979, p. 52.

Review of *Sweet Illusions, Kirkus Reviews,* February 1, 1987, p. 29.

Watkins, Mel, review of *Fallen Angels, New York Times Book Review,* January 22, 1989.

Webb, C. Anne, review of *Motown and Didi: A Love Story, ALAN Review,* Winter, 1985, p. 31.

Wilms, Denise M., review of *Won't Know Till I Get There, Booklist,* June 1, 1982, p. 1315.

Xavier, Becky Johnson, review of *The Nicholas Factor, Voice of Youth Advocates,* December, 1983, pp. 79-80.

Zvirin, Stephanie, review of *Sweet Illusions, Booklist,* June 15, 1987, p. 159.

■ For More Information See

BOOKS

Black Literature Criticism, Gale, 1992.

Children's Literature Review, Gale, Volume 4, 1982, pp. 155-60, Volume 16, 1989, pp. 134-44; Volume 35, 1995, pp. 295-99.

Contemporary Black Biography, Volume 8, Gale, 1995.

Contemporary Literary Criticism, Volume 35, Gale, 1985.

Dictionary of Literary Biography, Volume 33: *Afro-American Writers After 1955,* Gale, 1984.

Holtze, Sally Holmes, editor, *Fifth Book of Junior Authors and Illustrators,* H. W. Wilson, 1983.

Patrick-Wexler, Diane, *Walter Dean Myers,* Raintree, 1996.

The Schomburg Center Guide to Black Literature, Gale, 1996.

Twentieth-Century Children's Writers, 3rd edition, St. James Press, 1989.

PERIODICALS

Black Enterprise, December, 1982, p. 31.

Booklist, February 1, 1992, p. 1028; June 1, 1992, p. 1768; June 15, 1992, p. 1840; October 1, 1992, pp. 321-22; November 15, 1992, p. 588; September 1, 1993, p. 54; October 15, 1993, p. 438; June 1, 1995, p. 1788; April 1, 1996, p. 1373; September 1, 1996, p. 123.

Boys' Life, May, 1983, p. 19; July, 1990, p. 13.

Children's Digest, January/February, 1995, p. 23.

Ebony, September, 1985, p. 28.

English Journal, January, 1990, p. 90; March, 1990, p. 79; September, 1992, p. 95; October, 1993, pp. 80-81; December, 1993, p. 74.

Entertainment Weekly, February 5, 1993, p. 63.

Essence, December, 1981, p. 22.

Horn Book, June, 1980, pp. 301-2; December, 1980, pp. 636-37; August, 1981, p. 434; August, 1982, pp. 415-16; July/August, 1988, p. 503-4; January/February, 1989, pp. 73-74; May/June, 1990, p. 339; March/April, 1992, pp. 217-18; May/June, 1992, pp. 344-45; November/December, 1992, pp. 739-40; March/April, 1993, p. 209; September/October, 1993, pp. 626-27; January/February, 1994, p. 82, pp. 88-89; March/April, 1995, pp. 194-95, 200-1; July/August, 1996, pp. 452-53.

NEA Today, May/June, 1989, p. 33; May 20, 1990, p. 44; September, 1990, p. 32; December, 1991, p. 9.

New York Times Book Review, July 20, 1997, pp. 21-22.

People, December 18, 1995, pp. 30-31.

Publishers Weekly, May 8, 1987, p. 71; May 13, 1988, p. 277; June 10, 1988, p. 82; November 11, 1988; March 30, 1990, p. 64; November 1, 1991,

p. 82; March 9, 1992, p. 58; June 22, 1992, p. 65; July 13, 1992, p. 56; September 28, 1992, p. 80; November 23, 1992, p. 64; August 30, 1993, p. 94; May 8, 1995, p. 296; February 19, 1996, p. 215; November 4, 1996, p. 89; November 25, 1996, p. 76.

School Library Journal, June/July, 1987, p. 111; June/July, 1988, p. 118; September, 1988, p. 201; December, 1988, p. 110; July, 1990, p. 90; February, 1991, p. 54; March, 1992, pp. 263-64; April, 1992, p. 146; September, 1992, pp. 254-55; October, 1992, pp. 144-45; February, 1993, p. 102; May, 1993, p. 100; June, 1993, p. 120; June, 1994, pp. 24-28; March, 1995, p. 185; July, 1995, p. 67; September, 1995, p. 196; January, 1996, p. 65; May, 1996, p. 96; August, 1996, p. p. 186; November, 1996, pp. 116-17; February, 1997, p. 121.

Skipping Stones, Winter/Spring, 1994, p. 31.

Voice of Youth Advocates, October, 1997, pp. 266, 268.

Wilson Library Bulletin, October, 1987, pp. 62-63; March, 1988, pp. 76-77; May, 1990, p. 102; March, 1992, pp. 95-96; June, 1992, pp. 154-55; January, 1993, p. 88; October, 1993, pp. 120-21; April, 1994, pp. 125-26.*

—Sketch by Aaron Saari

Beverley Naidoo

Teacher for Cultural Diversity and English, Dorset, United Kingdom, 1988—; visiting fellow, University of Southampton. *Member:* British Defence and Aid Fund for Southern Africa's Education Committee, Writers' Guild for Great Britain, National Association for Teachers of English.

■ Personal

Born May 21, 1943, in Johannesburg, South Africa; daughter of Ralph (a composer and music copyright manager) and Evelyn (a broadcaster and theater critic; maiden name, Levison) Trewhela; married Nandhagopaul Naidoo (a solicitor), February 1, 1969; children: Praveen, Maya. *Education:* University of Witwatersrand, South Africa, B.A., 1963; University of York, B.A. (with honors), 1967, Certificate of Education, 1968; University of Southampton, Ph.D., 1991.

■ Addresses

Home—13 Huntly Rd., Bournemouth, Dorset BH3 7HF, United Kingdom. *Agent*—Gary Carter, Roger Hancock Ltd., 4 Water Lane, London NW1 8NZ, United Kingdom.

■ Career

Kupugani Non-Profit Nutrition Corporation, Johannesburg, South Africa, field worker; primary and secondary teacher in London, England, 1969; writer, 1985—; researcher, 1988-91; Advisory

■ Awards, Honors

Other Award, *Children's Book Bulletin*, 1985, Children's Book Award, Child Study Book Committee at Bank Street College of Education, 1986, Child Study Association of America's Children's Books of the Year selection, 1987, Parents' Choice Honor Book for Paperback Literature, Parents' Choice Foundation, 1988, and Notable Children's Trade Book in the Field of Social Studies, National Council on the Social Studies/Children's Book Council, all for *Journey to Jo'burg: A South African Story;* Notable Children's Trade Book in the Field of Social Studies, National Council for the Social Studies/Children's Book Council, 1990, and Best Book for Young Adults selection, American Library Association, 1991, both for *Chain of Fire.*

■ Writings

FOR YOUNG ADULTS

Journey to Jo'burg: A South African Story, illustrated by Eric Velasquez, Longman, 1985, Lippincott, 1986.
(Editor) *Free As I Know,* Bell & Hyman (London), 1987.

Chain of Fire, Collins, 1989.

FOR CHILDREN

Letang's New Friend, illustrated by Petra Rohr-Rouendaal, Longman, 1994.
No Turning Back: A Novel of South Africa, HarperCollins, 1997.

FOR ADULTS

Censoring Reality: An Examination of Books on South Africa, ILEA Centre for Anti-Racist Education and British Defence/Aid Fund for Southern Africa, 1985.
Through Whose Eyes? Exploring Racism: Reader, Text and Context, Trentham Books, 1992.

Contributor to academic journals, including *English in Education* and *Researching Language and Literature*.

■ Sidelights

South African expatriate Beverley Naidoo's books about the evils of the apartheid system and of homelessness in "the new South Africa" have brought her and the issues she writes about into the international spotlight. Prior to the May 1994 election of the first black majority government headed by African National Congress leader Nelson Mandela, Naidoo wrote a series of groundbreaking books intended to educate young people on the evils of racism in her homeland. In the years since the dismantling of apartheid, Naidoo has turned her attentions to more general concerns, chiefly the plight of homeless street children. She commented in *Twentieth-Century Young Adult Writers* (*TCYA*) that she now writes to challenge herself by broadening her perspective and to inform, educate, and entertain her readers, particularly children. "Writing is a journey. It is a way of exploring the country of my childhood from the perspective of the child I was not," she explained.

Beverley Naidoo was born into a comfortable lifestyle as a member of an upper middle-class family in Johannesburg, South Africa. She grew up in a world of privilege where whites patronizingly referred to African males—of any age—as "boys" and females as "girls." Naidoo was raised by a black nanny whom she knew only as

"Mary." As a girl, young Beverley was happily oblivious to the fact that her caregiver had three young children of her own who lived nearly two hundred miles away. Mary seldom saw her own family because she had to work in town to support them. One particular incident that occurred when Naidoo was eight or nine has stayed with her: "Mary received a telegram and collapsed. The telegram said that two of her three young daughters had died. It was diphtheria—something for which, I as a white child, had been vaccinated," Naidoo stated in her acceptance speech for the 1986 Award of the Child Study Children's Book Committee. It took Naidoo years to realize the significance of that event. She continued: "I must have continued to spout with the arrogance of white youth the customary rationalizations—that Mary and those who followed her, were lucky because we gave them jobs, sent presents to their children at Christmas, and so on. I still feel intensely angry about the racist deceptions and distortions of reality which the adult society passed on to me as a child."

Following her high school graduation, Naidoo attended the University of Witwatersrand, earning her B.A. in 1963. But it was what she learned outside the classroom that proved to be far more important than anything she learned in it. "It was a period of growing state repression and as I gradually began to see for the first time some of the stark reality all around me, I became intensely angry not only at the narrowness of my schooling, but at its complicity in perpetuating apartheid through not previously challenging my blinkered vision," Naidoo wrote in *Through Whose Eyes? Exploring Racism: Reader, Text, and Context.* She became politicized and joined in the anti-apartheid movement. Although she was a "small fish," as she puts it, Naidoo was detained by police in 1964 under the "Ninety Days" solitary confinement law. That experience forever changed the way she viewed life in South Africa. The following year, Naidoo moved to England to study at the University of York, supporting herself for a time by teaching school.

Naidoo had always resisted her mother's suggestion that she should become a teacher. Now having seen and experienced for herself the impact of education as a tool in the fight against apartheid, Naidoo pursued a career in the classroom. Almost as important, she continued to expand her own horizons by reading about what she terms "the reality [that] she had left behind" in South Africa. Two of the books that Naidoo found to be particularly influential in her own life were *The African Child* by Camara Laye and *Roaring Boys* by Edward Blishen. "The contexts were so different—Laye's memories of a West African childhood and Blishen's semi-autobiographical novel of a young teacher's initiation into the violence of schooling and youth culture in London's East End," Naidoo stated. "Within each of [these books] I hear a strong, implicit commitment to education as a process of opening out and questions being raised about the nature of schooling, power, young people and society." Inspired by these messages, Naidoo earned a B.A. with honors from York in 1967 and then received her teaching certificate the following year. For the next decade, she taught primary and secondary school in London. She also

became involved with an anti-apartheid group and began looking for ways to educate young people about the dangers of racism in general and of the South African apartheid system in particular.

Works to End Apartheid

During the early 1980s, Naidoo began doing research for the Education Group of the British Defence and Aid Fund for Southern Africa, an activist organization that aided victims of apartheid and worked to raise the world's awareness of human rights abuses in South Africa. Naidoo's efforts helped make people aware of the alarming shortage of suitable teaching materials about apartheid and resulted in the publication of a critical bibliographical study called *Censoring Reality: An Examination of Books on South Africa,* which Naidoo edited. When the Education Group decided to commission a work of "informed and helpful fiction" on apartheid, she volunteered to write it. "I wrote the text simply, quite deliberately," she explained. Naidoo penned the story as if she were telling it to her own children, she recalled, because "it seemed important to be able to explain at their level what was happening in South Africa."

The fruit of Naidoo's efforts was a juvenile novella called *Journey to Jo'burg: A South African Story.* The story deals with the adventures of a young black girl named Naledi and her younger brother Tiro when they travel to Johannesburg in search of their mother, who works there in a white household as a domestic servant—just as Naidoo's own caregiver Mary had done. The children set out on the three-day journey because their baby sister is critically ill and their grandmother, who cares for them in their mother's absence, has no money for medicine or a doctor. The journey is an eye-opener for the children as they encounter the ugly realities of life for black people under apartheid.

Reviews for *Journey to Jo'burg* were mixed. In *School Library Journal,* JoAnn Butler Henry found favor with the book. "A short story with a wealth to share, this well-written piece has no equal," she wrote. Gillian Klein, writing in the *Times Educational Supplement,* found the novel a work of "uncompromising realism." In *Booklist,* however, Hazel Rochman stated, "This is not great fiction: story and characters are thinly disguised mecha-

Naledi and her friend Taolo lead their schoolmates in demonstrations against apartheid—with frightening consequences—in this 1990 novel.

If you enjoy the works of Beverley Naidoo, you may also want to check out the following books and films:

Sheila Gordon, *Waiting for the Rain*, 1987.
Alan Paton, *Cry, the Beloved Country*, 1948.
Hazel Rochman, *Somehow Tenderness Survives: Stories of Southern Africa*, 1988.
Bopha!, a film directed by Morgan Freeman, 1993.
The Navigator, a film about time travel produced in New Zealand, 1988.

nisms for describing the brutal social conditions and the need for change." Whatever they thought of the quality of Naidoo's writing, critics and readers alike agreed that her subject material was as powerful as it was shocking. As a result, the book achieved the desired effect: it helped to draw the world's attention to the anti-apartheid struggle. *Journey to Jo'burg* was banned by the South African government, and it won several children's book awards in the U.S. and the United Kingdom.

Encouraged by the success of her first book, Naidoo pressed ahead in her literary efforts. She edited an anthology of poems, short stories, and extracts for young people called *Free As I Know*. Reviewer Bill Deller in the *Times Educational Supplement* explained the three criteria behind the selections: "The idea of the seminal experience whereby young people gain insight into themselves and society; the concentration on perspectives that may be passed over in a white monocultural society and the desire to include 'stimulating literature of an international character.'"

In 1989, Naidoo produced a sequel to *Journey to Jo'burg*. The book was an adolescent novel called *Chain of Fire*. In it, Naidoo revisits Naledi, the central character in *Journey to Jo'burg*, now fifteen years old. *Chain of Fire* tells of the ordeal of Naledi, her family, and their neighbors as they face eviction and enforced resettlement to a "black homeland" called Bophuthatswana. Apartheid laws prevented Naidoo from living in South Africa, so she did all of her research for *Chain of Fire* by interviewing other South African expatriates and by reading whatever books and articles she could find about the government's ethnic cleansing policies. "I immersed myself in the devastating data

on the mass destruction of the homes and lives of millions of South Africans by the apartheid regime through its program of 'Removals' to [these] so-called 'Homelands,'" Naidoo once commented in *Something About the Author*. "*Chain of Fire* is dedicated to all those who have struggled to resist and I hope it will enable young people in various parts of the world to feel links of both heart and mind to Naledi and others like her who refuse to let the flames of justice be smothered."

Most reviewers praised *Chain of Fire*. "The work flows effortlessly, with power and grace, as it succeeds in making a foreign culture immediate and real," wrote Marcia Hupp in *School Library Journal*. "*Chain of Fire* is not easy reading, nor should it be; it tackles tough issues head-on and presents them with superb dramatic tension," Diane Roback declared in *Publishers Weekly*. The book's "chief strength lies in the moving representation of family and village life," said Peter Hollindale of the *Times Educational Supplement*.

Naidoo's next book was *Through Whose Eyes? Exploring Racism: Reader, Text, And Context*, a collection of articles by English schoolchildren who were writing about literature they had read and about their own interactions with black visitors to their mostly white school; Naidoo served as editor. In 1994, she wrote a children's book entitled *Letang's New Friend*.

Exploring New Themes

Naidoo has said that for her writing is "a journey" of self-discovery in which she learns things about herself and about the world around her. Thus in the wake of apartheid's demise, she has begun to explore new themes as she has broadened her own horizons. "I want my writing always to be primarily a way of extending the limits of my own understanding," she told *TCYA*. Reflecting this, Naidoo's next book for young readers was *No Turning Back: A Novel of South Africa*. The story tells of the adventures of a twelve-year-old African boy named Sipho who flees an abusive step-father and runs away to a new life on the mean streets of Johannesburg. Sipho learns quickly about survival in the "new South Africa." He gets involved with a street gang, sleeps in the gutters, begs for food, and experiments with glue sniffing in an effort to escape his misery. In the end, he finds refuge in a shelter where he has the chance to go to school. *No Turning Back* is a stark, powerful, uncompromising look at the plight of abused and homeless street children. "The problems [Sipho] faces are those experienced by street children internationally. However they are also those of a child struggling to make sense of his world at a time of turbulent historical change," Naidoo wrote in the *Seventh Book of Junior Authors and Illustrators.*

Amy Chamberlain in *Horn Book* praised *No Turning Back* as "a can't put down account of an impoverished South African boy." In *Publishers Weekly,* Diane Roback and Elizabeth Devereaux felt the book was a "powerful novel" written "effortlessly from the boy's point of view, so that his confusion, eagerness and naïve wishes unfold naturally." A contributor in *Kirkus Reviews* was less impressed, describing the book as "bland [and] uninvolving" and noting "the story lacks the fire that made *Journey to Jo'burg* so compelling."

In the post-apartheid era, Beverley Naidoo has persisted in her struggle for human rights. She delivers lectures and holds workshops on anti-racist and multicultural themes. She also conducts creative writing seminars and has said that she intends to continue writing about life in the land of her birth. "South Africa is now in the process of great historical change but, as in the U.S., the rifts and scars of racism run deep. Writing allows me to use my imagination to challenge the segregation of experience caused through discrimination," Naidoo stated in *TCYA.*

■ Works Cited

Chamberlain, Amy, review of *No Turning Back: A Novel of South Africa, Horn Book,* March/April, 1997, p. 203.

Deller, Bill, "Breadth of Vision," *Times Educational Supplement,* May 20, 1988, p. B21.

Henry, JoAnn Butler, review of *Journey to Jo'burg: A South African Story, School Library Journal,* August, 1986, p. 96.

Hollindale, Peter, "Bound to Protest," *Times Educational Supplement,* March 10, 1989, p. B15.

Hupp, Marcia, review of *Chain of Fire, School Library Journal,* May, 1990, pp. 108, 113.

Klein, Gillian, review of *Journey to Jo'burg: A South African Story* and *Censoring Reality: An Examination of Books in South Africa, Times Educational Supplement,* April 26, 1985, p. 26.

Naidoo, Beverley, "The Story behind 'Journey to Jo'burg,'" *School Library Journal,* May, 1987, p. 43.

Naidoo, Beverley, comments in *Something About the Author,* Volume 63, Gale, 1991, pp. 108-12.

Naidoo, Beverley, *Through Whose Eyes? Exploring Racism: Reader, Text and Context,* Trentham Books, 1992.

Naidoo, Beverley, comments in *Twentieth Century Young Adult Writers,* 1st edition, St. James Press, 1994, pp. 479-80.

Naidoo, Beverley, comments in *Seventh Book of Junior Authors and Illustrators,* edited by Sally Holmes Holtze, H. W. Wilson, 1996, pp. 234-35.

Review of *No Turning Back: A Novel of South Africa, Kirkus Reviews,* December 1, 1996.

Roback, Diane, review of *Chain of Fire, Publishers Weekly,* March 30, 1990, p. 64.

Roback, Diane, and Elizabeth Devereaux, review of *No Turning Back: A Novel of South Africa, Publishers Weekly,* December 16, 1996, p. 60.

Rochman, Hazel, review of *Journey to Jo'burg: A South African Story, Booklist,* March 15, 1986, p. 1086.

■ For More Information See

BOOKS

Children's Literature Review, Volume 29, Gale, 1993, pp. 160-67.

Gallo, Donald R., compiler and editor, *Speaking for Ourselves, Too,* National Council of Teachers of English, 1993.

PERIODICALS

ALAN Review, Spring, 1997.

Booklist, March 15, 1990, p. 1430; October 1, 1990, p. 351.

Bulletin of the Center for Children's Books, May, 1986, p. 175; May, 1990, p. 223.

Children's Literature Association Quarterly, Summer, 1988, pp. 57-60.

English Journal, September, 1986, p. 81; March, 1995, p. 55.

Five Owls, May, 1990, p. 90; March, 1991, p. 70.

Kirkus Reviews, March 15, 1990, p. 428.

Los Angeles Times Book Review, January 28, 1990, p. 15.

Magpies, March, 1996, p. 36.

Publishers Weekly, May 30, 1986, p. 67; January 25, 1993, p. 88.

School Librarian, May, 1989, p. 75; February, 1996, p. 31; August, 1996, p. 96.

School Library Journal, February, 1997, p. 104.

Times Educational Supplement, October 2, 1992, p. 9; July 7, 1995, p. 20; July 5, 1996, p. R8.

Tribune Books (Chicago), February 26, 1989, p. 8.

Voice of Youth Advocates, August, 1986, p. 148; June, 1990, p. 108; October, 1996, p. 199; October, 1997, p. 246.

Wilson Library Bulletin, November, 1990.*

—Sketch by Ken Cuthbertson

Jan Needle

◼ Personal

Born February 8, 1943, in Holybourne, England; son of Bernard Lionel (an engineer) and Dorothy Mary (Brice) Needle. *Education:* Victory University of Manchester, drama degree (with honors), 1971.

◼ Addresses

Home—Rye Top, Gellfield Ln., Uppermill, Oldham, Lancashire, England. *Agent*—Rochelle Stevens & Co., 15/17 Islington High St., London N1 1LQ, England.

◼ Career

Portsmouth Evening News, Portsmouth, England, reporter, 1960-64; reporter and sub-editor for *Daily Herald and Sun,* 1964-68; freelance writer, 1971—.

◼ Awards, Honors

My Mate Shofiq was a runner-up for the Guardian Award; *Wagstaffe the Wind-Up Boy* was voted one of the best books of 1987 by the Federation of Children's Book Groups, 1987.

◼ Writings

FICTION FOR YOUNG ADULTS

Albeson and the Germans, Deutsch, 1977.
My Mate Shofiq, Deutsch, 1978.
A Fine Boy for Killing (also see below), Deutsch, 1979.
A Sense of Shame and Other Stories, Deutsch, 1980.
Piggy in the Middle, Deutsch, 1982.
The Wicked Trade, Burnett Books, 1983.
Going Out, Deutsch, 1983.
A Pitiful Place and Other Stories (short stories), Deutsch, 1984.
Tucker in Control, Deutsch, 1985.
The Thief (also see below), Hamish Hamilton, 1989.
The Bully, Hamish Hamilton, 1993.

PLAYS

(With Vivien Gardner and Stephen Cockett) *A Game of Soldiers,* Collins, 1985.
(With Vivien Gardner and Stephen Cockett) *The Rebels of Gast Street,* Collins, 1986.
(With Vivien Gardner and Stephen Cockett) *The Thief,* Collins, 1990.

FOR CHILDREN

Rottenteeth (picture book), illustrated by Roy Bentley, Deutsch, 1979.
The Bee Rustlers, illustrated by Paul Wright, Collins, 1980.

The Size Spies, illustrated by Roy Bentley, Deutsch, 1980.

Losers Weepers, illustrated by Jane Bottomley, Methuen, 1981.

Another Fine Mess, illustrated by Roy Bentley, Armada, 1982.

Behind the Bike Sheds, Methuen, 1985.

A Game of Soldiers (also see below), Deutsch, 1985.

Great Days at Grange Hill, Deutsch, 1985.

Skeleton at School, illustrated by Robert Bartelt, Heinemann, 1987.

Uncle in the Attic, illustrated by Robert Bartelt, Heinemann, 1987.

Wagstaffe the Wind-Up Boy, illustrated by Roy Bentley, Deutsch, 1987.

In the Doghouse, illustrated by Robert Bartelt, Heinemann, 1988.

The Sleeping Party, illustrated by Robert Bartelt, Heinemann, 1988.

Mad Scramble, illustrated by Kate Aldous, Heinemann, 1990.

As Seen on TV, illustrated by Kay Widdowson, Hamish Hamilton, 1992.

Wagstaffe and the Life of Crime, illustrated by Roy Bentley, Collins Lions, 1992.

Bogeymen, illustrated by Liz Tofts, Deutsch, 1992.

FOR ADULTS

Wild Wood, illustrated by William Rushton, Deutsch, 1981.

(Under name Frank Kippax) *The Scar* (dramatized as television series "Underbelly") HarperCollins, 1990.

(Under name Frank Kippax) *The Butcher's Bill,* HarperCollins, 1991.

(Under name Frank Kippax) *Other People's Blood,* HarperCollins, 1992.

(Under name Frank Kippax) *Fear of Night and Darkness,* HarperCollins, 1993.

A Fine Boy for Killing (restored and uncut version of the young adult title), HarperCollins, 1996.

OTHER

(With Peter Thomson) *Brecht* (criticism), Blackwell (Oxford), 1981, University of Chicago Press, 1981.

Also author of television series "A Game of Soldiers," 1984, "Behind the Bike Sheds," 1985-86, "Truckers" (for adults), 1987-88, and "Soft Soap," 1988. Author of radio plays broadcast in England and New Zealand between 1971 and 1980.

■ Sidelights

"Children's taste is not the same as adults'," writes Jan Needle in his autobiographical essay in *Something about the Author Autobiography Series* (*SAAS*). "That which adults prescribe for children is not necessarily going to do them any 'good,' nor is it what they really 'need,' nor indeed, will they even *read* it. If I have a mission as a children's writer, that could be it: Listen to the children." Needle has made a name for himself by writing tough-minded, sometimes controversial books that examine real-life issues such as violence, racism, and poverty.

As a child, Needle lived with his family in a comfortable home in a nice suburb of Portsmouth, England. His father gave it all up, though, to become a farmer in the north of Wales. However, the first winter there was a harsh one, and it nearly bankrupted the family. They returned to Portsmouth where they could only afford to rent a damaged room behind a dry-cleaning plant. From then on, his father had a variety of odd jobs and they were very poor. However, Needle found it exciting. "We lived in this shattered old wreck of a factory, no telephone, no radio that worked, often no gas to keep us warm, occasionally no electricity for the light. . . . I adored it. . . . I thought it was my private castle," he related in *SAAS.*

Perhaps the unusual environment helped develop Needle's imagination. In addition, the city of Portsmouth had been severely bombed during World War II, and the barren landscape provided an exotic playground. "For a person with a romantic turn of mind, who lived in fantasyland much of the time, it could hardly have been a better place," he confessed in *SAAS.* When he was out of school, he and his friends would explore bombed houses and other structures, imagining what had happened during the destruction. This landscape was to help him formulate his first published novel, *Albeson and the Germans.*

Needle's tendency towards fantasy and storytelling was well known in his family and community. "I was first published when I was about eight years old, but even before that I was known as being much better at making up stories than telling the truth," he related in *SAAS.* His first story was published in the Labour Party newsletter edited by his father, although his father's ulterior motive was to publish it because he thought the spelling in it was very strange. Still, Needle claims in *SAAS* that "there was never much doubt in anybody's mind that I would end up as a writer."

"To the adults who think I am treading n areas best left unexplored, I can only say this: if a problem exists in life and affects children, it exists to be examined through the medium of children's fiction."

—Jan Needle

Needle's family wanted him to get a good education, so they had him take an examination that would get him a spot in a private school. Much to his surprise, Needle performed well and earned a place at Portsmouth Grammar School. However, school was difficult for him because his classmates were the sons of naval officers, and they immediately knew he was not one of them. He was teased and taunted frequently. Needle admitted in *SAAS* that "it was the sea that saved my bacon in that school. The point was, that although my peers could talk about ships and things, I could sail. . . . When I did make friends, it was usually with the sons of naval officers who wanted to learn to sail but did not get the chance."

School Struggles

Despite Needle's keen imagination and talent at telling stories, he did not do very well in school. Before he was going to graduate, his Headmaster had a discussion with him. He was failing all the classes he needed to get into a university. After a discussion with his father, he decided to quit school and went to work as a journalist. "Journalism, I have to say it, suited me. . . . Unlike schoolwork, which I found hard, and boring, and irrelevant, I found journalism easy, and it gave me the space to grow up and develop." He soon had a better job in a city in the north of England and eventually became a sub-editor there.

For once, Needle was enjoying a middle-class existence, and the money he made helped him go to clubs and otherwise have fun. However, at the same time, he was also trying his hand at writing fiction. "I was aware that I wanted to tell some sort of truth about the world (or how I saw it), and it was very difficult," Needle told *SAAS*. "The dichotomy became clearer rather rapidly: I was being paid to write stories in a popular newspaper that basically I found distortions of the truth, and I was being paid extremely well for it. At the same time, I was trying very hard to express the real, essential truth . . . and nobody would pay."

Needle, now married, decided to enter a university to study drama. The path ahead of him was not easy. His poor grades in high school precluded him from getting into a university. So Needle commuted to a nearby town to take college preparatory classes. At the end of the year, when he took his examinations, he nearly failed English and general studies and pulled off a good grade only in economic history. He was devastated. Contacting Victory University in Manchester, he explained his situation. Fortunately, school administrators allowed him to attend.

In the university setting, Needle thrived, passing his first-year classes with top honors. The university let him enter the honors program after this showing, and he finished his degree with high honors. "I recount this story not to boast, but maybe to hearten other 'low achievers'," Needle related in *SAAS*. After finishing his degree, Needle realized that he had to make a living again, because his calling as a playwright was not paying the bills. He was able to secure a part-time sub-editor job and to write in his spare time.

One day an idea came to him that was to change his career. He began writing a parody based on the book *The Wind in the Willows*. Within weeks, he had a completed manuscript, and a realization: "From almost the moment I'd begun, I'd known that this was what my writing life had been lacking; I had found the form that suited my persona, or my talent, or my secret desires. . . . I knew from the moment I put pen to paper, that underneath it all I was a novelist. The die was cast." Because of potential copyright violations, the book would not be published until several years later, but it set everything in motion.

Finding His Niche

With the knowledge that he could write a children's book, within a few weeks Needle had knocked out his second work, *Albeson and the Germans* (1977). However, he was still surprised that he was becoming a children's writer, having considered himself only a writer for adults. "Like every other aspect of my becoming a novelist, it seemed, the process was more accidental than thought-through. But if it worked, why argue?" he wrote in *SAAS*.

Albeson and the Germans follows a young boy named Jimmy Albeson who is horrified that there are going to be two German children in his classroom. It is after the war and Albeson remains loyal to his dead grandfather, who told him that Germans were evil. He goes on a rampage of andalism with his friend Smithie when they hear the news of the German children. Albeson decides to run away, and he joins a ship that, ironically, is filled with Germans.

Reviewer Margaret Meek praised the novel's realism in the *School Librarian*, believing that "It will make us less comfortable, for a start, but young readers will see the point." Roy Blatchford, writing in the *Times Educational Supplement* found some of the plot unbelievable but nonetheless felt that Needle wrote a strong and convincing story: "It should not be long before Jan Needle appears on the Topliner list." However, the book also became quite controversial. Many reviewers and parents were outraged by Needle's realistic tone. "Letters were received from librarians and teachers who refused to give it houseroom. . . ." Needle related to *SAAS*. However, it has always been a popular book, "It is still in print and widely used in British schools."

"From my point of view, these reactions were fascinating," Needle confessed to *SAAS*. "I had written the sort of book I had felt the lack of as a child and in a way I assumed would have become completely standard in the newer, harder world we all perceived ourselves as living in." However, the reaction to his book didn't keep Needle from continuing this style in his next work, *My Mate Shofiq* (1978). This book tackled racism and class distinctions. Bernard, a poor white boy, initially finds himself disliking Shofiq, a Pakistani immigrant. Shofiq is involved in violence with the local gang because he wants to defend his sisters. Bernard gets drawn in to Shofiq's world and grudgingly admits respect for Shofiq; eventually they become good friends, or "mates."

If you enjoy the works of Jan Needle, you may also want to check out the following books and films:

Christopher Paul Curtis, *The Watsons Go to Birmingham—1963*, 1995.

Farrukh Dhondy, *East End at Your Feet*, 1976, and *Come to Mecca, and Other Stories*, 1978.

My Beautiful Launderette, a film starring Daniel Day Lewis, 1985.

Reviewers generally praised Needle's book for its realism and social consciousness. "Altogether this is a strongly committed, outspoken book. In one sense there can be no other kind on this theme because children born here are in the midground of all racial conflicts," wrote Margaret Meek in the *School Librarian*. Leila Berg was especially enthusiastic about the book, claiming in the *Times Educational Supplement* that Needle would be hard-pressed to top this work, "because nothing, *nothing*, will ever be better than *My Mate Shofiq*."

However, there was considerable backlash from parents and critics about the book. "The first shot was fired within a week of publication," Needle related in *SAAS*. "The headteacher of a London school where I was due to address a conference on 'Realism in Children's Books' (on the strength of *Albeson*) the following Monday, rang me at home on Saturday evening to say the teachers had 'voted democratically' to ban me from the school premises. So much for realism." Partly because of the criticism he was receiving, Needle decided to venture into a different realm, writing comedic novels. "Looking back on it, it was here I made probably the big mistake in my career as a writer for young people. After two books that were realistic, hard, difficult—and extremely popular with young readers, I am glad to say—what I should have done is exactly what critics, however much they may deny it, ever and always want a writer to do: produce more of the same."

Work Shows Variety

Instead, Needle wrote a comic adventure about a pair of children thwarting a group of spies in *The Size Spies* (1979), a harrowing work about a shepherd boy illegally pressed into work on a naval ship in *A Fine Boy for Killing* (1979), and a chronicle of the children of bee farmers in *The Bee Rustlers* (1980). In 1981, Needle's parody of *The Wind in the Willows* was published as *Wild Wood*. In this book, he turned the upper-class structure of the original book upside down, making the lower-class animals the ones who tell the story. Jessica Yates remarked in *British Book News, Children's Supplement* that *Wild Wood* "should become a favourite with adults as well as children."

Needle's *A Game of Soldiers* (1985) chronicles the dreadful events that happen to a group of children during the Falkland Islands conflict. They find an enemy soldier hiding in their land and can't decide what to do with him. Marcus Crouch, in a review in the *Junior Bookshelf* claimed that "Jan Needle's new novel is small in scale and big in ideas. There are formidable problems, social and moral with which the reader must grapple."

Wagstaffe the Wind-Up Boy (1987) was a true departure for Needle. He wrote it with the intention that reluctant readers would enjoy it. A repulsive child, Wagstaffe is despised by his parents who abandon him one day. In the confusion, he is run over by a car and rebuilt into a wind-up boy by a strange doctor. The doctor them sends him out to perform heroic deeds, including one where he saves his parents from certain death. Yet even this isn't enough to make his parents change their minds about him. Chris Stephenson remarked in the *School Librarian* that "I have to confess to the odd snicker. The eleven-year-olds in my class are finding it '*wickedly* funny'—and that just about sums it up."

Needle took aim at a growing problem in British schools—bullying—in his 1993 work *The Bully*. Simon Mason is a poor loner who most people in the school feel is capable of being a bully. He is ostracized by many, but the person who is really abusing other schoolchildren is Anna, a popular girl. Only after Simon ends up falling into a chalk pit and breaking his leg do school officials realize that he is the one who is being tormented. *Junior Bookshelf* reviewer D. A. Young found that if the book "should stimulate open discussion on the topic by pupils *and* teachers it will have served a very useful purpose." David Buckley, writing in the *Times Educational Supplement*, believed that the work "is a good case study and a cracking piece of storytelling."

> "I do remember, from my own childhood, wondering why no one ever wrote about people like me. . . . Not only do the underprivileged need a voice, but the privileged need to see and hear them suffering."
>
> —Jan Needle

In 1980, Needle commented in *Books for Your Children* that "When I started writing children's books about four or five years ago, I had no idea of the trouble I was letting myself in for. I suppose I should have guessed, because my main reason for starting was a vague feeling that so many books already on the market were soft in the extreme—middle-class, middle of the road, and middling awful. What I didn't realise was just how large and determined is the body of adult opinion intent on keeping them that way!" However, Needle claims that he will continue to do things his way: "To the adults who think I am treading in areas best left unexplored, I can only say this: if a problem exists in life and affects children, it exists to be examined through the medium of children's fiction. I always tread extremely warily, whatever some of them claim to think; but I shall continue to tread. I hope they'll try and understand."

■ Works Cited

Berg, Leila, review of *My Mate Shofiq, Times Educational Supplement*, March 26, 1982, pp. 28-29.

Blatchford, Roy, review of *Albeson and the Germans, Times Educational Supplement*, January 13, 1978, p. 22.

Buckley, David, review of *The Bully, Times Educational Supplement*, February 25, 1994, p. 14.

Crouch, Marcus, review of *A Game of Soldiers, Junior Bookshelf*, August, 1985, p. 189.

Meek, Margaret, review of *Albeson and the Germans, School Librarian*, March, 1978, p. 60.

Meek, Margaret, review of *My Mate Shofiq, School Librarian*, December, 1978, p. 361.

Needle, Jan, "On First Writing for Children," in *Books for Your Children*, Autumn-Winter, 1980, pp. 20-21.

Needle, Jan, autobiographical essay in *Something about the Author Autobiography Series*, Volume 23, Gale, 1997, pp. 179-95.

Stephenson, Chris, review of *Wagstaffe the Wind-Up Boy, School Librarian,* May, 1988, pp. 57-58.

Yates, Jessica, review of *Wild Wood, British Book News, Children's Supplement,* Autumn, 1981, pp. 25-26.

Young, D. A., review of *The Bully, Junior Bookshelf,* December, 1993, pp. 242-43.

■ For More Information See

BOOKS

Children's Literature Review, Volume 43, Gale, 1997, pp. 123-43.

Contemporary Authors, New Revision Series, Volume 28, Gale, 1990, pp. 344-45.

Something about the Author, Volume 30, Gale, 1983, pp. 162-63.

Stories and Society: Children's Literature in its Social Context, Macmillan Academic and Professional Ltd., 1992, pp. 84-96.

Twentieth-Century Children's Writers, 3rd edition, St. Martin's, 1983, pp. 712-13.

Twentieth-Century Young Adult Writers, 1st edition, St. James Press, 1994, pp. 484-85.

PERIODICALS

Books for Keeps, January, 1985, p. 19.

Book Window, Winter, 1979, p. 32; Winter, 1980, p. 29.

British Book News Children's Books, March, 1986, p. 31.

British Book News, Children's Supplement, Spring, 1981, p. 27; Spring, 1982, pp. 7-8, 12.

Children's literature in education, Summer, 1982, pp. 59-60.

Growing Point, November, 1978, p. 3417; May, 1980, pp. 3699, 3702-3; January, 1981, p. 3826; July, 1981, pp. 3906-7; March, 1983, p. 4029.

Junior Bookshelf, June, 1979, pp. 170-71; August, 1980, pp. 178-79; April, 1982, pp. 67-68; February, 1983, p. 51.

Magpies, July, 1994, p. 32.

New Statesman, December 3, 1982, p. 21.

Punch, October 21, 1987, p. 42.

School Librarian, March, 1980, p. 62; March, 1981, p. 54; March, 1982, p. 38; June, 1983, pp. 166-67; March, 1985, pp. 59-60; December, 1985, pp. 301-5.

School Library Journal, January, 1984, p. 87; September, 1984, p. 121.

Sunday Times (London), July 31, 1988, p. G4.

Times Educational Supplement, November 7, 1980, p. 24; November 20, 1981, pp. 31-32; June 8, 1984, p. 46; December 3, 1993, p. 29.

Times Literary Supplement, September, 29, 1978, p. 1082; November 20, 1981, p. 1363; August 24, 1984, p. 954; March 29, 1985, p. 354.*

—Sketch by Nancy Rampson

Colby Rodowsky

■ Personal

Born February 26, 1932, in Baltimore, MD; daughter of Frank M. Fossett and Mary C. Fitz-Townsend; married Lawrence Rodowsky (an appeals court judge), August 7, 1954; children: Laurie, Alice, Emily, Sarah, Gregory, Katherine. *Education:* College of Notre Dame of Maryland, B.A., 1953. *Religion:* Roman Catholic.

■ Addresses

Agent—Gail Hochman, Brandt & Brandt, 1501 Broadway, New York, NY 10036. *Home*—4306 Norwood Rd., Baltimore, MD 21218-1118.

■ Career

Writer. Teacher in public schools in Baltimore, MD, 1953-55, and in a school for special education, 1955-56; children's book reviewer, *Baltimore Sunday Sun*, 1977-84; librarian's assistant, Notre Dame Preparatory School, Baltimore, 1974-79.

■ Awards, Honors

Notable Book citation, American Library Association, *School Library Journal* Best Book of the Year award, Library of Congress Children's Book of the Year award, and Notable Children's Trade Book in the Field of Social Studies award, National Council for the Social Studies-Children's Book Council, all for *The Gathering Room*; Best Books for Young Adults citation, American Library Association, and *School Library Journal* Best Book for Young Adults award, both for *Julie's Daughter*; *School Library Journal* Best Book of the Year award, and *Booklist* Editors' Choice citation, both for *Sydney, Herself*; Best Books for Young Adults citations, American Library Association, for *Hannah In Between* and *Remembering Mog*.

■ Writings

What About Me?, F. Watts, 1976.
P.S. Write Soon, F. Watts, 1978.
Evy-Ivy-Over, F. Watts, 1978.
A Summer's Worth of Shame: A Novel, F. Watts, 1980.
The Gathering Room, Farrar, Straus, 1981.
H, My Name Is Henley, Farrar, Straus, 1982.
Keeping Time, Farrar, Straus, 1983.
Julie's Daughter, Farrar, Straus, 1985.
Fitchett's Folly, Farrar, Straus, 1987.
Sydney, Herself, Farrar, Straus, 1989.

Dog Days, pictures by Kathleen Collins Howell, Farrar, Straus, 1990.

Jenny and the Grand Old Great-Aunts, illustrated by Barbara Roman, Bradbury, 1992.

Lucy Peale, Farrar, Straus, 1992.

Hannah In Between, Farrar, Straus, 1994.

Sydney Invincible, Farrar, Straus, 1995.

Remembering Mog, Farrar, Straus, 1996.

The Turnabout Shop, Farrar, Straus, 1998.

OTHER

Contributor of fiction, essays, and reviews to periodicals, including *McCall's, Good Housekeeping, Christian Science Monitor, New York Times Book Review,* and *Washington Post.*

■ Sidelights

Teacher-turned-author Colby Rodowsky was already into middle age when she wrote her first young adult novel in 1976. "I was about forty, and at that time I thought if you hadn't done anything by forty, you never would. Now I know a lot better," Rodowsky told Jean W. Ross in an interview in *Contemporary Authors.* In the two decades that she has been writing, Rodowsky has produced sixteen books and has won numerous literary awards. In the process she has earned a reputation as one of America's most consistently interesting and entertaining authors of novels for young adults. Critics have praised her talent for bringing to life fresh, empathetic characters who grapple with real-life situations, difficult people, and the uncertainties of growing up in a society where values are shifting and uncertain.

Colby Rodowsky was born and raised in Baltimore, Maryland, where she lived for a time in a house across the street from the one in which she and her family currently live. Rodowsky recalled in a 1996 essay for *Something About the Author Autobiography Series* (SAAS) that she always dreamed of being a member of a large family and of having siblings. In part, she explained, this was due to being an only child of an unhappy marriage. "I remember fights and silences and recriminations," Rodowsky wrote. "Night after night I would curl up under the covers with my Raggedy Ann doll, talking over the events of the day, telling her stories, finding answers to the age-old questions 'What if . . .?' and 'How about . . .?' and 'What happened next . . .?'"

Young Colby's parents, Mary and Frank Fossett, separated (for the first of several times) when their daughter was in first grade. Afterwards, Colby and her mother stayed with her mother's parents in the Chesapeake Bay town of Cape Charles, Virginia. Life in this idyllic seaside community was sleepy, safe, and relatively carefree for a child. It was here that Colby discovered the magical world of books. On days when the town library was closed, she would retreat to the attic of her grandparents' large rambling white frame house, which was filled with boxes and old trunks of wondrous things to play with and books to read. "The importance in my life of [Cape Charles] can be seen by the number of times I have used it in what I have written," Rodowsky explained in her *SAAS* article.

When her parents temporarily reconciled in the fall of 1939, the Fossetts reunited in Baltimore. Colby enrolled at a private Roman Catholic school for girls called Notre Dame. She has said the next two years were among the happiest of her early life, despite renewed tensions between her parents. When Frank Fossett enlisted in the Army Air Corps shortly after the start of World War II, he was posted to Florida. Colby and her mother moved to New York. The city was a wonderful place for a youngster then, a "friendlier and safer place than it is now," Rodowsky recalled. She had always loved making up stories, and it was while she was residing in New York during this period that she began doing so "seriously." Rodowsky recalls how she awoke once in the middle of the night to ask to whom she should dedicate her first book. Her mother sleepily suggested that she write it first and then decide. When her daughter did just that, Mary Fossett was enthusiastic in her praise and sent the manuscript to a friend who worked for a New York publisher. The book was rejected, of course, but it was returned to the twelve-year-old would-be author with an encouraging letter explaining that the reason it could not be published was the paper shortage caused by the war. "The 'book' was insignificant and best forgotten," Rodowsky later acknowledged, but "my mother's faith in me was definitely significant and continues to be important to me to this day."

The Fossetts briefly reconciled after the war before splitting for the last time. Mary Fossett relocated to Washington, where her teenaged daughter attended Georgetown Visitation Preparatory

School, first as a day student, then as a boarder. Following graduation, Colby moved in with her father and his parents in Baltimore. There she attended the College of Notre Dame of Maryland, majoring in English. In her spare time, she wrote poetry and signed up for creative writing classes; she had always wanted to be a writer. "It was at Notre Dame that I met Sister Maura Eichner and had her as a teacher. Sister Maura, a fine poet in her own right, was without question the best teacher I ever encountered and had more to do with my becoming a writer than anyone else," Rodowsky recalled in her *SAAS* article.

At a Saturday night square dance during her junior year at Notre Dame, she met Larry Rodowsky,

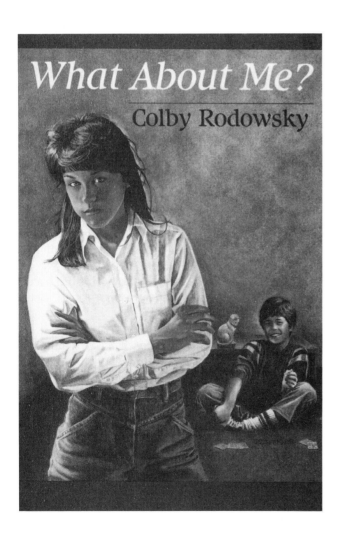

In this 1976 novel, a teenaged girl resents her little brother, "Fredlet," who has Down's syndrome, requires inordinate attention, and causes her public embarrassment.

a law student. The couple were married in August 1954, shortly after graduating from college, and Colby Rodowsky embarked on a teaching career. Following two years in the public primary school system, she took a job at St. Francis School for Special Education, working with developmentally handicapped children. Rodowsky loved the work, but when her first child was born in June 1956, she became a full-time homemaker. Five more children followed during the next nine years. By then, Larry Rodowsky had established his law practice and so the family moved to a large three-story house right across the street from where Colby Rodowsky once had lived as a girl. It was a dream come true for her. "At one point, in addition to the six children, we had three dogs and two cats. And suddenly there I was—in the midst of that LARGE EXTENDED FAMILY," Rodowsky said.

Inspired to Write

During the years that she was busy raising children, Rodowsky did little writing, other than "grocery lists." Then one day in the summer of 1972 she visited Sister Maura at Notre Dame. The teacher inspired her former pupil to enroll in a writing tutorial, something that Rodowsky had always longed to do. As part of this program, she wrote two novels. Neither of these initial efforts was publishable; however, Rodowsky was not discouraged. She signed up for another tutorial and by the end of the semester had written her third novel. *What About Me?* (which Rodowsky dedicated to Sister Maura) is the story of the love-hate relationship between a fifteen-year-old girl and her younger brother who has Down's syndrome. The story grew out of the author's experiences teaching developmentally handicapped children. "I . . . took that theme because I had taught the children and really loved them," Rodowsky told interviewer Jean W. Ross. "I didn't set out to write about a retarded child."

What About Me? was published in 1976 to excellent reviews. Zena Sutherland in *Bulletin of the Center for Children's Books* praised the work as "a good first novel" with "convincing characterization and dialogue." Jean Mercier of *Publishers Weekly* hailed it as "a profoundly moving, honest and tightly controlled, important novel." While Rodowsky continued to work part-time as a primary school librarian, the success of her first book

COLBY RODOWSKY

Julie's Daughter

aerial fiction

Told through three narrators—seventeen-year-old Slug, her mother who had abandoned her as an infant, and their dying neighbor, the artist Harper—this 1985 tale is about reconciliation and understanding.

inspired her to press ahead with her efforts to write fiction. "Eventually, after our eldest daughter married and moved away, I turned her room into an office and began to feel like a 'real' writer," she explained in an autobiographical sketch in the *Sixth Book of Junior Authors and Illustrators*. "Looking back on the books I've written, I see lots of things that have to do with my own life." Throughout the 1980s and early 1990s, although she writes "agonizingly slowly at times," as she puts it, Rodowsky penned more than a dozen young adult novels. Her own life experiences and emotions, aspects of her family life and

career, and intriguing characters she has met have all provided her with a wealth of literary inspiration.

The pattern of drawing upon her own life experiences for story material was set with Rodowsky's next two books, which appeared in 1978. Both of these novels proved popular with young readers and were well-received by the critics. *P.S. Write Soon* is about a spirited girl named Tanner who battles to overcome the twin handicaps of a brace that she wears on a paralyzed leg and the fact that she is the youngest in a family of bright, accomplished siblings. "Because the author deals so vividly with her characters and their problems, the book succeeds as an excellent family story," said a reviewer for *Horn Book*.

Evy-Ivy-Over is set in Cape Charles (although the town is never identified), and some of the characters in the story are modeled on people and situations the author knew in her childhood. The book tells the story of a young female heroine named Mary Rose October—affectionately known as "Slug"—and her grandmother Gussie, the town eccentric. The Slug character recurs in three of Rodowsky's subsequent books. In this, her debut, Slug struggles to find her identity while striving to reconcile the reality of who she is with the dream of the girl she would like to be. "Skilfully crafted, the story blends disparate themes into a coherent whole through a descriptive but not pretentious style and through the delineation of two unusual personalities," wrote reviewer Mary M. Burns of *Horn Book*. "Real and gripping, with penetration into unusual characters," said Betsy Hearne of *Booklist*.

Slug reappears in *H, My Name is Henley*, although not as the protagonist. This novel tells about the adventures of a twelve-year-old named Henley and her restless, footloose mother, Patti, who was loosely based on the character of Colby Rodowsky's own mom. "Henley is probably the most mature and perceptive twelve-year-old I've met in YA literature," noted *Voice of Youth Advocates* contributor Barbara Lenchitz Gottesman. "The tension and conflict between mother and daughter, the strain on a child forced into adult responsibilities, and the characterization of Patti are intensely real," reviewer Nancy C. Hammond of *Horn Book* commented. Reviewer C. Nordhielm Wooldridge of *School Library Journal* wrote that the book was "a bit short on plot and at times plausibility, and

If you enjoy the works of Colby Rodowsky, you may also want to check out the following books and films:

Bruce Brooks, *No Kidding*, 1989.
Patricia Calvert, *Yesterday's Daughter*, 1986.
Sharon Creech, *Walk Two Moons* 1994.
John Loughery, *First Sightings: Stories of American Youth*, 1993.
Zilpha Keatley Snyder, *Libby on Wednesday*, 1990.
The Breakfast Club, a film written and directed by John Hughes, 1985.

the characters, for all their idiosyncrasies, never quite emerge." Even so, the critic termed it "a fairly adept study of a particular mother-daughter relationship."

In *Julie's Daughter*, the sequel to *Evy-Ivy-Over*, Rodowsky reunites Slug with her long-lost mother Julie, who had abandoned her infant daughter in a bus station. The pair come to terms with one another and gain insights into life as they care for an irascible neighbor named Harper Tegges, an artist who is dying of cancer. Rodowsky tells this poignant story from the three viewpoints of the principal characters. "Many themes are discussed in this book: death, our responsibility to face life's crucial decisions, and sexual promiscuity," noted *Voice of Youth Advocates* reviewer Debbie Earl, who went on to praise *Julie's Daughter* for being "sensitively done and surprisingly humorous."

More Family Dramas

The theme of children losing one or both parents is a recurring one in Rodowsky's fiction. *Sydney, Herself* is the story of Sydney Downie, a free-spirited Australian girl whose father died a month before she was born. When an English teacher gives Sydney's class the assignment of writing a "self-awareness journal," Sydney invents a fanciful tale about being the daughter of a famous rock singer from a group known as The Boomerangs. When her story finds its way into the local newspaper, the confusion snowballs. "Rodowsky makes her readers work, never patronizing or condescending, yet always revealing inner layers that

poke through the surface," said reviewer Carol A. Edwards of *School Library Journal*. "The story is fresh, humorous, and believable. Sydney is interesting—bright, gritty, and sometimes sulky," wrote Elizabeth S. Watson of *Horn Book*.

Rodowsky offered a second installment of Sydney Downie's adventures in *Sydney Invincible*. The plot this time revolves around Sydney's tentative romance with Wally, the older brother of the child she babysits, and her unease at being in the high school history class taught by her own mother. "The emotional reactions of Sydney and her mom are poignant and easily imagined," wrote reviewer Betsy Eubanks of *Voice of Youth Advocates*. Brigitte Weeks of the *Washington Post Book World* agreed.

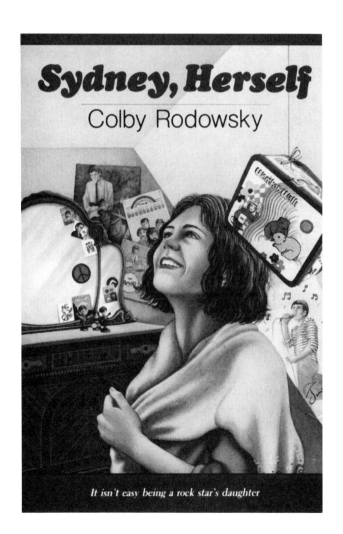

Sydney concocts a fanciful story about her father's career as the lead singer for an Australian rock group and discovers it isn't easy to have a famous dad in this 1989 work.

After being raped and condemned by her pastor father, Lucy runs away to Ocean City without money or any place to stay until she meets gentle Jake in this 1992 love story written for teens.

"Colby Rodowsky is an accomplished and sure-footed interpreter of what goes on in the mind of a teenaged girl," she observed.

The Rodowsky family's visits to the beach in Ocean City, Maryland, provided the backdrop for the novel *A Summer's Worth of Shame,* a story about a young man's summer holiday adventures working as a spook in a haunted house amusement facility. *Fitchett's Folly* also has a maritime setting. It is the story of Sarey-Ann, whose father drowns while he is rescuing a girl named Faith. When the foundling comes to live with Sarey-Ann,

her brother, and their aunt, Sarey-Ann is forced to come to grips with the deep resentments she feels towards Faith. "Rodowsky deftly balances adventure, pathos and surprising comedy in a tale about early days on the New England coast," said a reviewer for *Publishers Weekly.*

Keeping Time is an imaginative yarn about time travel back to sixteenth-century London. *The Gathering Room* is an offbeat story about the life, death, and a boy named Mudge, who lives with his reclusive parents in the gatehouse of a Baltimore cemetery. Rodowsky displayed the full range of her literary talents in creating what Jan Langton of the *New York Times Book Review* called a "simple, well-wrought story with a pleasant, if melancholy, sense of time and mortality." Reviewer Elizabeth Holtze of *School Library Journal* marveled at how "Despite the cemetery setting and the problem posed, there are no villains, and this is a happy book."

Explores Teens' Concerns

Not being content to merely entertain her young readers, Colby Rodowsky has also strived to make them think. In doing so, she has dared to explore the sometimes painful growing pains of today's teens in such gritty novels as *Lucy Peale, Hannah In Between,* and *Remembering Mog. Lucy Peale* is a love story about the seventeen-year-old daughter of a fanatically strict Christian evangelist. Lucy runs away from home when she becomes pregnant after being date-raped. When she meets a kindly young man named Jake in Ocean City, she moves in with him and struggles to build a new life for herself. A reviewer for *Kirkus Reviews* praised *Lucy Peale* as a "heartwarming love story" that is "gentle and appealing, [and] written with insight and skill." Stephanie Zvirin of *Booklist* wrote, "[Colby] Rodowsky fills the pages with talk and with Lucy's feelings and memories—of the date rape that resulted in her pregnancy, of her father's unbending rules, and of her sister Doris, whom she misses."

Hannah in Between delves into the troubled relationship between twelve-year-old Hannah Brant and her alcoholic mother. The book is an uncompromising look at a very painful social problem: alcohol abuse and its disastrous impact on family life. "The author constructs a believable story that weaves a young teen's limited understanding of

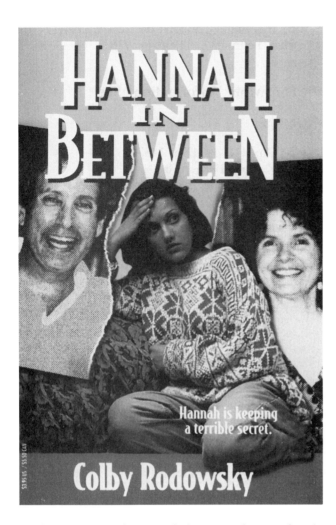

In this 1994 novel, Hannah is aware her mother is an alcoholic and needs help, but she doesn't know where to turn or how to begin looking.

the disease with her gradual acceptance that only her mother can begin to reverse her illness," stated Elizabeth S. Watson of *Horn Book*.

Remembering Mog is the story of a girl named Annie, whose older sister Mog was shot and killed by a stranger on the eve of her high school graduation. As Annie's own graduation day approaches, she is tortured by the recurring horror and fears brought about by her sister's murder. "Besides dealing with the protagonists's healing process, Rodowsky explores various manifestations of grief, including the state of denial experienced by Annie's mother and the suicidal urges of the boyfriend who was with Mog the day she was shot," wrote Elizabeth Devereaux and Diane Roback of *Publishers Weekly*. "A poignant, crystal-

line rendering of death's legacy for a parent and child, with a few powerful scenes that are unforgettable," remarked Stephanie Zvirin of *Booklist*.

Colby Rodowsky has said that she continues to derive a great deal of satisfaction from her work as a full-time writer. "I don't write books that are going to appeal to every child. Some, I think, are somewhat difficult and probably geared to good readers, but I don't see anything wrong with that. Every book isn't going to appeal to every child," she told interviewer Jean W. Ross. Asked to outline her future plans and goals, Rodowsky explained, "To get better. That's what we all want. What you always want somebody to say about your most recent work is that it's the best thing you've ever done."

■ Works Cited

Burns, Mary M., review of *Evy-Over-Ivy*, *Horn Book*, February, 1979, p. 65.

Devereaux, Elizabeth, and Roback, Diane, review of *Remembering Mog*, *Publishers Weekly*, March 25, 1996, p. 85.

Earl, Debbie, review of *Julie's Daughter*, *Voice of Youth Advocates*, April, 1986, p. 34.

Edwards, Carol A., review of *Sydney, Herself*, *School Library Journal*, July, 1989, p. 92.

Eubanks, Betsy, review of *Sydney, Invincible*, *Voice of Youth Advocates*, August, 1995, p. 164.

Review of *Fitchett's Folly*, *Publishers Weekly*, April 24, 1987, p. 70.

Gottesman, Barbara Lenchitz, review of *H, My Name is Henley*, *Voice of Youth Advocates*, April, 1983, p. 41.

Hammond, Nancy C., review of *H, My Name is Henley*, *Horn Book*, April, 1983, p. 167.

Hearne, Betsy, review of *Evy-Ivy-Over*, *Booklist*, November 1, 1978, p. 483.

Holtze, Elizabeth, review of *The Gathering Room*, *School Library Journal*, October, 1981, p. 146.

Langton, Jan, review of *The Gathering Room*, *New York Times Book Review*, October 25, 1981, p. 47.

Review of *Lucy Peale*, *Kirkus Reviews*, June 15, 1992, p. 784.

Mercier, Jean, review of *What About Me?*, *Publishers Weekly*, January 22, 1979, p. 371.

Review of *P.S. Write Soon*, *Horn Book*, August, 1978, p. 398.

Rodowsky, Colby, interview with Jean W. Ross for *Contemporary Authors*, *New Revision Series*, Volume 23, Gale, 1988, pp. 340-44.

Rodowsky, Colby, essay in *Sixth Book of Junior Authors and Illustrators*, edited by Sally Holmes Holtze, H. W. Wilson, 1989, p. 245.

Rodowsky, Colby, essay in *Something About the Author Autobiography Series*, Volume 22, Gale, 1996, pp. 225-39.

Sutherland, Zena, review of *What About Me?*, *Bulletin of the Center for Children's Books*, January, 1977, p. 80.

Watson, Elizabeth S., review of *Sydney, Herself*, *Horn Book*, September-October, 1989, p. 631.

Watson, Elizabeth S., review of *Hannah in Between*, *Horn Book*, September, 1994, p. 601.

Weeks, Brigitte, review of *Sydney, Invincible*, *Washington Post Book World*, July 5, 1995, p. 18.

Wooldridge, C. Nordhielm, review of *H, My Name is Henley*, *School Library Journal*, January, 1983, p. 87.

Zvirin, Stephanie, review of *Lucy Peale*, *Booklist*, July, 1992, p. 1933.

Zvirin, Stephanie, review of *Remembering Mog*, *Booklist*, February 1, 1996, p. 926.

■ For More Information See

PERIODICALS

Booklist, April 1, 1994, p. 1437.

Booktalker, May, 1990, p. 8.

Bulletin of the Center for Children's Books, January, 1983, p. 96.

Children's Literature in Education, June, 1992, p. 103.

New York Times Book Review, March 3, 1991, p. 29; July 3, 1994, p. 14.

Publishers Weekly, June 9, 1989, p. 70.

School Library Journal, October, 1978, p. 149.

Wilson Library Journal, February, 1990, pp. 84-85.*

—Sketch by Ken Cuthbertson

Danielle Steel

■ Personal

Born Danielle Fernande Schuelein-Steel, August 14, 1947, in New York, NY; daughter of John (a member of the family that owned the Lowenbrau Beer Company), and Norma (daughter of a Portuguese diplomat; maiden name, Stone) Schuelein-Steel; married four times; married fourth husband, John Traina (a businessman), in 1977; children: (first marriage) one daughter; (second marriage) one son; (fourth marriage) two stepsons, four daughters, one son. *Education:* Educated in France; attended Parsons School of Design, 1963, and New York University, 1963-67. *Religion:* Christian Scientist.

■ Addresses

Home—San Francisco, CA. *Agent*—Morton L. Janklow Associates, Inc., 598 Madison Ave., New York, NY 10022.

■ Career

Writer. Supergirls, Ltd. (public relations firm), vice-president of public relations, 1968-71; Grey Adver-

tising, San Francisco, CA, copywriter, 1973-74; has worked in other public relations and advertising.

■ Writings

NOVELS

Going Home, Pocket Books, 1973.
Passion's Promise, Dell, 1977.
The Promise (based on a screenplay by Garry Michael White), Dell, 1978.
Now and Forever, Dell, 1978.
Season of Passion, Dell, 1979.
Summer's End, Dell, 1979.
Loving, Dell, 1980.
The Ring, Delacorte, 1981.
Remembrance, Delacorte, 1981.
Palomino, Dell, 1981.
To Love Again, Dell, 1981.
Crossings, Delacorte, 1982.
Once in a Lifetime, Dell, 1982.
A Perfect Stranger, Dell, 1982.
Changes, Delacorte, 1983.
Thurston House, Dell, 1983.
Full Circle, Delacorte, 1984.
Secrets, Delacorte, 1985.
Family Album, Delacorte, 1985.
Wanderlust, Delacorte, 1986.
Fine Things, Delacorte, 1987.
Kaleidoscope, Delacorte, 1987.
Zoya, Delacorte, 1988.
Star, Delacorte, 1989.
Daddy, Delacorte, 1989.

Message from Nam, Delacorte, 1990.
Heartbeat, Delacorte, 1991.
No Greater Love, Delacorte, 1991.
Jewels, Delacorte, 1992.
Mixed Blessings, Delacorte, 1992.
Vanished, Delacorte, 1993.
Accident, Delacorte, 1993.
The Gift, Delacorte, 1994.
Wings, Delacorte, 1994.
Lightning, Delacorte, 1995.
Five Days in Paris, Delacorte, 1995.
Silent Honor, Delacorte, 1996.
Malice, Delacorte, 1996.
Special Delivery, Delacorte, 1997.
The Ranch, Delacorte, 1997.
The Wedding, Delacorte, 1997.
The Ghost, Delacorte, 1997.

POETRY

Love, Dell, 1981, revised edition, Delacorte, 1984.
Three-in-One, Piatkus (London), 1992.

JUVENILE FICTION

Martha's Best Friend Delacorte, 1989.
New Daddy, Delacorte, 1989.
New School, Delacorte, 1989.
Max's Daddy Goes to the Hospital, Delacorte, 1989.
Max and the Baby Sitter, Delacorte, 1989.
Max's New Baby, Delacorte, 1989.
Martha's New Puppy, Doubleday, 1990.
Max Runs Away, Doubleday, 1990.

OTHER

Having a Baby, Dell, 1984.

■ Adaptations

Twenty-two television movies have been based on Steel's works, including *Crossings*, 1986; *Kaleidoscope*, 1990; *Daddy*, 1991; *Secrets*, 1992; *Message from Nam*, 1993; *Once in a Lifetime*, 1994; *Zoya*, 1995; and *Remembrance*, 1996.

■ Sidelights

Danielle Steel is one of the most prolific and popular writers of our time. Her books are read by women and men, the young and the old, in forty-six countries and twenty-eight languages. To date, she has published forty-one romance novels, a book of poetry, and twenty fiction and nonfiction books for children. Twenty-two television movies have been produced based on Danielle Steel novels. Since 1981, she has been an almost permanent fixture on the *New York Times* hardcover, trade, paperback, and mass market bestseller lists, and has produced over 340 million books in print. Many of her novels have been adapted for television, and in 1981 Steel was listed in the *Guinness Book of World Records* for having one of her books on the *New York Times* bestseller list for 381 weeks. (Since that time, she has broken her own record by remaining on the list for over 390 weeks.) Today, there are Danielle Steel reading groups throughout the country and the author has her own Web site, complete with covers of her novels, audio samplings from her books on tape, a listing of her television movies, and a trivia contest.

Danielle Steel's life is every bit as unusual as the lives of the characters she creates. She was born in New York City in 1947. Her father, John Schuelein-Steel, was one of the owners of the Lowenbrau Beer Company in Munich, Germany, and her mother was the daughter of a Portuguese diplomat. She was an only child, and her parents divorced when she was eight years old. In an interview with *People* magazine in 1992, Steel described her childhood as "solitary and lonely."

As a child, Steel attended schools in New York and France. Later, she attended New York University and Parsons School of Design, but she left Parsons when she developed an ulcer. At the age of eighteen, she married Claude Eric Lazard, a wealthy French-American banker who was twenty-eight years old. They had a daughter, Beatrix, and Steel, along with three other women, formed a public relations firm and advertising agency in Manhattan called Supergirls. The agency was not successful, but one of Steel's clients suggested that she become a writer. Steel took his advice, wrote *Going Home*, her first novel, in three months, and has been writing ever since.

Troubled Marriages

In 1972, Steel and Lazard separated. Around that time she was asked to write an article about conscientious objectors to the war in Vietnam. When Steel interviewed a friend at Lompoc Correctional

Institute in California, she was introduced to a bank robber and inmate named Danny Zugelder. She married him in prison, and Zugelder was later released. However, the couple divorced shortly after Zugelder was convicted of robbing and sexually assaulting a woman. It is believed that two of Steel's novels, *Passion's Promise,* in which a socialite writer falls in love with a poor ex-con, and *Now and Forever,* in which the hero is accused of raping a woman he says consented to sex and then is imprisoned, are based in part on her relationship with Zugelder. In 1978, Steel married Bill Toth, a former convict and drug addict, and they had a son before the marriage ended. In 1981, she married John Traina, a real estate and investment manager who later became her manager. Traina had two sons from his first marriage, and the couple had five of their own children. Today, the couple is separated, but Steel is the mother of nine children. She lives in San Francisco in a fifty-five-room mansion that looks out over Alcatraz and the Golden Gate Bridge.

Steel often plans and researches her books for about a year, but she reports that she turns her ideas into completed manuscripts in ten to fourteen days. Because of her numerous family responsibilities, she generally writes from 9 P.M. until 3 or 4 A.M., and sleeps just three or four hours a day. In an interview with Nancy Faber of *People* magazine, Steel explained her writing schedule this way: "I start at nine and work in my bedroom. It drives everyone else crazy. People bring me food, and I shovel it in five hours later. Once a book is really going I can't get away from it." A rewrite generally takes her from three to five days to complete. It is not uncommon for three or four Danielle Steel books to be published in a given year.

To say that Steel is a popular writer is certainly an understatement; however, her work has not met with critical acclaim. Her novels are a diverse collection of love stories set in different places and times. In *Twentieth-Century Romance and Historical Writers,* Rachel Kumar states that Steel "turns out riveting, albeit occasionally farfetched, tales of love that hover dangerously on the razor's edge between works of serious romance and a frivolous dalliance with sentimentality. . . . In a typical Steel novel, the story is dominated by the presence of a single character, usually a heroine. . . . These women have everything, but are unfulfilled, their love affairs are essentially cathartic experiences

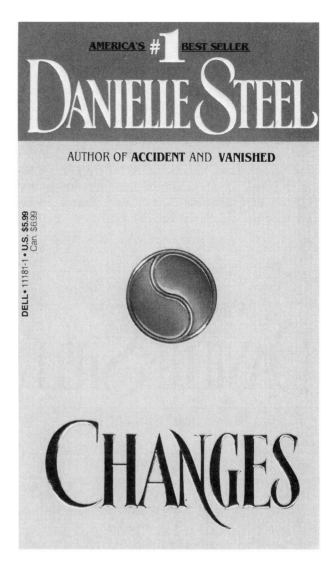

DELL • 11181-1 • U.S. $5.99 Can. $6.99

AMERICA'S #1 BEST SELLER

DANIELLE STEEL

AUTHOR OF **ACCIDENT** AND **VANISHED**

CHANGES

A famous television anchorwoman must decide between her career and a new love in this 1983 work.

that provide deeper enquiry by the heroine into herself. The predictable outcome in each of these stories is the emergence of a more resolute and strengthened being."

Novels Filled With Romance

Crossings is a novel set in both the United States and France. The heroine in this novel is Liane de Villiers, a blonde beauty from a San Francisco shipping family, and her husband, Armand de Villiers, who is twenty-four years her senior and French Ambassador to the United States. Right before the outbreak of World War II, the majestic ship *Normandie* makes a transatlantic voyage from Washington, D.C., to France, and Liane, Armand, and their two daughters are on board. It is on the ship that Liane meets Nick Burnham, an American steel magnate who is trapped in a loveless marriage to Hilary Burnham. After the fall of France, Liane and her daughters are forced to flee Paris, where they meet up with Nick again. The couple falls in love. In the *New York Times Book Review,* Ross Lipson notes "There is no writing to speak of. The costume morality clue is that Hilary wears backless dresses and flaunts jewels and furs her husband did not give her." In *Pub-*

lishers Weekly, Barbara Bannon notes that "Steel is in the habit of writing bestsellers, but her fans may be disappointed by her latest effort." On the other hand, in *Library Journal,* Rebecca Wondriska writes, "Steel has written another best seller. . . . Romance fans should love this."

Changes is the story of Melanie Adams, a New York anchorwoman and a mother of twins, who marries Peter Hallam, a Beverly Hills surgeon with three children. Over the course of the novel, Melanie must decide whether her career or a successful marriage are more important to her, and how to cope with the problems that occur when the two families merge. Judy Bass, writing in the *New York Times Book Review,* notes that Steel "succeeds in depicting the miseries threatening the Hallams' future without descending into melodrama."

The glamorous world of television was the setting for the novel *Secrets.* There are six major characters in the book—the producer, the leading actress, the female co-star, the young male and female supporting actors, and the leading man. Each of the characters is harboring a secret that, if it were discovered, could ruin their chance for success. As the novel progresses, the secrets are gradually revealed. In *Library Journal,* Barbara Kemp describes *Secrets* as "A sure-fire winner, bound to be in demand." David Bianculli, writing in the *New York Times Book Review,* was less impressed with the novel. He writes that "The secrets promised in the book's title range from laughable . . . to painfully predictable. . . . Danielle Steel even repeats herself."

In *Time* magazine, *Kaleidoscope* is described as "one of her [Steel's] better tear-stained efforts." The heroine of the novel is Hilary Walker, a woman whose father strangled her mother and then killed himself. Hilary is then separated from her two sisters and forced to live with her drunken uncle. She also lives in a series of foster homes, where she is repeatedly raped and beaten. But Hilary is a survivor—she becomes a television executive and falls in love with John Chapman, a man who she hires to find her sisters. Rosemary L. Bray, reviewing the novel in *People,* notes that "Ms. Steel's familiar themes of love and loss are here in abundance, along with exotic locales, expensive restaurants, titled Frenchmen, antique furniture and fresh flowers in every room." In *Publishers Weekly,* Sybil Steinberg notes that "The book gets

AMERICA'S #1 BEST SELLER

DANIELLE STEEL

AUTHOR OF **LIGHTNING** AND **WINGS**

ZOYA

In this 1988 work, a young woman is swept up in the events of the Russian Revolution, World War I, the Roaring Twenties, and the Great Depression.

off to a slow, overly sweet start, but by the midway mark Steel has given these tired characters a fresh look and a vibrant momentum all their own." In the *Los Angeles Times Book Review,* Karen Stabiner writes, "Steel seems to believe that neither a bankrupt environment nor a hereditary psychosis can keep a good woman down. . . . Steel's story is the perfect antidote to all those nasty nonfiction articles and books about how women can't have it all. . . ."

Zoya, a 1988 work, traces the dramatic life of the Russian countess Zoya Ossupov. Her story begins in Russia before the revolution, when the eighteen-year-old Zoya was a member of the Imperial family. The violence of the revolution causes her to flee Russia with her grandmother and lose most of her family, her position, and her wealth. She lives in Paris during World War I and joins the ballet to support herself and her grandmother. While in Paris, she marries a wealthy American. They move to New York and live an exciting life during the Roaring Twenties, but Zoya's life changes again when the stock market crashes in 1929, bankrupting her husband and contributing to his fatal heart attack. Zoya is again forced to make a new life, this time for herself and her children. Throughout the novel, Zoya is continually faced with crises and challenges, which help her to become stronger. Like most of Steel's books, *Zoya* met with mixed reviews. Peggy Hill, writing in the Toronto *Globe and Mail,* states that the author "has the ability to give such formula writing enough strength to not collapse into an exhausted state of cliche." Writing in the *New York Times Book Review,* William J. Harding notes that "*Zoya* is a riches-to-rags-to-riches story. But despite the topping of political, social and emotional turmoil, it's about as tasty as a mayonnaise sandwich."

Taking Chances With A Successful Formula

Daddy was a departure for Steel because the main character was a man. Oliver Watson is a middle-aged advertising executive with three sons who becomes a single parent when his wife leaves him to find herself. Soon after, Oliver's oldest son Ben gets a girl pregnant, and his father George suffers when his wife, who is suffering from Alzheimer's disease, is killed in an accident. Joyce Slater, reviewing *Daddy* in the Chicago *Tribune Books,* observes that Steel "relies almost entirely

on dialogue to advance her plot" and finds the book's "tidy, idyllic conclusion a bit unrealistic." In the *New York Times Book Review,* Edna Stumpf describes the moral of *Daddy* as "when bad things happen to good people everything still turns out great."

In *Message from Nam,* which Steinberg describes as "an audacious—and ill-conceived—departure from her usual glitzy settings," the heroine is Paxton Andrews and the setting is the Vietnam War. This native of Savannah goes to college at the University of California, Berkeley, where she

Three men—George Watson, his son Oliver, and his grandson Ben—must deal with the extraordinary changes in their lives in this 1989 novel.

majors in journalism and falls in love with Peter Wilson, a law student and son of a newspaper tycoon. Peter is later killed in Vietnam, and Paxton goes to Vietnam as a correspondent and writes a newspaper column. *Message from Nam* chronicles many important events such as the assassinations of John F. Kennedy and Martin Luther King, Jr., but according to Steinberg, it is marred by "gushing, breathless prose that trivializes serious events." In the *Los Angeles Times Book Review*, Don G. Campbell finds fault with the credibility of the novel's main character, but notes that Steel "has done her research well as far as the sights and sounds of Saigon, and the crackle of rifle fire in the jungles, are concerned."

Lightning is the story of Alexandra Parker, a woman who is a partner in one of New York's most prestigious law firms and has a loving husband and a beautiful daughter. Her life is shattered when, at the age of forty, she discovers she has breast cancer. After undergoing a mastectomy, Alexandra also loses her husband, who has left her for a younger, healthier woman. Alexandra then meets a younger man who helps her through this difficult time. She plans to remarry, but when she asks her husband (who is living with a girlfriend and going through an economic crisis) for a divorce, he suddenly realizes how much he needs her. In *Publishers Weekly*, reviewer Sybil Steinberg notes that "Steel's message—that women are stronger than men but more foolish in love—may annoy some readers, but Alex's brave struggle to survive is inspiring." In the *New York Times Book Review*, Barry Gewen writes, "The plot of *Lightning* creaks with every turn of the page and the characters have all the depth of a cookie sheet . . . , yet Ms. Steel is undeniably an expert manipulator of her readers' feelings. . . ." In *Booklist*, Kathleen Hughes notes that the author "is in her element here, using high drama, pathos, and unpredictable plot developments that will keep readers in suspense until the end."

In addition to her romance novels, Steel has also written a number of books for children. Her first books were written for her own children. Speaking to Ellen Creager of the *Detroit Free Press*, she said, "I was looking for a book about saying good-bye and couldn't find one. Then my husband went into a hospital and I couldn't find a book about a grownup going into the hospital, so I ended up writing them." The result was the "Max and Martha" series, illustrated storybooks which

---

If you enjoy the works of Danielle Steel, you may also want to check out the following books and films:

Michelle Magorian, *Not a Swan*, 1992.
Norma Fox Mazer, *Someone to Love*, 1985.
The works of Barbara Wersba, including *Beautiful Losers*, 1988, and *Wonderful Me*, 1989.
The works of Cheryl Zach, including *Looking Out for Lacey*, 1989, *Paradise*, 1994, and *Runaway*, 1995.
Casablanca, the classic film starring Humphrey Bogart and Ingrid Bergman, 1942.

---

include titles such as *Max Runs Away*, *Max and the Baby-Sitter*, and *Max's New Baby*. Steel's "Max and Martha" series was written to comfort young people as they face special problems in their lives. Although she loves writing romance novels, Steel believes that children are an important audience for her books. In *Preferred Reader Guide*, Steel explains that "Writing the children's books has been great, because my children love them, so they feel I've done something important."

Although Steel has not received much critical acclaim for her work, her books are read and loved by people around the world, and the numerous television adaptations of her works have garnered high ratings. Ellen Goodman, reviewing *Message from Nam* in the *New York Times Book Review*, admitted that many of Steel's fans "most certainly don't care that I regard this novel as a work without redeeming social value. . . . Nor do they care if the esthetes at writer's workshops . . . read passages to feed their paranoia about publishers and their scorn for success." In an interview with *Publishers Weekly*, Steel once said, "I think I have an instinctive sense for the feelings of others and that is what seems to hold the reader. What I write touches people."

■ Works Cited

Bannon, Barbara, review of *Crossings*, *Publishers Weekly*, July 2, 1982, p. 45.
Bass, Judy, review of *Changes*, *New York Times Book Review*, September 11, 1983.

Bianculli, David, review of *Secrets, New York Times Book Review,* November 17, 1985, p. 30.

Bray, Rosemary L., review of *Kaleidoscope, People,* November 15, 1987.

Campbell, Don E., review of *Message from Nam, Los Angeles Times Book Review,* May 20, 1990.

Chin, Paula, "Danielle Steel," *People,* June 29, 1992, pp. 90-96.

Creager, Ellen, interview with Danielle Steel, *Detroit Free Press,* December 1, 1989.

Gewen, Barry, review of *Lightning, New York Times Book Review,* July 9, 1995, p. 21.

Goodman, Ellen, review of *Message from Nam, New York Times Book Review,* June 10, 1990, pp. 14-15.

Harding, William J., review of *Zoya, New York Times Book Review,* July 17, 1988.

Hill, Peggy, review of *Zoya, Globe and Mail* (Toronto), July 9, 1988.

Hughes, Kathleen, review of *Lightning, Booklist,* April 15, 1995, p. 453.

Review of *Kaleidoscope, Time,* January 11, 1988, p. 76.

Kemp, Barbara, review of *Secrets, Library Journal,* October 15, 1985, p. 103.

Kumar, Rachel, *Twentieth-Century Romance and Historical Writers,* 3rd edition, St. James Press, 1994, pp. 619-20.

Lipson, Ross, review of *Crossings, New York Times Book Review,* October 3, 1982, p. 13.

Martin, Sue, review of *Changes, Los Angeles Times Book Review,* September 25, 1983.

Slater, Joyce, "Pop fiction: From lovely anchorwomen to charismatic billionaires," *Tribune Books* (Chicago), November 19, 1989, pp. 9-10.

Stabiner, Karen, "Best Seller Preview: Waiting for a Real Man," *Los Angeles Times Book Review,* October 25, 1987, pp. 12-13.

Steel, Danielle, comments in "Author Talk," *Preferred Reader Guide,* Volume 2, issue 1, 1990, p. 3.

Steinberg, Sybil, review of *Kaleidoscope, Publishers Weekly,* September 25, 1987, p. 96.

Steinberg, Sybil, review of *Message From Nam, Publishers Weekly,* April 13, 1990, pp. 56-57.

Steinberg, Sybil, review of *Lightning, Publishers Weekly,* May 1, 1995, p. 41.

Stumpf, Edna, review of *Daddy, New York Times Book Review,* December 10, 1989, p. 32.

Wondriska, Rebecca, review of *Crossings, Library Journal,* August, 1982.

Review of *Zoya, Bestsellers,* Volume 89, issue 1, Gale, 1989, pp. 59-61.

■ **For More Information See**

PERIODICALS

Entertainment Weekly, September 22, 1995, p. 18; November 29, 1996, p. 62.

McCall's, December 1991, pp. 62-65.

New York Times Book Review, June 10, 1990, pp. 3, 41.

People, October 3, 1994, p. 43.

Publishers Weekly, January 31, 1994, p. 13; December 12, 1994, p. 17; February 14, 1995, p. 21; September 15, 1997, p. 17.*

—Sketch by Irene Durham

Bram Stoker

■ Personal

Born Abraham Stoker, about November 8, 1847, in Dublin, Ireland; died April 20, 1912, in London, England; son of Abraham (a civil servant) and Charlotte (a social activist; maiden name, Thornley) Stoker; married Florence Balcombe, 1878; children: Noel. *Education:* Trinity College, Dublin, M.A. (honors in science).

■ Career

Novelist and journalist. Irish civil servant, 1868-78; drama critic for the Dublin *Evening Mail,* 1871-76; literary, art, and drama critic for various newspapers; barrister of the Inner Temple; business manager for the actor, Henry Irving, 1878-1905; later served on the literary staff of the London *Telegraph. Member:* National Liberal Club.

■ Awards, Honors

Medalist, Royal Humane Society.

■ Writings

The Duties of Clerks of Petty Session in Ireland (nonfiction), privately printed, 1879.

Under the Sunset (stories for children), illustrated by W. Fitzgerald and W. V. Cookburn, Sampson Low, 1881.

A Glimpse of America: A Lecture Given at the London Institution, 28th December, 1885 (nonfiction), Low, Marston, Searle & Rivington, 1886.

The Snake's Pass, Harper, 1890.

Crooken Sands, T. L. De Vinne, 1894.

The Watter's Mou', T. L. De Vinne, 1894.

The Man from Shorrox's, T. L. De Vinne, 1894.

The Shoulder of Shasta, Constable, 1895.

Dracula, Constable, 1897, Grosset & Dunlap, 1897.

Miss Betty, Pearson, 1898.

Sir Henry Irving and Miss Ellen Terry in "Robespierre," "Merchant of Venice," "The Bells," "Nance Oldfield," "The Amber Heart," "Waterloo." etc., Drawn by Pamela C. Smith (nonfiction), Doubleday & McClure, 1899.

The Mystery of the Sea: A Novel, Doubleday, Page, 1902.

The Jewel of Seven Stars, Heinemann, 1903, Harper, 1904.

The Man, Heinemann, 1905.

Personal Reminiscences of Henry Irving (nonfiction), 2 volumes, Heinemann, 1906, Macmillan, 1906.

Snowbound: The Record of a Theatrical Touring Party, Collier, 1908.

Lady Athlyne, Macmillan, 1908, Reynolds, 1908.

The Gates of Life, Cupples & Leon, 1908.

The Lady of the Shroud, Heinemann, 1909.

Famous Impostors, Sidgwick & Jackson, 1910, Sturgis & Walton, 1910.

The Lair of the White Worm, Rider, 1911.

Dracula's Guest, and Other Weird Stories, 1914, Hillman-Curl, 1937.

The Bram Stoker Bedside Companion: Ten Stories by the Author of Dracula, edited by Charles Osborne, Gollancz, 1973.

■ Adaptations

MOVIES

Dracula, (adapted as *Nosferatu*) Film Arts Guild, 1922, Universal Pictures, 1931, Dan Curtis Productions, 1974, Universal Pictures, 1979, Universal City Studios, 1979, Columbia Pictures, 1993; freely adapted as *Dracula's Daughter*, Universal Pictures, 1936, *The Return of the Vampire*, Columbia Pictures, 1943, *Son of Dracula*, Universal Pictures, 1943, *House of Dracula*, Universal Pictures, 1945, *Horror of Dracula*, Hammer Films, 1958, *The Brides of Dracula*, Universal Pictures, 1960, *Kiss of the Vampire*, Universal Pictures, 1963, *Dracula, Prince of Darkness*, Twentieth Century-Fox, 1965, *Dracula Has Risen from the Grave*, Warner Brothers, 1968, *Taste of Blood of Dracula*, Warner Brothers, 1970, *Scars of Dracula*, 1970, *Countess Dracula*, Twentieth Century-Fox, 1971, *Dracula, A.D.*, Warner Brothers, 1972, *Count Dracula*, three-part PBS television series, WNET-TV, 1978, *Love at First Bite*, International Pictures, 1979; *Dracula: Dead and Loving It*, Castle Rock Entertainment, 1995.

The Lair of the White Worm, Vestron Pictures, 1988.

PLAYS

Hamilton Deane and John Lloyd-Balderston, *Dracula*, Samuel French, 1960.

Ronald Bruce, *Dracula, Baby* (musical-comedy), Dramatic Publishing, 1970.

Leon Katz, *Dracula: Sabbat*, Studio Duplicating Service, 1970.

Ted Tiller, *Count Dracula*, Samuel French, 1972.

Crane Johnson, *Dracula*, Dramatist Play Service, 1976.

Bob Hall, *The Passion of Dracula*, Samuel French, 1979.

RECORDINGS

Dracula, Spoken Arts, 1974, Caedmon, 1975, Mark 56 Records, 1976, All Media Dramatic Workshop, 1976, Mind's Eye, 1983, World Tapes, 1984, HarperCollins, 1991, Random House, 1992.

Dracula's Ghost, Durkin Hays, 1993.

■ Sidelights

Abraham Stoker—better known to the world as Bram—created a century ago one of the most enduring figures of literary history. Patching together the works of earlier writers such as Sheridan Le Fanu and Guy de Maupassant, along with tales of Eastern Europe related to him by an adventurous Hungarian, Stoker published *Dracula* in 1897, bringing to the bright light of public renown the hungry, darkness-loving count of Transylvania. A success in its day, the exploits of Count Dracula have since that time inspired dozens of vampire novels, including a fabulously popular series by Anne Rice, and have also spawned a cottage industry with the world of film. Bela Lugosi, Lon Chaney, and Christopher Lee are but a few of the stars to hang their fame on the vampire legend. Such adaptations have taken the sexual subtext of the original novel and exploded it into an orgy of blood and bosoms. Literary criticism, taking Freud as its compass, has also had a field day with the original *Dracula*, reading into it all manner of subliminal desire and pent-up sexuality. As Brian Murray noted in an essay on Stoker in *Dictionary of Literary Biography*, "The publicly prudish Stoker—who once wrote an essay calling for the censorship of works that exploit 'sex impulses'—would probably be shocked to read of much of the recent criticism of *Dracula*." Stoker, a man of many means, would also most likely be peeved that his estate was not benefiting from the raft of spin-offs from his famous creation. But his reputation *has* benefited. Daniel Farson and Philip B. Dematteis put it quite bluntly in their essay on Stoker in a further *Dictionary of Literary Biography* entry: "Without *Dracula*, Bram Stoker would be forgotten. As it is, he is one of the least-known authors of one of the best-known books." The author of a dozen other forgotten novels and several nonfiction works, Stoker truly owes his fame to the infamous Count Dracula.

Bram Stoker was born on or about November 8, 1847, in Clontarf, a village just north of Dublin

Bay. In rural Ireland, this was the time of the potato famine when thousands of Irish were either dying from starvation or immigrating all over the world. The Stokers, however, were solidly middle class, with the father, Abraham, a civil servant, working as a chief secretary at Dublin Castle, the administrative center of the country. The mother, Charlotte Thornley, was two decades younger than her husband, and a rugged west-of-Ireland woman who had survived the cholera epidemic of 1832 in her native Sligo. She was a social activist who fought for the rights of impoverished women and was a formidable presence for her children.

As a child, Bram Stoker—born the third of seven children—was ill most of the time. As he recounted in his *Personal Reminiscences of Henry Irving,* "In my babyhood I used, I understand, to be often at the point of death. Certainly till I was about seven years old I never knew what it was to stand upright. I was naturally thoughtful and the leisure of long illness gave opportunity for many thoughts which were fruitful according to their kind in later years." Such an enforced bed-ridden state was clearly an influence on the course of Stoker's future life, much as invalidism was on that of another famous writer, Marcel Proust. During the long months and years of his illness, Stoker's mother would entertain her young son with grisly tales from her own youth, such as the story of the army sergeant who had apparently died of the plague. When the undertaker attempted to bury the enormous man, he found the corpse's legs were too long for the coffin. Determined to chop the legs off at the knee to ease the fit, the undertaker took an axe to the legs, but at the first hit, the sergeant suddenly revived. Such tales informed much of Stoker's youth.

But once healthy, Stoker never looked back. He grew into a strapping youth, and by the time he went off to Dublin's Trinity College in 1864, he was, as described by Farson and Dematteis, "a red-haired giant." He took to sports with a vengeance, as if to make up for lost time, and within two years had become the athletics champion of Trinity. But life was not all athletics for Stoker: He also studied mathematics, eventually graduating with honors in 1868. During his university years, two other influences came into his life. In 1867, Stoker first saw the actor Henry Irving perform at Dublin's Theatre Royal. Hugely impressed with the man's stage presence, Stoker would not

finally meet Irving for almost a decade, but that relationship would prove of utmost importance in his life. Also during his university years, Stoker fell under the spell of Walt Whitman's *Leaves of Grass,* freshly published in Britain and attacked for its supposed lack of morality. Stoker became an adamant defender of Whitman's work and began a correspondence with the American writer.

From Civil Servant to Writer

Upon graduation, Stoker won—with the assistance of his father—a clerk's position in the civil service at Dublin Castle. It was a secure position, yet Stoker found it terribly dull and allayed his boredom with Whitman, visits to the theater, and by writing essays. When Irving returned to Dublin in 1871, Stoker eagerly went to the theater but was disappointed that the local papers carried no reviews of the man's performance. Taking pen in hand, he cured that by submitting a review to the Dublin *Mail.* For the next six years Stoker held the position of unpaid drama critic for that paper. Also, in order to help finance his brothers' education at Trinity, Stoker began tutoring mathematics students. He also broadened his literary horizons by editing a small review and by writing a four-part serial about a "phantom" friend for the *Shamrock* magazine.

The next few years of Stoker's life swept him at breakneck speed into the literary world, marriage, and off to London. In 1876, Irving returned to Dublin for performances in *Hamlet.* Finally Stoker was able to meet his idol, and the two hit it off, beginning a close working friendship that would last for almost three decades, until the death of the actor. As Farson and Dematteis noted in *Dictionary of Literary Biography,* "Stoker had fallen in love. Throughout his life he needed heroes—Whitman, Lord Tennyson—but his attachment to the actor, ten years older than himself . . . was the most enduring." The following year, Stoker was promoted to a more interesting position in the civil service, as inspector of the courts of petty session. He began work on his first book, a "dry-as-dust" account, according to his *Reminiscences of Henry Irving,* entitled *The Duties of the Clerks of Petty Session in Ireland.* It was about this time, too, that he fell in love with his nineteen-year-old neighbor, the stunning Florence Balcombe. The two soon planned their marriage. Meanwhile, Irving had secured a lease on the Lyceum Theater in

London and intended forming his own theater company. Offered the job of manager, Stoker was quick to accept. Resigning his civil service position and marrying the young Florence in quick succession, Stoker set off for the bright lights of London, much to his mother's chagrin.

Novelist Emergent

For Stoker, a life-long theater enthusiast, such a position was a godsend. He was able to see the entire production arc at firsthand, to rub shoulders with not only famous actors such as Ellen

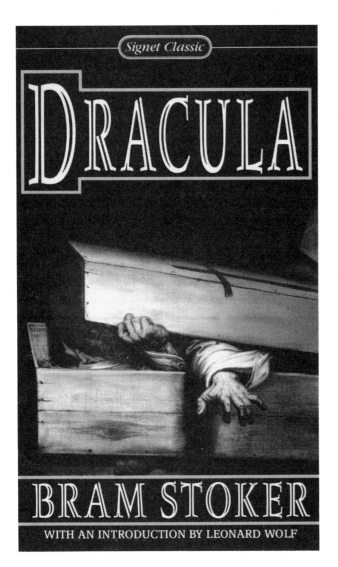

This 1897 novel introduced the world to the immortal vampire Count Dracula, one of the most enduring characters in literature.

Terry but also with royalty on opening nights. Though his duties were taxing, he still found time to study for the bar, lead a family life (his son, Noel, was born in 1879), and write books. The first of these was a collection of "highly unsuitable stories for children," according to Farson and Dematteis, *Under the Sunset*. One of the stories, "The Invisible Giant," about a coming plague, was obviously inspired by his mother's stories. The Stoker image as a man of action was reinforced when he dove overboard from a Thames steamer to save a drowning man. For this act of heroism, he earned a medal from the Royal Humane Society.

But all was not quite right with Stoker's life. His beautiful wife was more wedded to her good looks than to her husband. By all accounts a frigid woman, she was also a flirt, increasing Stoker's sense of isolation and frustration in that quarter. He made up for this by throwing himself into his work, writing several hundred letters weekly for the theater, and traveling extensively with the company. His new acquaintances included Mark Twain and Walt Whitman, whom he met on the company's American tours. And he continued writing. His first full-length novel, serialized in several magazines, was *The Snake's Pass*, published in 1889. Essentially a romantic novel, it is set in Ireland and tells the tale of a buried treasure, rivalry for the hand of a beautiful woman, and a sinister villain who finally gets his comeuppance by sinking into a bog. Though a reviewer for the *Atheneum* proclaimed the novel "dull," it was a popular success in its day, and convinced Stoker to continue with his writing career. Several other books followed, including *The Watter's Mou'*, a story of love and smuggling which another critic in the *Atheneum* found to have a "tendency to melodrama and stagey writing." But Stoker's main project for the next several years was his research into the bizarre world of vampirism.

Stoker did not invent his famous blood-sucking count out of whole cloth. There were, in fact, many influences to his work. Among the famous guests who would partake of late-night suppers with Irving's theater company were Henry Morton Stanley and Sir Richard Francis Burton who had translated *Vikram and the Vampire* from the Hindi. Another personal influence came from Arminius Vambery, a Hungarian adventurer and professor of Oriental languages who filled Stoker's head full of stories of vampirism in Eastern Europe. Four

In the 1931 film classic *Dracula*, Bela Lugosi portrays the Transylvanian vampire who thirsts for human blood.

months after meeting Vambery in April, 1890, Stoker was hard at work researching what would become *Dracula*. His researches led him eventually to Vlad, ruler of Wallachia (a part of Romania) in the fifteenth century. The man's nickname tells it all, for he is also known as Vlad the Impaler, after the tortuous manner in which he dispatched his enemies. Vlad's father had held the title of Dracul, for the Order of the Dragon given him by the Holy Roman Emperor. As son of Dracul, Vlad also became known as Dracula. Though a cruel man, Vlad was never historically associated with vampirism; that was a Stoker invention, as was the removal of Dracula's kingdom from Wallachia to the nearby region of Transylvania. Years of association with the Dracula legend have since given that region an ominous sound, though its meaning, "land beyond the forest," is actually quite bucolic. Daniel Farson, in his *The Man Who Wrote Dracula: A Biography of Bram Stoker,* noted that Stoker spent hours in the British Museum researching his tale. "I read [that] every known superstition in the world is gathered in the horseshoe of the Carpathians, as if it were the centre of some sort of imaginative whirlpool," Stoker wrote after such researches.

There were other, literary influences, as well, including the celebrated 1819 novel, *The Vampire,* written by a friend of Lord Byron, Dr. John Polidori; the short story, "Le Horla" by Guy de Maupassant; and most importantly another short story, "Carmilla," written in 1871 by another Dubliner, Sheridan Le Fanu. It is clear that Stoker was familiar with these earlier creations, especially with the Le Fanu story, for in his original notes for *Dracula,* Stoker placed the count's castle in Styria, the location of Le Fanu's, only later moving it to Transylvania. Other literary influences were in the air, as well, including the entire oeuvre of Gothic writing such as Horace Walpole's *Castle of Otranto* and Ann Radcliffe's *The Mysteries of Udolpho.* Numerous other writers had dealt tangentially with vampire themes: Johann Goethe, Samuel Taylor Coleridge, Sir Walter Scott, and even Lord Byron.

Dracula

Yet Stoker blended fable and tradition into a new stew, utilizing an epistolary style pioneered by Wilkie Collins. Rather than telling his tale in straight narrative form from the viewpoint of a single narrator, Stoker opted for a more episodic approach, accomplished by the use of letters, journal entries, telegrams, transliterated short-hand, newspaper clippings, and even—very up-to-date for the time—transcriptions of dictaphone recordings. Stoker worked on the book off and on for seven years, finally publishing it in 1897. Set in then contemporary times, the book's opening chapters are extracts from the journals of one Jonathan Harker, an English real estate agent off to Transylvania to the castle of Count Dracula. The count, it seems, wishes to buy property in London. Peasants of whom Harker asks the way become fearful at the mention of Dracula's very name and warn the Englishman off, but Harker is not to be put off. He assigns their fears to native superstition, and proceeds to the castle where he meets Dracula, "a tall old man, clean shaven save for a long white moustache, and clad in black from head to foot." Harker also notes Dracula's "peculiarly sharp white teeth" which "protruded over the lips." The count's complexion is very pale, except for his full, red lips and reddish eyes.

Harker stays at Dracula's castle for two months, part guest, part prisoner. During these months, Harker slowly begins to realize the abomination that lies at the heart of Count Dracula. The count is never to be found during the daylight hours, and never seems to eat or drink. There is no reflection in the mirror when Dracula looks into it, and history is not something read about by Dracula, but something apparently personally experienced, as if he had walked through time. Shaving, Harker once cuts himself, and the count suddenly lunges for his throat, only to be stopped short by a rosary. Three beautiful women also share the castle, and Harker meets them when, forgetting Dracula's dictum to only sleep in his guest room, he naps and awakes to find the beauties hovering about him with a "deliberate voluptuousness which was both thrilling and repulsive," their sweet scent offset by a "bitter offensiveness, as one smells in blood." As the women decide who will kiss Harker first, the Englishman lies back, filled with both fear and erotic expectation. However, the "kiss" is aimed at his neck, and Harker is saved at the last minute with the entrance of the count who chases the women off, yelling at them: "This man belongs to me!" Harker also sees the count slipping out of his castle at night, sliding down the walls head first like a lizard, only to return later with what

Harker thinks are bags filled with babies. When a protesting mother shows up at the castle, Dracula commands wolves to tear the pleading woman to shreds. Finally, seeing Dracula sleeping in a coffin in the castle crypt, Harker realizes that the count intends to have himself shipped off to England in this manner. Harker decides to escape the castle and try to make his way back to England. At this point, the first part of the novel ends.

With a scene shift to England, the reader is now transported back in time, as well, to the outset of Harker's stay in Transylvania. Several other characters are introduced, via letters and diaries: Mina Murray, Harker's fiancee, the handsome Lucy Westenra, who has just received three separate marriage proposals, and the three suitors—Dr. John Seward, who runs a lunatic asylum; Arthur Holmwood, an aristocrat, and Quincey Morris, a wealthy Texan. Holmwood is the lucky suitor chosen by Lucy, and through a series of letters and telegrams, the three male friends assure one another of their lasting friendship despite their recent rivalry. Seward, to forget his loss, throws himself into his work, especially the case of a patient named Renfield, a man who eats all manner of disgusting creatures. When Mina, awaiting Harker's return, joins her friend Lucy in Whitby on the south coast, events take a precipitous turn. A Russian ship runs aground one stormy night, with the captain lashed to the wheel and no other crew members about. They have disappeared, one by one, throughout the voyage, according to the ship's log. A large black dog on board, however, manages to run away, and some fifty boxes of earth are collected by a London agent.

Lucy at this point begins to act strangely, sleepwalking and plagued by nightmares. Mina discovers her one night huddled over a gravestone in the village church, a tall man with red eyes hovering over her. Mina discovers two small punctures in Lucy's neck, but thinks nothing of them. Meanwhile, Seward at his asylum is getting interesting messages from his patient, Renfield, who says "The Master is here." Lucy's sleepwalking continues, a bat is seen flying over her, and she grows weaker and weaker. But when a letter arrives from Hungary telling Mina that Harker has been in a hospital there for several weeks, she goes off to help him. The couple marry once he recovers from his supposed "brain fever" and head back to England.

Alarmed by Lucy's deteriorating condition, Holmwood calls Seward to have a look at her. Seward, in turn, calls in a colleague, Dr. Abraham Van Helsing, who transfuses Lucy with blood from Holmwood. Further transfusions follow from the other former suitors, and Van Helsing, something of an expert on vampirism, puts a wreath of garlics around her neck as protection. Lucy's mother however, takes the garlic off. She in turn dies of a heart attack one night when a giant wolf crashes through the bedroom window. Lucy, despite further transfusions from the Texan, Morris, ultimately dies and is buried in the family vault. Back in England, Harker and Mina see Count Dracula on the streets in London looking much younger, and then receive news of Lucy's death.

Newspaper reports also start recording the mysterious disappearance of children in London, lured away from the vicinity of a cemetery by a "bloofer lady." Meanwhile, Mina has read Harker's accounts of his time at the castle, which he had subscribed to hallucination. But when Van Helsing sees the journals, he assures Harker that these were not fantasies of the mind. He now realizes that the children in London have been lured away by Lucy, risen from the dead. Together with Holmwood, Seward, and Morris, the doctor goes to Lucy's tomb and drives a stake through her heart and chops off her head to stop her nocturnal ramblings and save her from the fate of the undead. The quartet also track down some of the mysterious boxes of earth and place holy wafers on them to make them uninhabitable for a vampire. Van Helsing is the repository for much vampire lore—just as the Hungarian Vambery was in real life—and explains to the others the precautions needed to be taken to ward off Dracula's attacks.

All this time, however, Dracula has been drinking Mina's blood, a fact unknown to the others until Seward's patient, Renfield—one of Dracula's minions—finally tells him of the count's activities. Bursting into the Harker bedroom one night, Van Helsing and Seward find Mina sucking blood from the count's chest and scare him off with a sacred wafer. The same wafer also purges the count's effects on Mina. In fact, the touch of the wafer on her forehead leaves a red mark. But if the count is not destroyed, they all know that Mina will share the same fate as Lucy. Harker discovers the location of one of Dracula's houses in London and finds more of the earth-filled boxes

Acclaimed illustrator Greg Hildebrandt turned his attention to the Dracula legend in this 1985 version of Stoker's classic novel.

there. Only one box now is unaccounted for, and the men lay a trap for Dracula only to have him escape at the last minute, screaming at them as he does so: "My revenge is just begun! I spread it over centuries, and time is on my side."

Now the action switches back to Transylvania, as the five men pursue Dracula, aided by the telepathic connection which Mina has with him. At the castle, Van Helsing drives stakes through the hearts of the three women in their coffins, and hard upon this, a band of gypsies draw up to the castle bearing the coffin of Dracula himself. Seward, Morris, Holmwood, and Harker are giving chase. Morris is killed in the ensuing battle with the gypsies, but Harker manages to open the casket just as the sun is setting and plunge a knife in the vampire's heart and cut off his head, ending his long tortured journey through time. As the count's body disintegrates, his face begins to take on a peaceful countenance, and the red mark on Mina's forehead, left by the holy wafer, also disappears. She has been saved. A postscript to the novel from seven years later tells that Harker and Mina have had a son and named him Quincey, after the Texan who lost his life saving Mina. Thus the curse has been wiped clean with new birth.

The Critical Response

A popular novel in its day, *Dracula* has had a long and varied critical reception. A contemporary review from the *Atheneum* was less than fulsome, calling the book "a mere series of grotesquely incredible events," and chiding the author for technique that was "wanting in the constructive art as well as in the higher literary sense." The anonymous reviewer concluded that "Isolated scenes and touches are probably quite uncanny enough to please those for whom they are designed." But a reviewer for the *Bookman* felt that Stoker had created a "closely woven" tale, and that despite some of the "hideous incidents," Stoker managed to aptly portray a battle between "human skill and courage" and "inhuman wrong and superhuman strength." Concluding the review, the writer advised that *Dracula* should be kept "out of the way of nervous children, certainly; but a grown reader, unless he be of unserviceably delicate stuff, will both shudder and enjoy." Some twenty years after publication, *Dracula* was still drawing new criticism. Montague Summers, in an essay in his *The Vampire: His Kith and Kin*, noted that from "a purely literary point of approach it must be acknowledged that there is much careless writing and many pages could have been compressed." He also commented on Stoker's characters, about whom it is "hardly possible to feel any great interest . . . they are labels rather than individuals." However, Summers felt, that in spite of such criticisms, "the fact remains that [*Dracula*] is a book of unwonted interest and fascination."

Stoker's most famous novel has never been out of print since its initial publication, nor has it been ignored by the critics during that century of life. Modern criticism looks at the subtext of the book, and finds all manner of meanings, from political to psycho-sexual. The American writer of horror tales, H. P. Lovecraft, wrote in 1927 that Stoker's novel was "justly assigned a permanent place in English letters." By mid-century, criticism of *Dracula* took this stature for granted and concentrated on the hidden and unconscious aspects of the novel. Maurice Richardson, in his essay "The Psychoanalysis of Ghost Stories," was one of the first to approach the book from a Freudian perspective, noting that "Death wishes all round exist side by side with the desire for immortality. . . . Behaviour smacks of the unconscious world of infantile sexuality with what Freud called its polymorph perverse tendencies. There is an obvious fixation at the oral level, with all that sucking and biting. . . ." Richardson pointed out also the father-figures Van Helsing and the count both represent, and the near incestuous relationship that Dracula and Mina thus share, and concluded that he doubted whether Stoker "had any inkling of the erotic content of the vampire superstition." A 1988 examination of the novel by the critic John Allen Stevenson follows up on this approach, revising the quasi-incestuous relationship between Mina and the count to an "interracial" one; Dracula is not a "monstrous father" but "a foreigner." Stevenson also draws attention to the central role of blood as a stand in for semen, something first remarked upon by Ernest Jones, the eminent psychoanalyst and biographer of Freud. Still other writers have noted the symbolic nature of the stake driven into the vampires—in Stoker's version an action committed by men on women. The count is dispatched by a knife, not a stake. As Farson and Dematteis noted in their *Dictionary of Literary Biography* entry, "This violent metaphor for sexual intercourse seems to associ-

If you enjoy the works of Bram Stoker, you may also want to check out the following books and films:

Annette Curtis Klause, *The Silver Kiss*, 1990.
The works of Anne Rice, including *Interview with the Vampire*, 1976, and *The Vampire Lestat*, 1985.
Near Dark, a film directed by Kathryn Bigelow, 1987.

ate the sex act with pain and with punishment of the woman for her seductiveness."

A different critical lens was employed by the critic Richard Wasson who looked upon the novel as a political allegory, with the count representing a foreign threat to the march of Western civilization. "While on the surface," Wasson wrote in *English Literature in Transition*, "Stoker's gothic political romance affirms the progressive aspects of English and Western society, its final effect is to warn the twentieth century of the dangers which faced it," including, according to Wasson, such horrors as the Nazi era. Other critics have focused on the psychological and artistic aspects of the novel, including Royce MacGillivray in *Queen's Quarterly*, who, though finding the book to be a "spoiled masterpiece" because of Stoker's poor characterization in parts, felt the book to be a "novel of alienation." MacGillivray noted that Dracula himself was "a towering figure who dominates the novel and appears utterly convincing." The Romanian-born author and critic, Leonard Wolf, echoed these sympathies in his *A Dream of Dracula: In Search of the Living Dead*, writing that *Dracula* "is a novel that lurches toward greatness, stumbling over perceived and unperceived mysteries."

Life After Dracula

Stoker continued to work with Irving and his theater company for eight years after the successful publication of *Dracula*, and these were years of decline for both the actor and his company, culminating in a fire at the theater and the ultimate loss of the Lyceum due to poor business practices. Irving died in 1905, with his best friend Stoker arriving two minutes too late to say good-bye. Thereafter Stoker's financial fortunes suffered ac-

cordingly. Though he continued to write novels and short stories, it is generally agreed that none of his creations match the timeless quality of *Dracula*.

Among other notable Stoker titles are *The Mystery of the Sea* from 1902, which "meticulously describes the hunt for lost treasure," according to Murray in *Dictionary of Literary Biography*, but which also "runs on, often laboriously, for nearly five hundred pages." Stoker's 1903 novel, *The Jewel of Seven Stars*, delves into mystery and magic, relating the story of a resurrected Egyptian queen, and is, according to Farson and Dematteis, "one of his most successful and popular books." A later book, *The Lady of the Shroud*, again takes up the theme of vampirism, but this time the female protagonist, a Balkan princess, only pretends to be a vampire. Wasson, in *English Literature in Transition*, called that book "one of the most entertaining bad novels ever written."

Stoker's last novel, *The Lair of the White Worm*, is "a literary curiosity," according to Farson in his *The Man Who Wrote "Dracula."* The story of Lady Arabella, who has the power to transform herself into a huge deadly snake, and of her neighbor in England's rugged Peak District, Adam Salton, who discovers her secret, the novel is rife with sexual implications. As Farson and Dematteis noted, "Hilarious throughout, without one line of intentional humor, it could still become a cult classic." A 1988 film adaptation of the novel by Ken Russell seemed to bear out that prophecy.

But Stoker was already seriously ill when writing that novel, and died not long after publication, on April 20, 1912. It has been conjectured that his death was caused by syphilis, most likely contracted from the prostitutes he visited as a result of his wife's active disinterest in conjugal relationships. Ironically then, the same frustrations that led to the powerful unconscious sexual symbolisms found in his work may have caused his death. A further irony is the fact that Stoker's own immortality rests on the creation of his most famous character, Count Dracula, prince of the undead.

■ **Works Cited**

Review of *Dracula, Atheneum*, June 26, 1897.
Review of *Dracula, Bookman*, August, 1897, p. 129.

Farson, Daniel, *The Man Who Wrote Dracula: A Biography of Bram Stoker,* St. Martin's Press, 1975.

Farson, Daniel, and Philip B. Dematteis, "Bram Stoker," *Dictionary of Literary Biography,* Volume 36: *British Novelists, 1890-1929: Modernists,* Gale, 1985, pp. 247-60.

Lovecraft, H. P., "Supernatural Horror in Literature," *Dagon and Other Macabre Tales,* edited by August Derleth, Arkham House, 1965, pp. 347-413.

MacGillivray, Royce, "'Dracula': Bram Stoker's Spoiled Masterpiece," *Queen's Quarterly,* Winter, 1972, pp. 518-27.

Murray, Brian, "Bram Stoker," *Dictionary of Literary Biography,* Volume 70, *British Mystery Writers, 1860-1919,* Gale, 1988, pp. 284-89.

Richardson, Maurice, "The Psychoanalysis of Ghost Stories," *The Twentieth Century,* December, 1959, pp. 419-31.

Review of *The Snake's Pass, Atheneum,* December 20, 1890.

Stevenson, John Allen, "A Vampire in the Mirror: The Sexuality of 'Dracula,'" *PMLA,* March, 1988, pp. 139-49.

Stoker, Bram, *Dracula,* Constable, 1897.

Stoker, Bram, *Personal Reminiscences of Henry Irving,* Heinemann, 1906.

Summers, Montague, "The Vampire in Literature," *The Vampire: His Kith and Kin,* University Books, Inc., 1960, pp. 271-340.

Wasson, Richard, "The Politics of 'Dracula,'" *English Literature in Transition,* Volume 9, number 1, 1966, pp. 24-27.

Review of *The Watter's Mou', Atheneum,* February 23, 1895, p. 246.

Wolf, Leonard, "Dracula: The King Vampire," *A Dream of Dracula: In Search of the Living Dead,* Little, Brown, 1972, pp. 171-224.

■ For More Information See

BOOKS

Carter, Margaret L., *Dracula: The Vampire and the Critics,* UPI Research Press, 1988.

Leatherdale, Clive, *"Dracula": The Novel and the Legend,* Aquarian Press, 1985.

Ludlam, Harry, *A Biography of Dracula: The Life Story of Bram Stoker,* Foulsham, 1962.

McNally, Raymond T., and Radu Florescu, *Dracula: A True History of Dracula and Vampire Legends,* New York Graphic Society, 1972.

Roth, Phyllis, *Bram Stoker,* Twayne, 1982.

Senf, Carol A., *The Critical Response to Bram Stoker,* Greenwood Press, 1993.

Twentieth-Century Literary Criticism, Volume 8, Gale, 1982, pp. 383-403.

World Literature Criticism, Gale, 1992, pp. 3461-78.

PERIODICALS

English Literature in Transition, Volume 20, number 1, 1977, pp. 13-26.

Journal of Narrative Technique, Fall, 1979, pp. 160-70.

Literature and Psychology, Volume 22, number 1, 1972, pp. 27-33.

Locus, May, 1994, p. 26.

Massachusetts Review, Summer, 1980, pp. 411-28.

Midwest Quarterly, Summer, 1977, pp. 392-405.

Nineteenth-Century Fiction, June, 1985, pp. 61-75.

Observer, July 7, 1991, p. 57.*

—Sketch by J. Sydney Jones

Martin Waddell

■ Personal

Also writes as Catherine Sefton; born April 10, 1941, in Belfast, Northern Ireland; son of Mayne (a linen manufacturer) and Alice (a homemaker; maiden name, Duffell) Waddell; married Rosaleen Carragher (a teacher), December 27, 1969; children: Thomas Mayne, David Martin, Peter Matthew. *Education:* "Almost nil." *Religion:* "Troubled agnostic." *Hobbies and other interests:* Chess.

■ Addresses

Home and office—139 Central Promenade, Newcastle, County Down, Northern Ireland. *Agent*—Gina Pollinger, 222 Old Brompton Rd., London SW5 OB2, England.

■ Career

Writer, 1966—. Has worked in several other occupations, including book-selling and junk-stalling. *Member:* Society of Authors, Children's Literature Association of Ireland, Irish Writers Union.

■ Awards, Honors

Federation of Children's Book Club Award runner-up, 1982, for *The Ghost and Bertie Boggin;* Carnegie Award nomination, 1984, for *Island of the Strangers;* Guardian Award runner-up, 1984, and Other Award, 1986, both for *Starry Night;* Smarties Grand Prize, 1988, and Le Prix des Critiques de Livres pour Enfants, Belgium, 1989, both for *Can't You Sleep, Little Bear?; Can't You Sleep, Little Bear?,* illustrated by Barbara Firth, received the Kate Greenaway Medal, Library Association, 1988; Kurt Maschler/Emil Award, 1989, for *The Park in the Dark;* Best Book for Babies Award, 1990, for *Rosie's Babies.*

■ Writings

FOR CHILDREN

Ernie's Chemistry Set, illustrated by Ronnie Baird, Blackstaff (Belfast), 1978.

Ernie's Flying Trousers, illustrated by Ronnie Baird, Blackstaff, 1978.

The Great Green Mouse Disaster, illustrated by Philippe Dupasquier, Andersen (London), 1981.

The House under the Stairs, Methuen, 1983.

(Editor) *A Tale to Tell,* Northern Ireland Arts Council, 1983.

Going West, illustrated by Philippe Dupasquier, Andersen, 1983, Harper, 1984.

Big Bad Bertie, illustrated by Glynis Ambrus, Methuen, 1984.

The Budgie Said GRRRR, illustrated by Glynis Ambrus, Methuen, 1985.

The School Reporter's Notebook, Beaver, 1985.

The Day It Rained Elephants, illustrated by Glynis Ambrus, Methuen, 1986.

Our Wild Weekend, Methuen, 1986.

Owl and Billy, Methuen, 1986.

The Tough Princess, illustrated by Patrick Benson, Walker Books, 1986, Putnam, 1987.

The Tall Story of Wilbur Small, Blackie & Son, 1987.

Alice the Artist, illustrated by Jonathan Langley, Methuen, 1988, Dutton, 1988.

Can't You Sleep, Little Bear?, illustrated by Barbara Firth, Walker Books, 1988, Candlewick, 1992.

Class Three and the Beanstalk, illustrated by Toni Goffe, Blackie & Son, 1988.

Great Gran Gorilla and the Robbers, illustrated by Dom Mansell, Walker Books, 1988.

Great Gran Gorilla to the Rescue, illustrated by Dom Mansell, Walker Books, 1988.

Our Sleepysaurus, Walker Books, 1988.

Owl and Billy and the Space Days, Methuen, 1988.

Tales from the Shop That Never Shuts, illustrated by Maureen Bradley, Viking Kestrel, 1988.

Fred the Angel, Walker Books, 1989.

Judy the Bad Fairy, Walker Books, 1989.

Once There Were Giants, illustrated by Penny Dale, Walker Books, 1989, Delacorte, 1989, Candlewick, 1995.

The Park in the Dark, illustrated by Barbara Firth, edited by D. Briley, Walker Books, 1989, Lothrop, 1989, Candlewick, 1996.

Amy Said, illustrated by Charlotte Voake, Walker Books, 1990, Little Brown, 1990.

Daisy's Christmas, illustrated by Jonathan Langley, Methuen, 1990, Ideals, 1990, Dell, 1993.

The Ghost Family Robinson, illustrated by Jacqui Thomas, Viking Kestrel, 1990.

The Hidden House, illustrated by Angela Barrett, Walker Books, 1990, Putnam, 1990.

My Great Grandpa, illustrated by Dom Mansell, Walker Books, 1990, Putnam, 1990.

Rosie's Babies, illustrated by Penny Dale, Walker Books, 1990.

We Love Them, illustrated by Barbara Firth, Walker Books, 1990, Lothrop, 1990.

Grandma's Bill, illustrated by Jane Johnson, Simon & Schuster, 1990, Orchard Books, 1991.

Coming Home, illustrated by Neil Reed, Simon & Schuster, 1991.

Farmer Duck, illustrated by Helen Oxenbury, Walker Books, 1991, Candlewick, 1992, Ingram, 1995, illustrated by Barbara Firth, Candlewick, 1995.

The Happy Hedgehog Band, illustrated by Jill Barton, Walker Books, 1991, Candlewick, 1992.

Herbie Whistle, illustrated by Anthony Ian Lewis, Viking Kestrel, 1991.

Let's Go Home, Little Bear, Walker Books, 1991, Candlewick, 1991.

Little Obie and the Kidnap, illustrated by Elsie Lennox, Walker Books, 1991, Candlewick, 1994.

Man Mountain, illustrated by Claudio Munoz, Viking Kestrel, 1991.

Squeak-a-Lot, illustrated by Virginia Miller, Walker Books, 1991, Greenwillow, 1991.

The Ghost Family Robinson at the Seaside, illustrated by Jacqui Thomas, Viking Kestrel, 1992.

Little Obie and the Flood, illustrated by Elsie Lennox, Candlewick, 1992.

Owl Babies, illustrated by Patrick Benson, Walker Books, 1992, Candlewick, 1992.

The Pig in the Pond, illustrated by Jill Barton, Walker Books, 1992, Candlewick, 1992.

Sailor Bear, illustrated by Virginia Miller, Walker Books, 1992, Candlewick, 1992.

Sam Vole and His Brothers, illustrated by Barbara Firth, Walker Books, 1992, Candlewick, 1992.

The Toymaker: A Story in Two Parts, illustrated by Terry Milne, Walker Books, 1992, Candlewick, 1992.

Baby's Hammer, illustrated by John Watson, Walker Books, 1993.

The Big Bad Mole's Coming!, illustrated by John Bendall-Brunello, Walker Books, 1993.

The Fishface Feud, illustrated by Arthur Robins, Walker Books, 1993.

Little Mo, illustrated by Jill Barton, Walker Books, 1993, Candlewick, 1993.

The Lucky Duck Song, illustrated by Judy Brown, Puffin, 1993.

Rubberneck's Revenge, illustrated by Arthur Robins, O'Brien Press, 1993.

The School That Went to Sea, illustrated by Leo Hartas, O'Brien Press, 1993.

Stories from the Bible: Old Testament Stories, illustrated by Geoffrey Patterson, Frances Lincoln, 1993, Ticknor & Fields, 1993.

Shipwreck at Old Jelly's Farm, Ginn, 1994.

Upside Down Harry Brown, Ginn, 1994.

The Big, Big Sea, illustrated by Jennifer Eachas, Candlewick, 1994.

When the Teddy Bears Came, illustrated by Penny Dale, Candlewick, 1995.

John Joe and the Big Hen, illustrated by Paul Howard, Candlewick, 1995.

Mimi and the Picnic, illustrated by Leo Hartas, Candlewick, 1995.

When Teddy Bears Came, illustrated by Penny Dale, 1995.

Small Bear Lost, illustrated by Virginia Austin, Candlewick, 1996.

What Use Is a Moose?, illustrated by Arthur Robins, Candlewick, 1996.

Sam Vole and His Brothers, illustrated by Barbara Firth, Candlewick, 1996.

You and Me, Little Bear, illustrated by Barbara Firth, Candlewick, 1996.

The Hidden House, illustrated by Angela Barrett, Candlewick, 1997.

Mimi's Christmas, illustrated by Leo Hartas, Candlewick, 1997.

"NAPPER" SERIES

Napper Goes for Goal, illustrated by Barrie Mitchell, Puffin (London), 1981.

Napper Strikes Again, illustrated by Barrie Mitchell, Puffin, 1981.

Napper's Golden Goals, illustrated by Barrie Mitchell, Puffin, 1984.

Napper's Luck, illustrated by Richard Berridge, Puffin, 1993.

Napper's Big Match, illustrated by Richard Berridge, Puffin, 1993.

Napper Super-Sub, illustrated by Richard Berridge, Puffin, 1993.

"HARRIET" SERIES; ILLUSTRATED BY MARK BURGESS

Harriet and the Crocodiles, Abelard, 1982, Little, Brown, 1984.

Harriet and the Haunted School, Abelard, 1984, Little, Brown, 1986.

Harriet and the Robot, Abelard, 1985, Little, Brown, 1987.

Harriet and the Flying Teachers, Blackie & Son, 1987.

"THE MYSTERY SQUAD" SERIES; ILLUSTRATED BY TERRY MCKENNA

The Mystery Squad and the Dead Man's Message, Blackie & Son, 1984.

The Mystery Squad and the Whistling Teeth, Blackie & Son, 1984.

The Mystery Squad and Mr. Midnight, Blackie & Son, 1984.

The Mystery Squad and the Artful Dodger, Blackie & Son, 1984.

The Mystery Squad and the Creeping Castle, Blackie & Son, 1985.

The Mystery Squad and the Gemini Job, Blackie & Son, 1985.

The Mystery Squad and the Candid Camera, Blackie & Son, 1985.

The Mystery Squad and Cannonball Kid, Blackie & Son, 1986.

The Mystery Squad and the Robot's Revenge, Blackie & Son, 1986.

"LITTLE DRACULA" SERIES; ILLUSTRATED BY JOSEPH WRIGHT

Little Dracula's Christmas, Viking Penguin, 1986.

Little Dracula's First Bite, Viking Penguin, 1986.

Little Dracula at the Seaside, Walker Books, 1987, Candlewick, 1992.

Little Dracula Goes to School, Walker Books, 1987, Candlewick, 1992.

Little Dracula at the Seashore, Candlewick, 1992.

FICTION; UNDER PSEUDONYM CATHERINE SEFTON

In a Blue Velvet Dress: Almost a Ghost Story, illustrated by Gareth Floyd, Faber, 1972, published as *In a Blue Velvet Dress*, illustrated by Eros Keith, Harper, 1973.

The Sleepers on the Hill, Faber, 1973.

The Back House Ghosts, Faber, 1974, published as *The Haunting of Ellen: A Story of Suspense*, Harper, 1975.

The Ghost and Bertie Boggin, illustrated by Jill Bennett, Faber, 1980.

Emer's Ghost, Hamish Hamilton, 1981.

The Finn Gang, illustrated by Sally Holmes, Hamish Hamilton, 1981.

The Emma Dilemma, illustrated by Jill Bennett, Faber, 1982.

A Puff of Smoke, illustrated by Thelma Lambert, Hamish Hamilton, 1982.

Island of the Strangers, Hamish Hamilton, 1983, Harcourt Brace, 1985.

It's My Gang, illustrated by Catherine Bradbury, Hamish Hamilton, 1984.

The Blue Misty Monsters, illustrated by Elaine McGregor Turney, Faber, 1985.

The Ghost Girl, Hamish Hamilton, 1985.

The Ghost Ship, illustrated by Martin Ursell, Hamish Hamilton, 1985.

Flying Sam, illustrated by Margaret Chamberlain, Hamish Hamilton, 1986.

Shadows on the Lake, Hamish Hamilton, 1987.

Bertie Boggin and the Ghost Again!, Faber, 1988.

The Day the Smells Went Wrong, illustrated by John Rogan, Hamish Hamilton, 1988.

The Haunted Schoolbag, illustrated by Caroline Crossland, Hamish Hamilton, 1989.

The Boggart in the Barrel, illustrated by Maureen Bradley, Hamish Hamilton, 1991.

Horace the Ghost, illustrated by Crossland, Hamish Hamilton, 1991.

Along a Lonely Road, Puffin, 1992.

The Ghosts of the Cobweb and the Skully Bones Mystery, Hamish Hamilton, 1993.

The Ghosts of the Cobweb Street and the Circus Star, illustrated by Jean Baylis, Hamish Hamilton, 1993.

The Cast-Off, Hamish Hamilton, 1993.

The Ghosts of Cobweb and the TV Battle, Hamish Hamilton, 1994.

The Ghosts of Cobweb, Puffin, 1994.

"IRISH POLITICAL" TRILOGY; UNDER PSEUDONYM CATHERINE SEFTON

Starry Night, Hamish Hamilton, 1986.

Frankie's Story, Hamish Hamilton, 1988.

The Beat of the Drum, Hamish Hamilton, 1989.

YOUNG ADULT NOVELS; UNDER PSEUDONYM CATHERINE SEFTON

The Kidnapping of Suzie Q, Hamish Hamilton, 1994, Candlewick, 1996.

Tango's Baby, Candlewick, 1995.

The Life and Loves of Zöe T. Curly, Walker Books, 1997.

FICTION FOR ADULTS

Otley, Hodder & Stoughton, 1966, Stein & Day, 1966.

Otley Pursued, Hodder & Stoughton, 1967, Stein & Day, 1967.

Otley Forever, Hodder & Stoughton, 1968, Stein & Day, 1968.

Come Back When I'm Sober, Hodder & Stoughton, 1969.

Otley Victorious, Hodder & Stoughton, 1969, Stein & Day, 1969.

A Little Bit British: Being the Diary of an Ulsterman, August, 1969, Tom Stacey, 1970.

OTHER

Author of a radio play, *The Fleas and Mr. Morgan,* 1969; contributor of sketches to "Bazaar" series, 1974, and "One Potato, Two Potato" series, 1975.

Owl Babies has been translated into Spanish by Andrea B. Bermudez as *Las lechucitas,* Compton, 1994; *Can't You Sleep, Little Bear?* has been translated into Spanish as *No Duermes, Osito?,* Ingram, 1996; *You and Me, Little Bear* has been translated into Spanish as *Tu y Yo Osito,* Ingram, 1997.

■ **Adaptations**

Otley was adapted for a motion picture starring Romy Schneider and Tom Courtenay, Columbia, 1969; *In a Blue Velvet Dress* was adapted for "Jackanory" reading, BBC-TV, 1974; *The Sleepers on the Hill* was adapted as a television serial by BBC-TV, 1976; *Fred the Angel* was broadcast on BBC-TV; *Island of the Strangers* was broadcast on Thames TV.

■ **Sidelights**

Catherine Sefton novels are popular among young adult readers, who enjoy the thrill of the supernatural or a first-hand experience of the "troubles" in Northern Ireland. These readers may not be aware, however, that Catherine Sefton is actually the pseudonym for Martin Waddell, the same author whose books for children delighted and enthralled them during their preschool and primary years. Waddell is frequently dubbed "two writers in one." Under his own name he publishes mysteries, ghost stories, light comedies, and picture books for children. As Catherine Sefton he has written more complex, emotionally charged books for young adults, several of which are ghost stories while others are political novels. For both audiences he relies on suspense, humor, colorful characters, and lively dialogue to engage the reader. At the same time he explores such themes as prejudice, self-reliance, and family problems.

Waddell has adapted easily to his two writing worlds. Growing up in Northern Ireland, which is a country separate from the Republic of Ireland, he became accustomed to divisions—nationalist versus loyalist, Catholic versus Protestant—that are a part of daily life in Ireland. However, Waddell has always considered himself to be an outsider in these conflicts, since he claims neither Catholic nor Protestant as his religion and he has not aligned himself with either side in the political struggle for Irish independence from Britain. In fact, Waddell wrote in an essay for *Something*

About the Author Autobiography Series (SAAS) that he hopes to "counter the 'Them' and 'Us' mentality which has cost so many lives and caused so much heartbreak to the people I live amongst."

"Why not? The books came first, the name was invented afterwards. The name had to fit the books and I think that it does."

—Martin Waddell, on why he chose a woman's name for a pseudonym

Although Waddell did not set out to become a writer, the craft came naturally to him, perhaps because four of his ancestors were noted writers. That his stories depict life in Northern Ireland also seems a natural consequence of his heritage, since his family has lived in County Down for more than two hundred years. Waddell was born in Belfast during the German bombing of the city in World War II. His parents fled to safety at Rock Cottage in the town of Newcastle, in County Down, where Waddell would later return to live as an adult. He spent his childhood exploring the woods near the town or walking along the seashore. At an early age he was introduced to stories by a local actor named Terence Pym, and he credits Pym's influence on his decision to become a writer. "Terence read to me from books, but he also told the stories as he walked, with dark eyes and an actor's intonation," Waddell recalled in the *SAAS* essay. "He was part of the stories, he was the characters, and I am sure that some of my love of story comes from those long days."

Waddell's parents took him to live in Belfast after the war, although they did not sever the connection with Newcastle, spending their summers at Rock Cottage. Although Waddell's father, a linen manufacturer, was frequently away on business, he always took the time to tell his son a bedtime story when he was home. Waddell remembered in particular a continuous tale about Dick Turpin the Highwayman which, he said in *SAAS*, "went on and on and on for years." He added that his father's storytelling also influenced his own career as a professional writer: "When I write books for the very small, books such as *Can't You Sleep, Little Bear* and *Farmer Duck*, I have this period in mind." However, this tranquil pe-

riod was interrupted when Waddell's parents began having marital problems. Waddell's mother took him back to Newcastle, and his father often commuted there from Belfast. In 1952, when Waddell was eleven, the family lived briefly in London, England, while his parents made an attempt at reconciliation. Finally he and his mother returned to Newcastle, where he remained for his schooling.

A Major Decision

At the age of fifteen Waddell made a decision that would have a lasting effect on his life, an act he would later regret: he quit school to take a job at a local newspaper. Although he enjoyed his writing duties, he was not cut out to be a printer's apprentice. He quit after only nine months, then tried to become a professional soccer player in England. Having had some success as a goalkeeper for a Newcastle team, he nearly secured a contract with a club in London. Soon he realized he was not destined for a career in the sport, and he found himself living in London without a job. At that point he turned to writing. "Why writing?" he asked in *SAAS*. "I suppose the answer is that writing had always come easily to me. I had never had to work at it at school; it was something I knew I could do. That goes back to the story, and reading. My love of story, of being told stories and being read to, had transferred to a love of books. . . ."

While working odd jobs Waddell wrote novels and stories for six years. Although he had accumulated a pile of unpublished manuscripts he did have an agent, Jonathan Clowes, who had faith in him. Clowes suggested that Waddell read books by Len Deighton, a spy novelist, as models for his own fiction. By 1966 Waddell had published *Otley*, a satirical adult spy-thriller, which was an immediate success. The novel was made into an equally successful film that in turn led Waddell to write other Otley books. After he had become financially secure he returned to Northern Ireland, buying a house in the seaside town of Donaghadee. In 1969 he married Rosaleen Carragher. Then his career took an unexpected turn: he began writing books for children. He published his first young adult novel, *In a Blue Velvet Dress*, under the name Catherine Sefton. He adopted a pen name because he had already established a reputation as a writer of adult thrillers and satires. Sefton had been his grandmother's maiden name, and he chose Catherine simply because he liked the name.

By 1972 Waddell had produced two Sefton novels, and he and his wife had had their first two children. That same year, however, he was nearly killed by the explosion of a bomb he discovered in a local church. His career came to a halt, as he was unable to write for six years. During that time he produced only one book, the Catherine Sefton ghost-adventure story *The Back House Ghosts*. Then, almost as suddenly as the bomb blast had altered Waddell's life, his ability to write came back to him. In 1978, with the assistance of his new agent, Gina Pollinger, he began producing the diverse range of children's stories that have become his trademark. He also resumed the Catherine Sefton ghost series, which later included novels about the Northern Ireland sectarian conflict. By the late 1990s, when he started publishing young adult novels under his own name as well, Waddell had produced more than one hundred books.

Tales of the Supernatural

Waddell's first Catherine Sefton novel, *In a Blue Velvet Dress*, is subtitled "almost a ghost story." The main character is eleven-year-old Jane Reid, who is spending a holiday with the Hildreths at their old house in the woods while her parents are sailing in Scotland. An avid reader, Jane realizes she has forgotten to bring her books from home. She can find nothing to read in the Hildreths' house, and she learns the little town has neither a library nor a bookstore. Just when Jane's visit is about to be ruined, a book begins to appear each night beside her bed, only to disappear before she wakes up in the morning. Seeing a thirteen-year-old girl in a blue velvet dress in her room, she surmises a connection between the apparition and the vanishing books. Eventually solving the mystery, Jane discovers that the girl is Mary Quinton, who died of grief a century earlier when her father drowned. Critical response to *In a Blue Velvet Dress* was mixed. Reviewing the book in *Growing Point*, Margery Fisher concluded that the present and the past "somehow don't mesh as they should," and Jane's character is not fully developed. Lucinda Fox stated in *School Librarian* that the book is written in "a pleasant style," and in *Junior Bookshelf* M. Hobbs

praised Sefton's "most endearing and effective humour." *In a Blue Velvet Dress* was later dramatized in a BBC television production.

The Sleepers on the Hill is also a ghost story involving a mysterious old house in a lonely location. This time the characters are Tom and Kathleen and the setting is a remote region of Ireland, where ancient ruins still stand and superstition is an integral part of local culture. The mystery begins when Miss Cooney, who lives alone in the large house on the hill, must leave her home after she has an accident. Assuming that the house is empty, Tom and Kathleen are soon caught up in a series of unsettling events. Their innocent discovery of a gold bracelet at a prehistoric site awakens the "sleepers," supernatural Celtic beings who live under the hills. Fortune-seeking villagers start hunting for other potential treasures, and real-estate developers concoct a housing plan that would displace people from their homes. The author also introduces problems faced by young people who are bored with small-town life or cannot find work in rural Ireland.

Noting that "these events wind up in a tense climax in the mysterious house," *Children's Book Review* contributor C. S. Hannabuss described *The Sleepers on the Hill* as being "approachable, clear, [and] concise." In a review for *School Librarian*, Harold A. Jester promised that the reader would find "some excellent surprises and dangerous moments." Nevertheless, Zena Sutherland cautioned in *Bulletin of the Center for Children's Books* that although the portrayal of social problems is interesting, it obscures the basic mystery story. Like *In a Blue Velvet Dress*, *The Sleepers on the Hill* was dramatized by BBC television.

The Back House Ghosts, which was published in the United States as *The Haunting of Ellen: A Story of Suspense*, takes place in a boarding house run by Mrs. Bailey at a popular seaside resort. Called a "combination of ghost story and the everyday adventures of several young people" by E. Colwell in *Junior Bookshelf*, the book opens with the unexpected arrival of thirteen members of the Mooney family. Having planned for only four guests, Mrs. Bailey moves with her daughters Bella and Ellen into a cottage, known as the back house, behind the main house. When a vacancy opens up Mrs. Bailey returns to the main house, but the girls remain at the cottage. Ellen then begins to notice disturbing occurrences: the view from the window often changes, and strange handwriting and words appear when she writes with her pen. After seeing women in old-fashioned dresses, she finds a dueling pistol in the chimney. She starts to wonder if the cottage is haunted by a ghost. Ellen and Bella soon befriend two of the Mooneys, with whom they embark on exciting adventures. Ellen and Violet Moody try to find information about the family who once lived in the cottage, while Bella and Paul Mooney track down the Mooneys' stolen mini-bus, which contains all of their belongings. Their investigations reach a climatic solution on the night of a fireworks display. Critics agreed

This 1973 novel, Waddell's first under the pseudonym Catherine Sefton, tells of a girl's ghostly encounters while visiting her relatives along the Irish seacoast.

that *The Back House Ghosts* is "full of excitement and humor," as Sylvia Mogg observed in *Children's Book Review*. Mogg also noted that "The author holds the reader's interest whilst the clues are gathered which lead to a romantic conclusion." Commenting that the story is "enlivened by a feeling of spontaneous gaiety," Colwell characterized the mystery as "intriguing" and the ghost as "not really frightening."

The following three Sefton novels—*Emer's Ghost, The Finn Gang,* and *The Emma Dilemma*—continued in the supernatural genre. In *Emer's Ghost* Emer, who is about twelve, lives with her sisters and widowed mother in a village on the border between Northern Ireland and the Republic of Ireland. Linking the present with the past, the story centers on the lost St. Aidan's chalice, which monks had hidden from Cromwell's troops during a British invasion. After meeting the ghost of a dead girl, Emer knows she can solve the mystery of the chalice. The plot gains momentum, at one point involving a fortune-teller, as preparations for a historical pageant at the convent school gradually reveal clues. Emer's discovery of an old doll belonging to the ghost is finally the key to the puzzle.

Emer's Ghost was published to nearly unanimous critical acclaim. In the *Times Literary Supplement* Ann Evans praised the "beautifully wrought story" as well as Sefton's "uncanny insight into the workings of a child's mind" and "acute ear for dialogue." Evans pronounced Sefton "a writer of a rare order." M. Hobbs was delighted by the mixture of drama and humor, writing in *Junior Bookshelf* that "For all its meatiness . . . , this is a very funny book." Hobbs concluded: "It is a lively and realistic narrative, with food for thought."

The Finn Gang, the story of a "gang" that consists of Dodger Finn and his sister Mary, was less successful. R. Baines noted in *Junior Bookshelf* that while the plot moves swiftly—the gang "improbably" uncovers a crime, stages a dramatic rescue, recovers stolen property, and captures the criminals—it is too "involved and confusing" for younger readers. Sefton's next book, *The Emma Dilemma,* received a mixed critical response. When nine-year-old Emma hits her head she is plunged into another world where she meets an identical Emma. Nobody else, except Dracula the family cat, can see the Other Emma. This leads to a series of unexplained incidents, such as a wrecked school room and seaweed on Emma's bed. Margery Fisher observed in *Growing Point* that "prosaic details . . . prevent the fantasy from taking off completely into a realm of psychological terror." However, Zena Sutherland gave the novel a more positive review in *Bulletin of the Center for Children's Books,* finding it to be a "nice blend of fantasy and realism, in a story written with vitality."

Island of the Strangers is more reality-based than the previous Sefton novels, yet it too contains a hint of the supernatural. The central character, Nora, lives in a remote village in Northern Ireland and is being cared for by Stella, a distant relative, while Nora's widowed father is away. Nora and Stella soon experience a personality conflict that parallels tensions in the village: the Gobbers, a group of toughs from Belfast, have taken over the town and caused a gang war. Reluctant to join her friends in opposing the Gobbers, Nora ultimately learns the importance of being true to oneself. She also reconciles with Stella in a warm, affecting scene. The plot builds to a violent, frightening conclusion that makes a comment on the political situation in Northern Ireland. In *Booklist*, Ilene Cooper described *Island of the Strangers* as a "strong, sure-handed effort" that offers a "dash" of mystery. Pauline Thomas, in a review for *School Librarian*, found Nora to be "a convincing heroine." J. Alison Illsley suggested in *School Library Journal* that the book offers a "springboard to a serious discussion on the nature of conflict and its resolutions."

In *My Gang, Blue Misty Monsters,* and *The Ghost Girl,* Sefton returns to familiar themes, yet from different perspectives. The author depicts gang warfare again in *My Gang*. But this time the emphasis is purely humorous as a young boy named Noel plots to turn his older sister and her friends against one another when they will not let him join their gang. Calling the book "funny and imaginative" in *Books for Keeps,* Colin Mills noted that the girls are "rounded and sparky characters." Rodie Sudbery claimed in *School Librarian* that the last chapter "demands applause." In sharp contrast to *My Gang, The Ghost Girl*—which critic Joanna Motion called a "serious and gentle" book in the *Times Literary Supplement*—utilizes the supernatural to depict contemporary Northern Ireland. However, the story takes place in Donegal, a county in the Republic, where Clare Campbell and her two sisters are vacationing with their

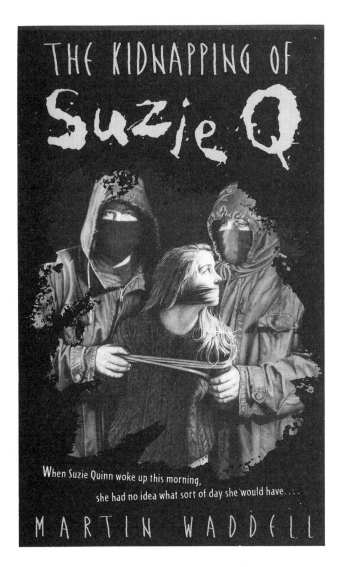

A botched robbery at a grocery store by a trio of amateur thieves becomes a dangerous hostage situation in this 1994 work.

parents after their shop has been bombed. Surrounding them is evidence of the current nationalist movement in the form of IRA grafitti. Past and present meet after Nora sees a ghost from the era of the Jacobite Rebellion, when Protestants seized control of Ireland from Catholics.

Clare and her family are staying at a guest house that was a garrison for British soldiers during the rebellion. Learning that a Catholic priest was also hanged nearby, Clare becomes immersed in the history of ancient sectarian divisions that have been passed down to the present day in Ireland. She befriends the Canon, a priest who helps her identify the ghost girl who, like Clare, also lived during troubled times. Motion commended Sefton for setting up "an illuminating device for writing about Northern Ireland," but went on to contend that "the sympathies of both Clare and the author seem more attuned to the past than to the present, and Catherine Sefton finds herself unable to give due weight to one period or the other." Motion also suspected too that much explanation of history would be required for young readers to understand the work. On the other hand, in *Books for Your Children,* George English called *The Ghost Girl* a "brave book," which "quite successfully" informs young readers about the history of the Irish "troubles."

Shadows on the Lake picked up the threads of *Island of Strangers* and *The Ghost Girl.* It is a realistic adventure story featuring Annie, a motherless girl who lives in impoverished rural Northern Ireland. However, noting Sefton's emphasis on social and family problems in the book, reviewer Celia Gibbs predicted in *British Book News Children's Books* that "many readers will find it oppressive and sad." Waddell continued to address the Irish "troubles" in the Sefton novels *Starry Night, Frankie's Story,* and *The Beat of the Drum,* which are frequently grouped together as a trilogy. The writer discounted this notion, however, in his autobiographical essay for *SAAS:* "These three have been called a trilogy, but they aren't really, each being a separate story. What they have in common is a set of ideas, laid out in *Starry Night* and observed in action in the other two. *Frankie's Story* and *The Beat of the Drum* are basically the same story: one about a Catholic girl resisting the forces of extremism in her world, and the other about a Protestant boy doing the same thing in his."

Examines the "Troubles"

Winner of the 1986 Other award, *Starry Night* depicts a crisis in the life of fifteen-year-old Kathleen Fay. While she was growing up Kathleen was told Irish fairy stories by her older sister Ruth. Yet, Kathleen comes to learn that the tales are all "blether" and Ruth is a different person than she had appeared to be. The sectarian conflict in Northern Ireland plays only a peripheral role in the plot of *Starry Night;* as Robert Leeson points out in the *Times Educational Supplement,* "politics were off-stage. In *Frankie's Story,* they are centre

stage." Frankie is a teen-age girl living on a Catholic estate in a tightly-knit neighborhood that includes the notorious Hagan family and Con, a menacing Provo (member of the radical Provisional IRA). The story, which is narrated by Frankie, revolves around her attempts to protect her Protestant ex-boyfriend from various threatening elements. In the process she is labeled an informer, nearly killed by a firebomb, and enmeshed in events surrounding the deaths of two Provos. The novel also depicts problems in Frankie's family that mirror the instability and violence in the outside world. Reviewing *Frankie's Story* in *British Book News Children's Books,* Caroline Heaton concluded, "The entire story is a forceful demonstration of the power of prejudice to fuel fanaticism and divide a community, a nation." Marcus Crouch noted in *Junior Bookshelf* that Sefton writes "in terse unadorned sentences, building up tension and rising to a disturbing climax. But it is the matter, rather than the manner, of this book which leaves its indelible impression on the reader."

The Beat of the Drum portrays the Protestant side of the Northern Ireland conflict. Set in Belfast, the novel is narrated by Brian Hanna, who has been orphaned and crippled by an IRA bomb. He is confined to a wheelchair and has been taught by his Auntie Mae not to hate his attackers, but instead to abhor the violence causing their act. As Leeson commented in the *Times Educational Supplement,* "Brian lives a whole life in a matter of days" in *The Beat of the Drum.* The story features a diverse cast of characters: marching Orangemen (hence the title of the novel), a preacher who stashes illegal arms in his church, the preacher's daughter who leads a secret life, Loyalist (pro-British) militants who bomb Catholic families, Mae's bigoted husband Billy, and Brian's doomed friend Hicky.

Leeson praised the book, stating: "The author has resolutely completed his aim, to help the teenage reader grasp the reality of Northern Ireland's tragedy. The trilogy is a real contribution to the understanding which must one day bring that suffering to an end." In a review for *Junior Bookshelf,* Crouch was critical of Sefton's tendency to stereotype people and situations in the novel—"the characters act as if operated by strings," he wrote. Nevertheless he found *The Beat of the Drum* to be a powerful novel: "There is little comfort in reading *The Beat of the Drum,* except that there are

---

If you enjoy the works of Martin Waddell, you may also want to check out the following books and films:

Joan Aiken, *The Haunting of Lamb House,* 1993.
Ann Head, *Mr. and Mrs. Bo Jo Jones,* 1967.
James Heneghan, *Torn Away,* 1994.
James Watson, *Talking in Whispers,* 1984.
Cal, a film set in Northern Ireland, 1984.
The Uninvited, a film about a haunted house, 1944.

---

people like Brian. . . . It portrays no heroes, few villains, many people bound to the wheel of traditional hatreds. It is not easily put out of the mind."

Sefton touches again on the IRA/Loyalist theme in *Along a Lonely Road.* Ruth, the fourteen-year-old main narrator, describes being held hostage with her family by the Gettigans on their farm in a remote part of Northern Ireland. At first Ruth thinks the Gettigans are involved with the IRA, but she soon learns differently: "they just didn't *feel* like the IRA," Ruth says, " . . . the IRA are *ordinary* ones, and the Gettigans were . . . *flash,* him with his yellow shoes and his leather jacket, and her with her made-up face you could leave footprints on if you were a fly." In a review for *Junior Bookshelf* D. A. Young observed that *Along a Lonely Road* moves beyond a depiction of the political situation, calling the novel "a masterpiece of suspense" and placing it in the category of "books that have to be read through in one sitting." Crouch reported in *School Librarian* that the book also addresses universal issues such as "human greed, courage and truth to oneself. It is a story not easily forgotten."

During the 1990s Waddell wrote other books for young adults under his own name. Among them are *The Kidnapping of Suzie Q, Tango's Baby,* and *The Life and Loves of Zöe T. Curly.* In *The Kidnapping of Suzie Q,* Suzie is running a last-minute errand to the grocery store when she is taken hostage by three masked gunmen. Bound, gagged, and blindfolded, she is whisked away in a van. The police are immediately wary because they do not know if this is an ordinary kidnapping or an IRA trap. The action becomes a study in inepti-

tude as the police fumble the investigation, the gunmen reveal their identity to Suzie, and Suzie makes a failed escape attempt. Frances Bradburn commented in *Booklist* that it is "difficult to muster much concern for Suzie simply because of the book's flippant tone" but, she concluded, it "will entice even the most reluctant reader." Similarly, Diane Roback and Elizabeth Devereaux stated in *Publishers Weekly* that the suspense is "liquidated by the format," yet readers should be kept "on the hook" by the "smart, breezy writing, jaunty heroine, and tense setting."

In *Tango's Baby* Waddell portrays Tango, a British teenager who is frequently in trouble with the law but is essentially good at heart. Narrated by one of Tango's former schoolmates, the novel features numerous characters who are dependant on the British welfare system. Tango falls in love with fifteen-year-old Crystal, whose father has died. The story unfolds as Crystal becomes pregnant and Tango must cope with his ill-fated love for the girl and the child. Roback and Devereaux noted in *Publishers Weekly* that the "oddly distant, choppy" story is "more suitable for adults than for the targeted audience." Waddell's next book, however, is definitely for teenagers. The format of *The Life and Loves of Zöe T. Curly* is a series of diary entries from a month in the life of the title character and her best friend Melissa. The novel has a slightly zany tone that is established with the nicknames of the characters: Zöe's writer father is The Creative, her brothers are Ob-noxious and Creep, though her mother is simply Mum. The family lives in the Kingdom of Zog, which is ruled by Mum. The "plot" consists of the ups and downs of Zöe's and Melissa's relationships with the opposite sex, along with everyday school and family problems. According to Jo Gordon in a review for *Magpies,* "Waddell economically conveys the dynamics of family life, its drama and rivalries, with more than a touch of irony."

Waddell continues his prolific output, writing books for both children and young adults. And he plans to keep up this pace for a very long time. In *SAAS,* Waddell wrote, "My stories are my mind-children, if you like. They are on my shelves, and growing in my head are others, waiting to attract my attention, fighting with each other about who-comes-first. It is a magic thing about stories that they come before the words . . . you can feel them stirring, but you don't know what form they will take. The good ones won't wait their turn to be written and thought about. The best ones, the really strong ones, pour themselves out on the page." Reflecting on his twenty-five-year career at the end of the essay, Waddell concluded, "I'm only fifty years old. That means I am halfway through my professional writing life, if I manage to keep going to seventy-five, which I hope to do."

■ Works Cited

Baines, R., review of *The Finn Gang, Junior Bookshelf*, August, 1982, p. 146.

Bradburn, Frances, review of *The Kidnapping of Suzie Q, Booklist*, May 1, 1996, p. 1499.

Colwell, E., review of *The Back House Ghosts, Junior Bookshelf*, April, 1975, p. 131.

Cooper, Ilene, review of *Island of the Strangers, Booklist*, January 1, 1986, p. 687.

Crouch, Marcus, review of *Frankie's Story, Junior Bookshelf*, April, 1988, p. 109.

Crouch, Marcus, review of *The Beat of the Drum, Junior Bookshelf*, August, 1989, p. 193.

Crouch, Marcus, review of *Along a Lonely Road, School Librarian*, February, 1992, p. 33.

English, George, review of *The Ghost Girl, Books for Your Children*, Autumn/Winter, 1985, p. 21.

Evans, Ann, review of *Emer's Ghost, Times Literary Supplement*, November 20, 1981, p. 1359.

Fisher, Margery, review of *In a Blue Velvet Dress, Growing Point*, November, 1972, p. 2036.

Fisher, Margery, review of *The Emma Dilemma, Growing Point*, May, 1982, p. 3895.

Fox, Lucinda, review of *In a Blue Velvet Dress, School Librarian*, September, 1972, p. 275.

Gibbs, Celia, review of *Shadows on the Lake, British Book News Children's Books*, March, 1987, pp. 33-34.

Gordon, Jo, review of *The Life and Loves of Zöe T. Curly, Magpies*, May, 1991, p. 35.

Hannabuss, C. S., review of *The Sleepers on the Hill, Children's Book Review*, December, 1973, pp. 179-80.

Heaton, Caroline, review of *Frankie's Story, British Book News Children's Books*, March, 1988, p. 32.

Hobbs, M., review of *In a Blue Velvet Dress, Junior Bookshelf*, December, 1972, p. 412.

Hobbs, M., review of *Emer's Ghost, Junior Bookshelf*, February, 1982, p. 32.

Illsley, J. Alison, review of *Island of the Strangers, School Library Journal*, January, 1986, p. 70.

Jester, Harold A., review of *The Sleepers on the Hill, School Librarian*, March, 1974, p. 99.

Leeson, Robert, review of *Frankie's Story, Times Educational Supplement*, February 26, 1988, p. 25.

Leeson, Robert, review of *The Beat of the Drum, Times Educational Supplement*, May 5, 1989, p. B7.

Mills, Colin, review of *My Gang, Books for Keeps*, July, 1987, p. 15.

Mogg, Sylvia, review of *The Back House Ghosts, Children's Book Review*, Spring, 1975, pp. 22-23.

Motion, Joanna, "Ancient Informers," *Times Literary Supplement*, April 12, 1985, p. 418.

Roback, Diane, and Elizabeth Devereaux, review of *Tango's Baby, Publishers Weekly*, October 30, 1995, p. 63.

Roback, Diane, and Elizabeth Devereaux, review of *The Kidnapping of Suzie Q, Publishers Weekly*, June 10, 1996, p. 101.

Sefton, Catherine, *Along a Lonely Road*, Puffin, 1992.

Sudbery, Rodie, review of *My Gang, School Librarian*, June, 1984, p. 138.

Sutherland, Zena, review of *The Sleepers on the Hill, Bulletin of the Center for Children's Books*, May, 1979, pp. 162-63.

Sutherland, Zena, review of *The Emma Dilemma, Bulletin of the Center for Children's Books*, October, 1983, p. 37.

Thomas, Pauline, review of *Island of the Strangers, School Librarian*, September, 1983, pp. 272-75.

Waddell, Martin, essay in *Something About the Author, Autobiography Series*, Gale, Volume 13, 1993, pp. 293-308.

Young, D. A., review of *Along a Lonely Road, Junior Bookshelf*, April, 1992, p. 79.

■ For More Information See

BOOKS

Children's Literature Review, Volume 31, Gale, 1994.

Seventh Book of Junior Authors and Illustrators, edited by Sally Holmes Holtze, H. W. Wilson, 1996.

Twentieth-Century Children's Writers, 4th edition, St. James Press, 1995.

PERIODICALS

Bulletin of the Center for Children's Books, October, 1983, p. 37.

Growing Point, September, 1981, pp. 3945-46; November, 1985, p. 4539; September, 1987, p. 4864.

Horn Book, August, 1975, pp. 383-84.

School Librarian, December, 1985, pp. 359-60; May, 1987, p. 159; August 3, 1989, p. 117.
Times Literary Supplement, April 17, 1987, p. 421.*

—Sketch by Peggy Saari

Patricia Windsor

■ **Personal**

Has also written as Colin Daniel; born September 21, 1938, in New York, NY; daughter of Bernhard Edward and Antoinette (Gaus) Seelinger; married Laurence Charles Windsor, Jr., 1959 (divorced, 1978); married Steve Altman, 1986 (divorced, 1987); children: Patience Wells, Laurence Edward. *Education:* Attended Bennington College and Westchester Community College; New York University, A.A.

■ **Addresses**

Agent—Amy Berkower, Writers House, Inc., 21 West 26th St., New York, NY 10010; and Patricia White, 20 Powis Mews, London W11 1JN, England.

■ **Career**

Novelist. Windsor-Morehead Associates (advertising agency), New York City, vice president, 1960-63; American Telephone and Telegraph, Washing-ton, DC, editor-in-chief of *Easterner* (company publication), 1979-81. Teacher of creative writing, Westchester, NY, 1975-78; Institute of Children's Literature, Redding Ridge, CT, faculty member, 1976—; instructor, University of Maryland Writers Institute, 1981-83, and OPEN University, Washington, DC; Family Planning Association, London, England, assistant director of central inquiries, 1972-73, counselor, 1974-75; correspondent, National Council of Social Service, London, 1974—; director, Wordspring Literary Consultants, 1987-90; counselor, First Call for Help, 1990-91; director, Summertree Studios, 1992—; active in YWCA and North Westchester Association for Retarded Children. Actress under the name Katonah Summertree for City Lights Productions. *Member:* PEN American Centre, Children's Book Guild, Poetry Society of Georgia, Georgia Historical Society, Savannah Storytellers, City Lights Theatre Guild.

■ **Awards, Honors**

Chicago Tribune Book World Honor Book award and Best Books for Young Adults award, American Library Association, both 1973, and Austrian State award for Books for Children and Youth, 1981, all for *The Summer Before; Diving for Roses* was named a notable book of 1976 by the *New York Times;* best newspaper story, United Way of National Capital Area, 1979; best photo presentation, United Way, 1980; Edgar Allan Poe Award, Mystery Writers of America, 1985, for *The Sandman's Eyes;*

Edgar Allan Poe Award nomination, 1992, for *The Christmas Killer.*

■ Writings

YOUNG ADULT NOVELS

The Summer Before, Harper, 1973.
Something's Waiting for You, Baker D, Harper, 1974.
Home Is Where Your Feet Are Standing, Harper, 1975.
Diving for Roses, Harper, 1976.
Mad Martin, Harper, 1976.
Killing Time, Harper, 1980.
The Sandman's Eyes, Delacorte, 1985.
How a Weirdo and a Ghost Can Change Your Entire Life, illustrated by Jacqueline Rogers, Delacorte, 1986.
The Hero, Delacorte, 1988.
Just Like the Movies, Pan Macmillan, 1990.
Two Weirdos and a Ghost, Dell, 1991.
Very Weird and Moogly Christmas, Dell, 1991.
The Christmas Killer, Scholastic, 1992.
The Blooding, Scholastic, 1996.

OTHER

Old Coat's Cat (short stories), Macmillan, 1974.
Rain (short stories), Macmillan, 1976.
The Girl with the Click Click Eyes (short stories), Heinemann, 1977.
(Under pseudonym Colin Daniel) *Demon Tree,* Dell, 1983.

Columnist, *Blood Review,* 1988-89, and *Savannah Parent,* 1990—. Lyricist for popular songs composed by Yseult Freilicher. Contributor of short stories to periodicals (in Sweden, Denmark, South Africa, Australia, England, and the United States), including *Seventeen* and *Scholastic Scope.* Windsor's manuscripts are included in the Kerlan Collection, University of Minnesota.

■ Work in Progress

A novel, *The House of Death.*

■ Sidelights

"Mystery writers hoping to hook teenagers could use (Patricia) Windsor as a model," according to reviewer Cathi Dunn MacRae in *Wilson Library Bulletin.* But being a leader in her field didn't come overnight for Windsor. "I began writing very early—at about age ten," she once told *Something about the Author (SATA).* "I always had a long list of titles for future novels . . . but never finished any of them (at least not until I was much older). . . . In high school I wrote poetry—have the honor of holding thirty-five rejection slips from *Seventeen* magazine. . . . For awhile I wrote a lot of science fiction . . . but never had any of it published." As an adult, Windsor began writing novels for young adults, and not only experienced the thrill of seeing her work published but was also honored with awards. Two of her works have been recognized by the Mystery Writers of America: *The Sandman's Eyes* received the 1985 Edgar Allan Poe Award, and *The Christmas Killer* was nominated for same award in 1992.

Like weaving a patchwork quilt, Windsor takes pieces of her own life and blends them together in her stories. The oldest of three girls, Windsor spent much of her childhood living in an apartment complex in New York City before her family moved to Croton-on-Hudson, which was a country town at the time. As a young girl, Windsor loved to read and hated when anything got in the way. In fact, she thought of school as an intrusion on a much more interesting life that she discovered through books and fantasies. Art and the theater, she thought, offered her this same kind of make-believe world, and she pursued both avenues. In fact, as a young adult, Windsor tested a few careers before settling in as a novelist. "This was my dream, to be a dancer, on the stage or in the movies," she wrote in *Something About the Author Autobiography Series (SAAS).* "It's curious that although I wrote 'novels' from the time I was ten—first they were handwritten, then banged out on an old manual typewriter—I never considered writing as a real career. Fame, stardom—that was what I wanted." She had taken ballet and tap lessons and studied dance seriously at Bennington College. A turning point came, however, after her freshman year when all underclassmen wrote a critique of the senior dance project. Windsor's teacher told her later that her writing was much better than her dancing.

Despite her teacher's assessment, Windsor didn't turn to writing just yet. Instead, she started making the rounds in the New York art world, showing her portfolio and landing a few jobs drawing book jackets and posters. Windsor hated watching art directors look through her work and sometimes make unflattering comments in front of her. After graduation she worked in the college department of *Mademoiselle* and *Living for Young Homemakers,* where she was a table-setting editor and did table set-ups for the magazine's photographers. While her two children, Patience and Laurence, were young most of her time was devoted to their care. She did, however, find time to teach modern dance at the YWCA and New York settlement houses. Windsor was also a member of the Citizen's Committee for Employment in Chicago and worked at finding jobs for released inmates from Chicago's Cook County Jail. Each job, all of the people she met, and their stories became seeds to be developed later, in her characters. If you want to know about Windsor "just read my books," she wrote in *SAAS.* "There's a part of me in every character, part of my experience in every event. Rarely do I write about people, places, or emotions I don't know." Like Windsor's life experiences, her reading also continued to influence her writing. Most of all she loved the work of James Joyce, Dylan Thomas, J. D. Salinger and T. S. Eliot; one of her favorite books is *Lolly Willows* by Sylvia Townsend Warner.

Windsor's own writing career was launched after reading *My Darling, My Hamburger* by Paul Zindel. She told *SATA* that she was amazed young adult books actually dealt with real problems and real people rather than the too-perfect Nancy Drew-like characters she read as a child. In Windsor's first book, *Three Flights Up,* she writes about three girls who are trying to get jobs in the theater. The twenty-page tale depicts life in New York's Greenwich Village. But the turning point of Windsor's career came in 1973 when *The Summer Before* was published. It was written just before she left for England with her two young children. When she arrived in London, Windsor felt like she had come home to a place she already knew. After just a few weeks in her home, Windsor learned that Harper and Row planned to publish *The Summer Before.* "Not only was a new life beginning for me, but what was to be my career for the rest of my life was launched," she told *SAAS.*

The Summer Before is about a girl, Alexandra, who suffers a breakdown after her boyfriend, Bradley, is killed in an auto accident. People often ask Windsor if that happened to her. Not exactly, she wrote in *SAAS,* but she does understand the emotions involved. "Every time we say good-bye and shut the door on a person or place, we experience grief and go through the same process of denial, anger, bargaining, depression and acceptance." All of her books tackle the issues young people face with the intent of letting them know others feel the same desperation. "I hope that my writing for young people helps them see they are not alone . . . that their heartaches, problems, pains and joys are shared by us all, adults included," Windsor once told *Contemporary Authors* (*CA*). *The Summer Before,* written in journal form, gives readers a clear idea about the emotions Alexandra felt. "The story is like a scream of an-

After spending two years in a reformatory, a young man returns to his hometown to clear his name for a murder he says he didn't commit.

Christmas cheer. Christmas fear...

THE CHRISTMAS KILLER

PATRICIA WINDSOR

In this 1992 mystery, Rose's strange dreams of a missing friend are a sign of terrible things to come.

guish and just as compelling," according to reviewer Jean Mercier in *Publishers Weekly*. According to Zena Sutherland in *Bulletin of the Center for Children's Books,* Windsor "has created a touching and credible protagonist in her first novel." The author hasn't revealed "startling news or insights from the flipped side of adolescence but other girls can still find fascination in the journey there and back," according to a critic in *Kirkus Reviews.*

Endless Possibilities

After the publication of her first book a flood of other novels followed. In 1974 *Something's Waiting*

for You, Baker D was published. Meanwhile, still living in England, Windsor worked for several social service agencies as a counselor, a writer, and in public relations. These and other new experiences in London, meshed with her old life in New York, was material for another book, *Home Is Where Your Feet Are Standing,* published in 1975. This book personalized her feelings about success as a novelist, her gutsy move to London, and the realization of her dreams. "And so I remained addicted to possibilities," she wrote in *SAAS.* "Like Colin Daniel in *Home is Where Your Feet Are Standing,* I saw them everywhere 'like a big explosion of glad in the sky.' In fact this book reflects one of my biggest adventures in possibilities: taking my two children and moving from the U.S. to England."

One year after *Home is Where Your Feet Are Standing* was published came *Diving for Roses,* which was cited by the *New York Times* as a notable book. The same year *Mad Martin* was published. In both works Windsor drew from her experience as a counselor at a walk-in advice bureau. "Many of the people who came to see me were young adults," she told *SATA.* "Some of their concerns and worries have been explored in my books, *Diving for Roses* and *Mad Martin.*" Then the torrent of emotions that came with her own divorce, she wrote in *Fifth Book of Junior Authors and Illustrators,* became someone else's break-up in her next novel, *Killing Time.* The plot centers around a sixteen-year-old boy, Sam Trevor, whose parents get divorced. Sam moves into an old house in the woods with his father, Duncan. Sam longs for his home in Manhattan, but his mother has no room for him in her small apartment. The turning point in the book comes when Sam is invited to a house party by the leader of the "in" group and his drink is spiked. This and other assaults on Sam and Duncan are linked to Duncan's discovery of Druid artifacts, proof of bloody sacrifices.

Critics gave *Killing Time* mixed reviews. "Windsor's new thriller adroitly fuses comedy and terror in the manner of her prize-winning tales," according to Mercier in *Publishers Weekly.* In *Bulletin of the Center for Children's Books,* Zena Sutherland stated, "the complexities of the structure and the relationships in the realistic portion are at times burdensome." Yet Sutherland went on to say that the work offers excitement, humor, suspense, and romance. *Voice of Youth Advocates* reviewer Frank Perry was less impressed. He remarked, "Readers deserve something more substantial to be frightened by."

Meanwhile, after some three years in England, Windsor moved back to the United States, taught writing for awhile and became editor of *Easterner*, a corporate newspaper for American Telephone and Telegraph in Washington, D.C. She also taught at the University of Maryland and OPEN University in Washington, D.C. But no matter where she lived, Windsor wrote in *SAAS*, ghosts haunted her homes. "The first house the estate agent showed us was definitely haunted, although the agent said not. But we knew. . . . Ghosts were not new to us. We had lived for years in a small Federal House on Commerce Street in Greenwich Village, and it was haunted by a benign ghost who walked the narrow halls at night. . . . It was my interest in ghosts and the paranormal that brought about many of my books." In fact, she said, when she moved from the north to Georgia she chose Savannah, one of the most ghost-ridden cities in the nation in which to live.

Haunting Death and Revelations About Life

Along those same haunting lines, Windsor wrote an acclaimed thriller, *The Sandman's Eyes*. The story focuses on a teenager, Michael Thorn, who has just been released from a two-year stay in a reformatory after having been suspected of murdering a young woman. A reviewer in *School Library Journal* called the book "A heartwrenching, unsettling reading experience." Michael learns that small towns, like Kornkill, aren't very receptive to a murder suspect and mental patient. With help from an investigative reporter, Michael looks for the real killer. Along the way Michael also looks for love and his own identity. "There is a taut psychological thriller aspect to this story," according to JoEllen Broome in *Voice of Youth Advocates*, who criticized the "too tidy ending. . . ." A critic in *Children's Book Review Service* remarked that the book has "complex relationships, but it is well-written and has well-drawn characters," and Pam Spencer, in a *School Library Journal* review, declared: "It's a bona fide suspense."

Relationships were a key element in a later work, *The Hero*. Sixteen-year-old Dale wakes to a terrifying nightmare, his first of many premonitions that ultimately saves several children's lives. Like some of Windsor's other work, this book met with

If you enjoy the works of Patricia Windsor, you may also want to check out the following books and films:

Peter Dickinson, *Healer*, 1983.
Lois Duncan, *The Third Eye*, 1984.
Joan Lowery Nixon, *Whispers From the Dead*, 1989.
Neal Shusterman, *Speeding Bullet*, 1991.
Scream, a film by Wes Craven, 1996.

both positive and negative reviews. K. Olson Fakih and Diane Roback in *Publishers Weekly* pointed to poor character development as a weakness of the novel: "at the end, we are left with little understanding of Dale or his gift." A critic in *Kirkus Reviews* said the conclusion is murky and leaves important unanswered questions, but also noted, "Windsor views this well-explored territory with a fresh eye and builds the tension expertly."

Like Dale in *The Hero*, Rose, the main character in Windsor's *The Christmas Killer*, receives startling images in her dreams. "A bit more gruesome than most young adult mysteries, this one is well plotted and has sufficient clues for astute readers," according to Jeanette Larson in a *School Library Journal* review. The story focuses on Rose's fears when her friend Nancy Emerson disappears. She has been missing for a couple of days when Rose sees her in a dream and gets hints about where the body is located. Police discover a pattern to the murder of girls during the Christmas season, with the only clue being a poinsettia found on each body. This 1992 novel also had mixed reviews. Stephanie Zvirin, writing in *Booklist*, said the reader cares about Rose "more than we do about the protagonists of most of the recent YA whodunits." Zvirin added, however, that Windsor seemed less in control of the plot. "But the story is riveting all the same, and elements of the supernatural double its YA appeal," Zvirin concluded. Sutherland wrote in the *Bulletin of the Center for Children's Books* that Windsor does a good job of building tension, "creating suspense, and disposing of red herrings. . . . While properly prepared, the revelation of the killer is somewhat lame, but the ending nevertheless provides an agreeable *frisson*." In *Publishers Weekly*, Diane Roback and Richard Donahue opined that Windsor vacillates between writing a detective novel and a ghost story. They added, however, that "readers are likely to enjoy the appealing characters, spooky atmosphere and aptly evoked small-town setting." Mary L. Adams in *Voice of Youth Advocates* called the work a "well crafted mystery" with clues "nicely paced and tantalizing with just enough false trails to keep the reader" in suspense.

Windsor creates another eerie plot, replete with werewolves, in her book, *The Blooding*, published in 1996. An American teenager, working as an au pair in England, witnesses strange events in her new surroundings: her employer's odd late-night treks into the woods; traces of blood and bits of flesh in the bathroom; a peculiar animal odor in the house. "The story moves quickly and has a haunting quality that stays with readers for some time," according to Charles R. Duke in the *ALAN Review*. In *School Library Journal*, Kelly Diller felt the plot was suspenseful, believing that "fans of horror fiction . . . will find the novel engrossing and generally satisfying."

Though Windsor has always had a taste for travel and changing addresses (during one period she moved eleven times within twelve years), she decided to plant roots after two years in Savannah, and began renovating an old cotton warehouse overlooking the Savannah River. She also maintained her lifelong passion for reading and writing. "Add to the list: skiing, horror movies, ghost stories, pizza, London, New York and my dog (an Australian Shepherd)," she explained in *Fifth Book of Junior Authors and Illustrators*. "I enjoy teaching people how to write as much as I do writing myself." And like her dream of endless possibilities in *Home is Where Your Feet Are Standing*, Windsor sees endless possibilities in life, too. She revisited her dream of becoming an actress when she played Mrs. Dudley, the crazy housekeeper, in a 1991 stage production of Shirley Jackson's *The Haunting of Hill House*.

After trying several different careers during her youth, Windsor has found happiness as an author. "I love to read books, and I'm pleased there are people who may right now be taking one of my books off a library shelf and getting ready to enjoy it as much as I enjoy the books of other writers," she told *CA*. "But if people don't like what I write, or hate the characters or the plot, that's all right with me (as) long as I made them think and react a little."

■ Works Cited

Adams, Mary L., review of *The Christmas Killer*, *Voice of Youth Advocates*, December, 1991, p. 319.

Broome, JoEllen, review of *The Sandman's Eyes*, *Voice of Youth Advocates*, June, 1985, p. 136.

Duke, Charles R., review of *The Blooding*, *ALAN Review*, Winter, 1997.

Diller, Kelly, review of *The Blooding*, *School Library Journal*, December, 1996, p. 40.

Fakih, K. Olson, and Diane Roback, review of *The Hero*, *Publishers Weekly*, June 10, 1988, p. 82.

Review of *The Hero*, *Kirkus Reviews*, May 1, 1988, p. 699.

Larson, Jeanette, review of *The Christmas Killer*, *School Library Journal*, November, 1991, p. 137.

MacRae, Cathi Dunn, review of *The Christmas Killer*, *Wilson Library Bulletin*, April, 1992, p. 99.

Mercier, Jean, review of *The Summer Before*, *Publishers Weekly*, June 18, 1973, p. 70.

Mercier, Jean, review of *Killing Time*, *Publishers Weekly*, November 21, 1980, p. 59.

Perry, Frank, review of *Killing Time*, *Voice of Youth Advocates*, June, 1981, p. 53.

Roback, Diane, and Richard Donahue, review of *The Christmas Killer*, *Publishers Weekly*, October 25, 1991, p. 69.

Review of *The Sandman's Eyes*, *Children's Book Review Service*, Spring Supplement, 1985.

Review of *The Sandman's Eyes*, *School Library Journal*, May, 1985, p. 111.

Spencer, Pam, review of *The Sandman's Eyes*, *School Journal Library*, March, 1992, p. 165.

Review of *The Summer Before*, *Kirkus Reviews*, May 15, 1973, p. 569.

Sutherland, Zena, review of *The Summer Before*, *Bulletin of the Center for Children's Books*, September, 1973, p. 20.

Sutherland, Zena, review of *Killing Time*, *Bulletin of the Center for Children's Books*, January, 1981, p. 103.

Sutherland, Zena, review of *The Christmas Killer*, *Bulletin for the Center for Children's Books*, November, 1991, p. 79.

Windsor, Patricia, comments in *Fifth Book of Junior Authors and Illustrators*, edited by Sally Holmes Holtze, H. W. Wilson, 1983, pp. 328-29.

Windsor, Patricia, comments in *Something about the Author*, Volume 30, Gale, 1983, pp. 216-18.

Windsor, Patricia, comments in *Contemporary Authors, New Revision Series*, Volume 19, Gale, 1987, pp. 486-87.

Windsor, Patricia, essay in *Something about the Author Autobiography Series*, Volume 19, Gale, 1995, pp. 305-17.

Zvirin, Stephanie, review of *The Christmas Killer, Booklist*, October 15, 1991, pp. 430-31.

■ **For More Information See**

PERIODICALS

Booklist, April 1, 1988.
Books for Keeps, July, 1996.
Wilson Library Bulletin, February, 1989.*

—Sketch by Diane Gale Andreassi

Acknowledgments

Acknowledgments

Grateful acknowledgment is made to the following publishers, authors, and artists for their kind permission to reproduce copyrighted material.

MARGARET BUFFIE. Cover of *The Warnings*, by Margaret Buffie. Scholastic Inc., 1989. Reproduced by permission./ Buffie, Margaret, photograph. Reproduced by permission.

MICHAEL CADNUM. Cadnum, Michael, photograph by Dave Thomas. Reproduced by permission./ Binger, Bill, illustrator. From a cover of *Ghostwright*, by Bill Binger. Carroll & Graf, 1993. Reproduced by permission.

CHRIS CARTER. Carter, Chris and David Duchovny, photograph. AP/Wide World Photos, Inc. Reproduced by permission./ Grecco, Michael, photographer. From a cover of *The X-Files: E.B.E.*, by Les Martin. HarperTrophy, 1996. Cover photograph (c) 1996 by Twentieth Century Fox Corporation. Cover (c) 1996 by HarperCollins Publishers. Reproduced by permission of HarperCollins Publishers, Inc./ Duchovny, David, Gillian Anderson, and Chris Carter, photograph by Reed Saxon. AP/Wide World Photos, Inc. Reproduced by permission./ Duchovny, David and Gillian Anderson, photograph by Michael Grecco. AP/Wide World Photos, Inc. Reproduced by permission.

CAMERON CROWE. Penn, Sean (holding microphone) in the film *Fast Times at Ridgemont High*, 1982, photograph. Archive Photos. Reproduced by permission./ Cusack, John and Ione Skye in the film *Say Anything. . .*, 1989, photograph. Archive Photos. Reproduced by permission./ Dillon, Matt, Bridget Fonda, and Kyra Sedgwick in the film *Singles*, 1992, photograph. Archive Photos. Reproduced by permission./ Cruise, Tom in the film *Jerry Maguire*, 1996, photograph. AP/Wide World Photos, Inc. Reproduced by permission./ Crowe, Cameron, photograph. AP/Wide World Photos, Inc. Reproduced by permission.

SALVADOR DALI. Dali, Salvador (with his painting *The Face of War*), photograph. AP/Wide World Photos, Inc. Reproduced by permission./ Dali, Salvador displaying a painting, photograph. U.S. Information Agency./ *The Persistence of Memory*, painting by Salvador Dali, 1931. The Museum of Modern Art, New York. Reproduced by permission./ Dali, Salvador (wearing pinstriped suit), photograph. AP/Wide World Photos, Inc. Reproduced by permission.

CHARLES DICKENS. Goodrich, Carter, illustrator. From an illustration in *A Christmas Carol*, by Charles Dickens. Books of Wonder, 1996. Illustrations (c) 1996 by Carter Goodrich. Reproduced by Books of Wonder, a division of William Morrow and Company, Inc./ *An Irish Immigrant Landing at Liverpool*, painting by Erskine Nicol. From a cover of *Oliver Twist*, by Charles Dickens. Bantam Books, 1991. Reproduced by permission of Bantam Books, a division of Bantam Doubleday Dell Publishing Group, Inc./ Browne, Hablot K., illustrator. From a cover of *The Life and Adventures of Nicholas Nickleby*, by Charles Dickens. Chapman and Hall, 1838./ Secombe, Harry and Mark Lester in the film *Oliver!*, 1968, photograph. AP/Wide World Photos, Inc. Reproduced by permission./ Dickens, Charles, photograph. The Library of Congress.

GREG EVANS. *Luann*, November 13, 1996, comic strip by Greg Evans. Reproduced by permission of Greg Evans./ *Luann*, August 30, 1997, comic strip by Greg Evans. Reproduced by permission of Greg Evans./ *Luann*, October 29, 1997, comic strip by Greg Evans. Reproduced by permission of Greg Evans./ Evans, Greg, photograph. Reproduced by permission of Greg Evans.

CYNTHIA D. GRANT. Archambault, Matthew, illustrator. From a cover of *Uncle Vampire*, by Cynthia D. Grant. Random House Sprinters, 1995. Cover art (c) 1995 by Matthew Archambault. Reproduced by permission of Random House, Inc./ Grant, Cynthia D., photograph by Rhonda Neuchiller. Reproduced by permission.

MARY DOWNING HAHN. Cover of *Daphne's Book*, by Mary Downing Hahn. Bantam Skylark Books, 1985. Reproduced by permission of Bantam Skylark Books, a division of Bantam Doubleday Dell Publishing Group, Inc./ Potter, J. K., illustrator. From a cover of *December Stillness*, by Mary Downing Hahn. Clarion Books, 1988. Reproduced by permission of Houghton Mifflin Company./ Cover of *Stepping on the Cracks*, by Mary Downing Hahn. Avon Camelot Books, 1992. Reproduced by permission of Avon Camelot Books, a division of William Morrow and Company, Inc./ Cover of *The Time of the Witch*, by Mary Downing Hahn. Avon Camelot Books, 1991. Reproduced by permission of Avon Camelot Books, a division of William Morrow and Company, Inc./ Cover of *Wait Till Helen Comes: A Ghost Story*, by Mary Downing Hahn. Avon Camelot Books, 1987. Reproduced by permission of Avon Camelot Flare Books, a division of William Morrow and Company, Inc./ Cover of *The Wind Blows Backward*, by Mary Downing Hahn. Avon Flare Books, 1994. Reproduced by permission of Avon Flare Books, a division of William Morrow and Company, Inc./ Hahn, Mary Downing, photograph. Reproduced by permission of Mary Downing Hahn.

M. E. KERR. Brown, Trevor, illustrator. From a cover of *Deliver Us from Evie,* by M. E. Kerr. HarperTrophy, 1995. Cover art (c) 1994 by Trevor Brown. Cover (c) 1995 by HarperCollins Publishers. Reproduced by permission of HarperCollins Publishers, Inc./ Sabin, Robert, illustrator. From a cover of *Dinky Hocker Shoots Smack!* by M. E. Kerr. HarperTrophy, 1989. Cover art (c) 1989 by Robert Sabin. Cover (c) 1989 HarperCollins Publishers. Reproduced by permission of HarperCollins Publishers, Inc./ McPheeters, Neal, illustrator. From a cover of *Gentlehands,* by M. E. Kerr. Harper Keypoint, 1990. Cover art (c) 1990 by Neal McPheeters. Cover (c) 1990 by HarperCollins Publishers. Reproduced by permission of HarperCollins Publishers, Inc./ Kerr, M. E., photograph by Zoe Kamitses. Reproduced by permission of M. E. Kerr.

DANIEL KEYES. Cover of *Flowers for Algernon,* by Daniel Keyes. Bantam Books, 1975. Reproduced by permission of Bantam Books, a division of Bantam Doubleday Dell Publishing Group, Inc./ Robertson, Cliff in the film *Charly,* 1967, photograph. Archive Photos. Reproduced by permission./ Keyes, Daniel, photograph. AP/Wide World Photos, Inc. Reproduced by permission.

BETTY LEVIN. Smith, Jos. A., illustrator. From a cover of *Fire in the Wind,* by Betty Levin. Greenwillow Books, 1995. Jacket art (c) 1995 by Jos. A. Smith. Reproduced by permission of Greenwillow Books, a division of William Morrow and Company, Inc./ Smith, Jos. A., illustrator. From a jacket of *Mercy's Mill,* by Betty Levin. Greenwillow Books, 1992. Jacket art (c) 1992 by Jos. A. Smith. Reproduced by permission of Greenwillow Books, a division of William Morrow and Company, Inc./ Levin, Betty (holding lamb), photograph by Kyle Bajakian. Reproduced by permission of Betty Levin.

GEORGE LUCAS. Howard, Ron, with Cindy Williams, in a scene from *American Graffiti,* photograph. The Kobal Collection. Reproduced by permission./ Ford, Harrison, in a scene from *Raiders of the Lost Ark,* photograph. The Kobal Collection. Reproduced by permission./ Bridges, Jeff, in a scene from *Tucker,* photograph. The Kobal Collection. Reproduced by permission./ Hamill, Mark, Carrie Fisher and Harrison Ford in the film *Star Wars,* photograph. The Kobal Collection. Reproduced by permission./ Lucas, George, photograph. AP/Wide World Photos, Inc. Reproduced by permission.

GERALDINE MCCAUGHREAN. Ambrus, Victor G., illustrator. From *The Canterbury Tales,* by Geraldine McCaughrean. Rand McNally & Company, 1985. Illustration (c) Victor Ambrus 1984. Reproduced by permission of Checkerboard Press./ McCaughrean, Geraldine, photograph. Reproduced by permission of Geraldine McCaughrean.

MARGARET MITCHELL. Cover of *Gone with the Wind,* by Margaret Mitchell. Warner Books, 1993. Cover illustration (c) 1939 Turner Entertainment Co. Reproduced by permission./ Gable, Clark and Vivien Leigh in the film *Gone with the Wind,* 1939, photograph. AP/Wide World Photos, Inc. Reproduced by permission/ Mitchell, Margaret, photograph. The Bettmann Archive/Newsphotos, Inc.. Reproduced by permission.

WALTER DEAN MYERS. Cover of *Fallen Angels,* by Walter Dean Myers. Scholastic Inc., 1988. Reproduced by permission./ Bacha, Andy, illustrator. From a cover of *The Mouse Rap,* by Walter Dean Myers. Harper & Row, 1990. Cover art (c) 1990 by Andy Bacha. Reproduced by permission of HarperCollins Publishers, Inc./ Bacha, Andy, illustrator. From a cover of *Scorpions,* by Walter Dean Myers. HarperTrophy, 1996. Cover art (s) 1996 by Andy Bacha. Cover (c) 1996 by HarperCollins Publishers. Reproduced by permission of HarperCollins Publishers, Inc./ Myers, Walter Dean, photograph by David Godlis. Reproduced by permission of Walter Dean Myers.

BEVERLEY NAIDOO. Velasquez, Eric, illustrator. From a cover of *Chain of Fire,* by Beverley Naidoo. HarperTrophy, 1990. Cover art (c) 1990 by Eric Velasquez. Reproduced by permission of HarperCollins Publishers, Inc./ Naidoo, Beverley, photograph. Kitchenham Ltd. Reproduced by permission of Beverley Naidoo.

JAN NEEDLE. Needle, Jan, photograph. Reproduced by permission of Jan Needle.

COLBY RODOWSKY. Cover illustration of *Hannah in Between,* Copyright (c) by Colby Rodowsky. Troll Medallion, an imprint and trademark of Troll Communications L.L.C., 1994. By permission of Troll Communications L.L.C./ Norman, Elaine, illustrator. From a cover of *Julie's Daughter,* by Colby Rodowsky. Aerial Fiction, 1992. Cover art (c) 1992 by Elaine Norman. Reproduced by permission of Aerial Fiction, a division of Farrar, Straus and Giroux, Inc./ Mosberg, Hilary, illustrator. From a cover of *Lucy Peale,* by Colby Rodowsky. Aerial Fiction, 1994. Cover art (c) 1994 by Hilary Mosberg. Reproduced by permission of Aerial Fiction, a division of Farrar, Straus and Giroux, Inc./ Nones, Eric Jon, illustrator. From a cover of *Sydney, Herself,* by Colby Rodowsky. Farrar, Straus and Giroux, 1989. Cover art (c) 1989 by Eric Jon Nones. Reproduced by permission of Farrar, Straus and Giroux, Inc./ Deutermann, Diana, illustrator. From a cover of *What About Me?* by Colby Rodowsky. Sunburst Books, 1989. Cover art (c) 1989 by Diana Deutermann. Reproduced by permission of Sunburst Books, a division of Farrar, Straus and Giroux, Inc./ Rodowsky, Colby, photograph by Sally Foster. Reproduced by permission of Colby Rodowsky.

DANIELLE STEEL. Cover of *Changes,* by Danielle Steel. Dell Books, 1983. Reproduced by permission of Dell Books, a division of Bantam Doubleday Dell Publishing Group, Inc./ Cover of *Daddy,* by Danielle Steel. Dell Books, 1989. Reproduced by permission of Dell Books, a division of Bantam Doubleday Dell Publishing Group, Inc./ Cover illustration of *Zoya,* by Danielle Steel. Dell Books, 1988. Reproduced by permission of Dell Books, a division of Bantam Doubleday Dell Publishing Group, Inc./ Steel, Danielle, photograph. AP/Wide World Photos, Inc. Reproduced by permission.

ABRAHAM STOKER. Hildebrandt, Greg, illustrator. From an illustration in *Dracula,* by Bram Stoker. The Unicorn Publishing House, 1985. Art work (c) 1985 Greg Hildebrandt. All rights reserved. Reproduced by permission./ Cover illustration of *Dracula,* by Bram Stoker. Signet Classics, 1992. Reproduced by permission of Signet Classics, a division of Penguin USA./ Lugosi, Bela in the film *Dracula,* 1931, photograph. AP/Wide World Photos, Inc. Reproduced by permission./ Stoker, Abraham, photograph. AP/Wide World Photos, Inc. Reproduced by permission.

MARTIN WADDELL. Cover of In a *Blue Velvet Dress,* by Catherine Sefton. Harper & Row, 1973. Reproduced by permission of Harper Collins Publishers, Inc./ Jones, Richard, illustrator. From a jacket of *The Kidnapping of Suzie Q,* by Martin Waddell. Candlewick Press, 1994. Jacket illustration (c) 1994 by Richard Jones./ Waddell, Martin (on desk), photograph. AP/Wide World Photos, Inc. Reproduced by permission.

PATRICIA WINDSOR. Cover of *The Christmas Killer,* by Patricia Windsor. Scholastic, 1991. Reproduced by permission./ Cover of *The Sandman's Eyes,* by Patricia Windsor. Laurel-Leaf Books, 1992. Reproduced by permission of Laurel-Leaf Books, a division of Bantam Doubleday Dell Publishing Group, Inc./ Windsor, Patricia, photograph. Reproduced by permission of Patricia Windsor.

Cumulative Index

Author/Artist Index

The following index gives the number of the volume in which an author/artist's biographical sketch appears.